FRONTIER POLITICS:
ALASKA'S JAMES WICKERSHAM

Books by Evangeline Atwood

83 Years of Neglect: Alaska's Struggle for Self Government, 1950 (editor)

Anchorage: All-America City, 1957

We Shall Be Remembered: the Story of the Matanuska Colonization Project, 1966

Who's Who in Alaskan Politics, 1977, compiled with Robert N. DeArmond

FRONTIER POLITICS:
ALASKA'S JAMES WICKERSHAM

By

Evangeline Atwood

Binford & Mort

Thomas Binford, Publisher

2536 S.E. Eleventh • Portland, Oregon 97202

*This book is dedicated to my fellow Alaskans
who are following in Wickersham's
footprints in his scholarly efforts to preserve
Alaska's historical heritage.*

PREFACE

This is the story of a man who has more living monuments to his memory than does any other in the state's history. These monuments will continue to contribute to the happiness and well-being of Alaskans for centuries to come. No other man has made as deep and varied imprints on Alaska's heritage, whether it be in politics, government, commerce, literature, history, or philosophy. A federal judge, member of Congress, attorney, explorer, author, and bibliophile—present-day Alaska is deeply in debt to him.

It was while researching for a sociopolitical history of Alaska that the author found the man, James Wickersham, looming so high on the horizon that he overshadowed his fellow Alaskans; he was their accepted leader and they his willing followers. Such a man deserved a biography and none had ever been written, hence the present effort to present him to the heirs of his multifaceted life.

As United States district judge for eight years; as Alaska's elected delegate in Congress for fourteen years; and as a lifetime historical researcher and scholar, Wickersham established the guidelines for Alaska's destiny. He rescued Alaskans from a bureaucratic dictatorship, winning instead their right to elect their own lawmakers. He sold his dream of a state university to his fellow Alaskans as well as to a reluctant Congress. He convinced the federal government that it should build and operate a railroad to aid in the territory's development.

He was the first to attempt to climb Mt. McKinley; to introduce a statehood bill; to develop an environmental impact statement; to advocate a native land claims settlement; to compile judicial opinions rendered in the Alaskan courts; to collect a comprehensive private library of Alaskana.

The story of James Wickersham's leadership in Alaskan affairs coincided with the federal government's empirical treatment of the territory, beginning with Theodore Roosevelt and ending with Franklin Roosevelt; whether the experiments succeeded or failed depended largely on how Wickersham viewed the issues involved.

Whether God created Alaska for Wickersham or Wickersham for Alaska, the land and the man were synonymous in the eyes and ears of the rest of the world. He did not bring calm and peace in his reign, but neither did the land offer them to him; times were stormy and unsettled for both man and land. It has been said that men, as ships, are measured by the waves which follow them. Wickersham was constantly "making waves." He called himself a rebel and said he was proud to be one. He believed, as did Thomas Jefferson, that "a little rebellion now and then is a good thing, and as necessary in the political world as storms in the physical."

Wickersham did not seek easy solutions but fought fearlessly for what he deemed best for Alaska. Undoubtedly he would have agreed with Harry Truman's maxim: "Do your duty and history will do you justice."

In an effort to give a true delineation of James Wickersham's life and times, the author has tried to avoid personal bias, as much as is humanly possible, and has included the bad with the good as Wickersham's character and personality unfolded through the years. Ten years of historical research provided a background for the narrative, with a minimum of personal interpretation, leaving that for the reader to make. The research was done primarily in the files of Alaskan newspapers published from Nome to Ketchikan, during his lifetime, plus his personal diaries kept during his thirty-nine years' residence in Alaska. The Seattle and Tacoma papers were used for portions of his life before coming to Alaska.

Special thanks are due the following persons for their kind assistance: Ruth Coffin Allman of Juneau, for the use of Wickersham's diaries; Mary Flinton of the Washington State Library in Olympia, for her dedicated research; Phyllis Nottingham and Richard Engen, of the Alaska Historical Library in Juneau; and Paul McCarthy and Ted Ryberg, of the Elmer E. Rasmuson Library at the University of Alaska in Fairbanks, for their cooperation in loaning me hundreds of reels of microfilm; Bob DeArmond of Juneau, for sharing his private research files.

And last, but not least, to my husband, Robert B. Atwood, publisher of the Anchorage *Times*, for his encouragement and patient sufferance during my determined effort.

E R A

CONTENTS

Contents

FRONTIER POLITICS:
ALASKA'S JAMES WICKERSHAM

PART I

WICKERSHAM'S PRE-ALASKA YEARS

Chapter I

American Genealogy

> . . .*I am busy while kept confined at home in reading Mac-aulay's History of England and I enjoy it by the hour. I understand why my oldest American ancestors came to Kennett Square, Pa. in 1700.* *(Diary, Dec. 27, 1932.)*

James Wickersham's American ancestry began with Thomas and Alice (Hogge) Wickersham. Thomas was born circa 1660. He became a farmer near Bolney, a village near Horsham, Sussex County, England, about sixty miles from London. The European Wickershams had migrated to England from the little town of Wickersheim in Alsace, France, near Strasbourg.

Thomas married seventeen-year-old Ann Grover on September 19, 1685 at a Friends' meeting at Hurstpierpoint in Sussex. They had four children—Humphrey, Thomas II, John, and Ann; the mother died in 1697.

On June 27, 1700 Thomas married Alice Hogge and two weeks later they left for America in a sailing vessel, taking his three younger children with them—Thomas, nine years, John, seven years, and four-year-old Ann.

The Wickershams were Quakers, a sect which was persecuted for its religious beliefs. They crossed the Atlantic in search of religious freedom. Thomas came to America with a deed for 1000 acres of virgin land which he had purchased from William Penn. They settled in East Marlborough, a mile northeast of Kennett Square, Chester County, Pennsylvania.

Thomas also carried a letter from the Friends in England to the Friends in America certifying that he was "an honest man," the highest credential a Quaker can have. He built himself a log home and in 1712 he was appointed an overseer for Kennett meeting; in 1714, when elders were first appointed, he was named the first elder of Kennett meeting; and in 1718 his friends made him a minister, the highest gift recognized by the Quaker meeting. He was also the first constable of East Marlborough township.

Through the years, the Wickersham family has held periodic reunions in Pennsylvania, the first one being held on October 23, 1920, at the old homestead of Thomas I; nearly two hundred persons attended. The Wickersham Printing Company of Lancaster, Pennsylvania printed a little booklet about the reunion listing those present. Judge Frank B. Wickersham of Harrisburg served as general chairman and George W. Wickersham, one-time United States attorney general, was chosen president of the Wickersham Association.

A second reunion was held at Old Kennett meetinghouse on October 10, 1925; James Madison Wickersham of Seattle, Washington was among those who signed the family register. The fourth reunion was held at the London Grove meetinghouse on October 5, 1935. Judge Wickersham did not attend these family reunions, but he sent greetings. For the 1935 reunion he wrote, "A History of the Wickershams in the Far West"; it was read to the group by Judge Frank Wickersham of Harrisburg.[1]

At the first reunion in 1920, three principal speeches were delivered describing the Wickershams of the past, present and future. George Wickersham delivered the one on the present Wickershams. He told of having written Judge James Wickersham, then of Tacoma, Washington and later of Alaska, asking him for the characteristics of the Wickershams in the state of Washington, to which the judge replied: "they usually have dark brown hair, gray or dark eyes, were slightly disposed to be skeptical in matters of religion, and they voted the Republican ticket as soon as they were born!"

He went on to relate that once when Judge Wickersham was hearing an important gold-mining case in Nome, he did not believe the witnesses on either side, so he adjourned court, traveled fifty or sixty miles through snow and cold, examined the mine himself, returned to the courtroom, and proceeded with the case.

Judge Wickersham had a keen curiosity about his forbears and took every opportunity to acquaint himself with their backgrounds. While serving as a delegate in Congress, he made several visits to his former home in southern Illinois and sought out genealogical information from his relatives; some vital statistics were found in old family bibles and church records. He checked the pension records in the Washington archives for ancestors who fought in the various American military engagements—the Revolutionary War, the War of 1812, the Black Hawk War in Illinois in 1832, and the Civil War.

On one of these expeditions he located a history of the Wickersham family in America in a book entitled *History of Chester County, Pa.* published in 1881 by Futhey and Cope and also in Pennsylvania Archives, part 2, sixth series, volume XV.

In 1917 Wickersham visited Kennett Square to experience firsthand the locale where his American ancestors established their first home. The excitement and emotional satisfaction which he derived from that visit is best portrayed in his diary entry:

> William Wickersham is tall, spare, scholarly and is a Quaker of the old stock. He received me in a very friendly manner and his sister, May or Mary, came in and met me. They sent for their brother Frank and sister Ann.
>
> William has been a teacher and scholar; Frank is a surveyor and contractor, road-builder, etc. They were all born and raised in and around Kennett, though Frank was in the West for some years in railroad work.
>
> After lunch with Frank at the Kennett Hotel, I secured the services of an automobile and we went out to see the old Wickersham family American birthplace. We passed "Cedarcroft", home of Bayard Taylor, noted author and journalist. Two miles north of Kennett is the old home place.
>
> Here Thomas and Alice Wickersham settled in 1700 and here today, more than two centuries afterward, we stood in their original rooms and wondered at the labor and effort put into the great walls of their low-ceilinged, old-fashioned English country house.
>
> The house was built on a sloping hillside, just above a stream of water. It faced east and a beautiful prospect. It was two-story, in part. Being on a sloping hillside, the front part of the house was two stories, while the rear part was only one story.

A great stone fireplace was built in each part, at the west end of the front ground floor—at the west end of the rear ground, raised story.

The big fireplace downstairs in the front room is the old hearthstone of the Wickersham family in America. The old fireplace stands out to four feet and covers the greater part of the west end of the first floor. It is big, wide, deep and built about 1700.

It is the old hearthstone beside which my great, great grandfather, James Wickersham, and my great grandfather Sampson Wickersham, sat as boys. They were raised here and went to school at Kennett meeting schoolhouse. Here in these rooms they were born. . . .

We then went over to the old Kennett meetinghouse, found the sexton, went in and examined its ancient seats, galleries, its old horse block and all made known to the world in "The Story of Kennett" by Bayard Taylor.

I got a copy of a little book entitled "1710-1910 Bicentennial of Old Kennett Meeting House," which contains a special account of the Wickersham family genealogy. I also bought a copy of "The Story of Kennett" in the Kennett bookstore.

I have had an unusually beautiful day—one of the most pleasant and I take away with me to our western homes, the most interesting traditions and pleasant memories of the old Quaker Thomas and his sons and daughters of Kennett.[2]

Wickersham's great-great-grandfather, James Wickersham I, fought in the Revolutionary War. His son Sampson left Pennsylvania in 1785, floating down the Ohio River to Harrodsburg, Kentucky. Once when Delegate Wickersham changed trains at Pittsburgh en route to Washington, he went to the Fort Pitt Hotel for dinner. While sitting on the veranda after dinner, enjoying a cigar and the background dinner music, his thoughts traveled back 120 years as he wondered what his great-grandfather looked like when he tied his canoe or flatboat to the bank in front of Fort Pitt and loaded his small outfit for the voyage down the Ohio River to the Boone country in Kentucky:

He was probably dressed in homespun; his wife in linsey-woolsey, and his outfit probably consisted of the aforesaid wife and children, some dogs, a squirrel rifle and an axe. What a change between the Fort Pitt waterfront of that day and this![3]

Sampson's westward move apparently was not a happy experience for his wife, as shortly thereafter a divorce terminated their twelve-year marriage. He remarried and had twelve children, including Delegate Wickersham's grandfather, James Lesenger.

On another visit to Harrodsburg, the Delegate learned about his grandfather's eldest brother, Daniel Boone Wickersham, who migrated to Arkansas territory. He was living there at the time of the Civil War and was hanged by members of the Union's Tenth Cavalry because he refused to disclose where he had hidden his gold. He was reputedly quite wealthy and he buried his gold with such care that none of his heirs were able to find it.

Delegate Wickersham's father, Alexander, the eldest son of James and Sarah (Smith) Wickersham, was born in 1825 in a log cabin on a farm near Mt. Carmel, Illinois, on the banks of the Wabash River. He served as a private in the Mexican War, and when he returned home he worked on a farm near Sandoval, Illinois.

He was tall and gawky in stature and walked with a clumsy step. His shaggy eyebrows, sunken eyes, pointed chin and beard reminded his neighbors so much of the President that they dubbed him "Abe Lincoln Wickersham." His son Frank also resembled the President, even to the mole on his chin, so strikingly that he was asked to play Abe Lincoln roles in the movies at Hollywood in later years.[4]

The Delegate's mother, Mary Jane McHaney, was born on October 12, 1837, on a farm near Lebanon, Tennessee. She migrated with her family from Tennessee to Salem, Illinois, when she was seven years old. She remembered driving a cow and calf behind the family's ox-drawn covered wagon.

Mary Jane Wickersham had four grandfathers who fought in the Revolutionary War—Terry McHaney, Isaac Ross, Thomas Sims, and John Wood. Judge Wickersham became a member of the Sons of the American Revolution in 1925, as a descendant of Thomas Sims of North Carolina.[5]

On the following pages, Wickersham's ancestry can be traced on both his paternal and maternal sides, terminating with his own three sons.

DESCENDANTS OF THOMAS AND
ALICE (HOGGE) WICKERSHAM (*Je 27, 1700*)

William   James = *Elizabeth Barker*
Isaac   = 2d Ann Achus

Sampson = Elizabeth Jackson (Nov. 20, 1775) div.
b.Jan.20,1751 = *2d Elizabeth Lessenger*
d.Nov.22,1819   b.Feb.2,1768
                              d.Apr.13,1834

Other Issue
Daniel Boone,Je 3,1790-circa 1861
Mary,Jan28,1791-1810
George,Mar.12,1792-Mar.21,1819
Jacob,Mar.21,1793-1880
Ruth Kirkland,Oct.29,1795-
Sampson (1st),Aug.15,1797-Aug.1,1798
Elizabeth,May20,1802-Apr.15,1808
Priscilla Isham,1805-
Phoebe Claunch,Apr.13,1807-Jan.18,1894
Sampson (2d),Oct.28,1809-July 6,1879
Jesse,Jan.7,1812-Sept.12,1887

James Lesenger = Sarah Smith (1824)
                              = 2d Elizabeth League
                              = 3d Mrs. Brown
                                   no issue

Alexander = *Mary Jane McHaney*
                 (Oct. 9, 1856
b.1825   n.Oct.12,1837
d.May29,1892 d.Apr.5,1924

Other Issue   Other Issue
Sampson Richard   James
     Thomas   William
                              Thompson

Other Issue
Sarah Nancy,Dec.25,1859-Je 23,1934
2 sons died in early childhood
Edgar,1866-Dec.14,1936
Harry,1869-Jan.1953
Clyde,1871-Aug.1893
Mary (May), 1873-Je 30,1921
Frank, 1875-
Jennie,1880-Aug.18,1927

Judge James = *Deborah Susan Bell*
                    (Oct.27,1880)
b.Aug.24,1857 b.Sept.25,1863
d.Oct.24,1939 d.Nov.23,1926
                      = 2d Grace Bishop
                      (Je 26,1928)

Darrell Palmer = Jane Avery (Sept.8,1920)
b.Apr.2,1882
d.Mar.9,1954
Arthur James: b.Feb.21,1886; d.Feb.20,1888
Howard Sullivan: b.Oct.19,1893; d.Jan.11,1902

DESCENDANTS OF ISAAC ROSS of Virginia (1712-1804)

Thomas Sims = *Molly Elizabeth Ross*

| Other Issue |
| Benjamin |
| Mathew |

Chesley Sims = Polly Brown

Other Issue	James McHaney = *Nancy Louisa Sims*
Martha (Patsy) m.Wyatt Parkman	
James m.Patsy Puckett	
Sanders m.Nancy Carter	
Jenny unmarried	
Betsy unmarried	
Susan m.John Dickerson	
Polly unmarried	
Sally m.John McHaney	

Other Issue	*Mary Jane* = Alexander Wickersham
Caroline	(Oct.9,1856)
Elizabeth King	b.Oct.12,1837	b. 1825
Robert	d.Apr.5,1924	d.May 29, 1892
Thomas	

Other Issue	*Judge James* = Deborah Susan Bell
Sarah Nancy, 1859-1934	(Oct.27,1880)
2 sons died in early childhood	b.Aug.24,1857	b.Sept.25,1863
Edgar,1866-1916	d.Oct.24,1939	d.Nov.23,1926
Harry,1869-1953	
Clyde,1871-1893	
Mary (May),1873-1921	
Frank,1875-	
Jennie,1880-1927	

Darrell Palmer,1882-1954
Arthur James,1886-1888
Howard Sullivan,1893-1902

Chapter 2

Early Years in Illinois

> *I continue to get the Patoka Register from my old home in Marion Co., Ill. and while all my boyhood friends are dead, it is a melancholy pleasure to read about their grandchildren and "Items" from all the surrounding places which I knew as a boy.*
>
> (*Diary, July 22, 1934*)

Wickersham's kinsfolk were among the first American settlers in southern Illinois, coming from Virginia, the Carolinas, Kentucky, and Tennessee. At the end of the Revolutionary War, Congress issued military warrants which entitled the veteran or his heirs to 160 acres of land, and the same was available to veterans of subsequent military engagements.

The first settlers were half hunters and half farmers. The Illinois and Wabash river valleys were major fur-bearing areas, yielding a wide variety of furs of commercial value.[1]

Low river land along the Kaskaskia River, in the vicinity of Patoka, was sold by the federal government for as low as twelve and a half cents an acre, in the 1850s. The financial panic of 1857, the year of Wickersham's birth, had driven many an Eastern city dweller to the Western frontier to start a new life.

When Alexander Wickersham returned from service in the Mexican War, undoubtedly he made use of the military warrants and bought cheap government land with them. According to the 1860 agricultural census of Marion County, his agricultural holdings consisted of the following:

> 120 A. improved land
> 80 A. unimproved land
> $4,000 estimated cash value of farm
> $75 value of farm machinery
> 2 horses - 4 milch cows - 2 mules - 2 oxen
> 11 other cattle - 4 swine

That year he produced 190 bushels of wheat, 47 bushels of rye, and 2,000 bushels of Indian corn.[2]

The Illinois federal census report for the same year gave the cash value of his real property as $6,000 and personal property as $800. His household consisted of ten persons: he and his wife and their two children, James and Nancy; his brothers, Thompson, 16, and Thomas, 14; and four farm hands.[3]

It was to this farm that Alexander Wickersham brought his bride on October 9, 1856, and where their two eldest children were born - James on August 24, 1857, and Sarah Nancy on Christmas Day two years later. Sarah Nancy was named for her two grandmothers - Sarah Smith Wickersham and Nancy Louisa McHaney. The next two boys died in early childhood.

Jim Wickersham was about five years old when his father sold the farm and moved the family into the town of Patoka. First he operated a sawmill at "Wilson's Switch" and later he built a mill at Fairman on the outskirts of Patoka, near the east fork of the Kaskaskia River.

Moving into town brought a new world to the five-year-old. He began wearing shoes for the first time. He also became aware that something was happening out in the big world which was taking his older playmates away from their homes. One of his earliest memories was of standing outside his home, clinging to his mother's hand, watching four of his relatives, the youngest only thirteen years old, walking across the fields to the railway station. Tears were in his mother's eyes; one of the boys was her brother Tom.

Another Illinois farm boy several years his senior, whose ancestors also had migrated from Kentucky and Tennessee, had just taken office as president of the United States, when he was forced to ask his fellow countrymen to take up arms in order to save the country from breaking apart. Young men from his home state were anxious to show their loyalty by volunteering to bear arms in support of their president. Farm boys were expert in the use of firearms, as wild game was the mainstay of their diet. Most of the volunteers were between eighteen and twenty-five years old, but many were younger.

As the Civil War progressed and victories failed to materialize, antiwar Democrats, popularly known as Copperheads (named for a snake that strikes without warning), began stirring up criticism of President Lincoln's administration. They were especially active in southern Illinois, but the Wickersham family remained loyal to the president and his newly launched Republican party.

Three years after little Jim had waved goodbye to his Uncle Tom and his other playmates, a long train of freight cars carrying hundreds of men clad in faded blue uniforms halted on the sidetrack at Patoka. When the train waited, these war-weary soldiers ate their morning meal and filled their canteens with water. Some came to the Wickersham well, where Jim willingly drew water for them. One soldier gave him a small American flag, the first he had ever possessed, and he was delighted. The man told him he had a little boy the same age whom he was anxious to see.

A few days later, most of the neighbors, including his father, draped their homes with black bunting; they had learned of President Lincoln's assassination.

As the weeks passed, the consequences of the Civil War bore in more closely on the Wickersham family. One of the four boys who had marched away that early morning as James watched with his mother now lay buried in a distant southern cemetery. Another, after two years' confinement in a military prison, had just returned home so broken in health that he soon joined his comrade on the last tenting ground.

In recalling these experiences from his early youth in a letter to J.M. McLaughlin, a Civil War veteran living in Fairbanks, Judge Wickersham wrote in conclusion:

> Thus, early in life I learned that the flag of our country stood for something more stern than happy songs and the music of the band. It stood for danger and death, as well as for the triumph of victory and the growth and greatness of our government and our people.
>
> The war between the states of the union - between our own people - involved principles of the right or wrong of human slavery and the dissolution of our country. Happily for all, freedom and unity won.[4]

When Jim was old enough to handle a team of oxen, it was his job to go into the nearby forest to cut trees and haul them back to the sawmill.

More brothers and sisters kept arriving: Edgar was born in 1866, then came Harry three years later; the next two were sisters - Clyde in 1871 and Mary, or May as she was called in later life, in 1873; then came Frank in 1875 and Jennie in 1880.

Apparently soon after the Civil War ended, Alexander Wickersham took his family to Kansas Territory for a brief interval as Jim Wickersham mentioned in his diary that he lived in Wyandot County, Kansas, in 1868.[5] The family returned to Patoka soon thereafter, as the family records indicate that his brother, Harry, was born in 1869 in Illinois and so also were the rest of the siblings.

As the eldest in a house full of little ones, Jim had to assume adult responsibilities at an early age. After graduating from eighth grade, he taught in a one-room country school a few miles from Patoka. In later years, Dr. B.F. Rodgers, who was a member of the school board when Wickersham was the teacher, recalled that Jim was "deeper" than most young men his age; he preferred reading books to sports activities, and his initiative to delve into and solve problems was outstanding.

His textbooks included McGuffey's *Readers*, Ray's *Arithmetic*, Pinneo's *Grammar*, and his geography was William Channing Woodbridge's *Universal Geography*, published by Beacher and Beckwith in 1835.

He was not yet eighteen years old when he submitted a bid for the construction of a coal shed adjoining the schoolhouse. He was awarded the job, which he completed satisfactorily and for which he received his contractor's fee.[6]

Wickersham visited his boyhood hometown several times while serving as Alaska's delegate in Congress, the last time being in March, 1933, at the conclusion of his fourteenth year in Congress. He and his second wife, Grace, were joined by his eighty-year-old cousin, John Wickersham, who lived at the Masonic Home for the Aged in Sullivan, Illinois. Wickersham and his cousin had attended the Patoka elementary school together.

The trio spent two days just driving around searching out old landmarks and taking pictures. They visited with a few former elementary school classmates. His diary entries reveal the nostalgia that he experienced in noting the drastic changes which had taken place through the years:

> My earliest home in Patoka has disappeared - the old mill yard is covered with stores, stables and houses, but our old lot is vacant and cheerless.

The old church where I went to Sunday School is yet standing, minus its steeple and is now used as the meeting place of the
American Legion.

The old schoolhouse of lumber frame was long ago moved to
another part of town and converted into a dwelling house. In its
place is a brick building, two stories high. . . .

Went out south of town to the old farm, where my father and
mother settled in 1856. The old buildings were burned some
years ago and another residence has since been erected on the
same spot. Only half a dozen large trees are still standing, which
my mother and father planted; orchard all gone, no fences
now. . . .

The cardinals, meadow larks, jay birds, flickers and many
other familiar birds and in the evening, the frogs, gave me
thrills such as I used to enjoy as a boy.[7]

In May, 1877, young Jim Wickersham shook the dust of southern
Illinois from his feet as he set out on a ninety-mile trek to Springfield,
the state capital. He was determined to seek wider horizons than those
the farm communities could offer him.

In Springfield he got a job as office boy and janitor in the law office
of former Governor John McAuley Palmer. He slept in a back room of
the office on a bed of his own manufacture, swept the floors, kindled
the fire, and washed windows; for this he received five dollars a month.
He didn't mind the meager wage as long as he could use the Governor's
law library and he was excited about being near such a dynamic personality.

Palmer had risen from probate judge, to state senator, to governor, to
United States senator, and to presidential candidate on the "gold"
Democratic ticket opposing William Jennings Bryan, the "silver"
candidate. In addition to his top political posts, Palmer served as a
major general in the Civil War and was the first national commander of
the Grand Army of the Republic (G.A.R.), which was born in Illinois in
1866.[8]

Besides reading law in Palmer's office, Wickersham taught school in
the little town of Berry in Sangamon County. He lived in the home of
Isaac Bell, the postmaster in nearby Rochester. Bell was a widower and
his daughter Lou kept house for him. Another daughter, Deborah
Susan, was attending high school in Springfield. One of her classmates
was Governor Palmer's daughter, Jessie. It was not long before the

Wedding picture of Deborah and James Wickersham, Rochester, Ill., Oct. 27, 1880.

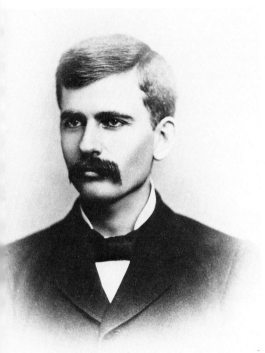 

Left: Wickersham in Tacoma, in 1880s. *Right:* Deborah Wickersham, 1st wife, in 1880s.

young schoolteacher began looking forward to Deborah's weekend visits to her father. She was in her second year in high school when they first met, and during her senior year, young Jim worked full time as a law clerk in Governor Palmer's office.[9]

Debbie graduated from high school in June, 1880, the same day that her father passed away; she returned to Rochester to live with her sister, Lou. Wickersham had passed the Illinois bar exam the previous January and was employed as a law clerk with the United States Census Bureau in Springfield.

Young Jim and Debbie were married in the little Campbellite church in Rochester on October 27, 1880. The Reverend A.T. Kane of Springfield performed the ceremony, after which the bridal party was entertained at the Springfield home of Wickersham's Aunt Kate and Uncle Tom Wickersham.

Wickersham had built a modest home on North Grand Avenue in Springfield, to which he brought his bride. On April 2, 1882, a nine-pound son was born in this home to the happy couple, and they named him Darrell Palmer.

Debbie's American ancestors dated back to Revolutionary War days. Her great-grandfather, Isaac Baker, was in the real estate business in Washington County, Maryland. Her grandparents first lived in Kentucky and then moved to Illinois. Debbie was born in Rochester, Illinois on September 25, 1862. She was the youngest of six daughters born to the Isaac Bells.[10]

Great changes were taking place in the nation, following the financial depression of 1873, causing widespread movement of populations. Transportation was the key. Transcontinental railroads were penetrating the Far West. Congress was generous with land grants - twenty square miles for every mile of track. By 1884 three railways had reached the Pacific coast.

As the railroads pushed westward in advance of settlers, they advertised for easterners and midwesterners to come West, transporting them at reduced rates and selling them land on credit; thousands obtained free homesteads from the federal government and bought tools, horses, and cattle with their savings. The terminals of these lines changed from villages into metropolitan centers almost overnight. Debt-ridden farmers of the prairies turned their eyes westward, dreaming of a new life rich in adventure and economic opportunity.

The young Wickershams responded to the call of the frontier and by the spring of 1883, they were ready to become pioneers in the wilderness of the Pacific Northwest. It is likely that they took a stern-wheeler down the Mississippi to New Orleans and there boarded a Southern Pacific train for San Francisco. When they arrived in San Francisco, they decided to follow the coast northward to the port city of Tacoma, in Washington Territory.

Chapter 3

Pioneering in Pierce County, Washington Territory

> *The Orr-Wickersham administration came into office at a crucial stage in Tacoma's history. The national financial panic of 1893 had thrown many local businesses into bankruptcy and the city itself was tottering on the brink of bankruptcy. . . .*
>
> *When the city's financial situation began to improve by 1896, community leaders referred to Wickersham as "a tower of strength during those troublesome times."* Herbert Hunt, Tacoma, Its History and Its Builders, *vol.II,p.150.)*

Tacoma was a sparsely settled wilderness when the Wickershams arrived; the townsite was spotted with stumps and brush; people waded through muddy streets, wooden plank sidewalks being a luxury reserved for one side of the downtown main street. Not infrequently a deer, driven out of the woods, dashed through the streets; men hunted pheasants on the downtown streets; black bear sauntered into the railroad yards.

Tacoma had been hard hit in 1880 by the bankruptcy of the Northern Pacific railroad when its population was only 1,098. Had Congress not granted a new charter to a reorganized company and given it an ample land grant, the "City of Hope" might have expired before the Wickershams arrived.

Their first winter was what the Indians termed the worst in its history. Beginning in mid-December, snow fell every day or so, for seventeen days, accompanied by sleet and low temperatures. More than two feet of snow covered the town. Several buildings collapsed. Only

16

one cutter was available to clear the streets. The railroad tracks were blocked and Tacoma was without mail for a month.

The first through freight train from St. Paul, Minnesota, via Portland, Oregon, arrived in Tacoma on October 1, 1883. From a population of approximately one thousand, it grew to four thousand in twelve months' time.[1]

Four years later, the city held a gala Fourth of July celebration welcoming the first direct train from St. Paul crossing over the Cascades via Pasco, North Yakima, and Ellensburg. *The Daily Ledger* proclaimed:

> Today which marks a new era in the history of Tacoma, will be celebrated in heroic style. . .Flags are flying everywhere. . . the screech of the American Eagle today. . .will be responded to by the shrill whistle of the American locomotive. . .as it rolls down into the fertile valleys of Puget Sea. . . .
>
> Lighted Chinese lanterns are strung the length of Pacific Avenue. . .The Coeur d'Alene band marches along the avenue, each member armed with Roman candles and rockets which they touch off at the rate of one a minute as they march.

Wickersham worked as a carpenter that first summer, shingling roofs and building fences; he built a home at 230 South C Street. There were already thirty attorneys in town. By fall he had formed a law partnership with Ezra Meeker; they were listed among the charter members of the newly organized Tacoma Bar Association in November, 1883.

Jim's letters home must have been full of praise for their new home because his parents and sisters and brothers joined them later that year. At first the Alexander Wickershams lived in Lakeview, south of Tacoma, and then they moved to a home in the same block on C Street, where their son Jim lived. In 1888 they took up an eighty-acre homestead bordering the Northern Pacific right-of-way, thirty-one miles east of Tacoma on the White River and the area was called White River Siding. But when Alexander Wickersham filed a plat of the townsite, subdividing his property into lots, he changed the name to Buckley in honor of J.M. Buckley, assistant general manager of the Northern Pacific.

When the town of Buckley was incorporated two years later, the district court appointed a board of trustees for the town and this board appointed James Wickersham town counsel.[2]

In the fall of 1884, scarcely more than a year after his arrival, Wickersham took his first step into the world of politics. He ran for the

Ruth Allman

Left: Wickersham's mother. *Right:* Wickersham and his mother in Buckley, Washington, in the 1920s.

county probate judgeship and won. His opponent, known as "Honest John," had held the office for years, and to be defeated by a rank newcomer amazed the townsfolk.

Wickersham served four years in that office, being reelected in 1886. He ran both as a Republican and as an Independent simultaneously the first time and on the People's ticket the second time.

The 27-year-old judge found himself in the center of a world of crime and corruption for which he had little preparation. The town had thirty saloons, one brewery, and seven churches. Until 1883 saloons never closed their doors, but in that year a territorial law was passed making it illegal to remain open on Sundays.

Gambling and prostitution were rampant. One man was tarred and feathered by his enemies, and a newspaper editor was shot by an irate reader. A Law and Order League was formed to control the town's morals, as it was generally suspected that the town marshall was allied with the underworld. An effort to have him impeached ended in acquittal because the moral forces were not united.

Upon the urging of the new judge, the city council passed an ordinance providing for the appointment of a chief of police in order to centralize responsibility for the increasing disorders.

A large Indian population surrounded the town, and the young judge was called upon frequently to make innovative decisions in translating Indian mores into white man's laws.

One of his first cases was that of an Indian with three wives. "Indian Henry Sicade," or Soo-too-lick, and his three wives were brought into court and Judge Wickersham told him to choose one. There are two stories of how Indian Henry complied with the judge's orders: one was that he beckoned the three squaws and led them into a clump of bushes, soon returning with only one squaw. To an inquiry put by Judge Wickersham, Indian Henry answered: "White man says keep one squaw, get rid of two squaws. I did."

The other version was that following the judge's order, Indian Henry picked out the youngest and prettiest, named Patoomlot, and, turning to the other two, said: "You come too. I pay you ten cents day wages." The next child born to Indian Henry was named William Waukisee Wickersham.[3]

The nation was facing a problem popularly referred to as the "Yellow Peril." With the construction of the transcontinental railroads, the floodgates of immigration had been opened wide to allow coolie labor to help build the railroads. This influx of oriental labor posed a dilemma during times of economic depression.

When the Northern Pacific was building westward to Tacoma, the Chinese came with it. While the chief objection was economic, the unsanitary living conditions of the Chinese were repulsive and contributed to a smoldering hostility. By 1885, the Chinese represented one-tenth of Tacoma's population of seven thousand.

Hatred toward the Chinese reached such fever heat that a series of mass meetings and torchlight parades were held in the fall of 1885. A "Committee of Fifteen" was formed to carry out the expulsion of the Chinese; Judge Wickersham was a member, as were other prominent city officials, including the mayor. All businesses were ordered to dismiss their Chinese employees.

Historian Hunt described the details of the plan:

> A secret "Committee of Nine" was organized. Each member of the Nine was to organize a circle of nine, no-one knowing

who belonged to another circle. . .all they knew was that he was a member of an organization set to drive out the orientals.

At an all-night session on November 2, the Committee of Nine. . .decided that all circle members would be instructed that when the whistles of the Lister Foundation blew at 9:30 the next morning, a general assault would be made on the Chinese shacks. The Committee of Fifteen were unaware of this plan.

The Chinese were herded aboard a train that carried them to Portland, Oregon. Several of the men who participated in their ouster were fined five hundred dollars and sent to McNeil Island prison where they served several months. . . .

Twenty-seven prominent citizens were arrested, including Judge Wickersham, the town's mayor, fire chief and two city councilmen. . .They were marched to the courthouse for the night and taken to Portland the following day, where their bonds were fixed at five thousand dollars each. They were charged with conspiring to insurrection and riot, depriving Chinese subjects of equal protection under the law, and of breaking open houses and driving out the oriental occupants.

The Portland judge sent the group back to Tacoma, where they were greeted with a torchlight procession and a cheering throng of fellow citizens.

A Seattle trial resulted in the acquittal of the "conspirators." A year later a federal grand jury reindicted nine of the original twenty-seven, including Judge Wickersham, but the case was never brought to trial. . . .

The first anniversary of the Chinese expulsion was observed with a parade and torchlight procession and at the meeting. . . Judge Wickersham was among the speakers. . .The members of the Committee of Fifteen became heroes in the public imagination, and they exercised a large authority in political affairs.[4]

When Hunt was writing Tacoma's history thirty years later, he wrote Judge Wickersham in Alaska, asking how he viewed his youthful involvement in the Chinese affair and the judge indicated he had no regrets; in fact, he felt he had done the right thing. He wrote from Fairbanks on April 21, 1916, as follows:

> To be quite frank with you I did not know the Chinese were
> to be expelled from Tacoma that day until the whistle blew and

the crowd began to gather. I well remember that Mayor Kaufman came to me as soon as he heard the whistle blowing and he saw the people coming toward us and said to me in his excitable way: "My God, Wickersham, there is going to be trouble here today. Are they going to put the Chinamen out of town?" I assured him that I did not know and that I was as ignorant that there was a plan already arranged as he was.

Kaufman and I stayed together all day and he was exceedingly nervous. He ran a large drygoods store in Tacoma and he felt just as I did that if by an accident or through any disorder on account of drunken men or otherwise, some Chinamen would be killed or some serious matter of that kind happened, the Committee of Fifteen would be on the road to Walla Walla (state prison).

With this horrible vision before us all day, we certainly did what we could to protect the Chinamen from imposition and assault and did the best we could to protect their property from destruction.

We sympathised with their willingness to remove themselves and their property to Portland and we greatly desired to have it done in such a way that we would not be compelled to retire to the privacy of a cell at Walla Walla, McNeil Island, or some other quiet retreat. Luckily we managed to control the situation during the day and while we were all indicted many times and had some interviews with the U.S. marshal backed by U.S. troops, we did escape sequestration of our persons as guests of the government.

I have always felt that we did a great and good work for the Pacific coast that day. There are on the Pacific coast of Asia millions of Chinese and even Japanese who would flood (our) Pacific coast, if the bars were once lowered.

I never objected to the Chinese because of their criminal activities or their immorality but rather the reverse. They appear to me to be a very hard-working, industrious and honest people. However, their system of development under intense suppression has made them much more to be feared than if they were criminals. A Chinaman can live on what an American family would throw from its table. He and every member of his family would work from early in the morning till late at night and live in a very modest hut.

The fear I have always had was not that the Pacific coast
would be overrun by criminals and a foreign race of base and
immoral character but that we would be confronted by millions
of industrious hard-working sons and daughters of Confucius,
who, if given an equal chance with our people, would outdo
them in the struggle for life and gain possession of the Pacific
coast of America. . . .[5]

As Tacoma emerged into a booming commercial center,
Wickersham's aggressive and ambitious personality won him a
leadership role. His swashbuckling manner earned him a reputation as a
"radical" in the eyes of the more sedate business community. When he
ran for re-election to the probate judgeship as a Populist and defeated
his Republican opponent, who had been nominated by the prestigious
Lincoln Club, he was ostracized from the Republican party. Two years
later he became a member of the new Labor Union party and was
thoroughly trounced by a Republican when he ran for a third term as
probate judge.

As one of the organizers of the Union Labor party, Wickersham
delivered such a firebrand speech that the meeting almost turned into a
riot. He contended that communism and anarchy could consistently be
embraced in the same party platform - a thesis which met with violent
objection from members of the audience. The group met again a few
days later when their anger had subsided and nominated a slate for city
officials to be elected; their ticket was overwhelmingly defeated by the
businessmen's ticket.[6]

Wickersham's reputation as a dynamic public speaker won him numerous invitations to speak on behalf of community projects. When the
Methodists were debating whether to build the Puget Sound University
either in Seattle or Tacoma, it was Wickersham's rousing talk which
turned the tide. He convinced his fellow Tacomans that they should
raise an endowment fund of $75,000 to induce the university's location
in their town and the university officials were so favorably impressed
that they decided on Tacoma.[7]

Wickersham became part-owner of the Tacoma *News* together with
Richard Roediger and Allen Mason; it was known as pro-Democratic as
opposed to its two competitors - the *Ledger* and the *Evening Telegraph* -
which were pro-Republican.[8]

During his interlude of political "radicalism", Wickersham changed
law partners three times within the same number of years: one was
James Palmer, the son of Governor Palmer of Springfield, Illinois;

another was D.F. Murray, and the third was Benjamin Sheeks. He was also the subject of front-page newspaper headlines for weeks on end because of his involvement with a woman who accused him of seducing her.

Fortunately for the sake of his future career, Wickersham's interlude of political radicalism and extramarital proclivities was short-lived and he reverted to his former conservative pattern of behavior. He moved to a farm in 1889 in the vicinity of Gig Harbor. Daily steamers and sailing vessels shuttled between Gig Harbor and the mainland so that he could commute readily to his law office in Tacoma. He bought acreage and subdivided it into residential lots. Today there is a "Wickersham Highway" leading off State Highway 16 going from Tacoma to Gig Harbor. The highway goes through Shore Acres, a fine-looking residential district.

He also filed a plat of 85-1/4 acres of land bordering Henderson Bay, naming it the city of Springfield. The name, however, was changed a few years later to Wauna. It was envisioned as a summer resort.[9]

After about two years, the Wickershams rented their farm and moved back into town. Their second son, Arthur James, born on February 21, 1886 had died two years later. His brief life coincided with his father's political and social interregnum! A third son, Howard Sullivan, was born on October 19, 1893.

The Wickershams were avid outdoorsmen; they loved to go hiking and mountain climbing in the Olympics and Cascade mountains. Once they walked from Cape Flattery along the beach to Grays Harbor, visiting the Indian villages along the way in order to study their language and mode of living. Sometimes they were joined on these expeditions by friends and relatives.

Wickersham described one of these backpacking trips in an article for *Goldwaite's Geographical Magazine.* For twenty days "they climbed mountains, waded torrents, slept above clouds and for the last seven days lived on water and flour cakes, having run out of provisions." His prose reached romantic heights as he recalled a moonlit evening when they were bedded down for the night on a frost-covered meadow and watched "the waving trees sparkle and flash like diamonds and the distant glaciers, glistening like burnished silver and the heavens ablaze with a myriad of diamonds - a picture never to be forgotten."[10]

It worried Wickersham to think that all this virgin beauty might some day be destroyed by man's encroachment. He is credited with being the first to propose that a national park be created in the Olympics. In November, 1890, he wrote articles for *Frank Leslie's* and *Century* magazines making that suggestion. At that time there were only three national parks - Yellowstone, Sequoia, and Yosemite.

It is not correct, however, to credit him with the first records made of the area, as that distinction belongs to naturalist John Muir. Wickersham's interest was more recreational than scientific. In urging the creation of a national park in the Olympics, he wanted the broad-antlered elk, deer, and bear protected, as well as the natural beauties of the mountain plateaus.[11]

Sometime during the summer of 1889 Wickersham returned to the Republican fold and from then on played an active role in the party's councils. Statehood for Washington Territory was imminent, and the politicians were vying for the first state offices. As a delegate to the county convention where delegates were chosen to go to the territorial convention, Wickersham showed surprising political influence, for having so recently been read out of the party. His prominence was noted in the local press:

> Did anybody say that James Wickersham was a dead duck? A few people might have said so a few weeks ago before Sadie's confessions, but there isn't a Republican in yesterday's convention to be found who will say so this morning.
> "The gentle James," as he has been affectionately called, had his oar in about every nomination, and with his friends, just about ran the convention. The other wire pullers did not suspect that there was so much solid Wickersham strength and the result was a surprise. . . .[12]

Wickersham was not chosen as one of the twenty-six delegates to the territorial convention in Walla Walla, but he attended, holding the proxy of Herman Jones of Minter district. Washington Territory became a state on November 11, 1889, when President Benjamin Harrison signed the enabling act.

Wickersham's political star regained some of its luster when his friend, Edward S. Orr, appointed him city attorney. Orr was elected mayor of Tacoma in 1894, in a bitter campaign against County Commissioner A.V. Fawcett. The Populist and Prohibitionist parties each entered the contest with a full ticket, as well as the Republicans and Democrats.[13]

Although the city council refused to confirm Wickersham as city attorney, Orr kept him in office for two years through recess

CITY OFFICIALS.

Edward S. Orr Mayor of Tacoma, was elected to his present position in April 1894, on the Republican ticket. He has been a resident of

Tacoma for six years, and in 1889 formed the real estate firm of Hill, Orr & Craig. He represented the First Ward one term in the City Council. Mr. Orr was born in Clarion County, Pennsylvania, in 1850. He received a common school education and later attended the Carrier Seminary at Clarion, Clarion County, from the eighteenth to the twenty-second year of his life. He then engaged in contracting in the oil regions of Pennsylvania, and in 1877 moved to Wichita, Kansas, where he was enga ed in stock raising and farming, but his health failing a year after went to Colorado, where he became interested in gold mining and milling and followed the business for eleven years, his operations being principally

MAYOR E. S. ORR

in San Juan and Trinidad. Coming further west he invested in mining properties in the British Columbia and Okanogan regions.

James Wickersham –City Attorney of Tacoma, is a young man

whose administration has been characterized by continuous effort and marked ability in looking after the legal rights of the "City of Destiny." Mr. Wickersham was born in Marion County, Illinois, August 24, 1857. Studied law in office of Senator John M. Palmer at S ringfield, Illinois, 1877-1880. Was connected with legal department of tenth census at Springfield, Illinois, from 1880 to 1883. Came to Tacoma in June, 1883. Was elected Probate Judge of Pierce County in 1884 and served two terms; appointed City Attorney of Tacoma in 1894.

JAMES WICKERSHAM

Ruth Allman

Wickersham as city attorney of Tacoma, 1894-96.

appointments. Orr ran for reelection in 1896 with Fawcett again as his opponent. The official canvass declared Fawcett the winner by two votes, but the city council ordered a recount, only to learn that the ballots were missing, though they had been locked in a vault.

Orr instituted legal action to oust Fawcett, and the superior court declared Orr the winner by fifteen votes. Orr held the mayoralty for about a year, when he had to surrender it to Fawcett following a reversal by the state supreme court, which declared Fawcett the winner by two votes.

Orr did not reappoint Wickersham during his second term. He appointed John A. "Jack" Shackleford instead. He was the brother of Lewis Shackleford, who years later became Alaska's Republican national committeeman and a bitter foe of Wickersham's.

Mayor Fawcett, with the city council's approval, employed Wickersham as special counsel to assist the city attorney in continuing the utility suit which Wickersham had instituted while city attorney in Orr's administration. It became known as the "million dollar suit." The city had purchased the private light and water system for $1,750,000 only to find that the company did not have clear title to the water sources and the real owners were threatening an injunction suit against the city for taking their water.[14]

The city was tottering on the brink of bankruptcy. The city treasurer had been found guilty of embezzling $109,000. But the utility company's executive officers, who were among the city's most influential community leaders, refused to accept any responsibility. As far as they were concerned, the company had consummated the sale and it was up to the city to solve its problems.

Wickersham, as city attorney, instituted suit against the utility company. It went to a jury trial and the jury found damages for the city in the sum of $787,500; Wickersham had asked for $1,000,000. Entering the courtroom shortly after the verdict had been rendered, he was given a standing ovation.

A year later the state supreme court reversed the decision, failing to find misrepresentation or fraud and holding that the purchaser was supposed to know what it was doing.

There was in Tacoma at the time a weekly paper called *The Sun*, edited by A.P. Tugwell and Frank L. Baker. Baker, who was known then and afterward as a rather testy radical, gave the supreme court, and particularly the judge, a pen-lashing in which he employed such expressions as "infernal rotten decision," "supreme simpleton," "conception of an ass," "vicious and vacillating." Baker and Tugwell promptly were cited for contempt and fined $300 each and carried off to jail.

Wickersham filed a motion for a rehearing, and the supreme court reversed its decision, awarding the city $797,500 in damages, which was $10,000 more than the jury in the superior court had awarded originally. Wickersham and his law partner, Benjamin Sheeks received a legal fee of $25,000.

The sheriff later reported that the Tacoma Light and Water Company was without property upon which levy could be made. Wickersham immediately alleged that the company had been organized with the aim of sequestration, and he obtained an execution on all its property, including the Tacoma gas plant, the Puyallup waterworks, and the company's franchises.[15]

Among the defendants in the utilities case was Charles B. Wright, president and chief stockholder, who, for years, had been called "the father of Tacoma" because of his philanthropic gestures, one being the establishment of Annie Wright Seminary, a girls' academy named for his daughter. In the final trial before the supreme court, the attorney for the defense, in his closing argument, urged the jury to bear in mind that Wright had invested much money in Tacoma and therefore was entitled to special consideration.

When the suit was finally settled, several of the major stockholders were reduced to bankruptcy; one committed suicide after embezzling $200,000 of trust funds. In recalling their former positions of wealth and power, Wickersham wrote in his diary:

> These men ruled Tacoma for twenty years with a rod of iron; they bankrupted the city, in the light and water deal, and other ill-advised and dishonest matters - and gained nothing by it in the end! They fought me politically and otherwise, and often and loudly threatened to run me out of town. Comment is unnecessary![16]

Wickersham was still fighting the city's case against the utility company when the Republicans of Pierce County nominated him for a seat in the state house of representatives in 1898. He made a successful race and had the unanimous support of the Pierce County delegation for the speakership of the house, but lost his bid to the nominee from King County, the traditional challenger of Pierce County.

Wickersham was not idle in his efforts to regain party prominence. He organized the first Benjamin Harrison Club to promote Harrison's reelection to the presidency. With the admission of six new states - Washington, Idaho, Montana, Wyoming, North and South Dakota - during Harrison's administration, western politicians gained prestige in the national councils. Harrison lost his bid for reelection to Democrat Grover Cleveland partly because of the strength of the Populist party in the West, which drew votes away from the normally Republican districts.

On another occasion he called a meeting at his home to organize a Republican Club, whose primary goal was the reelection of Frank Cushman to the United States House of Representatives.

Wickersham's quick-witted parliamentary maneuver at a party caucus won a United States Senate seat for his friend, Addison G. Foster of Tacoma, and his own Alaskan judgeship appointment. He wrote an account of the incident, entitling it "How Judges Are Sometimes Made."[17]

In those days, United States senators were chosen by their state legislators, with nominations made at party caucuses. Two prominent attorneys - Addison G. Foster of Tacoma and Watson C. Squire of Seattle, the incumbent and former territorial governor - had made statewide campaigns for the office. The nomination vote was expected to be very close. Not until the last vote was cast at the caucus was it known that the Tacoma candidate had won by one vote. The result was greeted with a roar of disappointment on the one hand and a wild cheer of exultation on the other. Wickersham recalled the subsequent maneuverings:

> Almost instantly the chairman threw his gavel on the desk, and in a loud voice declared the caucus adjourned. He shouted to those members who had lost to leave the meeting and gather immediately at their political headquarters. Great confusion followed as one-half the members and all their supporters rushed for the outer door. The one-man majority appeared to be stunned by this quick action of their adversaries and many of them began to follow the bolters from the hall.

> It just happened that my seat in the caucus was on the side line near the chair occupied by the bolting chairman. As he dropped the official gavel and shouted a dissolution of the meeting and rushed for the door, my fingers closed over the handle of the emblem of authority and its loud raps and my call for order came about so quickly as to arrest the flow towards the door.

Some of the quicker witted supporters of our candidate joined in the call for order, and urged our members to keep their seats. . .Seeing me in the chair, another of our faction took possession of the clerk's desk and a roll call was had, and to our discomfiture it disclosed that we had lost our single majority member - the out-rushing crowd had carried him away and we had one less than a majority left in the caucus.

Having the gavel in my hand it became my instant duty to appoint a committee of three influential members of our group and instruct them to go out and find our lost voter and persuade him to return to the caucus and to his promised allegiance to our candidate.

That committee found him in animated conversation in the midst of an excited and angry crowd of our opponents in the yard, but properly supported by the committee, he returned to our caucus. . .His return was greeted with great applause; the doors were closed and securely locked against a disorderly crowd of our opponents who seemed determined to return and break up further proceedings. . . .

The chairman was instructed to prepare a document for all to sign promising to cast his ballot in the next day's meeting of the legislature for our candidate. . . .

Foster won the United States senate seat after promising his opponent that he would share in the federal patronage. This agreement led to controversies and delayed appointments, one being Wickersham's. In gratitude for his help, Senator Foster recommended Wickersham for two alternative appointments - consul general to Japan or district judge in Alaska. There was a stable full of aspirants for both positions.

Foster endorsed Wickersham first for the judgeship and asked him to forward as many other endorsements as possible. This Wickersham did, and the list included judges, legislators, and other prominent politicians, including Washington's Governor John Harte McGraw of Seattle. Wickersham had campaigned for McGraw "almost at a risk of personal violence."

During the scramble for appointments, Wickersham's adversaries threatened "to file charges of my old troubles to prevent my appointment."[18]

Finally a wire arrived from Senator Foster congratulating him on being appointed to the judgeship at Eagle City, Alaska. Though disappointed in not getting the consulship, Wickersham telegraphed his reply: "Assignment perfectly satisfactory; wife specially pleased. Hurry commission and instructions. Am ready to go. . . ."[19]

Contrary to what he wrote in the 1930s in his book *Old Yukon* (page 2) to the effect that he declined the consular position preferring the judgeship, his diary entries at the time the two appointments were pending showed that he would rather have gone to Japan. On April 17, 1900, he wrote: "I telegraphed Foster saying, 'much prefer Japan, but leave everything with you.' " Then on May 4, he wrote: "E.C. Bellows of Vancouver, Wash. was today appointed consul general to Japan. I desired this place very much but my endorsements were all for judge in Alaska and evidently Senator Foster thought I ought not to have two choices."

With receipt of his commission as district judge, he took his oath of office and assumed his duties on June 12, 1900; his salary started from that date. He arranged to take his stenographer, George A. Jeffery, with him to Alaska.

He also hired Albert R. Heilig, a young Tacoma attorney and accountant to go with him as clerk of the court. Heilig had been elected city controller of Tacoma in 1892-94, and had served in the state House of Representatives with Wickersham and helped get Foster elected to the United States Senate.[20]

Chapter 4

The Sadie Brantner Affair

> *The verdict of the jury finding Judge Wickersham guilty of seducing Sadie Brantner last evening was the subject of much comment. . . Opinion is divided to a marked degree upon the justice of the verdict. . . .*   *(Seattle* Daily Press, *Feb.27,1889)*
>
> *Once more the Wickersham case is up before the public, this time because of a startling affidavit of Miss Brantner. . .in which she swears that Wickersham is not guilty of her seduction. . .that she had intercourse with other men before she saw Wickersham. . .She also swears that she was sent to James Wickersham for the purpose of injuring him. . . .(Seattle* Daily Times, *June17,1889)*

Wickersham was a handsome, virile young man, a popular personality about town. As county probate judge, he held one of the town's most prestigious positions. It was a heady time of life for the adventurous young frontiersman.

His wife was out of town - she had gone to visit her relatives in Illinois, taking their two sons with her - five-year-old Darrell and eighteen-months-old Arthur. It was the first time he and his wife had been separated during their seven years of marriage. He was at loose ends, not knowing what to do with himself after a day's work at the office.

One evening in October, 1887, he was eating dinner at Chilberg's restaurant and reading the evening paper when he noticed an attractive young woman sitting in a nearby booth. Their eyes met and a flirtation ensued. He sent a note to her and before the evening meal was over, they were conversing with one another. He learned that her name was Sadie Brantner and that she was a house-to-house book agent. She was selling a book entitled *The Royal Path to Life*. She said she was nineteen years old and unmarried. He suggested that she come to his office later in the week as he would be interested in buying a copy of the book.

Several office visits were required to consummate the sale, and they were followed by late evening buggy rides. As their buggy riding became more and more frequent, their relationship developed into serious lovemaking, including overnight rendezvous in Seattle hotel rooms. Sadie was flattered with the attention of such an important person, and the judge was enjoying a new experience.

It was not long before the young judge's political opponents learned of his extramarital excursions. As a matter of fact, he was so enamored with his new emotional involvement that he became careless about keeping it a secret.

For instance, one evening when he was leaving the courthouse, he encountered the county prosecuting attorney, who was one of his bitterest political enemies. The attorney asked Wickersham if he could have five minutes of his time to discuss a matter, whereupon the judge waved him aside, saying he had a date to go buggy riding with a young lady and was in a hurry. He even boasted about previous dates during which intimacies were discussed. The attorney cautioned him against continuing these buggy rides and threatened that he would tell his wife when she returned. Wickersham nonchalantly replied: "She won't believe you if you do," and went on his merry way to meet Sadie.[1]

The first stage of this philandering adventure allegedly took place between October and New Year's Eve, 1887. It is not known when Mrs. Wickersham returned to Tacoma, but it is known that the judge went to Washington, D.C. on business in January and was absent when his little son, Arthur, died in Tacoma on February 20, 1888. According to Sadie's story, she and the judge resumed their rendezvous in March, and they continued all through the summer.

Wickersham's term as probate judge was expiring in November, and he was running for reelection. Powerful interests were determined to defeat him, including Editor Radebaugh of the Tacoma *Ledger*, who wrote such scurrilous editorials about the judge that Wickersham filed a $50,000 libel suit against him during the campaign.

Then the bombshell exploded! Wickersham was arrested on a charge of seduction and Sadie Brantner was the complaining witness.

The Tacoma and Seattle newspapers devoted generous space to the judge's philandering escapades. He was defeated for reelection and was brought to trial on February 19, 1889, in the King County District Court in Seattle.

The trial lasted six days, during which the papers ran front page stories quoting almost verbatim the melodramatic testimony of the poor, helpless, innocent girl who had been seduced by the infatuated, knowledgeable jurist. The crime of the illicit intercourse which led to an illegal abortion operation was described in graphic detail by the girl and retold in the papers under such headlines as: "Eating Forbidden Fruit," "Man's Wiles and Women's Woes," "Courtroom Becomes Auditorium of Salacious Stories." The charge of seduction was based on the girl's chastity.

In addition to the seduction charge, Wickersham was also indicted for subornation of perjury for representing the Brantner girl as a married woman with a child and thus entitled to land on which to build a home, under the homestead law.

Wickersham did not deny his intimacies with the girl, but based his defense on the fact that she was not chaste and an array of male witnesses was produced who testified to having had intimate relations with Miss Brantner. Testimony also was produced to the effect that she had told the judge that she had been married and divorced.

Another defense argument was that the whole matter was spite work on the part of the judge's political enemies and that they had hired the Brantner girl to bring the case against him.

The jury was out almost seven hours; it returned with a verdict of guilty as charged.

The following May the case reappeared on the front pages when Miss Brantner told a reporter that Wickersham was trying to extort a written retraction from her. She told of being followed by detectives hired by him and of how she was kidnapped and forced to sign a retraction in order to save him from going to the penitentiary.

Her story appeared while a motion for a new trial was pending before the district court. During the ensuing weeks, the Brantner girl signed several conflicting affidavits, sometimes accusing Wickersham of duress and other times absolving him of all wrongdoing and admitting that she had lied at the behest of his political enemies.

On July 9, 1889, the prosecuting attorney moved to dismiss the case on the grounds that the contradicting affidavits proved Sadie Brantner "utterly unreliable." The judge agreed and dismissed the case.

In her final affidavit, Sadie said her pregnancy had been caused by another man and not the judge. In view of her conflicting stories, only the principals in the scenario know what part of her testimony was actually the truth.

But one fact is certain - Wickersham lived with this "skeleton in his closet" all the rest of his life. He referred to "that old 1888 affair" twenty-three different times in his diaries. It was aired during every political campaign, even in his last one in 1930 when he was seventy-three years old. Former Seattle and Tacoma acquaintances repeatedly threatened to blackmail him by retelling the story to a new audience. Wickersham took the position that he could not afford to accede to blackmail and instead would retell the story himself, trusting that the whole truth would exhonerate him.

The Brantner ghost kept reappearing. One day in 1915 Wickersham met United States Senator James Hamilton Lewis of Illinois in the House corridor. Lewis had been one of his defense attorneys in the seduction trial twenty-six years earlier. Lewis ruefully told Wickersham that Sadie was living in Washington, D.C. and he had seen her several times in the visitors' gallery in the Senate. Once he met and talked with her; she said she had married an army officer after the Wickersham trial and she was then a widow. She expressed regret over the shame and humiliation that she had caused Wickersham.

In his diary, Wickersham commented that the senator had neglected to give him Sadie's present name or her address.[2]

In 1928, when the Wickershams were guests at the Frye Hotel in Seattle, he had a surprise visitor - Mrs. Handsaker, who had been a star witness in the trial on behalf of Miss Brantner. She came to tell him how sorry she was about what had happened. Then she showed up again at the same hotel, just three days after his second marriage and begged for financial assistance. She said she was destitute, so he gave her a twenty-dollar bill and told her to go away and never show up again.[3]

Excerpts from the newspaper stories have been reproduced in Appendix A for those readers who desire more detailed information to decide how much of the Brantner story to believe.

Chapter 5

Family Relationships

When we drove up from Sandoval, we came by the old home where my mother went as a nineteen-year-old bride in 1856 and where I was born in 1857.

Four large silver-leaf trees are yet growing which mother tells me I brought from Grandpa McHaney's and planted there more than fifty years ago. . . .   *(Diary,Feb.20,1913)*

The Wickersham family ties were strong, with Mary Jane Wickersham the focal point. It was she who encouraged her eldest son to leave home to get additional education and it was she who kept the homefires burning while her children traveled far and wide.

Literally carving a new home out of the virgin wilderness, the Alexander Wickershams created a spirit of love and kinship which was to tie the individual family members together throughout their lives.

Mary Jane Wickersham's life was not an easy one, but she had the patience and courage to meet crises as they arose. Her son James once observed: "Mother is strong and healthy; she does not annoy one with nervous fancies, but is quiet and happy." She lost her husband and her twenty-two-year-old daughter Clyde within the same year. Shortly thereafter two sons and a daughter departed to make their homes in Alaska. Two sons and two daughters continued to live near her at Buckley.

The eldest daughter, Sarah Nancy, or Nan, as she came to be called, began teaching school in Tacoma as soon as the family arrived in the fall of 1883. She was one of the nine original teachers who were on hand to welcome 425 children when the new school opened its doors.

Nan never married, and when she tired of teaching school, she took up practical nursing or secretarial work. She often complained of feeling lonely, so Wickersham once brought her to Valdez to work in the office of the clerk of the court, but she was ready to return to Tacoma, at the end of three months. One day she came to his office to ask his advice on getting married to a local admirer. He laughed at her for considering such a thing at the advanced age of forty-five years. It was soon thereafter that she departed for Tacoma.

For years Wickersham sent her a monthly allowance of twenty-five dollars, but they became estranged in latter years when she demanded that he triple that amount. He tried to persuade her to sell the twenty-four acres of land which she owned in Buckley and buy herself a place in an old folks home, but she refused to do that. When she died in 1934, she named her brother Harry as her sole beneficiary to an estate valued at one thousand dollars. Wickersham arranged to have her buried in the family plot in the Tacoma cemetery next to his sister Clyde.

Wickersham's eldest brother Edgar, born in 1866, went to sea when he was about eighteen years old, making two or three voyages to the Orient. On his last voyage he brought home an English lad named Charles Edward Taylor; they lived at the Alexander Wickersham home in Buckley.

Taylor married Wickersham's sister May in 1896. Both he and Edgar joined the Klondike gold stampede the following year. Edgar was probably the first regular brakeman on the White Pass and Yukon railroad out of Skagway, and one of the first men in surveying and construction work on that line. He remained with the White Pass until Judge Wickersham came to Eagle City and had him appointed deputy United States marshal at Circle City and later at Fairbanks.[1]

Edgar married Lizzie Chamberlain on March 5, 1895; they had no children. She joined him in Circle after he got the marshal's job. Edgar's fondness for the bottle lost him his marshalship eventually, although his brother tried to keep him on the payroll as long as possible. He was chief of police in Fairbanks, but again the bottle cost him his job. He got in on the real estate boom when the town of Fairbanks was started and made enough to retire to California in 1905.

They returned to Fairbanks in 1918 and remained there until the early 1930s when they retired to Pasadena, California. The James Wickershams visited them each year as they traveled between Washington, D.C. and the West Coast. Edgar died in 1936. During his last illness, he ran out of funds and Judge Wickersham came to his rescue.

Brother Harry remained a bachelor all his life and lived in Buckley near his mother. He went to Fairbanks in the spring of 1914 hoping to get employment on the newly announced government railroad. He mushed over the trail from Chitina to Fairbanks.[2]

Harry's mind deteriorated in later years, and Judge Wickersham worried about him. He tried to get him to sell some of his property in Buckley, which he had inherited from his father, and enter an old folks home, but to no avail.

When Harry was made executor of his sister Nan's estate, he failed to file the will for probate, in accordance with the law, and was hailed into court to give an explanation. He refused to answer any questions, and when the judge asked him what he had done with his sister's will, he told the judge it was "none of your damn business," whereupon the judge remanded him to jail for twenty-four hours.

While serving his sentence, a complaint was drawn charging him with failure to produce the will, and he was held under one thousand dollars' bail. He was arraigned the following day but he refused to plead either guilty or not guilty or to be sworn. The judge found him guilty of contempt and sentenced him to ten days in jail. Judge Wickersham wrote the district attorney in Tacoma explaining that Harry was mentally incompetent, and no further legal action was taken against him. He died in the Pierce County Veterans Hospital in Tacoma in January 1953, at the age of eighty-four.

Sister May, born in 1873, joined her husband, Charles Taylor, in Skagway in 1897, where he was in the customs brokerage business. Later they went to Dawson where he worked for the White Pass and Yukon railroad until 1907, returning then to Skagway as claim agent for the White Pass.

He studied law and later went into private practice in Fairbanks. He was elected city clerk and police magistrate. He was in private practice in Iditarod when May died in Seattle in 1921, after a year's illness. The Taylors had two daughters, Clyde and Lucile.[3]

Taylor was appointed assistant United States attorney at Nome in 1927 but refused the promotion to United States attorney four years later, preferring to return to Fairbanks. He married Eva Lucille Randall, a Fairbanks schoolteacher, later that year and went into partnership with Major George W. Albrecht, who was narrowly defeated by Cap Lathrop for Republican national committeeman in 1928.[4]

Brother Frank, born in 1875, served in the Spanish-American War and was wounded in Manila. He also served in World War I, enlisting in the Engineers Corps as a bugler. He was forty years old when he enlisted and forfeited his thirty-dollar-a-month Philippine pension, but he craved the excitement of going abroad.

Frank visited his brothers in Fairbanks in 1904, on his way to Nome, where he had a job for the summer. He later became a tramp printer in San Francisco and Fresno, California. He was married and had a son, DeVere, who worked as an engineer on a tramp steamer in New York harbor.

Jennie, the youngest sister, born in 1880, married Charles D. Hanson of Enumclaw, Washington. He and his four brothers operated a sawmill and lumber business at Enumclaw, which they inherited from their father. The business provided a comfortable income for all five families.

The Charles Hansons had three children - Harold, Helen and Alice Elizabeth. When her husband died in 1919, Jennie moved to Buckley.

When Judge Wickersham received word in August, 1927, that his sister Jennie lay gravely ill in Providence Hospital in Seattle, he took the first boat south from Juneau to be at her bedside; she was suffering from Bright's disease. When he arrived at the hospital, he found that she was able to speak of her death calmly; she had made her will and requested her son Harold to continue giving financial assistance to her eldest sister, Nan, after she was gone.

When Jennie died, Wickersham felt the loss deeply as she was the last of his immediate family for whom he had real affection. That night he wrote in his diary:

> Mother, Debbie and now Jennie. I am now, indeed, an old and lonely man. Poor Jen, in half delirium, said to me, "I thought you would go next." She then shook her head as if perplexed and said to herself, "It's queer, aint it?" And it is, for I am twenty-three years older than Jen.
>
> Harry was here when Jen passed away, but he is almost wholly incompetent. I had to give him money to go home on to Buckley; he borrowed to get here on the car last night and Nan is worse. And in dealing with these I so depended on Jen - we divided the responsibilities and the expense - now it all falls on me. But Harold and Darrell will help me.
>
> Really, though, I will be seventy years old next week and am liable to be a burden myself in a few years. But Darrell has "money sense" and money and a strong sense of thoughtfulness and love - so it's all right.[5]

Driving over to Tacoma and then to Buckley a couple of days later to attend Jennie's funeral, Wickersham was overcome by loneliness - he had lost his mother three years before and his wife a year ago. Returning to his old hometown of his early manhood brought back memories of when he was young and virile. He stopped for lunch at the old Tacoma Hotel. The editor of the Puyallup paper recognized him and came over to visit. He had been a cub reporter with the Tacoma *Ledger* when Wickersham was city attorney.

His sister Nan and his brothers Harry and Frank, and all the Hanson family, were present for the funeral services. Jennie was laid to rest beside her husband and daughter Alice in the family plot in the old Tacoma cemetery.

Passing by the grave of Debbie and his two sons, he stooped down to lay a wreath of red roses. Later he wrote:

I feel old and deserted, with only Darrell left, but he is a dear and loving son.

I am always pleased at the fine crowd of boys growing up in the families. There are eight of them including Harold. Six of them acted as pallbearers at Jennie's funeral. They are all from eighteen to twenty-two years of age; are six feet tall, well-educated and all wellbred gentlemen.[6]

Four days later he took the stage from Seattle to Enumclaw to enjoy a dinner at Harold's home in honor of his birthday; it included his favorite dessert - fresh blackberry shortcake. Other Hanson relatives dropped in after dinner to wish him a happy birthday.

Son Darrell Palmer, the Judge's only child to reach adulthood, received an appointment to the naval academy at Annapolis in 1900 from Congressman Francis Cushman of Tacoma. He graduated in February, 1904, and was assigned to the S.S. *Tacoma* at Mare Island, San Francisco.

He was six feet, two inches tall and weighed 230 pounds. He had an introvertive personality which worried his father as he thought he was "too retiring and modest" for his own good. Darrell had a very close relationship with his mother, and she visited with him for weeks at a time, whenever she could arrange it.

During his seventeen years of active service in the U.S. Navy, he served aboard the *Nebraska*, *Iowa*, and *Minnesota*, either as chief engineer, navigator, or executive officer. He did a two-year stint as naval recruiting officer in St. Louis, Missouri and served aboard the

Paducah when it was doing hydrographic work along the coast of Nicaragua. He went on a two-year cruise around the world.

In 1909 Darrell contracted typhoid fever at Norfolk and from then on he suffered excessively from seasickness. This led him to start talking about resigning from the navy, much to his father's disgust and disappointment. He had hoped that his son would make the navy his lifetime career, assuring him of social and financial security.

In April, 1913, Darrell filed his first application for retirement on halfpay on account of disability from seasickness, but he was not granted it until eight years later. In the meantime, he served in the war with Mexico and World War I. He was made lieutenant commander at the outbreak of World War I, with the promise of retirement at the conclusion of hostilities.

Upon retirement in March, 1921, Darrell found employment with a marine insurance company in Philadelphia. He had married Jane Avery in Philadelphia the previous year; they had no children. In June, 1923, he was transferred to San Francisco to be in charge of the marine claims department of the Insurance Company of North America, for the entire Pacific Coast. His mother was overjoyed to know that her beloved son would be near her the remainder of her life. She went on frequent motoring trips with Darrell and his wife in the ensuing years.

Darrell was a devoted son during his mother's last years of illnesses. He took his father's place in showering her with attention as she lay ill in one sanitarium after the other. When he thought his father was remiss in writing to Debbie, Darrell took him to task. On one such occasion, Wickersham wrote in his diary:

> I am quite provoked about it, because I thought I was being so good for I write every boat and send the daily papers, but Darrell cannot bear to have his mother neglected. I just wonder if he thinks he loves her better than I do?[7]

Darrell and his wife visited his father twice in Juneau, after his mother passed away.

Darrell retired from his insurance job in March, 1937. Commenting on his retirement, the San Francisco *Chronicle* said: "Wick's deliberate, unruffled demeanor at loss meetings and his sound, cautious counsel will be missed."

He died in Ross, California, on March 9, 1954. His wife remarried and lived until April 6, 1970, when she passed away at age eighty-two.

Besides his immediate family, Judge Wickersham had half a dozen aunts and uncles who migrated from Illinois settling in the vicinity of Buckley. Whenever "the Judge from Alaska" came south for a visit, all of the relatives would gather in one of their homes, to listen to his tall tales about life on the northern frontier.

Today, in lot 22, block A, section 2, of the Old Tacoma cemetery, 4801 South Tacoma Way, there lie buried: Wickersham, himself; his parents; his two wives, Debbie and Grace; his three sons, Darrell, Arthur and Howard; his daughter-in-law, Jane (Wickersham) Lloyd; his brother Harry; and his sisters Clyde, May, and Nan.[8]

PART II

ALASKA PRE-WICKERSHAM

Chapter 6

Alaskans Seek Self-Government

The struggle of Alaskans for their rights as American citizens forms one of the gloomy pages of American history. (Hall Young of Alaska, the Mushing Parson, an Autobiography, *Fleming H. Revell,N.Y.,1927,p.272*)

While Wickersham was undergoing the vicissitudes of frontier life in the Puget Sound area in the 1880s and 1890s, when he was 26 to 43 years of age, other adventure-seeking Americans were heading north to seek their fortune in a land recently purchased by the United States from Russia. Little was known of this new possession, but that did not deter the fearless souls who were ready to forsake the security of their homes for untold fortune awaiting them beyond the horizon, just as the Wickersham families did when they left Illinois to pioneer the Puget Sound wilderness.

Unfortunately the American Congress was not as excited about the new territory and treated it more as a conquered province than a place for settlement and development. According to its second American governor, Alfred P. Swineford:

At the time of the transfer Sitka was a town of considerable importance from a commercial and industrial point of view, with a population of about 1,000 souls, exclusive of the native village. Its industries consisted of iron and brass foundries and machine shops, saw-mill, grist-mill, tannery, and a shipyard, besides the usual complement of shoemakers, bakers, tailors, etc. . . .

With the transfer, all the principal industries were abandoned, the buildings of the shipyard were demolished. . .there was no further use for the brass and iron foundries, and of all the industries then existing only the old saw-mill remains. . . .

From the time of the transfer the newly acquired territory was looked upon and treated by the President, and Congress as well, as an Indian country, and the rule of General Davis and succeeding military commanders was little, if any, less than absolute. . . .[1]

Alaska was designated a military and customs district and placed under the War Department for the first seventeen years. A customs act of July 27, 1868, extended to Alaska the United States laws regarding customs, commerce, and navigation, prohibited the sale, importation, and use of firearms and distilled liquors, and provided that offenders be prosecuted in the district courts of California, Oregon, or the Territory of Washington. Except for that lone bill, Congress took no action in extending civil government despite the promise contained in the treaty of cession extending to its civilized inhabitants "the enjoyment of all the rights, advantages, immunities of citizens of the U.S. and (they) shall be maintained and protected in the free enjoyment of their liberty, property and religion."

Alaskans' pleas for self-government, or home rule, began immediately after the transfer ceremony. On November 14, 1867, a public meeting was held in Sitka to formulate a city provisional government authorizing the creation of the offices of mayor, common council, fire department, etc. This local organic law was ratified by the citizens of the settlement and given official approval by General Jefferson Davis, who willingly promised to "give the citizens every assistance in his power compatible with his military duties."

The first issue of the *Alaska Times*, September 19, 1868, editorialized:

We are strongly in favor of a civil government and directly opposed to military rule. Give Alaska a civil government and you may soon expect to hear of rich minerals having been fully developed by our latent industry but not before.

At a mass meeting held in Sitka on the second anniversary of the flag-raising ceremonies, a resolution was adopted and sent to Congress reminding its members that civil rights and self-government were inalienable privileges of American citizens, therefore, "the citizens of Alaska, having for two years past been deprived of any voice in the making of laws, ask from Congress the formation of a territorial government."[2]

In June, 1877, the War Department relinquished jurisdiction to the Treasury Department. Anarchy reigned for the next two years:

> Brawls were incessant, and theft and murder stalked abroad unpunished. The settlement at Sitka barely escaped the horrors of Indian massacre. The Collector of Customs and his deputies constituted the sole official authority in the country - civil, military or naval. Urgent appeals were made to Washington, but to no avail.
>
> On March 1, 1879, deliverance came from a source the least expected, when a man-of-war, flying the tri-cross of the British ensign, dropped anchor in the Sitka harbor.[3]

A month later a United States naval ship took over the protection of the colony and that remained the sole government for the territory until passage of the Organic Act of May 17, 1884.

As settlers continued to arrive and attempted to establish communities, the need for local government became more acute. Town meetings were held and resolutions passed beseeching Congress for help, and unofficial delegates were sent to Washington to make personal appeals, to little avail.

During the first seventeen years following the purchase, some twenty-five bills were introduced in Congress providing for civil government in Alaska, but they remained buried in committee.[4]

Finally, in 1884, the Forty-eighth Congress passed a bill sponsored by Senator Benjamin Harrison, Republican of Indiana, constituting Alaska as "a civil and judicial district" with the seat of government in Sitka, and providing for a governor, a district judge, district attorney, clerk of court, four commissioners stationed at Sitka, Juneau, Wrangell, and Unalaska, a marshal, and four deputies.

The mining laws of the United States were to apply, but not the general land laws; a legislative assembly and delegate to Congress were specifically denied. The general laws of the state of Oregon were declared to be the law of the district. The secretary of interior was charged with inaugurating a school system for which $25,000 was appropriated for the biennium.

Though limited in scope, it was a significant first step in Alaskans' struggle for home rule. How inadequately it met their day-to-day requirements became distressingly clear as time went on and officials tried to perform their duties.

In October 1899, the Skagway and Juneau chambers of commerce sponsored a convention in Juneau at which a memorial was passed asking Congress for two additional judges, a delegate to Congress, added powers for the commissioners' courts, a civil code, amendments to the criminal code and a general municipal and incorporation law. A young Skagway lawyer, John Garland Price, was chosen to go to Washington to help Governor John Green Brady lobby for these requests.

They found an ally in Senator Thomas Henry Carter, Republican of Montana. He introduced legislation which revised the criminal code and provided for a civil code, all of which was enacted into law effective June 6, 1900. Alaska was divided into three judicial districts, with court headquarters at Sitka, Nome and Eagle City. Commenting on the comprehensive legislation passed on Alaska's behalf, the New York *Sun* editorialized:

> This is probably the longest law ever passed by Congress as a separate enactment. It filled more than 250 closely printed pages. . . .It is a notable example of the exercise in the highest degree, of the sovereign power of Congress to legislate for a territory belonging to the United States. . . .[5]

Thus, after almost a quarter of a century of continuous lobbying, Congress granted the territory the basic legal machinery which its citizens needed to build a stable American society.

Chapter 7

Alaska's First Civil Officials

> *Alaska became a political preserve for the payment of small debts owed by big politicians to little ones. . . .*
>
> *Alaska experienced the maladministrations of various appointees. Few were endowed with that understanding of conditions. . .which should have been a basic qualification for their office; many of them were seeking solace for uncomplimentary election returns. . . . Jeannette Paddock Nichols,* History of Alaska, *Arthur H. Clark Co., Cleveland,1924,p.83)*

It fell to President Chester A. Arthur, the twenty-first president of the United States, to nominate the first set of officials to inaugurate a civil government for Alaska. Three years earlier as vice president, he had acceded to the presidency following the assassination of President James A. Garfield.

Known as "The Gentleman Boss" of the Republican party in New York City, and a longtime collector of the port of New York, Arthur had become a symbol of the professional politican who handled patronage with a deft hand. He consulted with the Republican members of Congress in patronage matters and accorded the western senators the "courtesy" of priority selection for Alaska's new appointees.

It was a motley crew who came north in the summer of 1884. They knew their tenure in office would be brief since a new president would be taking office the following March. No one holding a position of merit would consider such a temporary assignment.

It did not take long after their arrival to note that these officials shared a common weakness, namely an addiction to tippling. This state of bibulosity posed a serious problem in a district where "the sale, importation, and use of distilled liquors" were prohibited by federal law. It was conducive to a brevity of tenure. The governor allegedly spent only two months in Alaska and the district judge departed after holding but one term of court. The district attorney was on a trip in California, when he became inebriated and fell off a train and was killed. The marshal was more of a gambler than a drunkard.

The picture was hardly an inspiring one for the poor Alaskans who had been pleading and waiting so long for the arrival of law and order to solve their problems!

The town of Sitka, which was to be the official headquarters for the officials, had little to offer in the way of diversion for these bibulous newcomers. Long gone were the days of gay parties at Baranof Castle and the spirited fur-trading rendezvous. Desolation reigned in the empty buildings as the winds blew through their broken window panes. To the three hundred white people living in the sleepy, little village, the greatest excitement was the arrival of an occasional steamer.

When the brass gun of the steamer boomed among the islands of the bay, the Stars and Stripes were run up from the marine barracks and customs house; the public officials opened their offices and a crowd of local residents ran down to the wharf to ogle the passengers.

The town's somnolence was no surprise to the new governor, John Henry Kinkead of Nevada, however, as he had served as its postmaster for three years, when the United States first took possession from Russia in 1867. He operated a trading post on the military reservation until the population dwindled so that it was no longer profitable.

He returned to Nevada and was elected its governor, serving from 1879 until 1883. In the intervening years, United States Senator John Percival Jones, of Nevada, had become a major stockholder in the Treadwell Gold-mining Company with quartz operations at Douglas, Alaska. Thus, when a governor was to be chosen for the district, he expressed interest in participating in the selection.

The Governor's bibulosity was humorously alluded to by Dr. S. Hall Young, a Presbyterian missionary who was in Sitka when the officials arrived. He wrote that Kinkead brought with him an immense supply of cases labeled "canned tomatoes." These "tomatoes" were proclaimed as tasting exactly like Scotch whiskey and producing the same effect.[1]

Kinkead spent most of his time in Washington. During his brief stay in Sitka, he fell on the icy street and broke his arm. He also suffered a paralytic stroke. When he returned to Sitka in the spring of 1885 he got orders, signed by the President, to relinquish the governorship.

According to his successor's appointment documents, Kinkead was "removed for cause, because he had refused to stay in Sitka."[2]

Alaska's first United States district judge was (Samuel) Ward McAllister Jr., a nephew of the famous social arbiter of New York Society of the same name. He held one term of court in the fall of 1884 and then left for Washington, D.C. and never returned to Alaska. When he was removed before the expiration of his term, he sued the United States government for the remainder of his salary which he contended was due him. The United States Supreme Court found no basis for his claim.[3]

Edwin W. Haskett, the district attorney who lost his life in a fall from a moving train near Needles, California, was described by Dr. Sheldon Jackson, Alaska's federal agent for education, as "uneducated, rowdyish in manner, vulgar and obscene. . .a gambler and confirmed drunkard, with little knowledge of the law."[4]

Marshall Munson Curtis Hillyer, also of Nevada, finished out his term and then returned to Nevada. Dr. Jackson described him as "a gambler although a fair man as politicians go."[5]

The second batch of carpetbag appointees sent north by the Democratic Grover Cleveland administration was a cut above the first group, except for the district judges, who combined embezzlement with tippling as character qualifications.

Governor Alfred P. Swineford, a Michigan newspaperman, developed a sincere interest in Alaska's welfare and eventually returned to the district to make his permanent home. He became convinced early in his term as governor that Alaskans were unjustly deprived of the basic rights to which all American citizens were entitled. He also concluded that this situation was largely due to the selfish interests of foreign corporations which sought to keep the district as their private fiefdom.

One of the first things he did as governor was to publish a weekly newspaper. The district had no papers at that time, as earlier efforts had collapsed for lack of financial support.

He wrote a history of Alaska in which he expounded on its great potential in the development of its natural resources:

> Alaska is possessed of all the material elements essential to the growth of a great and powerful state. . .she is fast coming to be recognized as the great storehouse of that which is the standard of value all over the world. . . .[6]

In his final governor's report to the secretary of interior, he declared that Alaska's civil government was "little, if any, better than a burlesque

Left: Governor John Green Brady, 1897-1906. *Right:* Governor Alfred Swineford, 1885-89.

both in form and substance," and that aside from preparing annual reports "there is really no duty enjoined upon the governor, the performance of which is possible, no power he can exercise, no authority that he can assert."

When he returned to Alaska and began publishing a newspaper in Ketchikan, he became a vigorous crusader for home rule which included an elective delegate in Congress and a local, elected legislature. He made an unsuccessful bid to become the territory's first delegate in Congress in 1906.

Governor Swineford's concern for Alaska's welfare was not shared by the other officials appointed to serve with him. Three different judges were appointed during the four-year tenure. The first one, Edward J. Dawne, skipped off to parts unknown, to avoid arrest for embezzling fifteen thousand dollars from his father-in-law. His wife and two children were left stranded in Sitka until local citizens "passed the hat" to return them to their former home in Salem, Oregon.[7]

Dawne's successor was Lafayette Dawson, an attorney from Missouri. He, too, had a drinking problem which his friends thought might be cured in "far-away prohibition-Alaska" but it did not work out that

way. When saloon-keepers were brought before him and tried for in-
fraction of the liquor laws, he would levy a heavy fine and then step
down from the bench to go have a drink with the defendant.[8]

Dawson was succeeded by John H. Keatley, a lawyer-newspaperman
from Council Bluffs, Iowa. He served the remaining fourteen months of
the Cleveland administration. Four years after leaving Alaska, he
offered testimony at a senate committee hearing in Washington in opposition to self-government for the district. He had no hope for the
future of the country.[9]

Mottrone Ball, a Sitka resident, received the appointment of district
attorney. He had come north originally to be the collector of customs
and chose to remain at the expiration of his term. He died two years
after becoming district attorney and was succeeded by Whitaker
McDonough Grant, an attorney from Davenport, Iowa. When his term
expired, he moved to Oklahoma and became the first mayor of
Oklahoma City and the state's Democratic national committeeman.

Barton Atkins, a railroad agent from Buffalo, New York, was
appointed the district's United States marshal. He served the full four-
year term in a quiet, sober fashion. His hobby was writing history.

When the Republicans returned to office nationally with Benjamin
Harrison as president, Alaskans were hopeful that local residents might
be appointed to some of the top offices. Both national party platforms
had endorsed the policy of appointing only bona fide residents to public
office. The Alaska press was vocal in resenting the riffraff being sent to
govern Alaskans as colonial subjects. The Juneau *City Mining Record*
editorialized:

> Alaska has been made the dumping ground for the political
> offal of the state of Oregon. Out of the half-dozen or more car-
> petbag appointments now in Alaska, not one of them has the
> necessary qualifications to fill the position he occupies.[10]

But the stateside politicians were loathe to waive the prerogative of
rewarding loyal party workers with such choice political plums as a
governorship or a judgeship, or even the post of district attorney or
marshal. Thus all of the major posts continued to go to outsiders.

Lyman Enos Knapp, a journalist-lawyer from Vermont was awarded the governorship and a San Francisco lawyer, John S. Bugbee won
the judgeship. When Bugbee resigned to go into private practice in the

booming mining camp of Juneau, Warren D. Truitt, an Oregon attorney, succeeded him.

Orville Tracy Porter, a schoolteacher from Albany, Oregon got the marshalship and Charles Sumner Johnson, a Nebraska lawyer, was given the district attorneyship.

Alaska was taking on a more promising economic future, particularly for lawyers, as gold discoveries were multiplying. A higher caliber of appointees were being recruited for the district. Bugbee was a Harvard graduate, the son of a prominent San Francisco architect. He was a regular contributor to the *Overland Monthly Magazine* and wrote articles deploring Alaska's neglect by the federal government, calling it "the Cinderella of the nation." He also was a water colorist of some note.[11]

Governor Knapp was a lackluster chief executive. His final report to the secretary of interior reflected a note of futility because his previous recommendations had been ignored in Washington. He was convinced that "in the apparent estimation of the legislative mind the lives and property rights of human beings were held of importance in the inverse ratio of the square of the distance" (from Washington).

He was unpopular with the local press as he lacked confidence in the Alaskans being able to govern themselves. He once observed that "an election would be a farce of the most ludicrous character, and he favored giving the governor the lobbyist role in Washington rather than electing a local resident as an official delegate. The Juneau *Record Miner* called him "a blatant hypocrite" and when his term expired, the Sitka *Alaskan* said "Thank God. Our only wish is that Alaska may not again be afflicted by him in any official capacity."

When Grover Cleveland returned to the White House for a second term, he promoted three of his former Alaskan appointees to higher posts. James Sheakley, a Pennsylvania oilman, was appointed governor. Six years earlier he had been appointed United States commissioner in Wrangell and assistant education agent to administer the public school system in the southeastern section of Alaska. He became active in Democratic party circles and was elected as one of Alaska's two delegates to the national convention at which Cleveland was nominated for a second term to the presidency. Sheakley was active on Cleveland's behalf at the convention.[12]

Sheakley proved to be a quiet, unobtrusive governor; his annual reports were brief and unimaginative. He stressed more aid for education, abolition of prohibition, and conservation policies for the salmon industry. At the conclusion of his term as governor, the Alaska Trade

Commission headquartered in San Francisco, in cooperation with the San Francisco chamber of commerce, hired him to go on a lecture tour to publicize the Klondike goldrush, urging men to go north to find their fortune.

The district judgeship went to Arthur K. Delaney, whose original appointment was as collector of customs at Sitka. He was in private practice in Everett, Washington when he received his second presidential appointment.

The marshalship went to Louis Littlepage Williams, formerly of Boonville, Missouri, who came north originally as United States commissioner in Juneau. He had stayed on and was chosen as Alaska's first Democratic national committeeman. It was in this capacity that he attended the national convention and helped get Cleveland nominated for a second term.

Nothing is known of Lytton Taylor, the new district attorney except that he arrived with his wife and departed a year later. He was succeeded by Burton E. Bennett, a Seattle attorney.

Chapter 8

Alaska Gets Its First Bona Fide Resident Governor

Had Brady exerted himself on behalf of the white people of Alaska one-half as much as he has on behalf of the Indian, Alaska today would be knocking at the door of statehood.

With Governor Brady, the Indian has always had the preference, and just as long as the Brady missionary element remains in charge of official affairs, just so long will Alaska remain as she is today. (Dispatch,Dec.27,1904,quote from Alaska Forum)

President William McKinley's choice of pioneer Alaskan John Green Brady of Sitka as governor, should have augured well for the region. For nine years, Brady had been an integral part of all that happened in Alaska, economically, socially and spiritually. He was the recognized authority on Alaskan affairs as far as Washington officialdom was concerned. The President would invite him to sit in on cabinet meetings when Alaskan issues were under discussion and he was given the privilege of the House floor, being introduced as "Governor Brady who represents the territory." In association with his friend, Dr. Sheldon Jackson, the district's federal agent for education, Brady's judgement was accepted as the gospel truth on what was best for Alaska.

Brady took office as Alaska's governor three months after President McKinley's inauguration. He and Jackson had gone to the nation's capital to lobby for Brady's appointment. A cabinet member, who was not aware of the two gentlemen's prestige in high places, suggested to Brady that he was wasting his time to think he could get the governorship. He told Brady that he might have influence in the "kingdom of heaven" but he had no political influence in Washington, whereupon Brady replied that he would go out and get some, if that was what was necessary.

He rounded up three of the most powerful United States senators - Mark Hanna, the Ohio millionaire who was largely responsible for getting McKinley elected president, and who was in charge of patronage; Knute Nelson of Minnesota and George Perkins of California, both of whom were closely associated with powerful business interests in Alaska. With this kind of backing, Brady's appointment was a cinch.

Brady's life story is a prototype of the old-time Hollywood film depicting the street waif mounting the ladder of success and living happily forever after in the governor's mansion.

Brady was born on Pearl Street in New York City on May 26, 1847. His longshoreman father was a drunkard who beat him mercilessly. The boy would run away from home and hide, sleeping under any available shelter, covering himself with horse blankets; he picked up pennies doing odd jobs.[1]

He did not remember much about his mother, who was separated from the father. One time when he was ill with smallpox he recalled a beautifully dressed lady who came to visit him - that was his mother. She died shortly thereafter. His face was so badly pockmarked from the disease that he wore a beard throughout his adulthood.

When he was nine years old he was picked up on the street by a worker from the Children's Aid Society and placed in an orphanage on Randall's Island, where he remained for two years. Then one day the Society received a letter from a Judge John Green of Tipton, Indiana, requesting "the homeliest and raggedest boy of the lot." A boy named Brady was delivered to the judge in 1859 and here the boy remained for the next seven years.[2]

At age eighteen Brady started teaching in the district schools and attended the Presbyterian Academy at Waveland, Indiana. Then he went East to Yale University, graduating in 1874. He did graduate work at the Presbyterian Union Theological Seminary at Princeton, New Jersey, finishing in 1877. A year later he was ordained a Presbyterian minister. That same year, he accepted the offer of the Board of Home Missions to go to Sitka, Alaska as a missionary.

His first project upon arrival in March, 1878, was to establish a vocational school for native children. This was the origin of present-day Sheldon Jackson Junior College in Sitka. Dr. Sheldon Jackson had preceded Brady by a year and was traveling from one end of the district to the other, establishing missions and schools.

Brady terminated his missionary career after a year, going into a variety of commercial enterprises on his own. He started with a sawmill and a general store, known as the Sitka Trading Company. Then he bought the United States Revenue Cutter *Reliance*, a two-masted schooner, renamed it *Leo*, and equipped it with a steam engine. The schooner carried freight and passengers between San Francisco and Seattle and Sitka; it also transported furs from western Alaska. All of his employees were Alaskan Indians.

He served as United States commissioner and ex officio register of the United States Land Office. He studied law and was admitted to the bar in October, 1885.

Two years later he married Elizabeth Jane Patton, who had come north to teach in the school which Brady had established. She was a graduate of Columbia University and fifteen years his junior. They had three sons - John Green, Jr., Hugh P., and Sheldon Jackson - and two daughters - Mary, and Elizabeth.

Brady's years as governor were turbulent ones. A new order was aborning. Thousands of newcomers were pouring into the district, hopeful that they might strike it rich and then return to their homes in the states. Many failed to find their fortune, but decided to stay in Alaska, either because they had fallen in love with the country, or because they didn't have the price of a steamer ticket back home.

A new breed of Alaskan was developing. No longer was it predominantly the land of the Indian and the Eskimo, whose welfare had been the primary concern of Brady and Jackson. The new white settlers resented a governor who appeared to favor the native people over the whites, and they also rebelled against the moralistic strictures with which he tried to govern the country.

A hostile Alaskan press began denouncing Brady as an "old fogy" who was out of step with the modern needs of the region; his resignation was called for but his strong political connections in Washington and New York City won him reappointment in 1901 and again four years later.

Brady was more fortunate than his predecessors in having a corps of sober, capable officials to handle the mechanics of government during his extended absences in Washington. General William Langmead Distin, as clerk of the court, surveyor-general and ex officio secretary of Alaska, was designated "acting governor." During his sixteen years' tenure in these triple offices, Distin served as acting governor longer than any other in the territory's history; he served under three successive governors.

Distin was the district's first surveyor general, a new title under the civil code of 1900 replacing clerk of the district court. He acquired his title of "general" from his brilliant military performance during the Civil War, when he achieved the rank of major general. The street on which the present governor's mansion in Juneau is located, is named Distin in his honor.

President McKinley chose Charles Sumner Johnson, another longtime Alaskan resident, as district judge. He was the former district attorney in President Harrison's administration and had gone into private law practice in Juneau, while the Democrats were in office. He was the first district judge to extend his jurisdiction beyond southeastern Alaska. The new mining camps in the Tanana Valley and on the Seward Peninsula required legal attention, especially in determining ownership of mining claims.

Accompanied by Governor Brady and the district attorney, Judge Johnson embarked on perhaps the longest circuit ever undertaken by a court. His itinerary began by ship from Sitka to Juneau and Skagway; from there he took the White Pass and Yukon train to Whitehorse, then by riverboat to Dawson, Eagle, Circle, Rampart, and St. Michael, holding court at each of the American villages; then to Nome, where he held the first court session ever held in that city; thence to Unalaska, Unga, and Kodiak by revenue cutter, thence back to Sitka. The circuit required three months to complete.

The judge was received with open arms at Nome in the summer of 1899. Men were arriving there with the idea that there was gold in every stream and they would go out into the countryside and stake miles of claims, ignoring the law which required a discovery of mineral before a claim could be legally staked. They staked by power of attorney, by agency, for their relatives and friends. They were called "pencil and hatchet" miners because they put in most of the season with a pencil, location notices, and a hatchet with which to cut willow branches for stakes to mark their claims.[3]

When Johnson resigned from the $3,000-a-year judgeship to go into private practice in Nome, President McKinley appointed Melville Cox Brown, an attorney from Laramie, Wyoming, as his replacement. He, too, proved to be of superior capability.

A native of Maine, Brown moved to the West Coast at age eighteen, first engaging in mining and merchandising in the placer mining district around Marysville, California. He later moved to Idaho Territory, becoming a member of the territorial legislature and serving as assessor of internal revenue for the territory.

Brown moved to Cheyenne, Wyoming in the later 1860s. He founded the town of Laramie, serving as its first mayor. He began his law practice there and was president of the Wyoming constitutional convention in 1890. He was married and had three daughters and one son.

The appointees to the offices of marshal and district attorney, during the Brady administration, were among the best in Alaska's territorial history. James McCain Shoup of Idaho held the office of marshal longer than any other appointee to that office; he served for twelve years. Normally if one survived one full term of four years without being asked to resign or being summarily removed, he was considered lucky.

Shoup was born in Pennsylvania in 1849 and spent his youth in Illinois. He served in the United States Navy during the final year of the Civil War, settling in Idaho Territory thereafter. He became an attorney and was a member of the Idaho constitutional convention and a member of the first state senate. His brother, George L., was the state's first governor and later a United States senator from Idaho. He was chairman of the Senate Committee on Territories when Alaska was provided both a criminal and a civil code.

Shoup's son, Arthur Glendenning, served as deputy marshal in Ketchikan and Sitka, under his father, and later as United States district attorney for the First Division from 1921 to 1926. The father and son practiced law together in Ketchikan until the father's death in 1927, when the son moved to San Jose, California.

For district attorney, President McKinley chose Brigadier General Robert A. Friedrich, a San Francisco attorney and former general in the Kansas National Guard. Friedrich was born in Kentucky in 1849. He enlisted in the Union Army at age thirteen and was made a lieutenant colonel at age sixteen. He moved to Topeka, Kansas in 1872, studied law, and began practicing in 1887. He served four years in the Kansas National Guard as adjutant general, achieving the rank of brigadier general.

He moved to San Francisco in 1889 and was practicing there when he received the Alaskan appointment. He died in Juneau in 1902.

PART III

WICKERSHAM GOES TO ALASKA AS U.S. DISTRICT JUDGE

Chapter 9

Inaugurates Law and Order in Interior Alaska

> *The honor and responsibility of aiding in founding American courts of justice in a vast new territory was accepted in the spirit that my forefathers shouldered their rifles in 1776 to aid in establishing the independence of the Colonies. (Old Yukon, Wickersham, p.3)*

It must have been with mixed emotions that the Wickershams left Tacoma, which had been their home for the past seventeen years. They were no longer young, he was 43 and she was 37, and Mrs. Wickersham's poor health made it necessary for her to be continuously under a doctor's care. Their eldest son, Darrell, had been appointed to the naval academy in Annapolis and so would not be accompanying them north. They were starting a new chapter in their life together, on a frontier where the physical comforts would be at a minimum. Hopefully, the prestige of being a judge would balance the drawbacks.

Had he been assigned to Juneau or Nome, their future would have been less obscure. But Eagle City - what would life be like there? Perhaps he could stake some gold claims and reap a fortune as other Tacomans had done. Reports of the Klondike gold discovery reached Tacoma in the summer of 1897, and people began leaving for the north. On August 22, F.P. Riley, a former railroad section boss who had been fired from his job, arrived in Tacoma from Alaska with $85,000 in gold; his story fired the community. Riley had formed a partnership with two other men and the three went into the Klondike district where from two claims they cleaned up $85,000 apiece.[1]

On July 2 at 4:30 in the afternoon, Judge and Mrs. Wickersham and their seven-year-old son, Howard, boarded the S.S. *Flyer* for Seattle. Many friends were on the dock to bid them bon voyage.

The Heiligs and their two children and Mrs. Heilig's sister, Mrs. Whittaker, a nurse, and George Jeffery were traveling with the Wickershams. At Seattle they were joined by Alfred M. Post, an attorney from York, Nebraska, who had been appointed United States attorney in Wickersham's district and George G. Perry, of Iowa, and his wife. Perry had been appointed United States marshal in the same district.

Also at Seattle, Wickersham met Arthur H. Noyes of Minnesota, who had been appointed to the Nome bench. The Justice Department had requested that the two meet in Seattle to jointly fix the boundary between the Nome and Eagle judicial divisions.

In recalling that one and only meeting which the two jurists had with one another, Wickersham was impressed with how much more exuberant the Nome group was than was his own modest contingent headed for the insignificant post at Eagle City. The crowds on the wharf paid no attention to the Wickersham party but "stood open-mouthed about those bound for Nome." Wickersham observed:

> The judge appeared to be an agreeable man, though he seemed to be immoderately fond of the bottle. Judge Noyes introduced. . .the members of his official party as well as Alexander McKenzie and several of his business associates who were going to Nome to engage in various mining schemes.
>
> On comparing the Nome group with the Eagle City group, it seemed to me that my companions were rather unimportant and probably blessed with only moderate ability. Members of the Nome group were alert, aggressive, and busily engaged in planning huge mining ventures.
>
> The members of my modest party felt that they were being shunted to an obscure place in the Yukon wilderness. The great Nome gold camp was everywhere the main topic of conversation, whereas no one knew whether our Eagle City division had mining possibilities. . . .[2]

Judge Noyes had been given the Nome judgeship following his defeat at the polls in his bid for the Hennepin County district judgeship, with headquarters in Minneapolis. His traveling companion, Alexander McKenzie, was a native Minnesotan who had risen from railroad section hand on the Northern Pacific Railroad to its receiver, becoming wealthy in the process. He also had risen high in North Dakota's Republican circles, becoming the party's national committeeman. Quite unabashedly he boasted that Judge Noyes owed his judgeship appointment to his (McKenzie's) political influence; a factor significant in their future Nome association.

Skies were overcast as the S.S. *City of Seattle* pulled away from Pier I on the Seattle waterfront and the Wickershams were Alaska-bound. They had good accommodations for which the government paid a modest rate of eleven dollars a day, from Seattle to Skagway, July 2 - 6, inclusive.

On the Fourth, as the ship was off the coast of southern Alaska, Howard joined the other youthful passengers in shooting off firecrackers on the upper stern deck and watching a practice fire drill by the crew.

Stops were made at Ketchikan, Wrangell, Treadwell, and Juneau. At Juneau Wickersham conferred with Judge Brown on a tentative boundary between the Juneau and Eagle districts. After a three-hour stop, the steamer left for Skagway. Here they disembarked for an overnight stop and were taken in a hack to the Fifth Avenue Hotel, a sprawling, three-storied wooden structure, overflowing with a restless crowd. There was but one topic of conversation - the Klondike gold fields.

Leaving Skagway early in the morning aboard the narrow-gauge White Pass and Yukon Railway, they wound their way up the Skagway Valley and along the steep mountain sides to White Pass summit, and thence down to Bennett, a busy town of tents and shacks at the head of Lake Bennett. There, with other anxious argonauts, they transferred to the steamer *Australian*, which carried them to Cariboo Crossing at the foot of the lake.

Large groups of men were blasting out a railway grade along the rocky walls on the south shore of the lake, hoping to connect Bennett and the Cariboo Crossing that summer. The railway was newly completed from Cariboo to Whitehorse, and so they were crowded into small passenger coaches and sent on to Whitehorse, where they arrived at midnight. The steamer *Yukoner*, bound for Dawson, was waiting for them, and the Wickersham party was fortunate enough to have berths assigned them; many others were compelled to sleep on the floor or to share berths on a half-time plan.

The sternwheeler *Yukoner* had acquired a colorful reputation during the Klondike gold rush days carrying passengers and cargo between St. Michael and Dawson. It was originally built in Victoria, British Columbia and taken to St. Michael in sections and re-assembled for use on the Yukon River. In 1897 and 1898 the cargo was mostly whiskey and her passengers chiefly dancehall girls and gamblers.[3]

Leaving Whitehorse early the next morning, with the sun shining brightly, the party marveled at the natural beauty surrounding them - clear river waters, wooded valleys, and distant snowcapped mountains. On the second day they came upon a steamer stuck on a sandbar in the middle of the river. The crew of the *Yukoner* stopped to help get the steamer off the sandbar, laboring all night long, not succeeding until ten o'clock the next morning.

At Dawson the party was obliged to occupy a bunkhouse as no vacancy remained in the hotels. There were no boats scheduled to go downriver to Eagle for severals days, so they got a good look at Dawson, in its heyday as the richest mining camp in the Yukon basin. According to Wickersham:

> Its streets were quagmires; its waterfront was jammed with hundreds of small boats and scows which had brought its inhabitants from Lindeman Bennett through the dangers of the Whitehorse rapids. . . .In Government Square, buildings for official use were going up; the mounted police barracks. . .and the dreaded woodpile hardby, gave warning that a sentence for crime meant hard work; two-story signs, which were lighted by kerosene lamps at night, inviting all and sundry to the saloons and dance-halls. . . .[4]

Wickersham met many former acquaintances from the Puget Sound area; among them was Ed Orr, the former Tacoma mayor who had appointed him city attorney. Orr had joined the Dawson stampede and had established a stage line from Dawson to the nearby mines. He invited the Wickersham party to take a two-day tour of the famous Bonanza and Eldorado mining camps. It proved to be an exciting experience, riding in a stagecoach drawn by four horses through spectacular mountain scenery. As they approached the mines, they saw a thousand men busily digging for that yellow metal which was to make them millionaires overnight!

Wickersham's animated diary account, indicated no regrets over the party's enforced lay-over:

> We arrived at the Grand Forks Hotel in time for lunch, and took rooms for the night in the sprawling, and sometimes brawling, log hotel. That afternoon we inspected Clarence Berry's rich claim on Eldorado Creek and others like it. These were the most valuable claims on the creeks - the exposed gravel pay-streaks fairly glowing with nuggets and heavy flakes of gold dust. Mr. Berry rather recklessly, it seemed to me, invited us to dig all the gold we wanted from the fully exposed golden pay-streak, limiting us, however to digging with our hands.
>
> Two greatly excited six-year-old boys, my son and Mr. Heilig's, and his young daughter Florence, at once began to hunt and dig like terriers after rats. Each child soon had a fistful of bright yellow gold nuggets, while the elders were satisfied with one or two larger nuggets of the value of ten dollars or so.
>
> It was an exciting hour for the three children, who greatly pleased the owner and other miners by their happy cries as they dug out some particularly bright nugget. When they had recovered all the nuggets their hands could hold, they were dragged out of the paystreak by their equally happy and excited mothers and taken to the creek for cleaning. . . .
>
> The Grand Forks roadhouse was a typical wild-west saloon and gambling house, without pistols or bad men. The main room on the ground floor had the office in one corner, the bar along one wall, gambling tables and games - said to be on the square - in the center and the dancing floor at the rear. . . .
>
> After a good dinner we viewed the dancing and gambling as nonchalantly as if we were quite used to such things. The strident music of the fiddles, the calls of the dance director, the whirling-dervish performances of some of the dancers, the promenade of the miners and their partners to the bar after each dance, the hazard of large sums on the turn of a card, the drop of a ball or the fall of dice stirred us, but official position and the presence of wives kept us merely spectators.[5]

After four days in Dawson the Wickersham party departed for Eagle aboard the steamer *John Cudahy*, arriving on Sunday, July 15, 1900. The entire population (383), headed by Mayor Emil Query, lined the riverbank to welcome the new judge and watch his official family disembark. The Wickershams were escorted to a furnished log cabin on the military reserve, for sleeping quarters, and they took their meals at the town's log cabin restaurant operated by Major Thompson.[6]

The town of Eagle was perched on the top of an embankment, thirty to fifty feet above the turgid waters of the Yukon River. The only access to the town was by river steamer; no roads or trails connected it with the rest of the district.

In 1874 a trading post was established on a small island midstream in the river just opposite the present townsite. Moses Mercier, a French-Canadian and one of the first fur traders on the upper Yukon for the Alaska Commercial Company, chose the site for its beauty and strategic position at the mouth of a beautiful, clear-water stream called Mission Creek; it was filled with grayling. It was six miles west of the Alaska-Canadian boundary. He called it Belle Isle. Wickersham was equally impressed by the beauty of this spruce-covered island and was inspired to describe it in poetic verse:

> A greenwood isle in the Yukon's flow,
> Lies 'neath an Arctic mountain crest;
> Eagles fly north when south winds blow,
> And raise their young in the old crag nest.[7]

When American prospectors in 1886 found gold along the creeks feeding into the Fortymile River, the Belle Isle trading post was moved to the river's bank. Wooden platforms were built for the unloading of passengers and cargo from the steamers, as they tied up one behind the other. The site was chosen by a group of American miners who had left Dawson in protest to their treatment by the mounted police. They resented being ordered about by foreigners and decided to establish their own American community on the left bank of the Yukon.

At first they considered naming it "American City" to emphasize their patriotism, but while conjuring that name they saw golden eagles swooping overhead and that inspired the name "Eagle" in honor of the national emblem. They discovered later that the eagles' nesting place was on the top of a 2000-foot bluff just half a mile north of the town.

By 1898 Eagle had become a bustling trading center for the miners on the nearby creeks; close to a million dollars was taken out from these diggings annually and the summer population would reach the thousand mark. Four customs officers were required to clear the cargo and passengers coming through Canada, as Eagle was the port of entry to the United States.

With the discovery of gold so near the Canadian boundary, the United States Congress decided to station military troops in the district to protect the national interests, as the boundary dispute remained unsettled despite diplomatic negotiations. Captain Patrick Henry Ray, with an assistant, Lieutenant Wilds Preston Richardson, was sent to Alaska in August, 1897, to investigate conditions and determine where army posts should be located.

Captain Ray recommended one site at the mouth of Mission Creek, which later became known as Fort Egbert. Overland transportation and communication became the next military project. The only established "roadway" in interior Alaska at the time was the Yukon River trail. In summer it was traveled by boat, raft, or paddle steamer; in winter it was used by dogsled, bobsled, and horse- or mule-drawn sleighs. Mail carriers drove their dog teams between Dawson and Nome 1,600 miles - in weekly trips by relays.

Soldiers from Fort Liscum (near Valdez) and Fort Egbert built a 370-mile trail from Valdez to Eagle during 1899-1901. Over this trail pack horses in summer and dog teams in winter carried mail twice a month.[8] Telegraph and cable lines were also strung between the various military garrisons.

The cable line between Eagle and Dawson was completed on October 29, 1900, and Judge Wickersham sent the first telegram from the American Yukon basin. He sent telegrams to Senator Addison Foster in Washington, D.C., the Tacoma *Ledger* and to Ed Orr in Dawson. Telegrams to the continental United States went to Skagway via Dawson, and thence to Seattle by a four-day steamer trip.[9]

When the Wickershams arrived, Eagle's downtown district consisted of two good-sized mercantile stores owned by the Alaska Commercial Company and the North American Trading and Transportation Company; a United States Customs Office, Presbyterian and Catholic churches, a Catholic hospital, two restaurants, and four or five log cabin saloons.

Wickersham and Heilig each rented a log cabin for living quarters until they could build their own. With the assistance of George Dribelis, a local logger, Wickersham set to work building his own log cabin; the logs cost him seventy-five dollars and the lot one hundred dollars. He was proud of his pioneering efforts:

It was sixteen feet wide, twenty-four feet long, seven feet high to the top of the side walls and ten feet from the floor to the center ridge pole, and, across the back, a lean-to kitchen eight feet wide, completed the structure.

The roof consisted of closely placed poles running from the ridge pole to the side walls, covered with a foot of moss, eight inches of turf and lastly gravel. The side walls were well caulked with moss; rough boards salvaged from an old Yukon riverboat were used for flooring; half-windows were installed and front and rear doors.

We made some of our furniture, bought a bedstead and some chairs, an air-tight heating stove for the large room, a cheap cookstove for the kitchen, made our shelves and a kitchen table, put down some carpets we had brought from the outside, moved in and had one of the best and warmest cabins in town. It was always comfortable, even when the temperature outside was sixty degrees below zero.[10]

Wickersham's judicial district covered 300,000 square miles but had fewer than 1,500 white residents. Its northern boundary extended along the Arctic Ocean, south to Mt. McKinley and Lake Clark, thence west to the Bering Sea. Its eastern boundary was from the Arctic coast to Cape St. Elias and the Pacific Ocean.

There was no courthouse, jail, school, or other public building and no money appropriated for such. The district judge was authorized to reserve two town lots for a courthouse and jail and to construct a courthouse not to exceed $5,000, all of which was to be paid for out of local license fees collected by the court. Thus, the day after their arrival, the judge and clerk started levying mercantile and saloon license fees; saloons were to pay an annual fee of one thousand dollars, and each store a fixed percentage upon its annual sales.

Wickersham sent men out into the woods to cut logs for the buildings, but actual construction had to await the unraveling of Washington red tape. Construction got underway the following February when a permit was received from the Justice Department allowing the court officials to use a lumber mill standing idle on the military reservation. The Justice Department had to get permission from the War Department to authorize the local military authorities to grant permission for the mill's use. This was Wickersham's introduction to federal red tape, which he was obliged to fight throughout his political career.

Left: Judge Wickersham at desk, Eagle City, 1900-02. *Right:* Wickersham on Mt. McKinley expedition. Note mosquito netting covering hat.

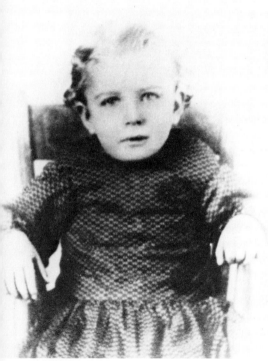

Left: Son, Howard Wickersham, *Right:* Mrs. Wickersham and Howard.

Judge Wickersham standing in doorway of his home in Eagle City, 1900, with Mrs. Wickersham to his left and Mrs. Heilig to his right.

Two views of interior of Wickersham's home in Eagle City, 1900-02.

Wickersham and his court officials experienced problems of a more personal nature, emphasizing the great geographical distance of Washington from Eagle, Alaska. Their first paychecks arrived in February, 1901, eight months after their departure from Seattle, and even then they were only for their first five months of employment; subsequent checks continued to be three to four months in arrears. It took at least four months by dogteams for a letter to travel between Eagle and Washington.

One official commented, gazing at his last silver dollar with its legend "In God We Trust," that it ought to read, "In the A.C. Co. (Alaska Commercial Co.) We Trust." That company extended credit to the financially embarrassed officials just as they did to prospectors and fur traders, who eventually paid-up with a "clean-up" or a winter's catch of pelts.

Wickersham spent three weeks splitting and piling wood in a tent by his back door to insure himself of an adequate winter's fuel supply. He banked the walls of his house with snow to keep the cold from creeping up through the floor boards. He hunted caribou and moose, putting in a winter's supply in an outdoor cache, where it was kept frozen all winter. He had a butcher cut the meat into steaks and roasts so all they had to do during the winter was to go out and get a frozen piece and drop it into a pot or skillet and they would have fresh meat for dinner.

The town had a unique water system during the winter months. When the river froze over in mid-October, a hole was cut in the main channel and a barrel injected into it. As the ice grew thicker, the hole was kept open by cutting it with an axe. The local waterman had a dog team and sled with which he delivered buckets of water at so much per bucket at the kitchen door, thus saving the householder the unpleasantness of going to the waterhole and carrying dripping buckets of freezing water up an icy bank.

Dispensing justice where none had existed previously, ofttimes demanded an innovative imagination and Wickersham proved himself equal to the situation. His first case in Eagle was settled on the town's main street, never requiring the formality of a courtroom. Chief Charley of the Tena Indian tribe came to the judge's cabin to report that his dog had been stolen by Eagle Jack. In the chief's words: "You big chief you get my dog; bring him me. If you not get my dog I get my dog. Maybe some Indian get hurt. Maybe you get my dog?"

Impressed by the chief's fearless honesty, Wickersham determined to help him get his dog in order to avoid serious trouble. Putting on his hat, the judge said, "Come with me, Charley," and the two set out for the Alaska Commercial store and located a deputy marshal. Charley described the dog and the thief and the judge told the deputy to get himself a folded piece of paper and walk to the Indian village about a mile from Eagle, find the dog and bring him back to the store.

The judge and Charley sat down on the store steps, exchanging fishing and hunting tales. In about an hour the deputy returned with the dog and delivered him to the chief. It was learned later that Chief Charley had a gun hidden in his canoe and planned to use it if necessary to retrieve his dog. The white man's "big chief" was proud of his successful solution to what might have resulted in a tragic incident.[11]

Wickersham decided to hold court in nearby Rampart and Circle City before winter set in, primarily in order to collect license fees from the businesses in those towns. Debbie and Howard accompanied him on the riverboat *Suzie*. Just opposite Coal Creek, the *Suzie* ran aground on a sandbar where it remained stranded for the better part of two days. The judge and his official family transferred to small boats and floated down to Circle. They left several old men aboard the *Suzie*, who had been drawn for jury duty, so Wickersham instructed the deputy marshal to take them a basket of food as it was uncertain when they would float off the sandbar. At the last minute he suggested that a bottle of whiskey be tucked into the basket to help keep them warm.

Later, when making up his official report, the deputy came to the judge to ask how he should itemize the whiskey, whereupon the judge advised that it be charged up as subsistence, the same as the basket of food. The next day, the deputy presented his account as follows: "basket of food, $10; one bottle of subsistence, $5." For over two years the marshal's office was in correspondence with the Justice Department about that "bottle of subsistence" and never did get reimbursement.[12]

While in Circle, Wickersham attended church services, which were held in the same room in which he held court on weekdays. He was fascinated by an incident which took place one Sunday morning during collection of the offering. Charley Claypool, a local attorney, was passing the collection plate and when he came to a young merchant, he stopped for several minutes, conversing with him in a low tone of voice. The next day the judge asked Claypool about his extended conversation while taking up the offering and received the following explanation:

> The young merchant put a five dollar gold piece on the plate, whereupon the deacon (Claypool) whispered "come again" and stood with arm and plate outstretched. . ."What do you want,

you blackmailer?" asked the merchant, as he put another five dollars on the plate. The deacon replied in a stage whisper: "I want the whole twenty-five dollars you beat me out of in the poker game last night," and remained patiently waiting with outstretched plate in front of the young merchant's face.

Everybody in the church turned to see what had caused the delay. Blushing like an embarrassed school girl, the young merchant hastily took from his pocket an additional fifteen dollars and dropped it on the plate, whereupon the now smiling deacon passed on his way.

Claypool explained that "Joe needed a little Christian chastening; the church needed the money; and I needed the happy glow of righteous satisfaction which I failed to get in the poker game."[13]

On his return to Eagle, Wickersham decided to go into the countryside to prospect for gold and hunt for Dall sheep. He and his companions returned home luckless in both respects, but the new judge was introduced to an unwritten tradition of the north. As they moved along the trails with their dogsleds, they passed prospectors' cabins, each with a latch string hanging on the outside of the door. That was an invitation to any traveler to walk in, build a fire, and make himself at home. Every cabin had a bunk covered with spruce boughs for a bed and a small sheet-iron Yukon stove. Before leaving the cabin, the visitor was expected to cut enough shavings from the dry wood always in the shelter of the door, and arrange the shavings and wood in the stove ready for a quick fire, and leave a square block of matches in sight, for the next visitor, who might arrive perishing from the cold and in need of a quick fire.

While her husband was away hunting for gold and sheep, Mrs. Wickersham settled into the social life of the little village, inviting the ladies in for afternoon tea. She attended Indian mission services at the Presbyterian church, where she heard the Athapascan Indian parishioners read the services from their own Takudh bibles.

The holiday season was heralded with the arrival of a shipment of toys for the two mercantile stores, and Howard was on hand to make his early selections and then relay his wishes to his parents. He and his dad went out into the woods to cut their Christmas tree and together they decorated it with apples, oranges, nuts, and candy. Howard invited the other four white boys in the village to his own holiday party.

The Wickershams' dinner guests on Christmas Day included Father Monroe, the Catholic priest, and the two Crouch brothers, Ed and Fred. Fred was the mail carrier, and he had brought them a twelve-pound turkey from Dawson, having traveled afoot all the way down the frozen Yukon River.

A special fresh vegetable treat for the dinner came as a surprise when the judge came home with a couple of frozen heads of cabbage which a neighbor had stored in his cache. The judge sawed the heads into quarters and Mrs. Wickersham dropped the pieces still frozen into boiling water; they tasted fresh out of the garden. After dinner they all attended a reception at the Presbyterian church, and thus concluded their first Alaska Christmas. [14]

Chapter 10

Goes On First Dog-Mushing Circuit and Floating Court

> *The first man he met was the proprietor of an old roadhouse, who had been in the interior for twenty years or so.*
>
> *"I'm to be the U.S. judge here," remarked Wickersham, modestly, but with judicial dignity. Then he waited for the man to spread out the doormat with 'welcome' on it. "The devil you are!" exclaimed the man. "Well, the thing for you to do is get right t'ell out of here. We don't need any of your kind. Understand? We've got a great country here, and we don't want it spoiled with lawyers and judges." (*Fairbanks* News-Miner, Feb. 20, 1913)*

When the holidays were over, Wickersham faced the stern realities of being a pioneer judge in a frontier land. His vast jurisdiction demanded that he forswear the comforts of home and strike out into the wilderness in order to dispense the fruits of justice to his constituency. Assured that Debbie and Howard would stay safe and warm in their new home, he set out on his first midwinter, snowshoeing, dog-team circuit, a 1,140-mile round-trip to Circle and Rampart, in temperatures fifty to sixty degrees below zero. He was away from home for forty-five days, twenty of them spent outdoors in the crisp Arctic cold, slugging along behind the dog sled or breaking trail for the dogs when the winds piled the trail high with drifts; he averaged twenty-six miles a day in this fashion. In addition to the court officials, his party included Ed Crouch, the mail carrier, and the judge's brother, Edgar, who was deputy marshal in Circle.

Wickersham's daily diary entries depict the stress and pain suffered by human beings unaccustomed to the rigors of trail blazing in interior

Alaska in midwinter. He traveled with a five-dog team loaded with three hundred pounds on the sled. It was a long, Indian-made spruce-basket sled filled with dog food, rice, bacon, dried fish, blankets, dry socks, and warm clothing, extra dog harness and soft caribou skin moccasins for trail-sore dog feet.

For the moderns who sail through the skies in comfort and ease, the trials and perils of the early-day circuit-rider offer a striking contrast:

Jan.21,1901   . . .I walked ahead of the team all day long with the wind in my face, breaking trail. The constant rolling all day pretty nearly lamed me in the ankles and I can hardly walk tonight. We reached Fox Creek cabin early, having traveled 25 miles. . . .

Feb.9   . . .As we came down the bank of the Seventy Mile river, I held back on the handle bars, the sled upset, caught me and turned my heels where my head was, and threw me several feet out into the snow-bank. Forty degrees below. . . .

Feb.14   . . .Forty-two below. . .My ankle hurt by fall the first day out is paining me badly and is very much swollen. Raised a bad blister on my other foot trying to shield the bad ankle; opened it and filled the hole with coal oil.

Feb.19   Thirty-five below. . .We open the blisters, fill them with coal oil out of our lantern which seems to effect a rapid cure. . . .

Mar.1   We remained last night in an old abandoned cabin, minus door and windows. . .frightfully cold . . .no landlord, no stove, no bed - we slept in the most sheltered corner on the packs and dog harness, while the dogs huddled on our feet and at our sides for such comfort as our bodily heat gave them. . . .

Mar.22   . . .Today I am suffering greatly with snow blindness; my eyes feel as if they are filled with sand

> and I keep them covered with a bandage and
> hold on to the handle bars of the sled for guid-
> ance. . . .[1]

Wickersham's capacity for perseverance under such physical discom-
forts was due partly to his love of the outdoors. Rarely did a weekend
pass that he did not go out for a hike just to enjoy the fresh air and
beautiful scenery. He enjoyed hunting trips whether it be for ducks,
deer, moose, caribou or sheep. Once on a mountain sheep hunt he
almost lost his life. After getting a couple of young bucks, he fell into a
raging river and was saved from drowning only by the quick thinking of
his three companions, who threw him a rope from the shore to tie
around himself under the arms. He was loaded down with his gun and
a pair of sheep horns.

Once landed on the shore, "a good drink of whiskey, a dry suit, and
in a few minutes I was eating a hearty supper."[2]

One problem which worried Wickersham when he first took over the
Alaskan bench was the behavior of the jurors - they were unalterably
lenient in their verdicts and vulnerable to bribery and blackmail. He
would lecture them and still they would refuse to return an indictment.
In his first court session in Circle, the grand jury refused to indict a
known murderer and the petit jury was equally adamant in returning a
"not guilty" verdict in the case of a rapist. He did not know how to
contend with this laissez-faire attitude, and yet he knew it had to be
changed.

As for the subornation of jurors, that stemmed partly from the system
by which they were impanelled. It was the prerogative of the United
States marshal to make the selection and his choice often was influenced
by his judgement as to the guilt of the accused. Attorneys did not
hesitate to confer with the marshal as well as with the jurors, on behalf
of their clients.

One Nome attorney, who was disturbed over the procuring of jurors,
wrote Wickersham:

> I have been practicing law in this district since June 1900 and
> the greatest evil we have had to contend with here is jury brib-
> ing, and I sincerely believe that unless some steps are taken to
> correct this evil, the administration of justice by the jury system
> will be a farce. . . .[3]

There was not enough litigation in his district to keep him busy, so Wickersham wrote the Justice Department offering to help out in the other two districts, which had heavy calendars. Whereupon, he received instructions in the summer of 1901 to proceed to the Aleutian Islands to hold court.

Before leaving on this extended trip, he arranged for his wife and son to go to Tacoma where he would join them in the fall, for a 60-day leave of absence. He got them comfortable accommodations on the new river steamer *Whitehorse*. As he stood on the river bank watching the steamer churn away with his loved ones, he was overcome with a sense of loneliness. This was their first long separation since coming north. Howard's dog Yukon sat beside him and howled as the steamer blew its departing whistle. He confided to his diary later that evening that when Yukon howled, he felt like howling also.[4]

A few days later, Wickersham and his court party took passage on the S.S. *Leah* for St. Michael. They spent the better part of two days stuck on sandbars in the middle of the Yukon River. As the steamer drifted slowly to her anchorage at St. Michael, a man perched on the outer edge of the dock shouted to the captain: "Is Judge Wickersham aboard?" Then seeing and recognizing the judge standing on deck, he heaved a sigh of relief. As the passengers disembarked, the man grabbed the judge, taking him aside to relate his predicament. He wanted the judge to marry him at three o'clock that afternoon. His bride-to-be had arrived from San Francisco with her parents and a party of friends only to discover that there was no minister or official in St. Michael to perform the ceremony. The bridal party was scheduled to return to the states on the last steamer of the season which was to depart at four o'clock. A hurry-up ceremony was arranged and at four o'clock the happy bridal couple stood waving goodbye as the steamer carried their friends and relatives far away to the southland.[5]

The Wickersham party proceeded on to Nome, arriving there the following morning. The sun was shining as they anchored half a mile offshore; the water was smooth, with only a slight swell rocking the boat. They went to the beach in a surfboat and were greeted by many former friends from Tacoma.

The town was in a turmoil. Contempt charges had been filed against Judge Noyes and he had departed for Washington four days earlier, to answer these charges. There was an intense, bitter feeling among the townspeople against the judge. They had held a mass meeting the previous evening and fifty members of the Nome bar association had signed a petition, asking the president to remove the judge and appoint a successor. The petition characterized Noyes as absolutely incompetent.

Wickersham was urged to remain in Nome and hold court during Noyes' absence. The docket was filled with important mining cases ready for trial, many longstanding ones. The night before, seventy-five armed men marched onto a valuable mining claim, ousting the owner; one man was shot during the melee. Such episodes were not uncommon as the court's orders had been treated with open contempt and disdain; a reign of anarchy existed. But Wickersham explained that he could not remain in Nome as he had been ordered by the United States attorney general to proceed to Unalaska to hold court. Before departing, he called on Mrs. Noyes to pay his respects. She was depressed by the attacks upon her husband and planned to go south on the next steamer.

Once out at sea, Wickersham was pleasantly surprised not to be seasick; they enjoyed a calm sea and sunny weather all the way to Unalaska. Nevertheless, he was overjoyed when he awoke one morning to the sound of land noises—cows and calves bellowing, cocks crowing, pigeons cooing and pigs grunting—all sounds of a farm that brought back memories of Patoka, Illinois.

Wickersham was charmed with Unalaska, the oldest commercial settlement on the Aleutians, which had been the main base for the Russian hunters of sea otter in the 1760s. Captain James Cook saw the settlement when he explored the shores about 1778, and Alexander Baranof wintered there in 1790.

Subsequently it was a thriving refueling center for whalers and other ships traversing the North Pacific. It was still an important waypoint when Wickersham was there, as the steamers carrying gold stampeders from Seattle to Nome used it as a refueling station.

Wickersham had several days on his hands while waiting for the arrival of the United States revenue cutter, which was bringing the district attorney and witnesses for the Hardy murder case. He would climb the nearby mountains, sit down when he reached an elevation, and read a book, gazing intermittently out over the scenic horizon. He mentioned reading a novel by Buchanan entitled "The Master of the Mine," which he found interesting. He enjoyed watching the red foxes come within fifty feet of him and then scamper away after barking at him sternly. The foxes played about in the meadows where bright-colored wildflowers grew in profusion.

The four-day-long Hardy murder trial ended in a guilty verdict of first degree murder, the punishment being hanging. Hardy had killed three prospectors and stolen their supplies. A fourth member of the party escaped and after wandering twenty days, finally reached town and reported the murders.

Just before leaving Unalaska, Wickersham got orders from the United States attorney general directing him to go to Nome to hold court during the absence of Judge Noyes. There went his 60-day leave and all hopes of joining his family in Tacoma. He dreaded spending the winter in Nome.

His next port of call was Dutch Harbor where he tried another murder case in which an Indian was accused of murdering his wife. At first the Indian witnesses played dumb, refusing to give any evidence for fear he would be hanged. When the interpreter explained that he would not be hanged but simply sent to the federal prison at McNeil Island, Washington, they willingly told what they knew. The jury found him guilty of manslaughter and the judge sentenced him to twenty years at McNeil.

The evening before he departed from Dutch Harbor, he was invited to attend a wedding in the Greek Catholic church. Actually, he was asked to lead the bride to the altar, but pleaded off for want of proper apparel. Upon arrival at the church he noted that the bride would be a mother in about four months and her silk wedding dress "displayed expansiveness." He firmly, but politely, insisted that he would not participate in the ceremony and was finally excused.[6]

When they left Dutch Harbor for Nome, they ran into a terrible storm, with high waves sweeping over the decks and the ship bobbing every which way. Wickersham was a poor sailor and for four days he "wished he were dead" as he noted in his diary:

Sept.11 . . .8 o'clock - seasick. Noon - sicker; evening - sickest; midnight - dying.

Sept.12 Morning - still dying. Noon - trouble with waiter; he said something about a farmer going to sea and laughed. Threw water at him, broke glass - two dollars - cheap. Still trying to die. Night - still have hopes of dying.

Sept.13 Still alive but very sick. Noon - damn Noah or Jonah or Columbus - or whoever it was who invented sea voyages. Overheard conversation day before yesterday in next room between P.C. Sullivan and John Corson (Tacoma-Seattle attorneys). . .The night we left Dutch

Harbor they had a "good jag" on - were drunk, in plain English.

When remorse and seasickness combined on them next day - between spells of eruptions and stomach retchings - both using the same bucket - Corson said - looking across at Sullivan with tears in his eyes - "By God, Charlie, if I get out of this alive, I'll swear off drinking."

As soon as he could speak, Sullivan replied, "No, John, we won't swear off drinking - we'll just swear off goin' to sea! Whoop!" and together they wh-o-oped into the same old bucket.

Noon - nobody dead yet. Night - sea calm, and see no immediate necessity for dying. Will be in Nome in the morning - may conclude to live again.

When the passengers awoke the next morning, the steamer lay at anchor in the Nome harbor and the sea was as smooth as glass and they saw the city of golden sands stretched out before them. After inspection by the health officer, they were taken ashore in a dingy and were never happier to set foot on land.

When they reached the shore, they discovered that the storm through which they had survived at sea, had wreaked widespread damage in the town. All the buildings on one side of Front Street were destroyed and the beach was littered with supplies scattered in all directions. They learned later that the storm had destroyed more than a million dollars worth of property and rendered hundreds of people homeless.

The beachcombers and scavengers came out in force, tempted by the valuable articles waiting to be snatched from the waves. Soldiers were assigned to guard against looting and to salvage property. Violent clashes took place between the scroungers and the military, and a number of arrests were made. Law and order was soon restored.[7]

Chapter 11

Corrupt Officialdom Creates Riotous Mood in Nome

> *The men who located the rich Anvil Creek mines were of that independent, vigorous character that they were able, notwithstanding their foreign birth and education (or lack of it), to fight the most astounding, vigorous and treacherous attack known in American jurisprudence and to so wisely and bravely conduct it as to eventually win and preserve their wealth.*
> *(Diary,Nov.24,1901)*

The townspeople of Nome were in a defiant mood toward formal law and order; it would take little for them to stage a riot in defense of what they considered their inalienable rights as American citizens. They had witnessed a coterie of judicial officials violate every article of justice and the people were in no mood to surrender their legal rights without a fight. A recital of some of the events which took place during Judge Noyes' tenure sets the stage for Judge Wickersham's arrival.

The gold stampede in the summer of 1899 was the result of discoveries by three Scandinavians who were not United States citizens. News of these discoveries leaked out and hundreds of prospectors rushed to Cape Nome, only to find that the richest claims were already staked by aliens. The Organic Act of 1884 stipulated that aliens enjoyed the same rights of land ownership as native citizens, but this did not stem the disappointment of the Americans.

Since there was no judicial set-up in Nome at that time, the disgruntled miners decided to handle the situation in their own way. They called a meeting in the Northern Saloon to discuss how they could take possession of the staked ground. They decided that they would pass a resolution vacating the present claims and throwing them open on a first-come basis.

This plan had been agreed upon preceding the assembly and miners had been stationed on Anvil mountain three miles away in readiness to rush to the claims and restake them. The prearranged signal was that when the resolution was passed, a bonfire would be lit outside the saloon to tell the mountain-toppers that they were legally empowered to go on their staking spree.

Word had spread during the preceding weeks that a crisis was developing, so a squad of soldiers was dispatched from Fort St. Michael to be on hand to avert bloodshed. The military contingent attended the miners' meeting and when the resolution was put up for a vote, the commanding lieutenant quickly stepped forward and ordered the resolution withdrawn and the meeting adjourned. When the miners refused to move, he dispersed the assembly at bayonet point and cleared the hall. The miners reassembled on the street, but they were redispersed by the military.

The situation was relieved with the discovery of gold along the Nome beach. The idle miners rushed to the area with hand rockers. By the end of the summer 2,000 miners had taken out more than one million dollars. It was the greatest poorman's diggings ever found.

But the "Lucky Swedes," as the original trio was called, were to face far graver attacks in their struggle to hold onto their mining claims. They and their friends organized the Pioneer Mining Company and the Wild Goose Mining Company, incorporating them in California, and they hired attorneys to protect their interests.

The trio represented striking contrasts as individuals. Jafet Lindeberg, a twenty-four-year-old reindeer herder from Lapland, Norway, had accompanied a reindeer herd purchased in Norway for the indigent Alaska Eskimos. Erik Lindblom was a forty-one-year-old immigrant tailor from Sweden, who had come north as a seaman on a whaling vessel and jumped ship when he heard of the gold strike. John Brynteson, a twenty-seven-year-old native of Sweden, had come north to work a coal prospect for a group of Swedish businessmen in Chicago.

The Nome gold rush attracted the attention of big-time politicians in the states and the ownership of the rich Anvil Creek property became a hot issue in the United States Congress. Alexander McKenzie, North Dakota's Republican National Committeeman, was chief lobbiest in pushing for legislation which would help him and his friends to share in the newly found Alaskan wealth. He worked through the two United States senators from North Dakota - Henry Clay Hansbrough and Porter James McCumber, both Republicans.

When they were foiled in their efforts to make it illegal for aliens to own property, the McKenzie cohorts set to work devising an alternate scheme for invalidating the Anvil Creek claims by permitting their relocation by "jumpers."

For years McKenzie was the recognized Republican boss of the Territory of Dakota; he ruled with an iron hand. He boasted of making governors, congressmen and senators. Thus when Congress authorized the creation of two new judicial districts in Alaska, including one for the Nome area, McKenzie prevailed on President McKinley to let him choose the court officials for Nome.

With all of the court officials owing their appointment to him, McKenzie anticipated no problem in gaining control of whatever mining claim he wanted by paying jumpers with stock in his Alaska Gold Mining Company.

Eighteen thousand men and a few women swarmed onto the beach of Nome during the summer of 1900.[1] No fewer than fifty saloons had opened their doors. Gunfights, thefts, and every kind of violence went unpunished as the city officials' efforts to maintain law and order proved futile. The local newspapers editorialized against asking federal troops to take over, claiming that martial law was not a democratic way for Americans to resolve their problems. The law-abiding citizens waited patiently for the arrival of the court party, expecting that then their problems would be given proper attention.

Finally the great day arrived on July 19, 1900, when the S.S. *Senator* came to anchor in the harbor and the townsfolk learned that the new judge and his party were aboard. The judge and his wife remained aboard the steamer for a couple of days while his officials located living quarters and courtroom facilities. McKenzie went ashore immediately with his paid jumper, Robert Chipps, and they arranged with a local law firm to give Chipps title to several choice mining claims, including those on Anvil Creek.

When the judge came ashore, McKenzie visited him in his apartment at the Golden Gate Hotel, and without any notice to Lindeberg, Brynteson and Lindblom, the judge appointed McKenzie receiver for their mining claims and instructed him to take immediate possession and begin mining the gold therefrom; those presently in possession of the claims were enjoined from interfering with his operations.

McKenzie had two wagons ready, and he and his men raced to Anvil Creek that night and took possession of the claims and all personal property thereon, to the surprise of the owners, who had not expected such quick action. Their attorneys tried to get the judge to revoke his orders and failing that, they departed for San Francisco to seek recourse from the circuit court of appeals.

In due time papers arrived from the circuit court directing McKenzie to return possession of the claims for which he was receiver, and Judge Noyes was commanded to stay all proceedings pending the hearing of the appeal. Both men refused to heed the court's orders, maintaining that Noyes had complete jurisdiction and the San Francisco judges were exceeding their authority.

A deputy marshal arrived from San Francisco to place McKenzie under arrest and take him south. He was tried and found guilty of contempt and sentenced to one year in the county jail. In passing the sentence, the court denounced what it characterized as high-handed and grossly illegal proceedings which had no parallel in the jurisprudence of the country. The judge congratulated the people of Nome on not having taken the law into their own hands.[2]

The United States Supreme Court refused to hear McKenzie's appeal and he went to jail. He walked out a free man, after serving a little over three months, having been pardoned by President McKinley. His friends had convinced the president that his health was such that he would not survive his full term of imprisonment.

McKenzie returned to North Dakota, where both his physical and political health were restored in short order. He resumed his office of national committeeman and was an active Washington lobbyist in Alaskan affairs. In 1908 he retired and moved to Chicago, where he lived quietly, reputedly worth millions, made on the stock exchange on pointers given him by his old friend, James J. Hill, president of the Great Northern Railroad.[3]

In commenting on the disposition of the McKenzie case, the Washington *Post* observed that Judge Noyes was the real culprit and should not remain unpunished because were it not for his "bulwark of authority" McKenzie "would have been powerless for evil." He could not have "despoiled the honest settlers." In conclusion, the *Post* editorialized that it was "the most detestable scandal that has ever smirched the record of any administration."[4]

With McKenzie in jail and the mining claims returned to the Pioneer Mining Company, it appeared that all charges made to the attorney general and to the president against Judge Noyes would be dropped.

Clearing the title to the ten million dollars worth of mining property put a stop to litigation for the time being. One claim alone had produced more than a million dollars worth of gold during the interval of McKenzie's receivership.[5]

During the testimony in the McKenzie trial, "Jumper" Chipps testified that the conspiracy to defraud had wide ramifications, and included Senators Carter of Montana, Hansbrough of North Dakota, Davis of Pennsylvania, and possibly Hanna of Ohio.

Governor Brady expressed fear for Judge Noyes' life if he remained on the Nome bench as the miners were so indignant over his rulings. Brady recommended that he be transferred to Juneau, whereupon the Juneau bar association wrathfully condemned such a contemplated move. Eventually Noyes was ordered to Washington, D.C. and also cited to appear before the circuit court in San Francisco.

Judge Noyes' departure from Nome became a classic in storytelling of early-day Alaska. A detailed description of his condition when he came aboard the S.S. *Queen* on the evening of August 13, 1901, was given to Judge Wickersham almost a quarter of a century later, by C.D. Harland, who was an assistant engineer on the *Queen* at the time. It was one of the last ships to leave Nome before the harbor became blocked with ice, and 1,200 passengers crowded aboard. Harland recalled:

. . .As he (Judge Noyes) came on deck from the boat or scow alongside, he was so drunk as to be unsteady on his feet; he was covered by a large overcoat and carried a heavy pack beneath its folds.

In walking along the deck, in the darkness, he stumbled and fell; he was carrying a grip also. He finally arose, picked up his grip and went into his room. He fell just opposite Harland's door, in a dark passageway where a door or barrier had just been erected to assist in controlling the great crowd of people who had pressed passage upon the vessel.

The great crowd of people, the mass of baggage, etc. and the stormy sea prevented the cleaning up of the passageway or the decks generally, on that day after Judge Noyes came aboard. He was supplied with liquor and remained in his room all that day, drunk and in a dazed condition.

The next morning, twenty-eight hours after Noyes had fallen in the passageway, and about four o'clock a.m., Harland came up from the engine room to go into his room, opposite where Noyes had fallen. He slipped on the wet deck, one foot struck something hard in the scupper, or drainway on the outer side of the deck, among a lot of small rubbish. He didn't stop to see what it was, but went directly into his room.

Then he began to wonder what it was his foot struck and his curiosity was so keen that he went out on the deck, lit a match, and looked for the object and found it. It was a large poke of gold dust, with a smaller poke tied to it. He carried the pokes into his room and put them under his pillow and turned in to sleep.

About nine o'clock he got up and had breakfast, then called the chief engineer and they carried the pokes of gold to the purser's room, weighed them carefully, and placed them in the purser's safe to await claimants.

In about an hour afterward, Judge Noyes came to the purser's office and declared that he had been robbed of a poke of gold dust containing thirty thousand dollars and gave the exact description - the exact weight of the large poke, and after careful consideration it was delivered to him.

He had made no mention of the smaller poke, but when it was mentioned, he claimed it but the purser refused to deliver it to him and it was afterward given to Harland as a reward for finding the large poke. The small poke contained gold nuggets of the value of six hundred twenty-five dollars.[6]

Judge Noyes was presumed to be leaving Nome bankrupt. How he could have accumulated $30,000 in gold, in one year, with an annual salary of $5,000 may best be understood by reading Rex Beach's famous article entitled "The Looting of Alaska: the true story of a robbery by law," appearing in Appleton's *Booklovers'* magazine, January - May, 1906, and his novel *The Spoilers*, written in the same year that Noyes appeared before the circuit court in San Francisco.

Judge Noyes was found guilty of contempt by the circuit court in January, 1902 and fined $1,000; a month later, President Theodore Roosevelt removed him from the bench. He returned to his former home in Baraboo, Wisconsin and died the following May from a hemorrhage of the lungs.

Commenting on the disposition of the Noyes' case, the Nome *Gold Digger* said in part:

Judge Noyes will long be remembered in Nome as an anomaly. Too honorable to be a scoundrel, too much of a scoundrel to be an honorable man; too strong to be a pliant tool; too weak to protect his own honor; brilliant and brainy, with many of the mental graces of a Chesterfield, but a fool.[7]

Shortly after Judge Noyes' departure, a riot took place on Glacier Creek in which a man was shot. The mine owners were fed up with the continuing harassment of having their claims "jumped" by casual trespassers, so one dark night they donned face masks and launched an attack on the intruders. Some nervous member of the party in the excitement shot one of the jumpers, wounding him seriously. An effort was made to keep the identity of the rioters a secret, but witnesses produced seven names of prominent mine owners, including Jafet Lindeberg, and all seven were indicted by the grand jury.

When word of the secret indictment leaked out, there was a sudden rush, by some of the principals charged, to get aboard the southbound steamer leaving that evening. The last lighter with passengers had left the beach, so they hired a small boat to get to the steamer just as it was hoisting anchor. Among the escapees were Lindeberg, who spent the winter in San Francisco, and Gabriel Price, who chose Mexico for his winter's vacation. There were insufficient funds in the marshal's budget to pay for extradition proceedings.[8]

When the remaining rioters were brought to trial, the cases ended in hung juries. By the time Lindeberg and Price returned the following spring, the cases had been dismissed as it was obvious that no jury would convict the rioters.

Chapter 12

Wickersham Takes Over the Nome Bench

. . .I have an opportunity to make a high and honorable record for myself as judge.

. . .The Nome court tangle has. . .annoyed and distressed the national administration and I have a chance to correct the evil, if I am of such weight and character as to manage the immense and wide-spread questions and interests involved.

I feel absolutely equal to the emergency and intend to take hold with an iron hand - encased in silk. My greatest task so far in life, begins Monday morning and I feel no fear. (Diary, Sept. 15, 1901)

Wickersham received a warm welcome from the people of Nome as they looked to him to end the turmoil over mine ownerships. It was reassuring to him to note their faith and confidence in view of their bitter disillusionment in his predecessor, and he hoped he would not prove a disappointment to them.

Wickersham took a room at the Golden Gate Hotel where there was a dining room. He disliked eating dinner alone and usually invited someone to join him. Frequently after dinner he and his guests would attend a social function in the hotel's ballroom. He was a member of the Elks, Masons and Arctic Brotherhood, each of which group held regular monthly social affairs. Though he did neither dance nor play cards, he enjoyed sitting around drinking beer, smoking cigars, and exchanging tales with the oldtime prospectors. Entertainment features ofttimes included boxing matches and/or musical and poetic renditions.

The hotel's thin room partitions caused him some problems of insomnia because, in his words "you can hear a man kiss his wife in the fourth room down the hall from yours. A young newly-married couple occupy the room next to me. They occupy a squeaky spring bed, just through a thin partition and they make me nervous."[1]

On weekends he would go for long walks or a mountain climb. Getting outdoors and enjoying nature's beauties helped him overcome a mood of loneliness because of his enforced separation from his wife and son. Returning to his hotel room on one such Sunday, which happened to be his twenty-first wedding anniversary, he confided in his diary that he "wrote a long, good letter to Debbie telling her that I love her more now than when I first took her into my arms twenty-one years ago."[2]

Wickersham's relationship with the opposite sex was awkward and self-conscious. His experience with the Brantner woman made him skittish toward women. He was both attracted to them and afraid of them, and particularly wary of a beautiful woman.

Living alone in a hotel, he was the object of interest among women guests who also were living there alone, and on several occasions he found it necessary to shun their attentions, fearing the dire consequences which might result. To him there were but two kinds of women - the morally good and responsible ones like his wife and mother, and the bad ones who were completely untrustworthy. Was it they or himself that he did not trust?

A case in point was a Mrs. Emma Downing who called on him in his hotel room; he described the visit as "strenuous." He considered her a "dangerous" woman and he told her to leave his room. Three weeks later he learned that she had had "a delicate operation." Grateful that he had recognized her as a woman of doubtful character, he wrote in his diary: "I only escaped blackmail by holding her off." In discussing the operation with her doctor, the latter explained that "it was done to save her life, having already been brought on." The judge described her conduct with him and the doctor said she had behaved the same way with him.[3]

Then there was another hotel guest, Mrs. Emily Dornberg, who "made eyes at me and even attempted nearer relations which I was too scared (even if for no other reason) to permit." She had been deserted by her husband and the proprietor of the hotel, feeling sorry for her plight, had taken her into the hotel to stay until navigation opened in the spring and she could go Outside.[4]

Fearing that she would subject him to unsavory gossip, he forbade her to come to his room. In his words: "She sought by the wiles of woman to get too near the judge - too near even for a mining camp and I put her out of my room to save myself from talk and told her not to come back and enforced my order."[5]

Years later Mrs. Dornberg became a professional actress; her stage name was Emily Ann Wellman. Once when Wickersham was in St. Louis, she saw his picture in the paper and telephoned him to invite him to have dinner with her at her parents' home, which he did, and another time he went to see her in a play and went backstage after the performance to congratulate her, whereupon he was invited to an after-theatre supper with the cast.

He went to see her at least two other times in plays in Washington, D.C. He considered her acting quite outstanding and marveled at how much more attractive she had become since leaving Nome.[6]

There was also Jennie O'Brien, a prominent Fairbanks business woman with whom he "passed some interesting hours." The two of them happened to be traveling north on the same steamer about ten years later, and when she saw him, she dashed to her stateroom and remained there all evening. Noting her hurried exit, he confided to his diary: "Verily conscience makes cowards of us all. Of course she married after our acquaintance, but she ought to know I never forget to be a discreet gentleman—even to my diary. Jennie is a very competent business woman and has made a fortune even in Fairbanks. She is a fine pioneer character and has the respect of the people of the Tanana and well deserves it."

Their ship remained anchored at the mouth of Wrangell Narrows the following evening due to a snowstorm, whereupon Jennie "came out of retirement" and they had a pleasant visit in the social salon. A year later, Jennie and her husband were aboard the same ship with Wickersham and they visited pleasantly again.[7]

On the bench, Wickersham had little sympathy for the call girls or prostitutes brought before him for robbing drunken miners of their hard-earned gold dust. One time when the male accusing witness decided to retract his charges and testify in the woman's defense, the judge got so angry that he decided he would teach the litigants that they could not make a farce of the court.

The evidence was clear that the man had been robbed in one of the rooms at the Gold Belt Saloon, which the two occupied, but her fellow "companions in infamy gathered to her aid and flooded the court with false affidavits on the motion of mistrial." The judge ordered the marshal to round up all the witnesses and hail them into court to give their testimony. The man was found guilty of perjury and the women sentenced to three years at the federal penitentiary on McNeil Island.[8]

Wickersham's feeling of righteous indignation was tempered somewhat when a beautiful, fashionably groomed woman of the demimonde was involved. Not that he would choose such a woman as a companion for himself, but his fascination was aroused when she was another man's object of affection.

One evening during the holidays, Magnus Kjelsberg, one of the millionaire partners in the Pioneer Mining Company, showed up at a party with a beautiful Russian woman on his arm. Kjelsberg had come to Alaska originally as a reindeer herder from Lapland. Sharing the same good fortune as his fellow countrymen, he spent his winters in San Francisco and there met "Russian Rosa," known for having made a fortune as an adventuress.

Wickersham was so intrigued by her physical and social charm that he inquired about her. He was told that she had been married to Kjelsberg for a year or more and that they were devoted to one another. To the judge they were "an interesting pair of beautiful animals."

As he continued to meet the Kjelsbergs at parties around town, he became increasingly captivated by her charm, as witness the following effusive diary entry, written one evening after returning to his hotel room, from a party at which he had enjoyed a long conversation with her:

> . . .She is really a remarkable woman. She has tact, taste and great talents. Her power with men is astonishing. Highly educated—a linguist—a woman of great physical charms and strength—strong in her natural mental endowments and skilled in the game of the world—she is such a woman as has in times gone by overturned thrones—Cleopatra—Sara Bernhardt—Delilah—these are the ingredients that enter into the composition of this Russian Adventuress, who made a fortune in San Francisco as the keeper of an assignation house—and in a year as the wife of one of the magnates of Anvil Creek, gets Nome society by the ears.
>
> She mentioned Metson, the San Francisco lawyer of the Pioneer Mining Company to me with a look that made me wonder if he brought about the marriage with his client to the beautiful tigress—and if so, why?
>
> . . .Will this bold, black-eyed woman rule (the Pioneer Company millionaires) like a barbarian queen? Is she in love with her great, strapping, silent husband, or is it only another

"graft?" There is a million or more in the pot—if she is playing
for it, and she certainly holds the winning cards.[9]

Three months later, Wickersham received a telephone call from the
"Russian Tigress" asking if she could come and see him privately that
evening. She came and after a long preliminary statement told him that
she and Kjelsberg were not married and she wanted the judge to
perform a marriage ceremony secretly so that the whole town would not
know about it; this he agreed to do. The ceremony was performed at a
friend's home, and the happy newlyweds presented him with a beautiful
diamond necktie stud for his trouble. Following a fine dinner, the three
attended a ball given by the Arctic Brotherhood.

Nome's social whirl heightened during the holidays, and the lonely
bachelor judge was not ignored. There was not only a dinner party
every evening, but later in the evening the guests attended a ball or a
theatre performance. Finally the time came when the continuous
partying lost its appeal and the judge vowed he had had enough. He
wrote in his diary: "I am tired of society in Nome and will not attend
anymore public functions and very few private ones. The town is
dance-mad but I have escaped that disease. This is the meanest town for
small talk I ever knew."[11]

Wickersham was determined that his tenure on the Nome bench
would be marked by incorruptible justice, despite the conduct of the
court's petty officials. A frequent complaint against Noyes was his
availability to designing attorneys who talked privately to him about
cases pending in his court. Wickersham admonished the attorneys, on
his first day in court, that "no member of the bar shall in my private
office or any other place except in the courtroom or in the presence of
the opposing counsel speak to me at any time upon any matter
connected with the litigation in this court."[12] There were 127 attorneys
in Nome at the time.

Judge Noyes left no written decisions made in mining cases during his
year of service; not an opinion on any subject was to be found in the
files, leaving Wickersham free to blaze his own legal trails. This he was
determined to do posthaste. When he discovered a tendency among the
attorneys to let their cases drag on indefinitely, Wickersham told them
he would not tolerate such delays. The records showed that about two
hundred cases were substantially ready for trial.

It was late in the season and many of the litigants, witnesses, and
attorneys were preparing to leave for the winter. It therefore came as a

shock to have the new judge insist on scheduling their cases on an immediate calendar. Wickersham instructed the attorneys that they must have their cases ready when they were called, or they would be dismissed for want of prosecution.

Court convened at nine o'clock in the morning and, if necessary, continued until ten-thirty in the evening. About one hundred cases were dismissed for want of prosecution. Counsel voluntarily dismissed many others rather than go to trial without witnesses who had already left for the states. Most of the cases involved "jumpers" who had taken possession of claims. The circuit court decisions in the Anvil Creek cases had clearly settled the rules of law applicable to them.

Wickersham also directed his attention to cleaning out some of the corrupt officialdom which had come north as stooges for Alexander McKenzie in his scheme for controlling the whole Nome judiciary. Some had failed to submit any account of their receipts and expenditures since their arrival and others had falsified such reports that they were part of a public scandal around town. As both United States commissioner and municipal judge, R.N. Stevens earned twice the salary of the federal judge and made him the next most important judicial officer in the camp. Evidence disclosed that Stevens had taken in about nine thousand dollars in fees and fines as municipal judge, without keeping any account of receipts and expenses. The judge removed Stevens from both offices.

It was ascertained that United States Marshal Frank Richards was handing in false accounts, defrauding the government of excessive reimbursements.

Wickersham had known Richards for many years, both having been active in Republican circles in the state of Washington. Both were natives of Illinois and migrated to the Puget Sound in the same year. Although he had been admitted to the Illinois bar, Richards had never practiced law. He served in the Washington state senate from Whatcom County from 1891 to 1895.

When Wickersham was being considered for the Alaska judgeship, Richards threatened Washington's United States Senator Addison Foster that if he (Richards) was not appointed collector of customs for Alaska, he would expose Wickersham's old Sadie Brantner affair to prevent his appointment. Failing to get the customs job, Richards went to Nome to prospect for gold and later landed the marshalship.

When Wickersham asked Richards to present his quarterly account to him for approval, the judge found it to be grossly padded. For example, he had charged fifteen dollars a day for board and room at the Golden

Gate Hotel where the judge was paying seven dollars. The hotel keeper was called in and frankly admitted that it was customary to sign vouchers against the government for the marshal and other officials for larger amounts than were actually paid; this had been done with the approval of Judge Noyes. When Richards was queried about the matter, he had nothing to say in his defense and agreed to submit an alternate account, minus hundreds of false items contained in the original copy.

There arose even more serious charges against Richards which could not be remedied as readily. Complaints were made by reputable members of the bar that he was engaged in "fixing juries" in cases where his friends were involved. When the regular panel was exhausted, it was the practice under the law to issue an open venire to the marshal to summon a sufficient number of persons to complete the jury.

The marshal, or one of his confidential deputies, would go out in town, often to Joe Jourden's saloon, and summon friends of the litigant whom he wished to assist and bring them into court as potential jurors. They would be advised how to qualify when questioned and thereby persons favorable to the litigant would get on the jury. Often these cases ended in hung juries.

Tampering with juries by the marshal's office reached the status of a public scandal in the acquittal of Joseph Wright, the Nome postmaster who admitted to his supervisor that he had embezzled $8,000. The case was tried before Wickersham. Suspecting jury fixing, the judge ordered the acting district attorney, John McGinn, to investigate. McGinn reported back his findings and Marshal Richards and Joseph Jourden, the saloon-keeper, were arrested and convicted; each was fined $300 for contempt of court.

Wickersham had been warned that Richards vowed he would bring up "the old trouble of 1888" if the judge held him guilty of contempt, but Wickersham concluded that he must meet it with fortitude and courage as it was bound to be brought up sooner or later; if he shrank from doing his duty on account of that threat, it would prove that he was unworthy to be a judge.[14]

In rendering his verdict, it took Wickersham almost an hour to read his opinion. He reviewed the evidence of the principal witnesses at great length, referring to the jurors as "rounders" and "bosom friends and fellow gamblers" of Wright.

Editor J.F.A. Strong of the *Nugget* charged that the judge was biased and prejudiced; that his language was not seemly but displayed a bitterness, lacking the dignity of a judge; that it partook more of the utterance of a special pleader than the dicta of a judge delivered from the bench.[15]

On the other hand, Editor Will Steel of the *News* commended the court on its fearless prosecution and conviction of a serious offense. Venting his personal venom on his rival journalist, he observed sarcastically:

> The *News's* defense of the court's action rankles in the feeble brain of the antiquated editor of our semi-weekly contemporary. . . . Jay Flop Around Strong, papsucking leach that he is, has used his paper as an organette for the marshal's crowd. . . . [16]

Jourden paid his fine but Richards refused to do so. Instead, he filed an appeal with the circuit court in San Francisco, and that court reversed Wickersham's decision on the ground that the record did not contain sufficient evidence to sustain the verdict. Stevens and Richards became implacable enemies of the judge and never missed an opportunity to injure him during the remainder of his career in Alaska.

By January Wickersham was sufficiently caught up with his court work that he decided to declare a month's recess, during which the clerk could prepare a new calendar for the February term. He wanted to get away from town for awhile and decided to go on a snowshoeing trip to Cape Prince of Wales and Bering Straits. Besides enjoying the Arctic scenery, the trip would afford him the opportunity to pursue his ethnological studies of the Eskimos.

He invited Louis Lane to accompany him as he would be helpful during the strenuous times along the trail. He was the son of Charles D. Lane, president of the Wild Goose Mining Company and an enthusiastic outdoorsman like the judge. They left Nome warmly clad in fur garments from head to toe, driving a seven-dog team.

They made twenty miles the first day, stopping overnight at Quartz Creek roadhouse. Wickersham slept poorly that night, suffering from an old neck ailment. His sleep also was disturbed by having to share his bedroom with Lane and the seven dogs; one of the dogs kept trying to get into bed with him. That developed into a point of contention between Lane and the judge as Lane insisted on the dogs' sleeping in the same room with them every night of the trip.[17]

It took them three days to get to the Cape. There they climbed a 2,300-foot mountain and had a spectacular view of the Straits and the two Diomede Islands, even seeing the Siberian shoreline. Wickersham suffered a painful eye injury when a flying fragment of granite hit his eye as he was chiseling out the words "The Cadet" on a slab of stone. He wanted to name the mountain in honor of his son who was a cadet at the Annapolis naval academy.

They spent ten days in the ancient village of Kingegan, where William T. Lopp, the government agent in charge of the reindeer herd and educational work among the natives, acted as their host. They visited the Eskimo igloo homes and were entertained in the men's "Kosga," an underground clubhouse where they watched plays and dances.

Wickersham bought a collection of artifacts, primarily utensils made and used by the Eskimos' ancestors; he also bought a bell said to have been made in Russia a hundred years before. Upon his return to Nome, he decorated his hotel room with these relics. He took copious notes so that he could prepare a paper on the lifestyle of the Eskimos living in this ancient village; he presented it at a meeting of the Nome Literary Society. In it he concluded that there was no obstacle to the migration of the Mongolian people via the Straits to America; in fact, there probably were a good many who crossed involuntarily as seal hunters drifting on the floating ice.

The weather was clear, but the subzero temperatures with a gale blowing from the east prevented them from hunting polar bear or sealing on the ice pack. One of their dogs broke through the ice and drowned; this frightened them away from venturing very far out onto the ice.

They returned to Nome on February 7, making forty miles the last day. The judge ran with the dogs about a fourth of the time at a pace of six miles an hour. He was happy to be back where he could get a hot bath, clean clothes, and a soft bed.[18]

He was disappointed not to find a letter from Debbie awaiting him as the last time she wrote, little Howard had been ill with typhoid fever, which left his lungs in a weakened condition. When a letter did arrive, Howard was again very ill - this time with pleurisy.

How desperately he wished he could be with his wife to comfort her. He recalled that she had been alone when their son, Arthur, died, and it was unfair that she should be alone a second time.

On March 3 came the terrible news - a telegram from Heilig in Eagle saying that Howard had died on January 11. Wickersham was beside himself with grief:

. . .The light of my life is gone. I held sweet Clyde's hand until she died (his sister)—and am robbed of the last look from my son's eyes.

Oh, Howard—Howard—I will never see your sweet face again.

The judge adjourned court without revealing his reason, but the word got out and the next morning, when he opened court, Acting District Attorney John McGinn arose and read a resolution passed by the Nome bar association, concluding with the recommendation that the court adjourn for a day as a token of respect for the judge's grief. The resolution read:

Whereas, Death has entered the home of our much-esteemed judge and taken from him an idolized son, the hope of his declining years,

Be it Resolved. . .that we do hereby tender to Judge Wickersham, wife and family, our sincere sympathy in this their sad bereavement. May they be comforted and sustained by the thought so truly expressed by the poet:

"There is no flock however watched and tended
But one dead lamb is there.
There is no fireside, howsoe'r defended
But has one vacant chair."[19]

Wickersham did not hear again from his wife until April 2, when a letter arrived dated in Tacoma on January 17. In the meantime, he had telegraphed Heilig to get word to her from Eagle asking her to come north and join him as early as possible. But when he received her reply, she had gone East to be with Darrell at Annapolis. She planned to remain there until spring and come north when navigation reopened to Nome.

The judge buried himself in his court work, hoping thereby to overcome his grief and loneliness. He spent evenings with close friends but shunned public gatherings. A favorite evening companion was Captain Hanson, commanding officer at Fort Davis, whose wife was also in the states. They enjoyed discussing politics, with the captain urging Wickersham to give up the judgeship and run for the office of Alaska's first delegate in Congress. A bill was before Congress providing for an elective delegate; were it to pass, Hanson and other friends wanted to start a movement to boom the judge for the office.

Though flattered by his friends' high opinion of him, Wickersham's first response was negative, he preferred to remain on the bench. But when the Nome *News* and the Council City *News* endorsed him for delegate, the idea began to be more appealing. However, he decided to make no public statement and await the turn of events.[20]

With the arrival of spring, Wickersham went on early morning hunting excursions, usually with Louis Lane and a couple of Eskimos who were experts in hunting on the pack ice. One morning they walked three miles out on the ice to open water and killed twenty-two eider ducks. Another morning they walked four miles to the edge of the "pack" to hunt seals; the ice was jammed and there was no open water - no seals.[21]

Wickersham's expeditious handling of court matters moved the town's business leaders and attorneys to start agitating for his permanent retention on the Nome bench. Over a hundred endorsements were sent to the attorney general urging that he remain in Nome; both local papers favored it, describing him as an "indefatigable worker on the bench."

But as time wore on and Wickersham was obliged to render controversial decisions, his enemies increased in number. According to the Washington correspondent for the Seattle *Post Intelligencer*, President Roosevelt decided not to appoint Wickersham to the Nome judgeship, after receiving representations from an unknown source contending that Nome was "divided into two hostile factions irreconcilably divided by rival mining interests and Wickersham was biased in favor of the Pioneer Mining Company and the Wild Goose Mining Company." Something like twenty-five candidates had applied for the judgeship.[22]

Wickersham was philosophically unconcerned about whether he would remain in Nome or return to his former post. He would continue to administer justice as he saw it and leave it up to the attorney general to decide where he should preside.

When the first ship of the season arrived on June 2, there was a letter from the attorney general ordering him to return to his post as judge of the third judicial district. Valdez and Unalaska had been added to his district, which meant he would not be confined to the Yukon interior. When it became known that he was soon to leave Nome, the local press showered him with accolades. Editor Strong of the *Nugget* editorialized:

. . .He has been a painstaking judge. The *Nugget* believes
that all of his judicial acts have been actuated by a sincere desire
to do that which he believed was in accordance with law and for
the best interests of the division over which he has presided. He
has done much to restore a confidence that was lacking, and his
single-minded efforts have taught most men that there is but one
application of the laws of the land - that which guarantees equal
rights to all and discrimination against none. . . .

As a jurist. . .he has exercized a discerning judgment, a
breadth of mind and a conscientious devotion to the trying duties of his office that are admirable.

No breath of suspicion has ever been directed against his honesty and integrity of purpose, though, perhaps in the discharge
of his multifarious duties, he has made stout enemies as well as
staunch friends. . . .[23]

The *Alaska Forum* in Rampart praised the judge for holding with the
original locator against the "jumper":

In every case he held with the original locator and swept
masses of technicalities aside. By his judicial acts in protecting
the individual miner from the ruthless maws of organized gangs
of jumpers, Wickersham has won the respect and esteem of
every respectable and honest man in the country.[24]

By the time Debbie arrived on June 11, Nome was alive again after a
long winter of hibernation; five large ships were in the harbor and
hundreds of passengers were pouring onto the beach, anxious to get an
early start in their search for that fabled yellow sand.

Wickersham remained in Nome another month, awaiting the arrival
of his successor, Alfred Stibbs Moore of Beaver, Pennsylvania, but departed the following day. Debbie was happy to leave as she had suffered
from attacks of pleurisy throughout her stay. It took them two weeks to
reach Eagle, stopping at Fort Yukon and Circle en route.

Once he knew he was to leave, Wickersham was glad to be on his way,
as he wrote years later in his book *Old Yukon*: "The evergreen forests
along the Yukon looked like the flowery fringes of Paradise to me after a
year's residence on the barren and tree-less tundra at Nome."[25]

Chapter 13

Court Headquarters Moved to the
New Town of Fairbanks

*On July 28, 1902 Felix Pedro "struck it." In no time stamped-
ers began pouring into the valleys near "Barnette's
Cache". . .Barnette built a large log store and cleared approximately ten acres for his trading site, including living quarters
for his employees. . .On September 8, 1902, at a miners'
meeting, "Barnette's Cache" became "Fairbanks" by official
sanction. (Fairbanks* News-Miner,*Golden Jubilee ed., Nov.8,
1951.)*

Wickersham's third judicial district was destined to overshadow the
other two districts. Instead of occupying the least important federal
bench, he was to become the czar of the territory's heartland. Here was
where the action took place during the following eight years—a new
metropolis was born; gold and copper discoveries produced hundreds of
millions of dollars; railroads and highways were constructed connecting
the rich interior with the coastal area. Judicial decisions reached out to
touch the lives of important personalities on the national scene.

The Wickershams remained in Eagle for only three weeks before
departing for a four-months' vacation in the states—the first he had had
in two years. They rented their home as Debbie's poor health would
keep her in Tucson, Arizona for the winter and the judge would be
traveling over his extensive circuit.

A brief court session took care of minor matters which had arisen
during his absence. His brother Edgar, a deputy marshal, embarrassed
him by challenging Marshal Perry, his superior, to a fist fight, while on

a drunken spree. During the fracas Wickersham took Edgar's marshal's badge and revolver away from him, agreeing with Perry that he should be fired. As usual, when Edgar sobered up, he apologized and begged to be given another chance, which Perry agreed to, in deference to the judge.

During his vacation, Wickersham started a long-planned project, namely, the compilation of all judicial opinions rendered in, or relative to, Alaska since it became a possession of the United States in 1867. The project resulted eventually in a multi-volume series. It meant searching through 115 volumes of the Federal Reporter, 30 volumes of the Federal Cases and checking the court reports in the states of Washington, Oregon and California, where Alaskan cases were most likely to be referred. But historical research was Wickersham's favorite hobby so he did not begrudge the hours spent on it.

On December 12 he placed Debbie on the train for Tucson and the following day he sailed north on the S.S. *Bertha*. The ship was heavily loaded with railroad construction supplies and mining equipment bound for Valdez; cockroaches were everywhere. He spent the major portion of his time with Captain Johansen in his cabin playing a card game called "cinch."

He received a warm welcome upon his arrival in Valdez. The townsfolk were excited about the town's prospect of becoming the terminus for an All-American railroad into interior Alaska, which would tap rich coal and copper deposits along the way. Its year-round, ice-free harbor made many predict that it would become the metropolis of southcentral Alaska. At least a dozen plans for rail routes out of Valdez were on the drawing boards of large commercial firms in the states.

With the discovery of placer gold and copper ledges, the town was attracting an influx of miners on each steamer. With these discoveries, construction of a railroad seemed inevitable and survey parties of rival companies began arriving.

Wickersham was swept into the festivities of the holiday season. On Christmas Eve a reception was held in his honor at the Moose Hall, during which he shook the hands of hundreds of people. The following day he and his court officials attended a dinner prepared by the Ladies of the Moose, after they had worked all day at the office.

He experienced some pangs of loneliness when he recalled past Christmases, especially those with Howard running about excitedly, opening his presents - the last one was in Eagle, their first Alaskan Christmas. He remembered his last sight of Howard, the picture of health, waving goodbye as the river steamer carried him and his mother downriver to Dawson.

Returning to his hotel room on Christmas night, he wrote in his diary:

> He was my pride, my love, and the hope of my future, and I am just now beginning to realize that he is dead. His death almost killed his mother and quite destroyed one half of my life— hopes and happiness. My ambition went with his dear, sweet baby face. I did not know how much I depended on him nor how much he meant to my life. Howard! Howard!

On New Year's Eve he attended a dance at the Knights of Pythias Hall for a couple of hours, and on New Year's Day he and District Attorney Harlan made some calls, including one to the newspaper office of the *Prospector*. Here they were served a brown-colored "lemonade" from a large tureen in the back of the shop. It had a familiar odor and taste as the two court officials helped themselves to cupsful, eyeing the demure editors with a quizzical look. Lemonade with a "stick" in it came as a pleasant surprise, despite its being an illegal concoction.

The Valdez bar association honored him with a banquet replete with printed menu and program and an assortment of wines, including Mumm's champagne served with a dessert of welsh rarebit.

Wickersham's admirers continued to promote him as the best qualified candidate for Alaska's first delegate in Congress, so much so, in fact, that he became sold on the idea himself and wrote in his diary: "I would rather be the first delegate from Alaska than judge."[1]

As he began to give serious consideration to the candidacy, it occurred to him that he better tell his supporters about "my old scandal." He first told the whole story to United States Commissioner John Lyons in Valdez, and his reaction was that it would not bar the judge's candidacy. Valdez attorney John Ostrander was living in Tacoma at the time of Wickersham's seduction trial, so it could not be a total secret around town.

Lyons even went so far as to voluntarily travel through southeastern Alaska to canvass the reaction to Wickersham's running for delegate. He returned with a favorable report and both the Juneau *Record-Miner* and the Douglas Island *News* editorialized in favor of his candidacy. Governor Brady said he would support the judge but former Governor Swineford said he was opposed.[2]

By the end of February Wickersham had cleared the court docket sufficiently that he could move on to other parts of his district. Reports of new gold strikes in the Tanana Valley required his going there to set up recorders' offices and appoint commissioners to handle the filing of mining claims.

Since the overland trail from Valdez to Eagle was restricted to military travel, the judge had to take the round about steamer route via Sitka, Juneau, Skagway and on into the interior. It took him a whole week to go from Valdez to Sitka, where he made an over-night stop. He stayed in Alexander Baranof's former home, kept by Mrs. Archangelsky, a Russian creole. He was awakened the following morning by the loud, sweet tones of the bells of the old Russian cathedral, and a girl pounding on his door to announce that it was ten o'clock.

It was a glorious, sunny Sunday morning and he had several calls he wanted to make before proceeding on to Juneau. He first paid a courtesy call on Governor Brady, who reiterated his support for the delegateship. The governor took him on a tour of the Sheldon Jackson museum to see the priceless collection of native handicrafts which Dr. Jackson had donated to the training school, when he departed from Alaska.

The judge then looked up his old friend, Captain David Jarvis, collector of customs, whom he had first met in Nome when the captain was with the United States revenue cutter service. Wickersham was not one to rave about the good qualities of another man but Jarvis was an exception. In a diary entry he expressed a great fondness for Captain Jarvis. He described him as "lovable, honest and competent" adding that he considered those three adjectives as covering about all the good that can be said about a man.[3] This is significant in view of his contrasting attitude in later years, which brought great sorrow to the captain.

Wickersham took the White Pass and Yukon train from Skagway to Whitehorse, and from there he traveled in a stage-sled drawn by four horses; it accommodated nine passengers and the driver. They made sixty-three miles the first day. From Dawson to Eagle he traveled in a one-horse sled over the frozen Yukon River, together with two other passengers.

He found Eagle practically deserted, everyone having stampeded to the new gold strikes in the Tanana Valley. He telegraphed the attorney general recommending that the court headquarters be moved from Eagle to the new mining district. He also recommended that the United States Army send a detachment of men to the Tanana diggings as he had heard that crime was rampant, with drunkenness a major problem.

After selling his home with all its furnishings, Wickersham set out for the Tanana with a six-dog team. He found the 350-mile trail lined with miners headed in the same direction. The second night out, he reached a roadhouse already filled to capacity and he was obliged to sleep on the dining-room table. He spread out his blankets and slept peacefully until the cook aroused him to say he would have to move as he needed the table for a five o'clock breakfast.

At Circle he met the E.T. Barnettes, who were en route to San Francisco for the winter, planning to return north in June. They had left Frank Cleary, Mrs. Barnette's brother, in charge of their trading post operations in the new town of Fairbanks. Barnette offered the judge a free lot if he would establish the court headquarters there.

Wickersham first met Elbridge Truman Barnette and his wife Isabelle in St. Michael in July, 1902, when the Wickershams were returning to Eagle from Nome. The Barnettes were assembling their boat, the *Isabelle*, which they had shipped north for use in their trading operations.

During that visit, Wickersham asked Barnette to name his new trading site on the Chena slough in honor of Charles Warren Fairbanks, Republican United States senator from Indiana, to whom Wickersham felt indebted for his Alaska judgeship. When Wickersham's friend, Senator Foster, began promoting him for the judgeship, the Washington state senator discovered that Senator Fairbanks also had a candidate for the same office. Senator Foster, accompanied by John P. Hartman of Seattle, another friend of Wickersham's, called on Senator Fairbanks and secured his consent to withdraw his candidate in favor of Wickersham, even agreeing to help get Wickersham appointed.[4]

Barnette agreed to Wickersham's request, and the judge promised in return to use his influence in getting the court headquarters moved there.[5]

When the court party arrived in Fairbanks on the evening of April 9, 1903, Cleary provided them with sleeping quarters in a side room of the large trading post and arranged for them to have their meals at Wada's restaurant.

Though the temperatures still dipped below zero at nighttime, spring was in the air; the days were sunny and the pussy willows were unfolding cattails. Wickersham gathered birch branches covered with swollen buds and they sprouted green leaves when he brought them indoors and placed them in a pail of water. The streams were opening -

the Tanana River was open and running for many miles above the town.

The first child to be born in Fairbanks made its appearance two days after the court officials arrived. The father was Dan McCarty and the mother was an Indian from Koyukuk. The town's first doctor, Dr. Fugard, a lady physician, arrived a day later, coming in over the trail from Circle.[6]

There were about five hundred residents and they were living mostly in tents. It was a motley crowd - miners, gamblers, Indians, Negroes, Japanese, dogs, prostitutes; lots of music and drinking! Town lots were selling at a premium. Cleary allocated a tract of land to the court officials on which to build homes for themselves and for a courthouse and jail. Before nightfall of their second day in town, Wickersham, assisted by his officials, had a pile of logs cut and a log jail was completed within the next few days.

Wickersham arranged for the construction of a 16'x24' log house on the corner of First and Cushman, for his own home. It was to be one story and would cost him $400 to build. He wanted a comfortable home for his wife, who was to join him later in the fall.

Except for his concern over his wife's health, Wickersham was a happy man at this point in time. He exulted in his role in pushing back the wilderness and creating a new civilization which soon would welcome thousands of his fellow Americans from the states.

He was exhilarated by the natural beauty around him - he called the Tanana Valley "the garden spot of Alaska." He took frequent walks into the woods to enjoy listening to the birds and squirrels talking with one another. He and Cleary and George Jeffery went out to the creeks and staked claims the whole length of an unnamed stream which the judge suggested naming "Isabella" after Mrs. Barnette.

It was only when he received letters from Debbie describing her illness that he wondered if he should remain in Alaska. He had offered to give up the judgeship the previous fall when her doctor advised her to spend the winter in Arizona, but she insisted that he not do so.[7]

When the local bar association honored him with a banquet, he wore his full dress suit - the first one to be worn in the Tanana Valley! He was not embarrassed to be the only one so formally attired as he considered it an indication of the high esteem with which he held the local legal fraternity. His appreciation of the gala affair was reflected in his diary notation:

. . .The large room was elegantly decorated with flags, curtains, evergreens and red, white and blue mosquito netting. The floor was carpeted with sweet smelling spruce boughs and the music - violin and guitar - was in an alcove behind curtains.

Dr. Whitney sang Annie Laurie and Ben Bolt. We all sang America and the Star Spangled Banner. Toasts were proposed . . .In response to a toast to me, I spoke of the courage and honesty of lawyers and defended them from the prevalent slander of trickery and dishonesty. The music was the feature of the evening. Morgan plays the violin like a master.[8]

Wickersham reciprocated a few days later with a banquet honoring the bar association. He had his secretary make menu cards out of birch bark and they used Felix Pedro's old gold pan—the one he used when he made his big discovery—to serve the "hootch." He later made a gift of the pan to Senator Fairbanks.

Wickersham decided to take the summer off from his judicial duties to climb Mt. McKinley. Preparing for such an expedition took weeks of planning.

Chapter 14

Wickersham Climbs Mt. McKinley

> In the faraway, frozen heart of Alaska stands the highest mountain in North America. We know it as Mount McKinley. Men of other races, however, have had other, and better, names for it.
>
> To many of the aboriginal Indian tribes of the region it was known as Denali - "The Home of the Sun." Others knew it as Tralaika, still others as Doleyka, and the Russians, when they came, called it Bulshain Gora.
>
> Significantly these three names, in three different tongues, meant the same thing - The Great One. (James Ramsey Ullman, High Conquest; J.B. Lippincott Co.,1941.)

When word got around that Wickersham was planning to climb Mt. McKinley, he was beseiged by men wanting to join his party. As an experienced mountain climber, he knew how important it was to have congenial trail mates. He also needed strong, healthy men and someone familiar with the Alaskan wildersness. It was not easy to turn away eager adventurers, but funds were limited so he had to keep the group small; in fact, he was the only one who had surplus funds to spend on such a project.

His final choice was four men whom he thought would make a satisfactory team. One was his private secretary, George Jeffery, with whom he enjoyed a close friendship and who was also a good photographer.

Another was Charlie Webb, a Tacoma boy who had been a pupil of Wickersham's sister Nan. He had known Webb in Eagle and on the Tanana for two years and knew him to be a good packer, hunter,

105

boatman, and guide. A third was Morton I. Stevens, a six-foot, all-around athlete, shot, and boatman.

The fourth was John McLeod, a twenty-six-year-old Canadian who had lived on the McKenzie and Yukon Rivers all his life. He had served as guide for Professors Stone and Hanbury on their expeditions gathering natural history specimens along the MacKenzie to the Arctic. He was a hunter, canoe-man, and trapper, and spoke the Tena Indian language; he knew the wilderness as well as the Indians did.

The two other members of the party were Mark and Hannah, thoroughbred Kentucky mules, young and strong. Wickersham named them in honor of United States Senator Marcus Alonzo Hanna of Ohio, a close friend of President William McKinley, for whom the mountain was named. The mules had been used to carry freight on the Dawson to Fairbanks trail, and their owners offered them to the party. Being the only mules in the Tanana Valley, their donation was accepted with sincere gratitude.

Once the party was organized, someone suggested the publication of a newspaper to raise funds for the trip. There had never been a paper in the Tanana Valley, and there was no reporter, no printing press, no newsprint. Wickersham was chosen editor, and Jeffery went to work on his typewriter and commandeered all the typewriting paper in town.

The Fairbanks Miner, Vol. I, No. 1, was completed on May 9, 1903; there were only seven copies as that was all the paper available. It sold for five dollars a copy and was a one-issue publication. It consisted of eight pages, eight inches by thirteen inches, typewritten double column on one side only. Wickersham wrote every word and was in complete charge of its format. Thirty-six ads were sold at five dollars apiece.

The limited supply required a judicious distribution in order to reap the maximum financial returns. Luther Hess, E.B. Condon, Frank Cleary, and Mort Stevens were chosen to arrange for its being read before the largest paying audiences, which usually were assembled in the various saloons; each listener paid a dollar to listen to its contents. A copy was sent to Senator Fairbanks, and Wickersham kept one for himself. The recipient of the seventh copy was not identified - perhaps it was reserved for general circulation, to be relayed from person to person, for a price, until everyone in camp was familiar with its contents.

The lead story narrated Felix Pedro's adventures culminating in his big discovery and the founding of the town of Fairbanks. The lead editorial described the editor as "a stampeder who is waiting for the snow to melt and the ice to go out of the river."

A second editorial lamented the wasteful killing of wild game and urged stricter enforcement of the game laws. There was even a social column, written in traditional society terminology, reporting the banquet which the judge hosted for the local bar. In his characteristically low-key humor, the editor wrote:

The table of whipsawed spruce boards was covered with a dainty napery of flour sacks, beautifully ornamented in large letters carrying name of mill and weight and brand of contents; nail kegs served as dining-room chairs, and the viands and liquors were the best the country could produce. . . .

The wine list included Hootch Albert's Best Brew, served in tin cups (no glasses in camp), Pedro's old. . .battered, long-carried discovery gold pan. . .was used as a tray; the menu was done by the official scrivener in his best letter-press on birch bark. . . .[1]

On a cloudless day, bright and warm, the mountaineers loaded their packs and Mark and Hannah onto the *Isabelle* and chugged downriver to Chena where they purchased their supplies and boarded the *Tanana Chief*, which was to take them to the mouth of the Kantishna River; here they were to disembark and proceed on their own.

Their stock of supplies consisted of flour, bacon, beans, dried apples, and prunes; 300 feet of rope; alpenstocks, mukluks, and 100 pounds of rolled oats and a bale of hay for the mules.

Arriving at the mouth of the Kantishna, they found it still gushing with the winter's ice. Captain Hendricks agreed to wait until morning; if it was gone by then, he would give them an extra ride up the river to save them some time. While they were tied to the bank waiting for the ice to slush past them, Webb noted a skiff stuck on a bar; he and McLeod crossed in the *Chief's* canoe and brought it alongside. To their delight they found it to be in good condition, needing only a little extra caulking. They borrowed oars from Captain Hendricks and they had a water craft which would come in handy for crossing streams and lakes; they dubbed it the *Mudlark*.

The following evening Captain Hendricks deposited the party on the riverbank near an Athapascan Indian camp. Here they settled down for the night after caching their supplies high in the trees away from reach of marauding malamutes. The Indians had never seen mules before and

took to calling them "white man's moose." The Indians thought the ex-
peditioners were fools to try to climb to the top of Mt. McKinley, observing that even mountain sheep fall off that mountain.[2]

The next day the party split up with Jeffery and Stevens traveling
overland with the mules and Wickersham, McLeod, and Webb rowing
upstream in the *Mudlark*, stopping at intervals to cook themselves a
meal. One early morning breakfast rated special mention in the judge's
diary:

> We had fried caribou steaks, purchased from a Tena hunter,
> garnished with crisp bacon, browned on the open fire, and
> Webb's best coffee and biscuits.
>
> The perfumes of Araby may be more agreeable to the olfac-
> tory nerves of the poet, but for good homey flavor to a woods-
> man's nose the odor of frying bacon on an early morning camp-
> fire in the wilderness cannot be excelled. . . .[3]

After five days of strenuous rowing and poling, the marine contingent
joined up with the cavalry. The *Mudlark* was cached and the united
party started out on foot, each carrying a heavy pack on his back, with
Mark and Hannah carrying their share. They tramped through swamps
and forests in a downpour of rain and waded icy cold rivers up to their
shoulders, finally reaching a beautiful birch hill sloping to a lake in
whose clear waters "Mt. McKinley was reflected like a great white
cloud, whose outer edges were tinted crimson by the descending sun."

The majesty of the mountain overwhelmed them as they stood gazing
at its beauty:

> Throw Mt. Hood, Mt. Helens, Mt. Tacoma and Mt. Adams
> together for mass, then pile Mt. Baker on their summits for
> height, and you will have a fair view of Denali (McKinley) from
> the upper valley of the Kantishna. We exposed several photo-
> graphic plates hoping to get a view of the great glacier-capped
> dome, now crimson and gold in the setting sun.
>
> To the west of Mt. McKinley, and joined by its tremendous
> ridge of stone, covered with external snow and ice, is a beautiful
> peak which from its lesser height renders it a feminine appear-
> ance as compared with McKinley. This splendid peak we named
> Mt. Deborah, in honor of my good wife.[4]

Later he learned that the mountain he had named for his wife had already been named Mt. Foraker by Lieutenant Herron, United States Army, in 1899. So four years later he selected a mountain fifty-five miles southeast of Healy to name Mt. Deborah, and that is still accepted as the official name by the United States Geological Survey.

Wickersham loved to commune with nature; he was never happier than when he was out alone, watching the birds and animals moving about in their private world. One evening after pitching camp for the night, he strolled away from the campfire and climbed a nearby hillside to meditate by himself:

> I sat long hours on the hillside listening to the cries of the waterfowl, the honk of the moving geese, the harsh notes of swan, and when the sun began its ascent in the northeast, to the grand chorus of the robins.
>
> Through the soft haze of fog, spreading low over the lakes and swamps in the valley at our feet, we could see muskrats quietly parting the waters as they moved in search of a morning meal; the warm south wind gently moving the waving branches of the surrounding birch, drooping like willow lace and red with ascending sun. . .the glow of resurrection in the balmy air of returning spring and the vast wilderness landscape, disclose the joy of life that primitive man has in his surroundings.
>
> Whether man is happier as a wanderer in the wild, or as a cog in the complicated machinery of civilization is a question.[5]

Stops were made along the way to add to their larder. One time they were walking beside a lake and noted that it was full of pickerel. McLeod's wilderness experience came in handy. He fired his rifle, the bullet just skimming the water, then he waded in, knee deep, reached down bringing up a three-pound, sixteen-inch pickerel. The shot stunned the fish and they were easily seized and thrown onto the shore. In half an hour they had a dozen large pickerel. They built a campfire and soon were eating a meal of juicy fish steaks.

Another time when Webb and McLeod killed two bull caribou, they made camp and stayed a couple of days to hang the meat to dry, for use when climbing the mountain.

They also stopped occasionally to do a little prospecting. They found colors in Chitsiah Creek and proceeded to stake claims. Discovery claim at the mouth of the Two Bull Moose gulch Wickersham staked for himself; No. 4 above for Debbie and No. 5 below for Darrell.[6]

It was mid-June when they reached the base of McKinley. The nights were so balmy that they didn't bother pitching tents but would make themselves beds out of spruce boughs. As they lay gazing into the sky they could see McKinley's great white dome gilded by the moon and the rising sun.

At ten o'clock on the evening of June 19, Wickersham, Webb, Jeffery, and Stevens left camp to start their ascent of the mountain; McLeod remained at the base to care for the mules and their cache of supplies. The climbers chose nighttime for climbing as avalanches were less likely. They started their ascent by following a medial moraine in the center of the main glacier which protruded ten to forty feet above the surface of the glacier, serving as a safe and solid causeway.

About five miles up the main glacier they came to the confluence of a branch glacier coming down from a high bench; it seemed a more direct ascent, so they chose to follow it rather than to continue on the main glacier. The mountain was glaciated from summit to base. They thought that once they reached that bench, they could continue right on to the summit.

They trudged through the sunlit night in single file, fifty feet apart in Indian style; their leader kept sounding for crevasses with the long hickory handle of his alpenstock. At seven o'clock the next morning, after traveling for nine hours without resting, they reached the bench they were aiming for only to discover that they were 8,100 feet above the mountain's base and were on a precipice beyond which they could not go. The alternative was to climb the vertical wall of the mountain and that was impossible; the wall reached an elevation of 16,500 feet.[7]

It took them three days to return to base camp; there they found McLeod sleeping soundly high on a platform in the spruce trees, safe from attack by animals. A council was held as to what further efforts should be made to climb to the top of the mountain, and the decision was unanimous to defer any further attempt. Their food supply was almost exhausted and the long, hot June and July days were making the snow fields dangerous to cross for fear of avalanches and the time was running short until the opening of the term of court at Rampart.

After a good sleep on spruce boughs, they arose the next morning entirely refreshed. After an early breakfast, they packed the mules for the homeward journey down the McKinley Fork to the Kantishna River.

When they reached the river, they built a raft and Webb, Stevens, and McLeod went as the raft crew. Wickersham did not trust the safety of the raft for himself and the mules, so Jeffery joined him on the overland trail. The raft was wrecked, the men falling overboard and swimming for their lives. Everything on the raft was lost except the two axes, auger, and McLeod's gun, which had been tied onto the raft. The grub box, dishes, pots, pans, and supplies of all kinds were lost, including all the blankets except the two which were tucked under the saddles of the mules.

This accident brought to a crisis the undercurrents of dissension which had been brewing among the members of the party. Wickersham was the recognized leader, and his dignified but stern behavior had prevented physical violence but could not eliminate seething hostility. He was unhappy to note Jeffery's transfer of loyalty from himself to Stevens. Following the raft incident he commented in his diary:

> Stevens' arrogance has received somewhat of a set-back, but is so supreme that nothing can quite dampen it.
>
> George has entirely abandoned all idea of loyalty to me and has become his most sycophantic. . .It is all owing to a "bull con" idea that Stevens has suggested to George that in a year they start on a journey around the world on bicycles for a newspaper at a big salary, and that during the circumperambulation they take photos of all remarkable places and upon their return they start a studio in New York and live happily ever afterward!!
>
> George is thoroughly infatuated with Stevens and his scheme and it is amusing, though disappointing, to me to watch his abject slavery to Stevens.
>
> McLeod was nearly hysterical after the wreck—laughter and crying—he lost all his belongings except his gun and this seemed a ray of sunshine to him for without it he is lost, but with it never. He sleeps with it—never allows it beyond reach of his hand and is now cleaning and talking to it.
>
> Stevens openly criticizes Webb for the disaster and boasted of his skill and nerve until I was forced to call him down and told him that his nerve was wholly in his mouth. . . .[8]

They made a new start in the morning—Stevens, George, and John on the raft—Wickersham and Webb with the mules on the trail through the woods. The damaged raft would be repaired when they got to the Kantishna and then, hopefully, they would all float down the river on the raft, including the mules.

This was accomplished and they all climbed aboard the raft except McLeod, who didn't trust it and was afraid of the mules. He made himself a canoe out of spruce bark and paddled his way down the river. They had nothing to eat but moose at every meal, roasted at the end of a stick over the campfire. They floated placidly down the river at about three miles an hour. When they reached the mouth of the Chitsiana, where they had cached the *Mudlark* and some beans and flour, they found that McLeod had rescued them and was busy preparing supper for the party. He had found an old bucket at the abandoned Indian camp, which he used for cooking the beans.

They continued floating down the river, stopping once a day for the mules to go ashore to eat grass and drink fresh water. The men did not bother to stop to camp, preferring to sleep on a bed of spruce boughs and grass aboard the raft, two members alternating in steering the raft.

They landed at the mouth of Baker Creek, where they loaded the mules and McLeod onto the steamer *North Star*, bound for Fairbanks, while the rest of the party started afoot along the overland trail for Rampart, fifty miles away. They stopped one night at a miner's camp.

Upon arrival at Rampart, Wickersham passed a lighted cabin where he saw Debbie sitting waiting for her wandering husband. He continued on to the house of the town's barber to get his two-months-old beard shaved off and have a warm bath in a tub with soap, truly a luxury after so long out in the woods. He sent home for clean clothes, and the barber heaved his dirty wardrobe into the Yukon, with his hundred-dollar gold watch tied thereto by a moosehide string—the bundle was seaward bound and the judge was bound for the little log cabin to take his beloved wife into his arms after being separated for five months.

Thus ended the first attempt of white men, and probably any other men, to climb mighty McKinley. Though they failed to reach the summit, they enjoyed a healthy two months in the invigorating and soul-refreshing outdoors.

The following year many prospectors went to the Kantishna to mine for placer gold, using trails made by the Wickersham party. Camps were located and the Kantishna mining district added its share of placer gold to the material development of the territory, thanks to the information brought back by the mountain climbers.

Chapter 15

Wickersham's Reappointment In Question

I have had word from Valdez about many complaints which were going to Washington against me from disappointed litigants and political strikers who desire to prevent my reappointment. . . .

I have held the office for four years and am satisfied with the result. If I am reappointed, very well. If not, I have some mines in this district which now bid fair to be much more valuable in a financial way than the office here. . . .(Letter from Wickersham to Senator Charles Fairbanks,Diary,May 17,1904)

All was in readiness for a court session in Rampart when Wickersham returned from his Mt. McKinley expedition. A large warehouse had been rented as a courtroom; the seating facilities consisted of barroom chairs and rough benches.

Wickersham had just gaveled the court to order on the morning of July 20 when the army transport *Jeff C. Davis* whistled its arrival with a committee of United States senators who were to hold a public hearing in the same warehouse in which the courtroom was located. The judge adjourned court so that he and his officials could assist in welcoming the party of dignitaries.

In the group were Senators Willingham of Vermont, Nelson of Minnesota, Patterson of Colorado, and Burnham of New Hampshire. They had come north to investigate conditions in the district and were holding hearings in each community. John E. McLaine, editor of the Minneapolis *Journal* and Will H. Brill of the Scripps-McRea Press were traveling with the senators.

The senators were in high spirits, enjoying their Alaskan junket with its accompanying hospitality. They were out to savor any and all unique Alaskan experiences coming their way. All four being attorneys, they asked to be admitted to the Alaska bar and Wickersham readily responded to their request. He asked United States Commissioner Charles Claypool of Circle to move their admission, and he administered the oath.

Then when the local members of the Arctic Brotherhood lodge honored them with a smoker, the senators were so intrigued with that organization's uniqueness that they asked to be made members of it also. The mystique of the Arctic was upon them!

The senators were initiated in due and regular form but Brill, the newspaperman, was chosen to receive the rougher embellishments of the initiation ceremony. After a "wet" lunch, the A.B. members, dressed in their long white parkas, escorted their distinguished guests to the riverbank and gave them the "malemute howl" as they boarded their steamer for Nome. [1]

After clearing the court docket in Rampart, the judge took off on his annual "floating court" circuit. For thirty-seven days aboard the United States revenue cutter *Rush*, the poor judge suffered through frequent bouts of seasickness. As the ship rolled through the high seas, he moaned to his diary: "They who go to sea on ships see the wonders of the Lord, however, they who go to sea on the *Rush* catch hell!!" [2]

It was with relief and thanksgiving that he stepped ashore at Valdez at the conclusion of his marine cruise. Debbie had remained in Rampart while he was traveling along the Aleutian Islands, stopping at the various villages to transact legal matters, but she was on hand to greet him upon his arrival in Valdez. She was suffering from heavy chills and high fever, suggesting a resurgence of the lung infection she had had the previous winter. They declined social invitations and lived quietly at the Imperial rooming house.

He found time to write up his McKinley trip for both the *National Geographic* magazine and the *Alaska Geographic* magazine. The Alaska Geographic Society was holding its fifth annual meeting in New York in October and the president wanted to feature the judge's article at that meeting.

Wickersham received a copy of his first volume of *Alaska Reports* and was delighted with its appearance. Now he had achieved "a historical standing" in Alaska's judiciary! The United States attorney general authorized the purchase of seventy-five copies for each of the three judicial districts.

Attorneys were arriving from all parts of the country preparatory to the hearing of the Bonanza copper case. They were bringing their wives with them as they expected it to last for several weeks. There was United States Senator Heyburn of Idaho, Congressman Cushman of Washington, Andrew Burleigh and Frank Arthur, New York City attorneys specializing in railroad litigation, and John Carson of Portland, Oregon. Alaskan attorneys Lewis Shackleford of Juneau and John Ostrander and Fred Brown of Valdez had been retained by the two contending parties.

The case promised to be one of the most crucial of Wickersham's career as a jurist. It rivaled the Anvil Creek gold cases in Nome which sent a federal judge and two of his court officials to prison and Wickersham had to step in to create law and order out of chaos. Just as in that case, the Bonanza suit would net him a whole new crop of political enemies intent on blocking his reappointment to the bench. He was well aware of these political overtones as he readied himself for the opening of the session of court. His four-year term was expiring and his political enemies were busily laying plans to get rid of him and have him replaced by someone sympathetic to their cause. Millions of dollars and the careers of national political figures were involved in the decision he was obliged to render.

The dramatic story of the accidental discoveries of these rich copper deposits became the plot of Rex Beach's novel entitled *The Iron Trail*. Wickersham presented a brief summary of the discovery in his *Old Yukon* tales:

> In the summer of 1900, Jack Smith and Clarence Warner, prospecting independently, wandered up a small and muddy stream coming from underneath a great glacier. One day they sat down on some boulders. . .to eat their lunch, and while thus engaged gazed idly at the mountain side.
>
> Jack called his partner's attention to a large green spot on the side of a distant mountain, and inquired what it could be. After carefully scanning it, one of them suggested it might be a field of grass. The other declared it could not be grass since grass would not be growing on such a high mountain, surrounded by glaciers and snow fields.
>
> They became so interested in the strange-looking green spot that out of curiosity they climbed up to it the next day and dis-

covered that it was the outcrop of an enormous copper vein of very high grade. In the next few days they located twelve mining claims covering this green spot, and extensions of the Bonanza copper deposits, in their own and their partners' names.

The War Department was just then engaged in surveying a route from Valdez to the Yukon River for an All-American roadway. This expedition was then at work along the Copper River in the vicinity of the mines in question. . . .

One of the employees in the expedition was Stephen Birch, a bright-eyed young New York engineer who had made a special study of copper. . .When he heard about the location of the Bonanza claims by the McClellan party and saw some of the ore, he made a visit to the green spot and carefully examined the Bonanza claims located over it. . .He got an option to purchase the claims at a very reasonable price.[3]

Smith and Warner had been grubstaked by R.F. McClellan, an employee of the Chittyna Exploration Company, which owned nearby copper claims. When the Company learned of Smith and Warner's rich finds, they claimed ownership on the basis that McClellan's grubstaking them made them employees of the Company. The two men contended that they were acting independently.

Judge Wickersham ruled in favor of the miners, holding that they had discovered the deposits without any assistance from the company.[4] His decision was affirmed on May 16, 1905, by the United States circuit court of appeals, and the United States Supreme Court refused to review it.

Once the decision was sustained, the miners completed their sale to Birch, who was representing the J.P. Morgan-Guggenheim interests in New York. That led to the formation of The Alaska Syndicate; the construction of the Copper River and Northwestern Railroad; and the establishment of the Alaska Steamship Company which carried the ore from the famous Kennecott copper mines to a smelter in Tacoma.

After five months of almost continuous courtroom sessions, Wickersham put in for and was granted a three-month leave of absence, which he spent in the Seattle-Tacoma area and in Washington, D.C. Debbie's doctor in Seattle diagnosed her illness as tuberculosis and advised that she spend the winter in a warm, dry climate. Worry over his wife's health and the vigorous fight being made against his reappointment revived his uncertainty about remaining in Alaska. If he had the money to develop his mining property he would gladly leave the bench as it was such a poor-paying job that he could scarcely save anything out of a year's salary.

Wickersham's first term expired on June 6, 1904, and if his enemies failed to prevent his reappointment, their alternative was to have his power diminished by splitting his judicial district into two parts, assigning the southern section to a fourth judge. The Alexander McKenzie crowd saw that as an opportunity for them to exploit the new copper discoveries and railroad construction.

When Wickersham came to Washington, D.C., Senator Foster and Congressman Jones of the state of Washington volunteered to serve as his official escorts, introducing him to the president, the cabinet officers, and other members of Congress. President Roosevelt's warm reception augered well for his reappointment and established a rapport that was mutually beneficial through the coming years. The judge recorded his first impression of the dynamic "Rough Rider" president in these words:

> He is a strenuous and rapid talker and began at once to ask questions and to answer them. He was much interested in the big Kodiak bear. I finally told him that I had a picture of Mt. McKinley which I wanted to give him. . .He accepted it and said he would hang it on his office wall.
>
> He volunteered the remark that every Alaskan official had been accused of every crime imaginable but laughingly referred to his experiences on the Little Missouri in an early day and said that notwithstanding these charges he thought Alaskan officials came up to the average.
>
> He was really good-natured but talked of everything else than conditions in Alaska. He is not as ugly as the pictorial papers and his photographs make him appear.[5]

While in Washington, Wickersham was admitted to practice before the United States Supreme Court on the motion of Congressman Lacey of Iowa. He also appeared before the House Committee on Territories, and after delivering an hour and a half speech on Alaska's needs, the chairman congratulated him, saying: "You have illuminated these Alaskan questions for us in a way that no man has done before, and we are very much indebted to you." This was the first of many similar compliments which he was to receive from members of Congress, who were impressed with his encyclopedic knowledge of the district and with his dramatic style of presentation.

He made a call at the Justice Department to learn what, if anything, was happening to the corrupt court officials he had left behind in Nome. It irked him to think that a fellow like Frank Richards could continue in the office of United States marshal when his corruption was so widely recognized in the community. In checking through the Richards file, he came upon a letter from Nome attorney George Grigsby to his father, Colonel Melvin Grigsby, United States district attorney in Nome. George was acting district attorney while his father was in Washington fighting Wickersham's reappointment and defending Richards' conduct in office. In the letter George boasted of his success as acting district attorney in getting certain gamblers convicted by "fixing juries." Wickersham asked to have a copy of the letter but was refused on the grounds that it was a personal letter which had been inadvertently placed in the official file. He planned to make a formal written demand for the letter in order to push charges against both Gribsby and Richards for "fixing juries."[6]

Later that spring Colonel Grigsby's resignation was in the hands of the president and was accepted immediately. It had been over a year since Attorney General Knox had recommended to the president that Grigsby be dismissed for leaving his post in Nome without permission. Subsequent charges were preferred against him in which it was alleged that he received $10,000 from the Pioneer Mining Company to secure immunity for the company from prosecution by the federal government. He admitted receiving the money but said it was for attorney's fees.[7]

While on the East Coast, the Wickershams visited New York City where they were entertained by Stephen Birch and other Guggenheim associates. They attended the theatre almost every evening with their hosts. A weekend with Darrell at Annapolis found him in high spirits, looking forward to graduation in February and his assignment to the S.S. *Tacoma* at Mare Island near San Francisco.

In Washington they were dinner guests at the home of Senator and Mrs. Fairbanks and frequently dined with Walter E. Clark, newspaper correspondent for a number of papers, including the Seattle *Post-Intelligencer*. Clark was boosting the judge's reappointment in his dispatches to the Seattle paper.

When his leave of absence was over, Wickersham left his wife in San Francisco where she could enjoy frequent visits with Darrell, and he headed north to resume his judicial duties. While in Seattle he helped his friend Barnette organize a bank under the laws of the state of Washington, but it was to be located in Fairbanks and known as the Fairbanks Banking Company. Barnette had sold his trading post to the

Northern Commercial Company and planned to devote his time to developing his mining property and to the operation of the bank, which was the first in the Tanana Valley.

As his ship moved northward from Seattle, he was pleasantly surprised at the degree of interest which his fellow Alaskans showed in having him as a candidate for either delegate in Congress or governor. Even his former critic, ex-Governor Swineford in Ketchikan, proferred his support for the governorship. At Treadwell, McDonald, the mine superintendent, strongly urged him to run for delegate, and at Juneau he found the same support from Judge Brown, Bill Maloney, a pioneer miner from Nome, and Juneau attorneys Shackleford and Lyons. All this latent political support was reassuring, in case he failed to be reappointed to the bench.

One of his first projects upon arrival in Fairbanks was to start construction on a new home. He figured that if he could provide Debbie with a warm, comfortable home, she would stay with him for longer periods of time, despite her ill health. He decided to keep it a secret and have it as a surprise when she arrived in Juneau. There were no wagons in the area as there were no wheels available. He had to carry the lumber on his back from the sawmill. Labor costs were high, so he did most of the work himself. He worked night and day to get it finished by the time his wife was due to arrive. No doors or windows were available until navigation opened on the Yukon. He sowed timothy, bluegrass, and clover in his yard. He built a picket fence—the first in the Tanana Valley—of real planed pickets which he painted white.

He donned work clothes and dug postholes, sawed lumber, and hammered nails. Except for doors and windows, he had the house finished by the time Debbie arrived on June 17. It consisted of a fourteen-by-sixteen-foot living room and a twelve-by-fourteen-foot bedroom; it did not have indoor plumbing, but the walls were covered with a bright, floral wallpaper and the floors with Japanese matting; there was a good spring bed, a cookstove and a hat rack made of moose horns. He planted a flower garden by the front walkway.

He received encouraging letters from his friends in Washington, who were lobbying for his reappointment. Then came word that the president was sending an investigator to Alaska to check on the charges which had been filed against all three district judges, Governor Brady, and Marshal Richards.

Midway during the term of court, William A. Day, assistant attorney general, arrived in Fairbanks to investigate the charges filed against the judge. He placed an ad in the paper, inviting one and all to appear before him at the city hall and express their opinions about the judge's conduct on the bench. When Wickersham called on him to offer any assistance, he was politely rebuffed. Collector of Customs Jarvis was Day's official escort while he was in Alaska, and he assured Wickersham that he had not hesitated to tell Day that he was wholeheartedly in favor of the judge's reappointment.

After a day and a half of hearings, Day came to Wickersham and told him that he had concluded them because there seemed to be no great interest in bringing charges against him. Day enumerated the charges which had been made and the judge offered an explanation for each of them:

> The old scandal of 1887-89 in Tacoma was the principal charge—the conviction of Richards was another - the re-instatement of Kellum as an attorney—the employment of Whittlesey— and a dozen small and insignificant matters.
>
> But not a single charge of incompetency, dishonesty or wrongdoing in my office. I am simply disgusted at the "small talk" which disappointed litigants and narrow-minded enemies imagine are worthy of consideration by the Department of Justice. . . the mountain has labored and it's a mouse. . . .[8]

Confident that he had provided Day with adequate answers to the various charges, Wickersham proceeded with his court calendar, trying to maintain a calm outward composure.

At this term of court, Wickersham rendered a decision which has become a classic in the annals of frontier justice, especially because of the humor involved. It is the case *McGinley v. Cleary* and was rendered on August 8, 1904. It is in Appendix B. The case was one in equity to set aside a bill of sale of a one-fourth interest in a hotel, allegedly made during a gambling game with dice, while the plaintiff was under the influence of liquor.

Wickersham's brother Edgar's fondness for the bottle was a constant problem. Each time Edgar "made a fool of himself" in public, the judge would threaten to force his resignation as deputy marshal, only to give in later to his brother's entreaties to give him one more chance.

But later that fall, when Marshal Perry removed Edgar from office without consulting the judge, Wickersham was surprised and hurt. Coming as it did when the judge was under investigation, it made him wonder if perhaps Perry, too, was working against him behind the scenes. Even when Perry explained why he had removed Edgar, the judge's resentment deepened and he was convinced that his brother had been treated unfairly.[9]

At the conclusion of the court term, Wickersham went out to the creeks to check on his mining operations before going south with his wife. He would be gone two months as he was taking a month's vacation and President Roosevelt had designated him a delegate to the Universal Congress of Lawyers and Jurists to be held in St. Louis. He was also a delegate to the national bar association convention, meeting in St. Louis at the same time. He would visit friends in Springfield and Chicago while in that vicinity.

Following the telephone trail to the creeks, Wickersham walked the fourteen miles in four hours, without sitting down to rest. Traffic was heavy along the trail; pack trains of mules loaded with the winter's provisions for the camps, passed him; miners going and coming meant frequent delays as they stopped to exchange greetings.

At Cleary Creek Wickersham met a friend whose wife had died that morning and he asked the judge to help him give her a proper funeral. Seeing how overcome with grief his friend was, Wickersham, without a moment's hesitation, took full charge of all arrangements.

He spent the afternoon whipsawing and planing lumber to make a coffin. The women in camp donated their black sateen underskirts for lining the coffin. The next morning he held graveside services, delivering the eulogy himself. The coffin rested on two upturned mining buckets encased in soft green moss. He spoke of the loss to the husband and community of a fine young wife, the first white woman to be buried in the Tanana region.[10]

It was with a sense of relief that the Wickershams departed from Fairbanks that fall. Debbie had been bedridden much of the time. They had slept in a tent which he pitched just outside the front door, believing that the dry, fresh air would be beneficial to her health.

Chapter 16

Continues Under Recess Appointments

> *My conclusion is that Judge Wickersham is an able, honest
> and upright judge; that he administers justice promptly and
> firmly; that he possesses the confidence of the people of his
> division; that his long residence in western communities, and
> his familiarity with mining laws and customs peculiarly fit him
> for the position he holds; that he deserves reappointment, and
> the best interests of the people of the third division - and all of
> Alaska for that matter - would be served by his continuation in
> office.*　　　　(Day's report to the President,Diary,Nov.14,1904)

Wickersham was in Valdez when he learned from Walter Clark that
Special Investigator Day had made a favorable report to the president
and the latter had reappointed him. The Day report recommended the
reappointment of Judge Moore in Nome and Governor Brady as well,
and the removal of Judge Brown in Juneau and Marshal Richards in
Nome. Elated that Richards was finally ousted for "jury fixing" and
padding his expense accounts, the judge observed: "the mills of the gods
grind slowly, but they grind."

Wickersham was so happy over his reappointment that he threw a
dinner party for his friends that evening, celebrating "with a quart and
good birds!"

Congratulatory telegrams began arriving, including ones from
Attorney General Moody and Stephen Birch. He felt deeply grateful for
the president's support:

> I feel now that I can say, modestly, but to my own private
> diary—that notwithstanding all the mistakes which I have

122

made, my life is now fairly a success—not that I have reached
the end, but that I am now in that sphere where successful men
stand, and from which I can do more and better work.

I am particularly proud of my reappointment because of Darrell—he can now always be reasonably satisfied to say who his
father is and my good, clean, pure-minded wife is to be credited
with nearly all of it. . . .[1]

Wickersham did not have long to savor his happiness however. When
the "lame duck" session of Congress adjourned without taking any
action on his nomination, he realized that his enemies intended to fight
his confirmation by the Senate. The president gave him a recess
appointment on December 24.

The judge felt helpless in defending himself against his political
enemies who were free to assemble in Washington to lobby for his
removal. Here he was thousands of miles away and forbidden to leave
his post unless he had official permission to do so. If only he could be
there in person, he might defeat their efforts. He sank into a slough of
self-pity.

Being alone during the holidays added to his despondent mood.
Debbie wrote that she would not be joining him until in June as she had
read newspaper stories about the terrible blizzards that raged over the
Tanana Valley in which several persons had frozen to death in the
snowdrifts. He had planned that she would join him in Valdez and they
would travel together over the Richardson trail to Fairbanks in the
month of January.

Debbie also wrote urging him to give up the Alaskan judgeship so
they could be together. In meditating on his marital problems, he
decided that they began with the death of Howard—that marked the
end of any kind of family life for him—his son was gone, and his wife
had contracted the same disease from which he had died and could no
longer live in the severe Alaskan climate. He observed: "It seems to me
like a century and as if I were transported to another world; it will soon
be four years of discomfort."

Torn between self-pity and anger at his wife's continued refusal to
come north, he wrote her: "My darling wife: Damn it. Your loving
husband." He knew it was a brutal letter but he was half-mad. In
thinking about it later, he concluded he was getting cross and cranky
and hoped she would take his letter as a joke and not be offended.[2]

When he was depressed, he could not sleep and developed an upset
stomach. In his determination to conceal his inner feelings of despair, he

assumed a stern exterior which made some people afraid of him, for they thought him insensitive to their problems.

His critics in the Alaska press became louder in their denunciation as they noted the reluctance of the Senate Judiciary Committee to recommend his confirmation.

Editor Strong of the Nome *Nugget*, who had lived in Tacoma during the Brantner trials, suggested that his past record was sufficient to warrant his removal from the bench:

> We who know something about his character and past record, even before he came to Alaska, can well believe that there are grave and serious foundations that justify the senate in wanting to investigate further into this man's past life. . . .
>
> For the sake of the judiciary of Alaska. . .we hope that the appointment of Wickersham will be rejected. . .and that the applicant will be returned to the oblivion from whence, by one of those infrequent and inexplicable turns of political fortune, he came.[3]

Wickersham had a formidable group of United States senators opposing his confirmation, each for his own personal reasons. Both senators from the state of Washington were old-time political foes. His friend Addison Foster had lost his bid for reelection to Samuel H. Piles, Seattle attorney; Piles was one of Sadie Brantner's attorneys. The other senator was Levi Ankeny, a Walla Walla banker who had been in an opposing faction in the Republican party when Wickersham was active in Pierce County. Recalling his Pierce County politicking days:

> Senator Ankeny, through John Forbes, offered me five thousand dollars to vote for him for senator six years ago when I was conducting the campaign for Senator Foster. I called him a "son-of-a-bitch" and other things; P.C. Sullivan who packed the jury at Nome with Richards is Piles' manager and is to be district attorney for the state of Washington.[4]

Senator Ankeny was promoting Thomas J. Humes, former Seattle mayor, to succeed Wickersham in the Alaska judgeship. Richard A. Ballinger had succeeded Humes as mayor of Seattle.[5]

Senator Heyburn of Idaho was antagonistic toward Wickersham because of the verdict in the Bonanza case which went against his client, Helms of New York. Senators Hansbrough and McCumber of North

Dakota were creatures of Alexander McKenzie, who was still smarting from his Nome experience and associated Wickersham with his ill fortune.

Senator Carter of Montana had two brothers-in-law in Nome who had not fared well during Wickersham's tenure. One was James Galen, a deputy under Marshal Richards, whom the judge had removed as commissioner at Kougaruk. The other was Lang, who owned the building in which the Nome jail was located; when Wickersham learned that Richards was paying him an annual rent of $3,600, the judge reported to the Justice Department that it could be built for $1,800, and the rent was reduced to that amount.

Senator Knute Nelson of Minnesota felt unfriendly to the judge because of a series of adverse verdicts which he had rendered involving some of his constituents, who were mining in Nome and Valdez. Also the senator resented the judge's having reneged on his support for a fourth judicial division in Alaska.

After winding up his work in Valdez the latter part of February, Wickersham set out on the trail for Fairbanks, accompanied by Bob Coles, a young Valdez prospector, who helped him handle his six-dog team. It took them fourteen days to make the 371-mile journey, and they experienced the usual hardships of fighting snow blizzards, wading through icy streams and sleeping in uncomfortable roadhouse facilities. One day they walked fifty-one miles, the last fifteen in the face of a raging snowstorm. (This was the trip he wanted his sick wife to make with him!)

One dark night their sled struck a pole lying across the road, throwing dogs and all into a deep ravine; their supplies went in all directions:

> We finally righted the sled, found and re-packed our supplies by lantern light, and cut the brush back to the trail. With much shouting, pushing and pulling we regained the trail but little injured, though my hands and face were bleeding and my hip felt as if it had been cracked when I landed on a log after my flight through the air. We rough-locked the sled, proceeded more cautiously to the valley below, and reached the Copper Center roadhouse at midnight.
>
> Here a hot bath and a roll of sticking plaster made me new again. The next morning, however, my ankle was so badly sprained and swollen that we concluded to lay off a day for rest

and hospital treatment, though the sourdough hotcakes we had for breakfast may really have been the strongest inducement.[6]

Another overnight stop was at the Chippewa roadhouse, which consisted of a one-room cabin and a tent lean-to in which the owner's mule team was lodged. Meals were two dollars and a place to spread your blankets for the night was an additional dollar. Finding the roadhouse filled with stranded guests waiting for the Gakona River to recede, and whooping it up with a generous supply of liquor, the judge chose to bed down with the mules: "I betook myself to the mule-tent, where there were half-a-dozen bales of hay safely stowed away from the mules. I spread my blankets on these hard but level bales of hay and passed the night more agreeably than those who remained in the shelter of the cabin."

At Nigger Bill's roadhouse Wickersham had an experience which Debbie would be glad to have missed! He was awakened at five o'clock in the morning when the chef lighted the fire in the Yukon stove and prepared to mix the dough for biscuits:

> With half-closed eyes I watched him mix the dough for biscuits. Balancing it in his hands he expertly mixed and kneaded it, until by accident, he dropped the whole mass upon the gravel floor which was carpeted with evergreen needles and dirt. Hastily recovering it, he brushed off as much of the dirt as he could without too much labor, picked out most of the evergreen needles, and then quickly turned it inward to conceal the soiled parts.
>
> Having finished the kneading he put the dough on the table, first wiping off the tobacco leavings, rolled it out with a bottle and cut it into squares for the pan. Though I am particularly fond of biscuits for breakfast, my menu that morning consisted of fried lamb chops and coffee.[7]

At Salchakat Wickersham received a telegram saying that President Roosevelt had given him a third recess appointment; the president was determined to keep him on the bench despite the opposition of a handful of senators.

Before leaving Valdez, Wickersham bought himself the latest model of a phonograph with a horn amplifier and a hundred tubular records. He packed it carefully in a wooden box filled with excelsior to take with him on the trail to Fairbanks. It became an exciting object of curiosity to the Fairbanksans. He presented the first mechanical outdoor concert in the Tanana Valley when one evening he set the machine in an open window with pillows stuffed around it to keep out the cold and the whole town was entertained with strains of grand opera, Sousa's marches, and other popular melodies floating through the frosty winter atmosphere.

Listening to phonograph music after dinner while smoking cigars and drinking Scotch whiskey became a routine when he invited friends in for dinner. He built a sideboard on which to mount the phonograph in the living room and he laid new carpeting to give the room a gayer appearance. When spring came he planted flowers around his home so it would present a pleasing picture for Debbie when she arrived in June.

His mining claims were panning out well, but not well enough for him to retire from public office. His friends kept urging him to quit the judgeship and go into private practice, which would net him a greater income. He was torn between freeing himself from the continuous criticism or remaining on the bench as long as the president wanted to keep him there. He hated to quit under fire as that might suggest that he was guilty of some wrongdoing, which he was not. By the end of 1905 the president had given him five recess appointments while his enemies kept his confirmation bottled-up in the Judiciary committee.

His mood of indecision was reflected in his diary entries. One evening he wrote: "I hope I can make enough money out of my property and mines to enable me to retire from official life soon, for it is hell in Alaska." And yet another time he wrote: "Everyone asks me 'why don't you quit the office and make some money?'—as if money were the one great object of life! I would rather have the first and second *Alaska Reports* as a monument of my work in Alaska than to have money!"

Wickersham rendered an opinion in his Fairbanks term of court in 1905 which revolutionized gold mining in the Tanana Valley and which also made him a whole new host of enemies. He declared that an actual discovery of gold was necessary to make a valid location of a mining claim and said the discovery must be made within ninety days of the staking of the claim.

This decision practically eliminated the much-hated "power of attorney" device which had been in existence ever since the first discovery. No longer could an unlimited number of claims be staked by an individual on behalf of his friends and be held indefinitely without any work being done on them. The miners were jubilant over the decision, as now they could go to work on ground which heretofore remained in a state of "reservation" only being held by stakes and a notice.

Wickersham's "discovery" opinion was not only revolutionary in its significance to the hardworking local prospector, but it wiped out the hopes and dreams of many influential men in high places in whose names claims had been staked.

Placer mining in the Tanana was different from that elsewhere in the states, hence the need for a new legal definition of "discovery." In a camp where the gravel deposits that contain gold are on or very near the surface, there is little trouble with the mining laws, but in the Tanana a new situation existed. The bedrock there was from thirty to three hundred feet below the surface, and over it there was a layer of muck, a sticky kind of mud, with nothing on the surface of the ground to indicate that there was gold within a thousand miles.

When the Tanana district camps were first located and the presence of gold in paying quantities was determined, people rushed in from all directions bringing with them their ideas of liberal mining laws, which they applied there. One man without prospecting the property would stake a whole creek, swear that he had made discovery, tie up the creek for a year, and hold back the development of the camp. It was two years before the camp found any degree of stability. Prospectors had to find new creeks or pay tribute to the grafters who had the country tied up.

With the miners came camp followers who behaved as birds of prey; many were lawyers criminally inclined. They lay in wait in their offices or in saloons until some hardworking miner demonstrated at his own expense the existence of "pay" on a creek, and then they would jump his claim or cause it to be jumped. The miner was out of money by the time he had made his bona fide discovery of gold, and any lawsuit brought against him meant to him the loss of half or part of his claim in fees to some lawyer, or a division of the claim with the grafters to prevent a suit. The courts were full of such cases, and the camp was full of perjurers waiting for the opportunity to beat some honest prospector out of his discovered ground.

It was soon demonstrated that a true discovery could only be made in the Tanana by sinking to bedrock or after going down through the non-mineral-bearing muck to the bedrock, to the gravel where the gold was, and Wickersham ruled that a locator must actually find gold before swearing that he had discovered it. That threw the country open to the working miner and the camp came alive.

With the working miner protected by an honest court, the grafters were thwarted and they howled, naturally. They saw that their only hope of easy money lay in ousting the square judge and getting a crooked one in his place, or one whom they could use to further their own selfish ends.

They appealed to the old prairie crowd of grafters who backed the notorious McKenzie-Noyes outfit at Nome to ruin that camp, and the fight upon the reappointment of Wickersham as judge began in the Senate. McKenzie's two North Dakota senators and Nelson of Minnesota, were in the vanguard.

Wickersham spent his twenty-fifth wedding anniversary in Seward, while his wife was in New York visiting Darrell, who was on shore leave. The judge had just returned from a moose hunt on the north shore of Kenai Lake. He never forgot anniversaries or birthdates of his loved ones and invariably commented on them in his diary. On his twenty-fifth wedding anniversary he wrote:

> I love my clean-minded, good wife with a stronger love than I did when she came as my bride. If our three boys were all alive how happy I would be, but our eldest is left and he is so strong and manly that I cannot complain. Though Howard's death was the greatest loss of my life, it also seems to have been almost the end of my home life.[8]

Wickersham's failure to win Senate confirmation made him both a controversial and a popular political figure. However much he tried to stay out of politics, sooner or later every issue took on a pro- or anti-Wickersham interpretation. His supporters were as ardent as his enemies were bitter.

The grand jury at Valdez, on two different occasions, noted that the third division had been singularly free from any judicial scandals, in marked contrast to the other divisions, declaring:

> Much of the credit for this is due to the judge. . .His fearlessness and sterling qualities as a man, and his known abhorence of anything that taints of graft or official corruption, has had a salutory effect upon the other officers of this division. . . .
>
> Judge Wickersham has proven himself to be just, able, honest, dignified, patient and fearless. . .Property rights and the liberties of the people have been safe in his hands and justice has been fairly and honestly administered.

We feel that we, as American citizens, have a right to demand that this man who has served us so faithfully, conscientiously and well shall continue in his present position. . . .[9]

Chapter 17

Goes To Washington To Answer Charges

> *Judge Wickersham, I have read everything in or about your case. . .and I understand the whole case fully. . .I am satisfied with you and will reappoint you - go back to Alaska and continue your work as judge. . . .*
>
> *I will be President yet for two years and eight months and I will support you that long - you shall be judge in Alaska as long as I am President - you can depend on me, so go home and go to work. . . .(Conversation between President Roosevelt and Judge Wickersham,* Old Yukon, *p.460.)*

Wickersham was in Buckley working on his second volume of *Alaska Judicial Reports* when a telegram arrived from the attorney general authorizing him to come to Washington to appear before the Senate Judiciary Committee, which was considering his reappointment.

He was delighted to be given an opportunity to face his detractors and answer their charges face to face. The day of his departure, the *Post-Intelligencer* ran a story saying that Senator Nelson had made a formal list of charges against him, the main one being that gambling was taking place on property owned by the judge. Actually, Wickersham owned the land but the lease specifically stipulated that it should not be leased for a saloon or gambling purposes.[1]

En route on the eastbound train, Wickersham bought a copy of the Fargo (North Dakota) *Forum* which carried a story with a Seattle dateline saying that "a petition has been sent to President Roosevelt by a number of Alaskans in the city (Seattle) asking that Judge Wickersham be appointed governor of Alaska to succeed Governor Brady."

Wickersham considered it an unwise move by either his "fool friends" or his "astute enemies" as it was bound to complicate his present confirmation fight and at that point he preferred to win the fight rather than be governor.[2]

When he arrived in Washington, a reporter asked him about the governor story and Wickersham was quoted as saying: "I am not now, nor ever have been a candidate for governor of Alaska." He was determined to fight for Senate confirmation.

Wickersham's friends in the Senate told him that Senator Nelson had opposed his coming to Washington and also objected to providing him with a written statement of the charges filed against him, but the other committee members countermanded him and insisted that the judge be given full opportunity to prepare answers to the charges.

Angry and frustrated by Nelson's unfair and treacherous tactics, Wickersham wanted to have a face to face encounter with the senator but his friends advised against it, saying it would be a violation of "senatorial courtesy." The senators themselves referred to Nelson behind his back as "that Swede son-of-a-bitch" but were adamant that strict senatorial protocol be observed in face to face confrontations.

Once he got a copy of the charges, he worked day and night for a week compiling his answers. He went into great detail explaining the Brantner affair. In his words: "I brought out my personal 'skeletons' and set them up on the highway—a humiliating thing to do, but I did not shield myself in any respect—just did what Mr. Cleveland did when they accused him—he said to his friends—'tell the truth about it.'[4] and that's just what I did—at length—also sent copies to the Fairbanks *News* and also to Debbie. He had copies printed and attached therewith thirty-one exhibits; he had to look up the law in some of the decisions which he had made in several cases. His friends John McGinn and E.T. Barnette distributed the document to the committee members and to the Washington press.

In summary, the charges as drafted by Senator Nelson consisted of the following:

1) That Wickersham owned a lot in Fairbanks on which the Exchange saloon was located and in which gambling was conducted. Answer: That he owned the ground and the lease stipulated a saloon could not be located on it.

2) That he accepted a lot in Fairbanks from Captain Barnette, who was a party to a suit which was tried before him. Answer: That he

staked the lot himself and had a cabin built thereon, which cost him $400.

3) That he showed favoritism in his decisions while on the bench. Answer: Have decided 250 cases, involving all kinds of litigation, and not one of these have been reversed by the circuit court of appeals.

4) That he favored the "big interests" in a harbor case in Tacoma. Answer: The attention of the committee is directed to the record in the case, which shows that there is no truth in the charges.

5) That he appointed W.H. Whittlesey clerk of the court after his removal as commissioner for embezzlement. Answer: This appointment was made by the assistant district attorney.

6) Concerned indictment involving expulsion of Chinese in Tacoma. Answer: Simply did his duty in matter and also tried to protect the Chinese who were law abiding; the indictment was quashed for lack of evidence.

7) Concerned an indictment for subornation of perjury in the Sadie Brantner case in Tacoma. Answer: The woman who won the case afterwards admitted that her testimony was false, leading to the indictment.

8) That he was indifferent to the violation of gambling laws in his district. Answer: That federal officials have no authority in this matter in incorporated towns, under a recent act of Congress and even if they did, it was not the duty of a judge to police or do secret service duty; this duty lies wholly within the province of the marshal.

9) Concerned the approval of accounts alleged to be inflated and presented by the marshal for the support of prisoners at Nome. Answer: Had no knowledge of this alleged inflation until the charge was made.

10) Some newspaper clippings charge that the judgment in the case of *Nelson v. Macham* was not in accordance with the law and evidence. Answer: Denied the charge and said that it was unworthy of consideration.[5]

Wickersham had to wait a month before being invited to appear before the committee. He tried to keep busy by volunteering testimony before congressional committees on behalf of various Alaskan bills, including the Cushman bill providing for an elected delegate in Congress, which finally passed on May 7, 1906, while he was still in

Washington. He browsed in old bookstores, buying rare histories of old Russia, and he spent days doing research in the Library of Congress.

He was twice a dinner guest at the home of Vice President and Mrs. Fairbanks. Captain and Mrs. Barnette were fellow guests at the first party, which he described in his diary:

> Dinner this evening at eight o'clock. I am sorry that I have not a dress suit, but I intend to go with Prince Albert coat. . . .
>
> A most elegant dinner party. Mrs. Barnette was seated at the Vice President's right, while Mrs. Patterson of the Chicago *Tribune* was at his left. Ex-Speaker Keifer of Ohio was at Mrs. Fairbanks' right and Captain Barnette was at her left.
>
> After dinner we retired - the ladies to the parlor and the gentlemen to the library to smoke. Had pleasant and instructive talk with Ex-Speaker Keifer about his experiences as one of the generals in our army in Cuba, the yellow fever plague and how it was fostered and spread by mosquitoes. We also talked Alaska. . . .
>
> We returned to the parlor whereupon Vice President Fairbanks and Keifer, who is an old man, white-haired and patriarchal - talked of Lincoln and McKinley, comparing them and telling personal experiences about them and pointing out their differences.[6]

Wickersham bought a new dress suit to wear to the second dinner at the Fairbanks' home, feeling proud "to look in conventional shape" because it was the "most beautiful scene of my life: "

> There were thirty-two people at the table. Vice President Fairbanks sat at one side of the table, in the center, and just opposite him on the other side sat Mrs. Fairbanks. On the Vice President's right was Mrs. Nellie Grant Sartoris and on his left Mrs. Senator Clay.
>
> On Mrs. Fairbanks' right, Senator Clay and on her left, James A. Garfield, the son of President Garfield whom Groteau assassinated.
>
> I had the honor to sit with Mrs. Timmons, daughter of Vice President and Mrs. Fairbanks and the wife of Lieut. Timmons, U.S.N.—a most pleasant and beautiful woman.
>
> The great dining room was fairly gorgeous in its appointments—flowers, lights, beautiful silver and tableware—and

some handsome men and beautiful women—dressed in the height of fashion. It was a beautiful function—the most beautiful I ever attended and I thoroughly enjoyed the evening.[7]

The following day Wickersham joined the crowd milling around the White House to get a glimpse of the distinguished bridal couple - President Roosevelt's eldest daughter, Alice, and Congressman Nicholas Longworth, of Cincinnati, were married at noon. A thousand guests were invited to the reception, and thousands more circled the White House. It was a beautiful, sunny day and the crowd was excited and happy. Wickersham sent Debbie clippings from the Washington *Post* describing the wedding gowns and all the other social trivia so important to women readers.

The hottest political issue for the Alaskans in Washington was the appointment of a new governor, following Brady's resignation. The top candidates were David Jarvis, Wilford Hoggatt, John Clum, and Colonel William T. Perkins. The president had offered the governorship to both Jarvis and Washington newsman Walter Clark but both declined, whereupon the president asked each of them whom he would recommend among the remaining aspirants. They both agreed on Hoggatt, a former officer in the United States Navy, who owned mining property in the vicinity of Juneau and made annual visits there to overlook the mining operations.

When Hoggatt got the presidential nomination, Wickersham was pleased as the two had become good friends, eating dinner together most evenings while the judge was in Washington. Hoggatt was an active lobbyist on behalf of the judge's reappointment.

When Wickersham was finally called before the committee, he testified for nearly two hours. He felt satisfied with his presentation thinking perhaps he had won over Senators Pettus and Foraker to his side although Nelson was "as virulent and poisonous as a rattlesnake."[8]

Six weeks later the subcommittee reported to the full committee, and another three weeks lapsed before the latter group voted six to four in favor of Wickersham's confirmation, three members were absent.

President Roosevelt called Nelson to his office and extracted a promise that the senator would cease to oppose the judge inasmuch as the Judiciary Committee had voted favorably for his confirmation.

Prospects for favorable Senate action appeared good when the May issue of Appleton's *Booklovers* magazine appeared on the newsstands

Left: Governor Wilford Hoggatt, 1906-09. *Right:* Governor Walter Clark, 1909-13.

with an article by Rex Beach entitled "The Looting of Alaska," in which the North Dakota Senators McCumber and Hansbrough and the McKenzie group were bitterly denounced.

The North Dakota senators were fighting mad, holding Wickersham responsible for providing the material for the Beach article. When a summary appeared in the Washington *Times*, they accused Wickersham of hand-carrying it to the paper. McCumber vowed he would launch a filibuster when the judge's confirmation came up for debate on the Senate floor.

Wickersham telegraphed Rex Beach in New York urging him to come to Washington to get first-hand the sequel—the climax—to his two stories of the Nome court scandals—"The Spoilers" and "The Looting of Alaska: "

I wanted him to see for himself how the Dakota Boss (Alexander McKenzie) is yet able to "pack a jury" in the United States Senate, and when he loses in that way, to filibuster and defy the Senate through his power and influence on North Dakotan and Minnesotan politicians.

The "Boss of Dakota" personally urged the president not to appoint me, and his senators objected to my confirmation. Through senatorial courtesy it was passed for the session. The president knew, however, and reappointed me - and has reappointed me six times - and says he will continue to do so.

While the president, the Department of Justice and the large majority of the senators favor confirmation, "unlimited debate" however, gives them an advantage and the end is not yet. . . .

The McKenzie senators cannot get hold of Beach, or of *Everybody's* magazine or of *Booklovers* so I am being offered as a vicarious atonement, and I think they ought to have some one here to see me roasted. Especially, as I am answering for their sins as well as my own. . . .[9]

Beach's book *The Spoilers* was in its fourth edition, 40,000 copies having been sold; it had been made into a stage production to appear on Broadway.[10]

Wickersham was in a mood of indecision about whether or not he should voluntarily resign from the bench. He was a man who appreciated the amenities which accompanied personal wealth. Stephen Birch kept urging him to resign and become general counsel for the Morgan-Guggenheim interests in Alaska. On a visit to New York, Birch introduced him to Daniel Guggenheim, who later became a United States Senator. They had dinner together one evening with A.J. Robertson, owner of the copper mine at Latouche and of the St. Andrews Hotel at Seventy-second street and Broadway. Wickersham was impressed that Robertson was his own age and a millionaire.

In Washington he encountered a number of former Alaskans who had prospered in subsequent years. One was Key Pettman, formerly of Nome and now a wealthy miner from Tonipah, Nevada, and who was to become a senator from that state. Another was Tex Rickard, who ran a gambling house in Nome; he told the judge about how all the gamblers in Nome paid Marshal Richards and his deputy, Al Cody, 15 percent, and sometimes even a higher percentage, for protection; he offered to show Wickersham his account book listing his payments. Rickard was now promoting prize fights in Madison Square Garden in New York and rolling in wealth.

While in this quandary about whether or not he should remain on the bench, he received word from the attorney general's office telling him that he would not be paid his salary for the five months he had been in Washington as he was "merely defending himself from personal attack."

This struck Wickersham as totally unfair since every attack upon him came from the performance of his official duty; that the principal charges were the outgrowth of decisions as judge, and the Justice Department ought to assist him in defending the action of the court. He calculated that with the loss of five months' salary plus $2,500 in travel expenses in addition to his per diem costs, he would have worked a whole year for nothing![11]

On the last day of May the confirmation battle started in earnest on the Senate floor. The Senate went into executive session and Senators Nelson, McCumber, Hansbrough, and Pettus held the floor for four hours enumerating the reasons why they opposed the judge's confirmation. Senator Piles of Washington led the fight for confirmation. He presented "the old Brantner charges" so strongly, according to Senator Foraker, that the senators believed Wickersham was "more sinned against than sinning."

Day after day the Senate went into executive session for hours to discuss his confirmation. Senator Foraker, who had charge of the case, declared that he intended to call it up every day and make the opposing senators talk, and that when they quit he would call for a vote, but they never quit.

It became abundantly clear that Nelson and McCumber were intent on filibustering it to death as they were certain that if it came to a vote on the floor, Wickersham would win confirmation. Congress was due to adjourn on June 30, and there were several important pieces of legislation awaiting action; the senators were weary and resented spending so much time on this one item, as the Washington *Times* noted editorially:

> The big business of the session is jammed. . .into the last days of a session of which everybody is wearied. . .it is a great opportunity for manipulation and trades.
>
> Back of all these features of the greater legislative program lies the Wickersham federal judgeship case, before the senate in its executive capacity. Nothing in years has aroused such intensity of feeling in the executive sessions as this case, and trades and influences otherwise unexplainable are accounted for by reference to it.[12]

After three weeks of executive sessions, Wickersham called on Senator Foraker to ask if he thought a vote would be taken on the Senate floor. He was told that it was no longer up to the Senate as the president had taken charge. Recognizing that Senator McCumber planned to filibuster the issue through the session, the president instructed the attorney general to have it withdrawn as he intended to reappoint the judge when Congress adjourned.

Foraker confided to Wickersham that when he was appointed to the subcommittee, together with Nelson and Pettus, he was prejudiced against the judge by statements of Nelson and Pettus; only after hearing the judge's testimony before the subcommittee did he change his mind and realize that they had tried to mislead him. As Wickersham recalled the visit:

> He made it perfectly plain to me he was prejudiced and would have even signed a report against me before that hearing. This did not mean as much to him as it did to me, since it shows me conclusively that Nelson and others "packed the jury" on me solidly—all three members of the subcommittee were known in advance to be against me. And yet—with the start—with secret sessions and secret records and all, they failed to down me! Well, I had some pretty good friends. . . .[13]

A few days later the judge was summoned to the White House. Upon arrival, the president's secretary told him the chief executive was busy with some other visitors and he would have to sit down and wait. However, the president saw the judge through the half-opened door and quickly stepped out into the hall to greet him and assure him of his continued confidence. He told Wickersham to go home and go to work, and that ended the interview. With that, he packed up and headed for the West Coast. There was nothing more that he or his friends could do at this point.

The friendly Fairbanks *News* editorialized that Wickersham's presidential support was a higher honor bestowed on him than senate confirmation would have been and then roasted Senator Nelson for his obduracy:

> No greater rebuke could have been given a public man than the words of the President bore to Senator Nelson, whose hate alone served to prevent confirmatory action by the Senate and nullified the overwhelming desire of a vast majority of its members.
>
> That vicious thing known as "senatorial courtesy" which Senator Nelson so boldly and foolishly misused, could hardly have been dealt a blow more severe. . . .

Alaska, with the aid of a strenuous president, had scotched the snakes that lie in pothouse politics, and the fair, square way of the North has been uplifted.[14]

Chapter 18

Judgeship Armageddon

Well, I've done the best I could on this wild frontier and have the absolute approval of my own conscience and that is a victory of itself.

I will heave a sigh of relief when I yield the burden to other shoulders. I would rather be in my own position than to have done as Hoyt did - try the issues against a man in secret and condemn him without giving him the names of his accusers or the witnesses against him. . . . (Diary, Dec.20,1906)

Wickersham had scarcely departed from Washington when Senator McCumber wrote the president that he had new evidence against the judge based on "record evidence that is conclusive and unassailable." He wrote in part:

As you are undoubtedly aware, I joined Senator Nelson in his effort to prevent the confirmation of Judge Wickersham for the office of territorial judge in Alaska. I opposed him because I am absolutely certain that his appointment is very unjust to the people of Alaska, the miners, and all persons except a few of the wealthy men and corporations that have fastened on to nearly all of the valuable property in the district.

I am aware that you think he is a good man for the position. I am also aware that the department of justice so thinks. I am absolutely certain that if you had investigated the matter personally as I have, you would be as certain as I am that he should not hold this place and should not be imposed upon any community whatever. . . .

> Judge Day did not investigate the principal matters at all. I
> will give you a few facts that neither Judge Day nor any other
> person on earth can meet, or has attempted to meet. . . .
>
> I write this letter in an earnest endeavor to secure justice for
> these people. While you do not know it, Mr. President, I know
> as well as that I am living that the appointment of Mr. Wicker-
> sham is a wrong to all the people in his district and places them
> under the complete domination of Barnette, the Northern Com-
> mercial Company and Judge Wickersham, with their astute at-
> torney, McGinn. . . .[1]

Henry Martyn Hoyt, district attorney at Nome, was dispatched by the
Justice Department to look into the new charges against the judge. He
arrived in Fairbanks in September unbeknownst to Wickersham. His
presence in town was discovered by an alert newspaper reporter who
noticed an unusually large gathering of miners and businessmen around
Bion Dodge's cabin. Dodge was an attorney who had had his trouble
with the judge and was known to have spent weeks in Washington
trying to prevent Wickersham's confirmation.

The reporter knocked on the cabin door and Hoyt invited him in. He
admitted that he was investigating the case of the miners and merchants
who were opposed to Wickersham. The following day, the reporter
telephoned Wickersham to ask if he could see him. "What do you want
to see me about - the weather, or what?" Wickersham asked. When the
reporter explained his mission, Wickersham retorted: "I think you
better see Judge Hoyt if there is anything to be said," and "bang" went
the telephone receiver.[2]

For a week, Hoyt conducted interviews with Wickersham's adversaries, steering clear of the judge, who was busy hearing a group of Dome
Creek cases involving disputed ownership of claims worth millions of
dollars. Although Hoyt tried to keep the new charges secret, Wickersham's friends managed to ferret out a few of them and reported back to
the judge. One was that Wickersham owned claims on Dome Creek,
hence a conflict of interest existed in his hearing the present cases.

Wickersham denied vehemently that he had any such claims and
asked his friends to search out what documentary evidence there could
be for the charge. They reported back that indeed his name was on file
in the recorder's office naming him as one of eight owners of a placer
claim of 160 acres on Dome Creek.

Upon further inquiry, it developed that a man, unbeknownst to the
judge, had made a trip up the Tanana River and set a few stakes on an

unknown creek which he named "Dome Creek" and he marked a 160-acre association claim blanketing the creek with eight names, including Wickersham's. The creek was more than one hundred miles south of the true Dome Creek. A certified copy of this location on the fictious "Dome Creek" had been sent to Washington.

Another charge was that the majority of the newspapers in his district were opposed to him. If that were true, what would it prove? Actually, of the four papers in his district, two supported him—the Fairbanks *News* and the Valdez *Miner*—and the other two—Fairbanks *Times* and Fairbanks *News-Miner*—were against him. When he served on the bench in Nome, the *News* supported him while the *Nugget* was critical of him.

Captain L.B. Anderson, owner of the Fairbanks *Times*, was a mine owner whose claims were in litigation and who boasted publicly that he bought the paper primarily so that he could express his personal opinion of Wickersham. The Fairbanks *News* was owned by Wickersham's good friend, E.T. Barnette.

When Hoyt completed his investigation, he told Wickersham that although he did not consider any of the charges serious, he had concluded that in view of the unfavorable public sentiment which existed in the town toward the judge, he was going to recommend that he not be reappointed. That angered Wickersham, and he told Hoyt what he thought of a lawyer who presumed to try a judge on sentiment, observing later in his diary:

> The judges in Alaska are alone without support and if the (justice) department sets up the standard of public sentiment, the courts are doomed.
>
> I said that his presence here had destroyed this term of court - had created distrust - encouraged the enemies of law and order and that the action of the department in again investigating me after two years of investigation - trying me by secret inquiry - by a method that no court in America would adopt in trying a tramp for vagrancy, was unfair, unjust, un-American and an outrage and I protested against it as an American citizen and as a judge. . .I intend to write fully to the department about it.[3]

Hoyt revisited the judge the following day, giving him a copy of Senator McCumber's letter to the president enumerating a long list of charges. Hoyt told him confidentially that he thought the senator's claims were tommyrot! He admitted that he had met with McCumber and Fairbanks attorney Nye in St. Paul at which time his present investigation was planned.

Wickersham decided to write to the president, enclosing an interrogatory addressed to McCumber, in which he would ask the president to insist that the senator answer. He would make the interrogations so vitriolic that McCumber would feel compelled to answer them in self-defense and then the president would see how groundless and unwarranted his charges were.

In his letter to the president he said it was not important to Alaska that he remain on the bench, but it was overwhelmingly important to the administration of justice that the courts in Alaska be protected from exploitation and from unwarranted assaults by those who cannot control them. He also said that he resented McCumber's inquiry into his "alleged want of popularity."

In his letter to McCumber he prepared 248 interrogations based on the list of charges which the senator had made in his letter to the president. The charges dealt with the Frank Richards contempt case; the judge's partiality in the Bonanza copper case; his partiality toward Barnette; his unpopularity with the Alaska press.

In his interrogations in connection with the Bonanza case, Wickersham explained why he changed his mind about supporting the creation of a fourth judicial district, which allegedly was the basis for Senator Nelson's venemous opposition to the judge. He contended that immediately after his court decision was affirmed by the circuit court of appeals, every effort was made by the defeated litigants to secure the passage of a bill dividing his district so that they could secure the appointment of a new set of court officials who, like the McKenzie officials at Nome, would be friendly to them and have the case re-heard, with the decision going to the eastern corporate interests.

He added further that from the date of his decision in the copper case to the present, these defeated litigants, with the assistance of Senators Nelson, Heyburn, McCumber, and Hansbrough, had unitedly maligned, traduced and fought him, protesting his continuance on the Alaska bench.[4]

When Walter Clark learned of Hoyt's report recommending that "for the good of the service" a new judge should be appointed for the Fairbanks district, he wrote the judge that the president had been told of Hoyt's interest in becoming Wickersham's successor. He indicated also that there had been a good deal of criticism of Hoyt's selection to investigate the judge on the grounds that it was a matter of questionable propriety for a minor member of the judiciary to investigate the conduct of a federal judge.

The president received petitions from citizens of the other two judicial districts praying that Wickersham be transferred to either Nome or Juneau.[5]

Hoyt's report displeased President Roosevelt so much that Hoyt found himself transferred to Seattle and shortly thereafter to Puerto Rico.

The voluminous interrogatories which Wickersham submitted to Senator McCumber proved to be such a thorough exposé of the senator's false accusations that President Roosevelt ordered the attorney general to stop any further investigation of Wickersham.

The second short session of Congress, December 3, 1906, to March 4, 1907, took no action on the Wickersham confirmation, and the president gave him an eighth recess appointment.

After finishing his work in Fairbanks, the Wickershams departed for Valdez over the Richardson trail. It was forty-five degrees below zero and Debbie had a nervous headache. After three days in the stage-sled, they reached Donnelly's roadhouse where they changed into "double enders" a smaller single sled with the runner curved up the same at either end and pulled by one horse. There were five such sleds, forming a tightly organized procession along the nearly invisible trail. Had they not had experienced leaders in charge of their party, they might not have survived the severe snow blizzards through which they had to travel.

The wind cut like a knife and clouds of snow filled their clothing and blinded the horses as they floundered in the snowdrifts. The horses and sleds had to be pulled out of snowbanks and water holes and the passengers had to be watched carefully to make certain they were not freezing. Three of the party suffered frostbite, and Mrs. Wickersham came close to freezing her hands had the judge not picked her up in his arms and held her close to him.[6]

Debbie was ill when they arrived in Valdez, and she decided to go south with the other court officials' wives. Darrell was stationed at Bremerton, Washington and she looked forward to visiting him as they had not seen one another for almost a year. Wickersham made a quick visit to his wife and son in between court sessions in Valdez and Juneau. They celebrated Darrell's twenty-fifth birthday by buying him a suit of civilian clothes, going for an automobile ride around Seattle, and to dinner at the Rainier-Grand Hotel and then to the theatre.

Steve Birch was in Seattle, and they had dinner together, during which he renewed his suggestion that the judge resign and become Alaska counsel for the Guggenheims. Wickersham told him he would not be satisfied as then he would be subservient to the corporation's general counsel in Seattle. Birch then asked if he would consider the Seattle counselship and Wickersham said yes whereupon Birch promised to take up the proposition with his superiors in New York.

When Wickersham returned north to Juneau there was a strike on at the Treadwell mine, and seventy-five soldiers from Fort William H. Seward, near Haines, were on hand, at the request of the governor, to prevent rioting. Five strikers were arrested for beating up a nonunion man at Douglas. John Frame, editor of the *Transcript*, had a street fight with Levinsky, president of the strikers' union.[7]

Wickersham was a frequent dinner guest at the governor's house. George Irving, a Ketchikan attorney, was staying with the governor to keep him company, as the governor was a widower and did not like living alone in the large house.

In the case of Decker Brothers v. Berner's Bay Mining and Milling Company, Wickersham decided in favor of the prior lien of the mortgage bondholders instead of the local receivers' certificate holders. In so doing, he said: "I expect that a new crop of kickers will now stand up like weeds from the muck patch."[8]

He won accolades from the Juneau press for his prompt disposition of important litigation which had been hanging fire for many years. The *Record-Miner* editorialized:

> The court now in session will go down in history as the turning point between dull times and prosperity. It is now clearly seen that it is very important to have a real live court if you want good times around. Long live Judge Wickersham![9]

The Dispatch was equally praiseworthy:

> It looks as if Teddy Roosevelt knew right from wrong when he carried the Wickersham banner into the face of the enemy and planted it on the hill of reappointment.
>
> We are glad that southeastern Alaska, with few exceptions, stood solidly behind Wickersham. He is certainly making good in this section.[10]

Debbie paid him a surprise visit, saying that she felt he needed her to keep him from working too hard. He complained about being tired all the time:

> Sometimes in court I feel as if I must adjourn and go out to the mountains and rest. My friends tell me that I work too hard —too many hours on too many days and months. But I can't stop for a while—not till the annual investigator has come and finished. . . .[11]

Two Juneau attorneys, John Cobb and Lewis Shackleford, were feuding, and Wickersham got caught in the crossfire. First Cobb sued Shackleford; this case the judge decided in the latter's favor as he considered it a "spite" case based on the barest and most unfair technicality. Then Shackleford brought disbarment proceedings against Cobb, and Wickersham ruled in Cobb's favor, never conceiving what a drastic effect that decision would have on his own political future.

Cobb had been practicing in Juneau since 1898 and was considered one of the ablest attorneys in the territory. He was known as the first division's Democratic warhorse. He represented various large absentee corporations and in this instance it was claimed that he had secretly represented both sides in the Berner's Bay cases. He proved to Wickersham's satisfaction that he had followed instructions of the agents representing the bondholders all the way through, and the case against him was dismissed.

Cobb had made some bitter enemies among the Juneau Republicans, including Shackleford, the would-be Republican boss of the territory and close personal friend of the governor. Fearing that Judge Gunnison, the regular first division jurist, would not go along with the disbarment of Cobb, Shackleford had made a special application to the Justice Department to have Wickersham come and try the case.

Minutes after rendering his decision, Wickersham was told by Marshal Shoup that Shackleford and the governor were furious that he had not disbarred Cobb. The governor was so angry that he canceled his plans to accompany Wickersham on that evening's boat to Seattle, as had been previously arranged. He vowed that their friendship was finished and he would do nothing further to help get the judge confirmed.

Wickersham was astounded to find the governor so ready to break off what he had come to believe was a deep and lasting friendship, just because of a court decision with which he disagreed. Regretting his plight, the judge felt he had done right as he reviewed the case:

> I am sorry the governor feels that way, but I have the strong-
> est sense of having done right and will stand the consequences
> . . .I did not disbar Cobb, but I did criticize his actions and lec-
> tured him and his senior partner, Maloney, unmercifully. I also
> criticized Shackleford for bringing the disbarment proceedings
> up. . . .
> Now that I have decided against disbarment, they are ugly.
> Well, they can go to hell. I did right and that is that and ends
> it.[12]

Wickersham had to return to Valdez and in those days it was necessary to go from southeastern to the westward via Seattle. While in
Seattle, he was invited to address the Washington bar association. For
the first time he spoke publicly of the difficulties facing Alaskan judges.
A Seattle *Times* reporter described the judge as "tired, disgusted and dis-
heartened" but his speech as "the sensation of an otherwise prosaic
banquet. . .in comparison with the sledge-hammer ultimatum of Wickersham, the speech of Vice President Fairbanks partook of secondary
importance." Quoting directly from the speech:

> I want to request the assistance of the lawyers of the state of
> Washington to remedy a system of government insufficient and
> unsatisfactory to the people of Alaska. I know that it is a bad
> government and that it is resented by American citizens.
> What we want to do is to reach the senators and the represen-
> tatives of the state of Washington. Will you help us? When I
> went to the North, there were no courthouses; there were no
> records, no jails, nothing. There was merely a broad expanse of
> territory, and the only thing between Alaska and Siberia that
> looked like a semblance of government was the commission I
> bore signed by President McKinley. I began up there with only
> the assurance of the government at Washington that it would
> support every good thing I did. . . .
> The governor of Alaska has no powers. He is a mere figure-
> head. He has authority to appoint his own secretary, to name
> notaries public, and make reports to the president, and there his
> authority ends. He is sworn to see that the laws are enforced,
> but if they are not, he has no authority to enforce them. All he
> can do is to report to Washington.
> The judges of Alaska have all the power. They lay out all
> commissioner districts, appoint all justices of the peace and

other officers in that country. It is a wrong system and never should have been allowed. . . .

As a judge in that country, I want to be rid of the duties of governor. I want to be free from politics.[13]

Wickersham had a pleasant twelve days with his family before heading north again; Debbie would remain in Tacoma during his court session in Valdez. They visited with Darrell at the Bremerton Navy Yards and with his mother and sisters and brothers in Buckley. The large Queen Anne cherry tree in his mother's yard was loaded with fruit, and the strawberries were ripe so he had his favorite meal—fried chicken and strawberry shortcake!

He moved his collection of Indian artifacts from storage in Seattle to the Ferry museum in Tacoma and took his year's collection of Alaska books to his C Street home in Tacoma. He found that the renters were taking good care of the house, but it made him sad to walk into his old library and see the bookcases filled to bursting with his treasured books all locked and bolted.

Wickersham found Valdez in a feverish pitch of excitement over future prospects. Promoters were spreading rumors about new railroad and mining ventures in the making. The boom spirit extended to Katalla and Cordova. The discovery of coal back of Katalla caused the Alaska Syndicate to move its railway terminus from Valdez to Katalla. Still later they moved from Katalla to Cordova, sixty miles further west, as Katalla's harbor did not provide enough protection from wind storms.

With rival companies bent on reaching the rich mineral resources of the interior before their competitors, local disputes were frequent and the court was kept busy trying to settle them before violence broke out. For instance, at Katalla the syndicate wanted to cross the Katalla flats with their railroad tracks, but the Alaska Pacific Company claimed it as its right-of-way. Wickersham ruled that the Guggenheim road could not be restrained from crossing the flats. Shortly after the decision was rendered, a Guggenheim piledriver was blown up on the flats, and it was alleged that the agents of the Alaska Pacific were responsible. Wickersham's decision was sustained by the court of appeals in San Francisco.[14]

In Valdez the hero of the day was one Henry D. Reynolds. He was buying up the town and selling stock in his new railroad company, to be known as the Home Railroad, to distinguish it from the foreign rival corporations, thus appealing to the local residents' chauvinism. Reynolds bought out A.L. Levy and Company and S.A. Hemple and Company, the leading banking and mercantile establishments, the sale price said to be $300,000. He also bought another $100,000 worth of real estate and invested another $100,000 in the Keystone wharf, a wharf and railroad terminal—all this in ten days time.

At a mass meeting, Reynolds delighted his audience with the announcement that his electric railway to the summit up Lowe River would be built "before the snow flies." Ex-Governor Brady was on hand to swell the applause of his business partner. Together they condemned the outside "trusts" and pleaded for local support for their own companies. They raised $100,000 in subscriptions at the meeting and the townsfolk were out staking lots the next morning to be sure they were in on the big money.

The meeting reminded Wickersham of the old-fashioned revivals he used to attend back in southern Illinois in his early youth:

> Governor Brady opened the meeting by reading from the Bible, likening Reynolds to Nehemiah, who rebuilt the wall of Jerusalem—Reynolds was rebuilding the wall of protection from the "trusts"—the Morgan-Guggenheim badmen who are threatening to capture Alaska by building a railroad for the purpose of hauling the Bonanza copper ore to the coast.
>
> Both of them denounced the "trusts" in the name of the Bible and the People, yet only a few hours before the meeting, they had both signed an iron-clad trust contract for joint and high rates between their Keystone and the Lathrop wharves, thus creating a monopoly.
>
> The whole "revival" meeting is so ludicrous and funny to one who is able to stand aside and look on—but the gullibles flocked to their "mourners' bench" with subscriptions.[15]

Wickersham viewed Reynolds with distrust when he learned that he was paying dividends on his stock out of subscriptions! He considered Reynolds either crazy, an unappreciated genius, or an ass, as he went about spending money so recklessly.

Reynolds came to Wickersham with a written offer to serve as his general counsel at a salary of $12,000 a year plus a percentage of the company's profits, but the judge declined the offer.

Reynolds went south on the same steamer as Wickersham, and his behavior aboard ship did not increase the judge's confidence in this

"Alaskan Monte Cristo." Wickersham wondered where he was getting all of his money and how long it would last.

Reynold's affinity for underworld characters made him suspect. His steamer companion was from the Horseshoe Dance Hall, and Wickersham was disgusted with their conduct:

> In his attempts to organize the industries of Valdez, he has entered into a dance-hall scheme with "Kid" Brown, and proposes to include a vaudeville organized by himself and the "Kid."
>
> But more reckless than this attempt, is his to join hook-shops and dance halls to his legitimate schemes. He is even flaunting one of the graduates from the Horseshoe dance hall, who now offers fancy millinery as her mask for more respectable prostitution. She is with Reynolds—he seats her at his elbow at the dining room table, talks with her confidentially, and their affair is so bold, open, defiant, foolish as to call forth much criticism.
>
> He is easy—for she is a cheap flower—and lacks both style and sense. His hotel manager, his newspaper manager, and other heads of his various departments are on board and even "Kid" Brown is disgusted with the cheapness and commonness of his vices. It is even too poor and cheap to attract those who would excuse a fair display of vice. . . .[16]

Just a month after Wickersham and Reynolds went south, an incident occurred near Valdez which was destined to cause reverberations in Alaskan politics for years to come. The incident became the central plot of Rex Beach's novel, *The Iron Trail.*

When the Guggenheims abandoned Valdez for Katalla as their rail terminal in 1906, they left watchmen in charge of their Keystone canyon property where they had laid some track. The Reynolds Company wanted to use the same canyon for its Alaska Home Railway, which they were constructing from Valdez into the interior. Reynolds sought through negotiations to get permission from the Guggenheims to use their right-of-way without success, whereupon he decided to go ahead and use it anyway. His attorney, Charles E. Ingersoll of Ketchikan, advised him that the Guggenheims' right-of-way permit had expired. According to legislation passed by Congress on May 14, 1898, a railway company must complete twenty miles of track within a year and this had not been done; the act further stipulated that no company could have a monopoly of any pass or canyon.

Backed by this legal opinion, some two hundred workmen for the Alaska Home Railway set out for Keystone canyon on the morning of September 25, to take possession of the abandoned right-of-way; Ingersoll accompanied the group. They planned to establish construction camps in and beyond the canyon and were equipped with picks, peaveys, shovels, and mattocks. All went well until they arrived at a rock barricade which the Copper River and Northwestern Railway men had erected across their right-of-way. At this point, Edward C. Hasey, foreman for the C.R. & N., came out of his tent with a rifle in his hand; he had been deputized as a United States marshal by Marshal Perry in order to prevent any rioting, as there had been rumors floating around Valdez for weeks that the Reynolds people planned to proceed with force.

When Hasey ordered the men to halt and they kept marching toward him, he shot into the group and five men fell injured, four of them being hit in the limbs and the fifth just above his heart. Rescuing their wounded fellow workers, the Reynolds men turned and ran for town.

Hasey was indicted on five counts of "intent to kill." Threats of retaliation were subdued only by the promise of immediate court action. The United States attorney general ordered Governor Hoggatt to Valdez to investigate, and in his report he wrote:

> I cannot find that there was sufficient justification for the appointment of a deputy marshal for the purpose of protecting the right-of-way. District Attorney Harlan and his assistants do not appear to have made proper efforts to prevent this occurrence.
>
> I am of the opinion that Hasey exceeded his duty and authority and should be prosecuted for manslaughter, and that the leaders of the crowd of employees of the Alaska Home Railway, who attempted to take possession of the grade of the C.R. & N. . . .should be prosecuted for riot to the end that all parties hereafter will secure their rights through lawful and peaceable channels.[17]

The case did not come to trial until the spring of 1908. In the meantime, Chris Olsen, the workman who was hit above the heart, mysteriously disappeared and was never heard of again; Fred Reinhardt, who was hit in the thigh, died. Wickersham had left the bench and the case was tried in Juneau rather than in Valdez because of the tense emotional feelings among the townspeople.

Hasey was first tried for murder and was acquitted. A year later he was tried for assault with a dangerous weapon, convicted, and sentenced to eighteen months at McNeil Island.

Two district attorneys and two United States marshals lost their jobs in connection with the case. Charges of jury fixing, bribery, conspiracy and perjury were filed against the officials. Wickersham testified to the corruption of the officials, when he returned to Washington for his second term as delegate in 1911.

Chapter 19

Alaska's First Delegate Election

> The struggle (of Alaskans) for home rule. . .brought on the Pinchot-Ballinger investigation in Congress; destroyed the friendship between Theodore Roosevelt and President Taft; split the Republican party into two great factions, defeated President Taft for reelection in 1912, elected Woodrow Wilson president of the United States; and changed the course of the history of our country. (Jeannette Paddock Nichols, Alaska: A History of Its Administration,Exploitation,and Industrial Development, Cleveland: Arthur H. Clark Co.,1924,Introduction by Wickersham,p.17)

After agitating for years to be permitted an official delegate as a member of Congress and seeing the legislation die either in committee or in one of the houses of Congress, President Roosevelt became convinced that the Alaskans were entitled to an elective delegate. With this presidential support, Alaska's friends in Congress took heart and determined to push through a bill making that possible. The bill first passed the Senate on February 1, 1906, after Senator Cabot Lodge, Republican of Massachusetts, was assured that it would not lead to eventual statehood. And a month later it passed the House, survived a conference committee, and became a law on May 7 with the signing by the president.

The bill designated Alaska as a "territory" rather than a "district" and allowed its residents to elect a voteless delegate. Thus, despite the powerful lobbying of the taxable corporations, Alaskans won their right to elect their own representative in Congress.

An election was to be held on August 14. Two terms were to be filled - a short term, December 1906 to March, 1907 and a long term, March, 1907, to March, 1908. It was left to the Alaskans to decide whether to elect two delegates, one for each term or one for both terms.

The Alaskan press urged that the selection be made on a non-partisan basis and public opinion was generally in agreement. It was also generally conceded that if the miners' unions in the Tanana Valley and the Seward Peninsula combined forces, their candidates would win over the southeasterners with little difficulty.

The Seattle Alaskans, on the other hand, insisted that the choice of candidates be made along party lines as then they would be in a better position to control political affairs in the territory. The political leaders in Juneau tended to agree with their Seattle mentors, and so both the Republicans and the Democrats scheduled conventions in Juneau in July.

The miners of the Seward Peninsula and Tanana Valley agreed to unite their efforts, one region choosing a candidate for the short term and the other for the long term. They also agreed on three basic qualifications: he would be selected on a nonpartisan basis; he would be a practical miner; he would not be a lawyer or anyone connected with the courts as their past troubles made them suspicious of the legal profession.

The honor and distinction of being recorded in history as Alaska's first delegate in Congress made the newly created office an attraction to a number of ambitious office seekers. The financial remuneration was a lesser attraction, the salary being $4,383, with an additional $1,500 for mileage.

A formidable array of aspirants were hoping the nomination lightening would strike them. There was ex-Governor Swineford of Ketchikan; Henry W. Mellen, a brother-in-law of Governor Hoggatt and a mining attorney at Coppermount on Prince of Wales Island; Republican National Committeeman John G. Heid, a Juneau attorney; A.F. Wildt, a machinist in Skagway; John McGinn, former district attorney in Nome and Fairbanks; William T. Perkins, attorney and auditor in Nome; James M. Shoup, United States marshal for the first division, in Juneau; Judge James Wickersham of Fairbanks; Robert J. McChesney, manager of the Fairbanks *News*, the most metropolitan newspaper in the territory; Frank E. Youngs, Seward businessman, whom the Seward *Gateway* boosted on the grounds that he was a sourdough and not a summer boarder or tourist in Alaska, as were most of the others. Governor Hoggatt reported that forty names had been mentioned in Washington.

Frank Hinman Waskey, a thirty-one-year-old successful miner, was unanimously chosen by the Seward Peninsula miners for the short term. He had been in Alaska since 1898 when he landed at Portage Bay, now known as Whittier. He walked over the mountains, spending his twenty-second birthday pulling a sled over Portage glacier. He mined in the Cook Inlet region around Hope until 1900 when he joined the stampeders to Nome.

At Nome he made his first mining fortune, owning claims on the celebrated third beach, the richest deposit of placer ground ever found in the north. He was married and had two sons.

At a nonpartisan meeting in Fairbanks, four men were nominated: John "Jack" Ronan, Ernest Bilbe Collins, Dan Sutherland, and Tom Cale. All were well-known miners, Ronan, Cale, and Sutherland having come north during the Klondike gold rush and Collins having come to Fairbanks in 1904. Ronan, Collins, and Sutherland were in their thirties and Cale was fifty-eight.

Sixteen ballots were taken at the meeting before a final decision was reached. Ronan could have been the winner on the first ballot, but he refused the nomination unless he - received two-thirds of the total vote. When it became obvious that he would not get his two-thirds majority, he withdrew in favor of Cale.[1]

Before joining the Klondike stampeders in 1898, Cale worked for the Pinkerton detective agency, as did his brother. The brothers went to Colorado to arrest a man. In the ensuing scuffle, Cale's brother was shot dead, but before the man could turn the gun on Tom, he was killed by Tom. Cale decided to go to Canada to escape any legal entanglements and later crossed over into Alaska. He left a wife and seven children in Fond du Lac, Wisconsin. At the time he was nominated for delegate in Congress, it had been ten years since he last saw his family![2] The story came out during the campaign but apparently did not turn the voters against him.

The Republicans in Juneau nominated Cornelius D. Murane, a Nome attorney, for both the short and long terms. They hoped a Nome resident might appeal to the northern miners. Murane's nomination did not receive any applause from the Republican press in Alaska. *The Dispatch* observed that he had "buncoed the party leaders into thinking that Cale had a cinch on the political steeplechase and maneuvered himself into the limelight but most people do not think he casts much of a shadow."[3]

The Juneau *Record-Miner*, also a Republican organ, bolted the ticket and came out for the Democratic candidates.

Murane went to Nome in 1900 and had lived there ever since. The Fairbanks *Times* referred to him as "a peripatetic office-seeker" who had held out his "big mitt to grab a berth in the public service" ever since he came to Nome.

The Democrats nominated ex-Governor Swineford for the short term, and Henry Mellen, Hoggatt's brother-in-law, for the long term. The impression prevailed in many quarters that the Democrats purposely sacrificed two of their members in order to defeat Cale and help the Republicans elect Murane.

Cale was a tall, rugged pioneer miner-woodsman, who spoke in simple, unaffected language of his hopes for success. The *Dispatch* called his sincere manner "as refreshing as a Taku wind on a hot summer day." His lack of sophistication seemed more of an asset than a drawback.

During the next few weeks the five candidates crisscrossed the territory telling the voters why they should get their votes. The major newspapers espoused their favorites.

The miners' candidates won overwhelmingly. For the short term, Waskey received 4,849 out of a total vote cast of 8,882; Swineford received 1,572 votes and Murane 2,252. For the long term, Murane got 2,324 votes, Mellen 1,095, and Cale 5,819.

When Waskey and Cale left for Washington, they were determined to put their best effort toward winning a locally elected legislature for their constituents, as they had found that issue uppermost in the minds of the voters. They also hoped to have the mining laws changed to protect the working miner from unfair practices by speculators.[4]

It did not take long for them to discover that there was another voice from Alaska to which Washington officialdom lent an attentive ear. Governor Hoggatt was in Washington for the winter, appearing before congressional committees and interviewing top agency officials. One of his favorite themes was that the "solid business interests" were opposed to territorial government and the proponents were composed largely of the "saloon and gambling element" and "political demagogues."

As time wore on the delegates became convinced that Hoggatt was a tool of the Guggenheims who were opposed to any semblance of self-government in Alaska. Another reason for this accusation was his opposition to federal aid to private railroad ventures in the territory.

The Guggenheims did not need such assistance but neither did they want their competitors to benefit from it.

The Alaska press began sounding a warning to the people that a corporate octopus was in their midst. The concentration of corporation lawyers spending their winters in Washington lobbying against the people's elected delegates should be viewed with alarm. The Nome *Pioneer Press* warned that "the Guggs are after Alaska - they want this country for their own greedy devouring, and unless soon stopped they will have reached their desired end."[5]

Cale introduced a territorial government bill which was similar to one Representative William Sulzer, Democrat of New York, had introduced during the previous session. Wickersham had written Cale's bill and had publicly announced his support for it. Cale was optimistic about its chances for passage in view of President Roosevelt's urging that Alaskans be accorded home rule.

But Hoggatt remained vigorously opposed, and his testimony before committees tended to cancel anything Cale had to say. Hoggatt threw a bombshell into the committee room one day when he pulled a letter out of his pocket and read it aloud. It was a letter written to him by Judge Wickersham opposing home rule for Alaskans. Cale and the committee members were shocked and puzzled by the obvious inconsistency in Wickersham's private and public positions on home rule.

The letter was dated January 9, 1907, about ten months preceding his drafting of the territorial government bill introduced by Cale. In the interim, President Roosevelt had come out for home rule and the Alaskans themselves had launched a crusade for it, as a counter movement to the governor's opposition. In the letter, Wickersham wrote:

> I regret very much that Waskey and Cale have started off on the mistaken idea of putting territorial government ahead of all other things for Alaska. It is certainly a great mistake and one which will cost the territory dear. You are right in opposing it and you ought not to hesitate. The population is too sparse and the taxable wealth is too small to sustain local self-government. The population is unsettled, and probably out of the six or eight thousand men in this mining camp not a hundred of them would admit that they intend to remain in the territory the rest of their lives, nor would one-tenth of them remain if the placer mines were worked out, as they are in Dawson and will be here inside of a few years. . . .

It is my judgment that a large majority of the people of this district are opposed to local self-government, although there is no difficulty in scaring up resolutions in Fourth of July language in favor of it. You should pay no attention to such resolutions except to try to explain to Congress and the President that they come from a smaller number of people with nothing else to do and are simply good-naturedly mistaken about what to do. They are generally good citizens, but their theories are a long ways ahead of the needs of the country.

This letter is confidential and is not intended for anyone but you, since I always refrain from expressing my opinion on matters of public interest on account of my position. I only wish to encourage you to stand by the true needs of the territory. . . .[6]

Hoggatt did not only try to influence legislation but also patronage, which angered Cale. When Cale submitted a list of names to the appropriate official, Hoggatt followed up with his own list. In this controversy, Cale received assistance from a surprising source—it was none other than Alexander McKenzie, Republican national committeeman from North Dakota, of public repute from his Nome escapade! McKenzie operated in coalition with Alaska's Republican national committeeman, John G. Heid, a Juneau attorney affiliated with an opposing faction to Hoggatt and Shackleford in party affairs.[7]

Hoggatt became increasingly unpopular with the Alaskans, who considered him an obstacle to the territory's development. Editor W.F. Thompson, of the Tanana *Miner*, came right out editorially and said:

We don't like you, any more. You don't sound good to us.

You appear to me as a menace to the advancement of Alaska, a brake on the wheels of progress, and a relic of the old and worst feature that has attended the advancement of any territory of the United States—carpetbaggism. . . .[8]

Chapter 20

Wickersham Leaves the Bench

In the years to come, when the smoke of battle has cleared away and people are able to look at the acts of Judge Wickersham and view his record without emotion, the verdict of the Alaskan historian will be that he was a man to whom the adjective great must be applied; that he is the one who stands preeminent among his contemporaries for the good he has accomplished.   (*Fairbanks* News, Jan. 2, 1908)

After finishing his term of court in Valdez in August, 1907, Wickersham had a week to relax with his family in Tacoma before heading north again to hold court in Fairbanks. He had time to do some serious thinking about his future. He was pleased with the Valdez grand jury's flattering commendation and its urgent plea that the senators in Washington lay aside personal feelings and confirm him, in compliance with the wishes of the great majority of Alaskans. But such urgings had been relayed to Washington time and again during the past three years and still a handful of senators remained unyielding in their opposition to him.

He was tired of the constant disputation; he suffered from a nervous stomach which interrupted his sleep and left him weary the following morning. There was no money in being a judge; he could earn more in private practice. Discussing his problems with his family led to a unanimous conclusion—he would resign the Alaskan judgeship and return to Tacoma to make his home. Tacoma was a slow, sleepy place— it had not kept pace with Seattle, but he loved it just the same.

Once the decision was made, he felt relieved. He and Debbie went out and bought themselves new fur coats for the coming winter. It was agreed that he would go north to take care of his business investments and return to Tacoma in February. He suggested that Debbie remain south, but she insisted that she wanted to accompany him on their final Alaskan trip, even though it meant her coming out over the Valdez trail in the midst of raging blizzards.

The day before their departure, Darrell joined them for a carriage ride out to their farm in the Puyallup Valley. After dinner they went to the theatre, where they saw many of their friends.

In Seattle the next day they saw Governor Hoggatt on the pier as they were to board the S.S. *Humboldt* for Juneau; he was cold and unfriendly. The Wickershams had had dinner with the Jarvis family and it was evident from their conversation that Hoggatt and Shackleford had been at work trying to destroy the Jarvis-Wickersham friendship. This grieved the judge as he hoped for the respect and goodwill of the handful of Alaskan leaders with whom he shared a common concern for Alaska's future. He had never intentionally provoked their disfavor but had simply performed his duty as he saw it as a jurist.

Arriving at Juneau at four o'clock in the afternoon, he went to the courthouse and held a session, working till midnight when the steamer was scheduled to leave for Skagway. The attorneys found him short, sharp, and severe in his manner, even threatening disbarment in a couple of instances. According to the Ketchikan *Miner*, the Juneau attorneys dubbed him "James the Terrible."

When the Wickershams were settled in their Fifth Avenue Hotel room in Skagway, he sat down to compose his letter of resignation. With Debbie at his side to offer suggestions when he worried over the right word or phrase, he wrote out his first draft. He was suffering from dysentery—an ailment that bothered him frequently—and had to summon a doctor, who washed him out with salt water.

Deciding to sleep over his letter, he took it with him to Whitehorse, where he had his stenographer, George Jeffery, type and mail it for him. The final version read as follows:

Dear Mr. President:

I wish to resign the office of district judge of Alaska to which you have so frequently appointed me. Several things make it desirable to do so at this time besides the fact that I am a poor man and now have a reasonable and proper opportunity to re-enter the law practice with a fair prospect of accumulating a small competence before opportunity fails or old age overtakes me.

The first of these is that it seems hopeless to expect those senators who have opposed my confirmation to ever cease to do so.

At a recent term of court held by me at Juneau, upon special request of the attorney general, I had the misfortune to decide an important case involving the career of a young lawyer in a way contrary to Governor Hoggatt's views. Thereupon, the Governor withdrew his friendship, which I had highly valued and has criticized me so that his loss of confidence became publicly known. His views were both unjust and presumptuous but his opposition and refusal to support the court added greatly to my burden.

I have greatly desired a confirmation by the senate and appreciate your action in reappointing me as judge in this frontier district, but I now think it is in vain to expect it. However, since you have approved my service by several recess reappointments, and have thus repeatedly given your high endorsements thereto, and since the senate would have confirmed by a large majority except for the rule of unanimous consent which permitted two senators to prevent it, I shall bear this injustice with patience.

I do not wish to abandon my post, however, without your consent nor until you can supply my successor. By repeatedly appointing me in the face of opposition, you have assumed a responsibility that places me under such obligations that I do not wish my resignation accepted without it is entirely satisfactory to you.

It will be some time before you can get my successor to Alaska, and I shall deem it a duty to keep court in active progress until you can do so. He can come into Fairbanks via Valdez at any time after January first, 1908, and could take the oath of office at Valdez. It is highly necessary to keep court open in that way.

I have the honor, therefore, to request that my resignation. . . be accepted to take effect not later than March 1, 1908.

Pushing the letter aside, he reached for his trusty diary and confided:

Some other considerations appeared important enough to mention for my action—Debbie's health—and my inability to give her the care and attention she needs. But I concluded to base it only on those mentioned. . . .

And the end of my political career was reached without a pang of regret—with real genuine feeling of relief—I can now begin to organize my home—library and my own private fortune.[1]

President Roosevelt's response reached him in Fairbanks five weeks later:

I am in receipt of your letter of the 7th instant and accept your resignation, with deep regret.
I appreciate fully, however, why you feel that you must leave.
With all good wishes for your future, believe me,

Sincerely yours,[2]

Reaction to Wickersham's resignation in Alaska was one of relief both among his friends and his enemies—his friends were glad because he would no longer be the target of abuse, and his enemies felt his departure from the bench would help restore confidence in the judiciary.

The Wickershams enjoyed a relaxing seventeen day journey from Whitehorse to Chena, with a nine-day stopover in Dawson. Chugging along the Yukon River, they reveled in the vivid hillsides resplendent in the yellow, golds, and reds of the trees and shrubs which the early frosts had colored - it was like Joseph's coat of many colors; the air was crisp, but with the sunshine they were able to remain out on deck during the daytime.

Major Richardson was aboard and when the judge confided to him that he had sent in his resignation, the major expressed regret and mildly criticized Hoggatt for his unfriendliness toward the judge following the Cobb disbarment case. He told Wickersham that Hoggatt was angered because the judge had criticized his friend Shackleford so severely and also because the judge had not come to him to explain his decision.

The steamer remained nearly a day at Eagle and the Wickershams strolled around town and visited Fort Egbert, reminiscing about their first winter in Alaska. There were not half as many people in Eagle as there had been in 1900, and were it not for the military post, the town would be deserted.

Press reaction to the judge's resignation was varied and revealing. The Seward *Gateway* commented that the resignation ended in a drawn battle with the judge vindicated before the people and the Senate though the "senatorial tools of the most disreputable gang of blacklegs who ever invaded Alaska were able to defeat his confirmation."[3]

The *Dispatch* predicted:

> Wickersham has a future in private life and politics in Alaska which will allow him to repay in kind for the savage attacks of unpopular officials after he has given up a fight that was unfair and distasteful to himself and friends.
>
> Wickersham is and always will be a danger to every politician who aspires to high office. He is today the strongest public official in Alaska before the people. He will be heard from in Alaska when those that now seek to belittle him are snowed under by popular vote of the people.[4]

One of the most succinct evaluations of Wickersham's career on the bench came from the pen of E.S. Harrison, a former Nome newspaperman and one intimately acquainted with Alaskan affairs as editor of the *Alaska-Yukon* magazine:

> Wickersham's resignation is not a surrender. . .For some time he has wanted to relinquish the official position which he held. But there is too much fight in his nature for him to retire. . .in a way that would permit his enemies to claim a victory.
>
> The salary of the federal judge in Alaska is very much less than the earnings of a first-class lawyer in the same locality. He has given up several of the best years of his life to the faithful and conscientious discharge of his duties as a government official and during this time he might have acquired a competence. As a lawyer there would have been many opportunities for making money.
>
> And one of the best evidences that Wickersham has been faithful and conscientious in the conduct of his office is that he is a poor man, and that his chief reason for resigning is the necessity of doing work that will bring larger financial returns.
>
> I know something about the fight against Wickersham. I was in Nome in 1900 when the department of justice sent him there . . .He was confronted with a very difficult task. The people. . . were wrought up to a high pitch of excitement over the actions of the court in arbitrarily granting injunctions and appointing

Alexander McKenzie receiver involving the richest claims in the district. . . .

When Wickersham arrived to unravel the tangled skein of Judge Noyes' judicial actions, it soon became apparent to the people that he was a tireless worker; a man of great executive ability; an independent, forceful and fearless man.

His decisions did not please everybody, and among the people whose enmity he incurred were some U.S. senators who were associated with Alexander McKenzie in an attempt to use the federal court and the cloak of the law to illegally obtain possession of properties worth millions of dollars.

These distinguished officials have pursued Wickersham vindictively and relentlessly; they have attacked his character. . . they have made accusations against him as a judge; but I have never seen where they have proven a single contention. The animus of their action is apparent. The friends of Wickersham may say of him as it was once said of Grover Cleveland: "We love him for the enemies he has made. . . ."[5]

Another understanding editorial appeared in his former hometown paper, the Tacoma *News*, interpreting the reasons for the continuous harassment he had suffered:

The opposition has been only such as ever was and ever will be the fate of judges serving in Alaska. The judges of that territory have many appointive and administrative powers, not possessed by judges elsewhere. It is those powers that create enmities.

His opponents may be divided into two classes: those who have applied for appointments under him and have been refused; and those who have a grievance at his decisions in litigation. In the latter cases there are those whose egotism convinces them they know more law than all the courts or where personal interests cause them to take issue with him upon the question - what constitutes discovery or questions involving title?

About twenty-one positions worth from three hundred to thirty-five hundred dollars apiece—five of them worth three thousand dollars a year were at his disposal. When he was appointed there were no divisions or districts in the territory but soon afterwards the judges made three divisions with headquarters at Juneau, Nome and Fairbanks.

Perhaps the most important case Wickersham was called upon to decide was that of the Chitina Exploration company against McClelland and others, involving the title to the Bonanza mine. . .

His decision was in favor of the poor proprietors. It was this decision that seemed to particularly arouse the enmity of Senator Nelson of Minnesota, and he wrote a brief as a lawyer of the senate committee which had Wickersham's nomination under consideration, in which he said in effect that Wickersham did not know any law. Nevertheless, the decision was sustained by the ninth circuit court of appeals as in all cases of importance that were ever carried up from his court. . . .[6]

Wickersham appreciated the letter he received from William Day, the special investigator whose report had exonerated him. Day had moved into the vice presidency of the Equitable Life Assurance Company in New York City. He wrote the judge:

It's a man's work you have been doing there administering justice on the frontier, and Alaska, not you, will be the loser by your laying it down to take up again the practice of your profession.

The men who shall follow you as judges in Alaska will find their pathway easier and safer for the trails which you have broken or blazed through a country little known to white man when you entered it.

You have had a stormy experience. That was to be inevitable to the man who first carried the law into mining camps on the outskirts of civilization and there enforced it fearlessly and without favor. It required great moral and physical courage to do that. . . .[7]

The Fairbanks *News* ran a story about the disposition of the 1,726 final judgements which Wickersham rendered during his almost eight years on the bench, pointing out that of the forty-three which had been appealed, only ten were reversed.[8]

The newspaper story which bothered Wickersham most of all was one appearing in the *Daily Record* in Juneau, in which Hoggatt was part owner, declaring that the judge's resignation came in response to Hoggatt's demand to the president. Under the headlines—"Wickersham

Steps Down"—"Wearies of Long Wait for Confirmation by the Senate"
—"Prop Removed from Judge," the story read:

> After all the talk from North Dakota to Minnesota all along
> the line to Washington, D.C., it only took one word from one
> man to bring a call for Judge Wickersham's resignation. It is
> easy when you touch that right button to accomplish results. . .
> This instance goes far to show the influence of Alaska's gover-
> nor with the present administration and serves rather as an
> object lesson for those who are prone to call the executive of
> Alaska a "figure-head." He evidently figures considerably with
> the head of the government.[9]

Hoggatt was in Juneau when the story appeared and did nothing to
disabuse the public of the true facts of the case, which made the judge
confide his disappointment to his diary in these words:

> I am greatly disappointed in his character for I thought he
> was both courageous and truthful. . .I knew Shackleford was a
> poor little Apache, but I thought the governor was too brave to
> stoop to adopt a lie to hurt even his bitterest enemy. . . .[10]

Wickersham queried Secretary of Interior James R. Garfield regarding Hoggatt's letter to the president and learned it was dated September
13, just one week after the judge's letter of resignation, proof that the
governor had nothing to do with forcing the resignation. The secretary
wrote that he was authorized to say that Hoggatt's letter had nothing
whatever to do with the acceptance of his resignation; still the governor
continued to boast publicly that he was responsible for the president's
requesting Wickersham's resignation.[11]

During the confirmation fight against Wickersham, the Alaska
attorneys became increasingly disrespectful to him, in and out of court.
One of the worst offenders was Louis Kossuth Pratt, who came to
Skagway in 1898 to practice law. He imbibed freely and delighted in
picturesque expectoration in the ritual of tobacco chewing. He had been
a district judge in Kansas and had practiced in Denver, Colorado before
coming to Skagway.

He moved to Fairbanks in 1904 and soon earned a reputation for
unconventional courtroom behavior, especially in being rude to the presiding judge. Wickersham fined him three times for contempt and
finally suspended his practice in his court for the remainder of the

judge's term on the bench. The last fine was $1,000, which Pratt appealed but the ninth circuit court of appeals affirmed the judgement.[12]

Ironically, once Wickersham was off the bench and was running for delegate, Pratt became one of his staunchest supporters, accompanying him on the campaign trail and making speeches on his behalf.

Wickersham closed his records and adjourned court for the last time on December 31, 1907. John Dillon, as spokesman for the Fairbanks bar association, presented him with a gold watch, appropriately inscribed, covered with small gold nuggets. Wickersham expressed his thanks for the gift and after declaring the court adjourned, he and the attending attorneys enjoyed a smoker together, during which they entertained one another with stories of the early days when the judge first arrived in Fairbanks in 1902.

Thirty years later, Wickersham commented on his difficulties while serving on the Alaskan bench:

> Lust for gold when frustrated by an adverse decision not infrequently turns to malice towards the judge. Then no slander is too vile, no means of revenge is too base to satisfy the thirst for vengeance. It was my misfortune to be required to decide more cases involving great fortunes than any other judge in Alaska at that time; consequently my enemies were numerous and particularly vindictive. . . .
>
> There was never a closed season for protection of the district judges in Alaska as there was for brown bear and other varmints. Most of our early Alaska judges were removed from office upon secret charges without notice or a hearing; all of them were maliciously assailed and more or less intimidated in the performance of their judicial duty without an opportunity to defend their judicial acts or character from the secret malice of disappointed litigants.[13]

PART IV

ALASKA'S DELEGATE IN CONGRESS

Chapter 21

*Wickersham Announces Candidacy
for Delegate*

> *I will be a candidate for delegate if the people of the Tanana want me. I have declined to enter the race before for the reason that I did not feel certain of this support, and it is only upon the strongest assurance of a great many friends that I make this statement now. (Telegram sent to the Alaska press, June 24, 1908)*

Wickersham was in an halcyon mood on January 4, 1908, as he removed his jurist's robes and became a private citizen once again after seven and a half long years on the bench. The Wickershams had enjoyed a happy holiday season, having had dinner guests on Christmas Day and a New Year's Eve party at their home. Their party guests consisted of Debbie's bridge and whist club members and their husbands. They had a gay time "drinking the old year out and the new one in." On New Year's Day they called on their friends to wish them a Happy New Year, as was the custom of the day.

He was so financially solvent that he made a $10,000 loan to his friend Barnette and his banking partner, James Hill, for one year on their joint note, drawing 10 percent interest.[1] Debbie was feeling better than she had for the past six years. She had gained 16 or 18 pounds, so that she weighed 130 pounds, and she looked well. His successor, Judge Silas H. Reid's first official act was to admit Wickersham to the Alaska bar and he had many clients waiting for him to open his law office. The future looked good.

Apparently he had discarded the idea of returning to Tacoma to practice law. His financial future in Fairbanks looked bright. Almost ten million dollars worth of gold was being mined from the area annually. The Tanana Valley Railroad had been completed from Fairbanks to Chatinika, replacing the six-horse wagons for hauling supplies to the mining camps; it contributed a monthly payroll of $25,000 to the town.

The town boasted a population of approximately five thousand and had successfully survived a flood in 1905 and a fire the following year. Walking along the wooden sidewalks on Front and Cushman Streets, one saw fine merchandise displayed behind plate glass windows. Grocery advertisements listed pâté de foie gras, crabmeat, Russian caviar, and imported anchovies.

The two-story, 100-room Pioneer Hotel was furnished with steam heat, electric lights, baths, and flush toilets, and there were eleven other hotels. Two dailies, the *Times* and the *News*, a weekly and a monthly magazine provided their readers with telegraphic news service and local gossip columns.

Wickersham fitted up a spacious office for himself in the Red Cross Building, having decided not to go in with McGinn, who was Barnette's retainer; he preferred his independence in being available to a diversified clientele. Although he liked Barnette socially, he had reservations about being too closely associated in a business way. He had felt uncomfortable about Barnette ever since the Anderson jury-fixing case when Anderson's lawyer allowed Barnette's brother-in-law to stay on the jury on the promise he would guarantee a "hung" jury.[2]

Wickersham practiced alone the first month and then invited Heilig to become his partner. Among their first clients were W.H. Parsons, president of the Washington-Alaska Bank and Jesse Noble of the Dome City Bank; Wickersham agreed to take some stock and become a director of the former.

With an annual retainer fee of $1,200 from the Washington-Alaska Bank and $1,000 from the Dome City Bank, plus the usual fees for specific assignments, his cash income for his first twenty-two days in private practice was greater than his judge's annual salary.

Acting on the repeated suggestion of Stephen Birch, manager for the Guggenheim Alaska interests, Wickersham wrote him offering to become the company's general counsel in Alaska for a three-years' contract at $15,000 a year, with offices and office maintenance supplied by them. He didn't really care whether his proposition was accepted or not as his legal business was more than he had anticipated. Birch replied that they had just hired Bogle of Bogle and Spooner of Seattle as their Alaskan counsel for $1,000 a month.[3]

Wickersham joined the Tanana Club, a men's social organization comprised of the town's socially elite; Barnette was president. He became a charter member of the local Arctic Brotherhood camp, of which his brother-in-law, Charlie Taylor, was secretary; Wickersham was already a member of the Nome camp.

He took up curling as it afforded an opportunity to spend more time outdoors. Two new rinks had been built on Second Street between Wickersham and Cowles Streets. Later when he was a delegate in Congress, he provided an annual Wickersham trophy for the champion curler.

As heavy machinery took over mine operations, the day of the lone prospector-miner gave way to mine operators who hired men to work the claims. This led to the organization of a miners' union and a mine owners association.

The United Mine Workers of the Tanana, a branch of the national Western Federation of Miners, was organized in the spring of 1907 to give the miners a united front. Mining under permafrost conditions was dangerous and costly, and the working miner felt the need of protection. He also wanted an eight-hour workday, which was customary in most other occupations in the territory, and a minimum daily wage of six dollars.

The mine operators organized the Mine Owners and Operators Association in order to hold the line on a ten-hour, five dollar workday. With the announced positions of these two forces, the unionists went out on strike and the operators arranged to bring in workers from Seattle, where unemployment was widespread. John Ronan, association president, was in charge of the recruiting program. The territory-wide association had successfully broken strikes at Treadwell and Nome by this means.

The summer mining season passed without incident despite the strike. It was an abnormally dry summer, which made gold-washing almost impossible, and the Innoka stampede drained off a large percentage of the unemployed miners from the Fairbanks creeks. Also, the Tanana Valley Railroad absorbed a goodly number of miners as construction workers.

But as winter approached and the threat of violence loomed, Wickersham was urged to assist in arbitration efforts. W.F. Thompson, editor of the *Miners' Union Bulletin*, the union's weekly newspaper, proposed that Wickersham organize a group of businessmen to find a means of ending the strike. The judge recruited a five-man panel to work out a compromise agreement; this the operators accepted but it was rejected by the union.[4]

When the miners learned that the operators were bringing in strike-breakers over the trail from Valdez, they went out to meet them, threatening their lives if they continued on their way to the creeks to take their jobs. The marshal tried to protect the newcomers, threatening the strikers with drawn revolvers if they attacked the new men. The strikers armed themselves with rifles, and the situation became critical.

Wickersham commented in his diary that "things resemble the old 'Chinese Exodus' days of Tacoma - only here the marshal is not in sympathy and is acting with vigor and 30-40 Winchester rifles!"

The town's businessmen denounced the miners' union as a menace to the camp and declared they would support the operators. Gold production had dropped a million dollars during the strike, and businessmen were facing bankruptcy. Several hundred strikers gathered outside the lodging house where the nonunion men were staying and threatened their lives. The citizens formed three companies armed with rifles to assist the United States marshals, when the rioters threatened to burn down the town.

Rifle shots were fired one morning at the railway depot when George Dribelbis and Phil North, deputy marshals, were ushering a group of strike breakers onto the train bound for the creeks. According to Wickersham:

> When the marshals attempted to prevent a crowd of strikers from assaulting the non-union men, a Slavonian (Louis Doazat) striker fired five shots at the deputies, then ran into the Miners' Home saloon.
>
> The marshals beat up a few heads but got the men off on the train. They then went to search for the fellow who did the shooting and found him in a backroom of the Western Federation union hall. . . .
>
> Warrants were issued for the union leaders. . .and a telegram was dispatched to Judge Reid asking him to revoke the saloon licenses of the Miners' Home and the California saloons, both of which were resorts of criminal agitators and hotbeds of crime. . .
>
> I am satisfied that a revocation of those two licenses will do more to settle the pall of crime, intimidation and fear which now hovers over the camp than a dozen U.S. deputies.[5]

Although he refused to represent either side as its attorney, Wickersham's personal sympathy was with the operators. Fearing for the lives of innocent bystanders, he joined the local law enforcement officers in signing the telegram to Judge Reid.

The two dailies took opposite sides in the controversy, just as they usually did, the *News* supporting the owners and the *Times* the rioting miners. The businessmen canceled their ads in the *Times* and in Wickersham's words, the paper's editor "was whining like a whipped dog."[6]

The situation was finally brought under control when the union leaders were indicted and found guilty of "felonious riot" and sentenced by Judge Reid. At the expiration of their sentences, they left town and the nonunion workers were unmolested. Instead of continuing their strike efforts, the union miners decided to organize their own political party and fight their battles through the ballot box.

1908 was an election year—a United States president was to be elected and Alaskans would elect a delegate to Congress. The major political parties would elect delegates to the national conventions, who in turn would help choose a national committeeman to serve for the next four years.

Wickersham's supporters began urging him to run for delegate to Congress as soon as he resigned from the bench. His repeated response was that he was out of politics and meant to remain so. There was a time when the delegateship appeared attractive to him, he said, but after all that he had gone through in his efforts to gain senate confirmation as judge, he was enjoying the political independence of being a private citizen.

He was happy to sit on the sidelines and watch the struggles taking place at the political caucuses where delegations were chosen to attend the territorial convention in Juneau. That convention would be a test of who was in control of the party in the territory - Hoggatt or Cale. The stakes were high for three reasons: the faction in control might be strong enough to nominate the next delegate to Congress; that President Roosevelt had indicated that he would look to that individual for advice in federal appointments; national convention delegates would be chosen and they would influence the choice of national committeeman, who was a powerful man in patronage matters. Wickersham announced himself in favor of Cale's reelection, if the latter decided to run.

The Republican primary in Fairbanks was a victory for the Cale-Wickersham forces, with both factions of the party pledged to abide by the results; this meant dropping the fight against Wickersham, making him a delegate to the territorial convention, and giving Cale solid support in his efforts toward territorial government.[7]

Preceding the primary the *Times* had editorialized that the main issue was Wickersham and warned against giving him too prominent a role. If he were elected a delegate to the territorial convention, it warned, he would be in a position to control one or more of the delegates to the national convention for Vice President Charles Fairbanks, who was a candidate to succeed President Roosevelt. If Fairbanks were elected president, Wickersham would be reappointed to the bench. This argument failed to defeat the Wickersham candidates.

The Wickersham delegates called themselves the Roosevelt Republicans, and the opposing ticket was called the "Square Deal Republicans"; Henry Roden was a "Square Dealer."[8]

The territorial convention was heralded as important enough to attract reporters from each of the Seattle papers. Though Hoggatt was the alleged target, it really was the corporations largely based in Seattle which inspired the antagonism among resident Alaskans. Those who were fighting the governor charged that he was the tool of these corporations to the detriment of Alaskan residents.

The meeting was opened in the opera house in Juneau by John T. Spicket, chairman of the territorial central committee and an anti-Hoggatt man. The fight started when Shackleford stood up to oppose the voting of proxies in the temporary organization.

He argued that until such time as a credentials committee was appointed, it was not possible to determine who was entitled to vote. Spickett ruled, however, that the central committee constituted the credentials committee and proxies could be voted in the temporary organization. He was sustained by a roll call vote, and at this point about fifty delegates from the southeast walked out; those from Skagway and Haines and a portion of the Ketchikan delegation remained. The bolters decided not to hold a convention but to take their grievance to the national convention and protest the delegates sent there from the Juneau convention.

The convention elected as delegates to the national convention: John G. Heid, Juneau, from the first division; William T. Perkins, Captain Johnson, and Dick Ryan, of Nome and Seattle, from the second division; Wickersham and John E. Ballaine, railroad promoter from Seward, from the third division.

The press called the convention "a disgusting affair" because of the poor sportsmanship of the Juneau delegation in walking out, and special ire was directed at Juneau for taking up a collection to pay for the convention expenses, including rental of the hall. The Seward *Gateway* commented:

> No man in the convention could remember that he ever before heard of a convention city compelling the delegates to pay for the hall in which they met. Cities usually offer free halls and other inducements to get conventions. In this case, Juneau reaped a fair harvest in the money dropped at its third rate hotels and its bars by the delegates, who were mostly good spenders. . .It will probably be several years before another convention will be held in Juneau.[8]

The matter of nominating a candidate for delegate did not come up as Cale's future plans were still a mystery. One week he was quoted as planning to run for reelection and the next he insisted he was through with politics.

The Hoggatt-Shackleford forces got the national committee to declare the Juneau meeting null and void on a technicality. State conventions were forbidden to be held prior to thirty days after a call had been issued for the national convention, so a new call was issued for a convention to be held in Ketchikan the following spring.

The Ketchikan convention proved to be more or less a repetition of the one in Juneau, only more bitter. Both factions met separately in the same hall, trying to out-shout one another. The *Dispatch* observed that the Juneau convention was "a choir meeting compared to this one."[10]

Cornelius Murane of Nome served as chairman and did such a commendable job for the Hoggatt-Shackleford group that he was rewarded with a federal judgeship under the new administration. But the controversy of proxies versus personal attendance made harmony impossible between the two factions, so they split up and elected separate delegations to the national convention.

Elmer E. Ritchie, Valdez attorney-editor, served as chairman for the 103 anti-Hoggatt delegates. Cale received the nomination for delegate to Congress and the group named the same delegates to the national convention as had been chosen at the Juneau meeting, with the exception of Wickersham and Ballaine, who had wired that they would be unable to attend.

The Hoggatt group nominated John W. Corson, attorney-miner of Nome and Seattle, as its candidate for delegate to Congress. Their delegates to the national convention included: Shackleford and H.Z. Burkhardt of Ketchikan, first division; A.W. Johnson and George A.

Shea of Nome, second division; Judge Silas H. Reid and Bion A. Dodge of Fairbanks, third division.

When Wickersham learned that his successor on the bench had been elected a delegate to the national convention, he observed:

> That beats hell a mile! Dodge has complained of the federal officials in Alaska meddling with politics and the first clatter out of the box he puts poor Judge Reid into the position of partisan follower of his faction. . .Now, I **am** glad I kept out of the delegate fight![11]

Just as the two groups were about to adjourn, a row developed between rival delegates and it took the intervention of two deputy marshals to prevent the fracas from turning into a riot.[12]

The Hoggatt delegation was recognized by the national committee, and Shackleford became national committeeman for the territory. Not content with that position of authority, he had himself elected chairman of the territorial central committee as well.

With William Howard Taft's nomination for the presidency, Taft clubs began springing up in the territory; one of the largest was the one organized in Fairbanks by Louis K. Pratt and Henry Roden.

Shackleford had been in private practice in Alaska since 1900, having come from Tacoma, where his brother Jack was assistant prosecuting attorney for Pierce County at the same time that Wickersham was Tacoma's city attorney. Shackleford's principal clients were absentee corporations doing business in the territory, including the Treadwell gold mine.

Corson had mined and practiced law in Nome since 1900. He was associated with Captain E.W. Johnston in the Copper Gulch properties, which produced half a million dollars in gold in 1907. He was known as "Seattle John" Corson, as he lived in Seattle during the winter months.[13]

Fairbanks Postmaster John P. Clum was a nominee for delegate on an independent ticket. His chief claim to fame was the capture and placing in irons of the Apache Chief Geronimo in 1877 while an agent of the Apache police force. He also was the first mayor of Tombstone, Arizona when Wyatt Earp, as peace officer, engaged the Clanton boys in a shoot-out in which thirty-four shots were fired in thirty seconds and three men lay dead. Clum's Alaskan experience consisted of traveling through the territory establishing forty post offices from 1898 to 1906, spending the summer in Alaska and his winters in Washington.[14]

John Ronan, who had withdrawn in favor of Cale in the first nominating convention for delegate, was the Democrats' nominee for delegate. Ronan had had his court hassles with Judge Wickersham and had worked hard to have him removed from the bench. He came north in 1898 from Butte, moving from one strike to the other. He was politically vulnerable as he was the organizer and president of the Mine Owners and Operators Association, when it recruited 5,000 miners as strikebreakers during the miners strike in Fairbanks.

The Miners' Union nominated Joseph Chilberg on the labor ticket. He had come to the Seward Peninsula in 1897 from Olympia, Washington. He prospected and mined until 1907 when he opened a small general mercantile store in Nome. He was having a hard time staying in business in competition with the all-encompassing Northern Commercial Company, which operated trading posts throughout interior Alaska.

The five avowed candidates presented an intriguing challenge to Wickersham and his supporters. With the possible exception of Cale, there wasn't a strong one in the lot. What if Cale decided not to run. Should he make a try for it? There were so many who had been urging him to do so for the past six months, that he was beginning to waver.

A surprising incident occurred at a Clum rally which propelled Wickersham into affirmative action. In the audience was Ferdinand de Journal, a bitter antagonist of Wickersham while on the bench. De Journal was the attorney for the original locators on Dome Creek who were plaintiffs in the cases against Captain E.T. Barnette, in which the judge was accused of personal bias in favor of Barnette.

When de Journal accepted the invitation of the Clum boomers to attend the meeting, he said he would attend but warned them not to ask him to make a speech. Despite this warning, he was called upon, and when he got up on the stage, he told the audience that he favored Clum with one proviso - that Wickersham was not a candidate. He went on to say that he had heard it rumored on the streets that Wickersham might be a candidate. If that proved true, he, de Journal, would be for him heart and soul because he believed Wickersham was the man needed for the job. The idea took like wildfire, with Wickersham's friends going wild with cheers and stomping feet; poor Clum sat on the stage not knowing what had happened to his rally.

The next day Wickersham sent for de Journal and asked if he really meant what he had said at the meeting. He admitted that he was sincere and would even be willing to go out to the creeks to campaign on his behalf.

Wickersham's office was besieged by callers urging him to enter the race, until finally he agreed to do so if the people of the Tanana would support him. His friends called a mass meeting at which he made his formal announcement, and he sent telegrams to the newspapers reaffirming his decision to run.

Chapter 22

1908 Delegate Race

> *I favor a territorial form of government in Alaska and have done so since I took an oath to support it eight years ago. . . I also favor such congressional amendments and additions to the organic laws of the territory as may be necessary from time to time in the evolution of a progressive and liberal form of government therein. . . .(Wickersham's Alaska Day speech in Fairbanks, Oct.18,1907)*

The auditorium was filled to capacity, with a generous sprinkling of women in the audience. On the platform were John Dillon, local attorney who had been Cale's campaign leader, and Falcon Joslin, who had supported Clum financially as well as by personal endorsement. It was a rally to launch Wickersham's first race for delegate in Congress.

In his introductory remarks, Chairman Dillon read from a Corson dodger denouncing Wickersham as a "traitor to his party" and describing him as a man who had been "housed and fed by the Republican party." Dillon scored the statements as a low grade of campaign trickery. Joslin hailed Wickersham as the one man, who, in the halls of Congress, would be without a peer.

When Wickersham arose to speak, the crowd jumped to its feet, hailing him with tumultuous cheers. Since he was running as an independent candidate and thus did not have a party platform on which to campaign, he told the crowd what he considered the important issues in the campaign.

First he explained why he was not the Republican candidate, pointing out that the party had split in its territorial convention, nominating two different candidates, Corson and Cale. As for Cale, he considered him an honest and good man and if he had come north to launch his candidacy, Wickersham would not have been a candidate. In his opinion, Corson was not an Alaskan resident.

As for Clum, the independent candidate, he had the highest respect for him as well. He was his neighbor and they were personal friends. He considered him an excellent postmaster for Fairbanks, and Wickersham pledged his support of his continuance in that office. (Applause.)

Then he launched into his support of home rule, criticizing Governor Hoggatt for his opposition. All of the nominees for Congress had declared themselves in favor of territorial government. And last, but not least, President Roosevelt had announced his support for local self-government.[1]

Wickersham was greeted by enthusiastic audiences at the various mining camps. De Journal traveled with him as he promised he would and explained to the audiences why he was a Wickersham supporter, after having opposed him on the bench. He said:

> I fought him for a reason. . .I think he is not a good judge because he insists on interpreting the law, not as it is but as he thought it should be. He legislated on the bench. I think that the place for Wickersham is in Congress and I am doing all I can do to help him get there.
>
> I believe he will make an ideal representative. He is energetic, resourceful, aggressive; a good fighter where a fight is necessary; that he is better equipped than any other man I know in Alaska to accomplish things for Alaska in Congress. . . .
>
> Those who were against him as judge unite upon him for Congress. We believe in Wickersham's integrity - it was never questioned in all the fight against him as judge.[2]

The campaign was only ten days old when Wickersham began having second thoughts about the advisability of his having entered it. Old friends wrote him criticizing him for having betrayed his support for Cale and vowing their continued allegiance to the incumbent. Cale was still vacillating between whether or not he should run for reelection and at the same time made no move to campaign for the office.

Both Fairbanks papers were supporting his adversaries and he lacked a fund-raising organization. Judge Reid's court officials were opposing him as a disloyal ingrate to the Republican party by opposing Corson.

On top of all this, he had been offered a lucrative law case by a New York outfit which owned a $6 million copper mine at Latouche on Prince William Sound. Acceptance of the case would be sure to prove an embarrassment in a political campaign.

Overcome by these misgivings, Wickersham authorized the *News* to announce his withdrawal from the race. He was chagrined in doing so and felt like "a damn fool for getting myself into such a fool position." In a completely deflated mood, he confided to his diary:

> I greatly regret my unhappy position - I hate a weak man and I now appear in that role. . . .With both local newspapers against me, no money and no organization and with my friends in Skagway, Valdez and Nome for Cale. It is a mistake to continue longer in the scramble. . . .
>
> I am sorry that I made such a damned weak display of myself. I went up a little ways in a little balloon and forgot to take the parachute along.[3]

A week after his withdrawal, Wickersham received the wire he had been waiting for, from Cale stating that he had definitely decided not to run due to the illness of his wife and daughter. In it he endorsed Wickersham for delegate, requesting his friends to support him. Telegrams began pouring in urging him to reenter the race, contending that he was the only one who could save Alaska from the exploiting Guggenheims and who could challenge the autocracy of Governor Hoggatt.

His friends took over his law office as a campaign headquarters and refused to accept no for an answer. He was still dubious about his chances to win, but surrendered to their optimism. The support which went over to Corson upon the retirement of Wickersham and Cale was offering to return to Wickersham. With this encouragement, he announced to the press that he was again a candidate for delegate. So, off again he started on the campaign trail!

Just as he began composing a platform which his campaign committee could use in its publicity, Wickersham got a letter from David Jarvis strongly advising him to keep out of the political race as his companies would be supporting Corson. That so infuriated him that he emphasized an anti-Guggenheim position in his campaign literature.[4]

Wickersham realized that in so doing, he stood to have a real fight on his hands at Cordova, where the Guggenheim railroad employed several hundred workmen whom they would take to the polls to vote, even though they were not American citizens. Since there were no legal poll

Left: W. F. Thompson, Fairbanks newspaper editor-publisher, 1906-26. *Right:* Wickersham's campaign portrait for 1910 delegate races.

Wickersham with group of oldtimers, Fairbanks, circa 1905.

watchers, the fraud would go unchallenged unless his friends put up a hard fight.

That also closed the door to a source of financial help he had counted on. But just when he was about to sink into another morass of doldrums, a wholly unanticipated support made a surprise appearance on the horizon, in the form of a firebrand newspaper editor named William Fentress Thompson. He announced his unexpurgated opposition to the Guggenheims and all that they stood for in their efforts to fleece the Alaskans, and his unequivocal support of Wickersham.

Thompson had come to Fairbanks two years before to be editor of the *News* but lasted only a couple of months in that job. He then started his own weekly called the Tanana *Miner,* which he published in Chena during the winter months and at Ridgetop during the summer. Ridgetop was not a community but merely the junction of the two main highways leading to the mining camps along the creeks.

He promised to publish a daily during the campaign in order to counteract the lies which the other two dailies were telling about Wickersham. He noted that though the *News* and *Times* saturated the Fairbanks market with both a morning and evening paper, they had limited circulation on the creeks and it was there that the *Miner* would do its work.[5]

In announcing his projected editorial position, he wrote with characteristic vehemence:

> The *Miner* isn't in politics, and has no use for politics or politicians. Politics is hell, and most politicians are hellions. In a political sense, we don't care what name the man who is elected bears or what his politics are, so long as Alaska and Alaskans are not harmed, but benefitted.
>
> The grafters on the outside, represented in the Guggs and the "big interests," who already possess our governor and use him to thwart our wishes, now want to own our congressman, and have picked a Seattle lawyer and sent him to Alaska to buy the delegateship. If he gets it, he will work hand in hand with Hoggatt to protect and enrich the "big interests," and the trimming Alaska will get will make it too small for the honest Alaskans.
>
> The Gugg man has purchased the columns of all the big newspapers of Tanana - has bought the right to use the newspapers you take to peddle lies to you and deceive you into delivering yourself and your heritage, Alaska, into his hands.

> The Alaskans who are also candidates for delegate, and who
> have a moral and legal right to fight for election - Wickersham,
> Clum, Ronan and Chilberg - have been shut out of the columns
> of Tanana's newspapers, and nothing but misrepresentation of
> those men appears in those newspapers. . . .[6]

A favorite newspaper trick during political campaigns was to publish
fake or "homemade" telegrams purportedly coming from other towns
telling how overwhelmingly popular their favorite candidate was in
those localities, hoping thereby to convince their readers that a vote for
his opponents would be wasted. With poor communication between the
various sections of the territory, these forged telegrams were hard to
dispute.

Forced to run as an independent Republican, Wickersham actually
launched a new political party, the Wickites, which was to remain a
virile force in Alaskan politics for the next quarter of a century. With
factional splits in the two major party organizations, the Wickites had
the advantage of having but one binding cord - the person of its leader -
and no other issue mattered when final decisions had to be made;
loyalty to Wickersham as a person was all that counted.

The *Miners' Union Bulletin*, a weekly published in Fairbanks, in
promoting Chilberg's candidacy disposed of his opponents in simplistic
fashion: Wickersham's court decisions had all too often gone against the
workingman; Corson was the bosom friend of Hoggatt, who brought
troops to the Treadwell mine during a strike; Ronan's repudiation of the
eight-hour day labeled him an operators' nominee; Clum didn't have a
chance, so no need for further comment.[7]

The miners on the creeks were the prime target for all the candidates.
Wickersham was the first to make the circuit over the new wagon trail.
He rented a stage from his friend Ed Orr, and with a party of twelve
went from one camp to the other, stopping to speak to audiences put
together by his advance men. The mine whistles would shriek a shrill
welcome as the stage approached, and his enthusiastic supporters would
contribute their share of noise by hammering the big anvils in the blacksmith shops. Wickersham was given to lengthy orations in which his
satire and humor entertained the crowd.

Wickersham's final speech in Fairbanks before traveling to the
Seward Peninsula was a real "roaster." He had a large audience, and he
spoke for an hour and a half. He commenced by complimenting the
Times on its consistency in attacking him ever since it came into
existence, and then turned on the *News*, accusing it of printing lies

about him. He chastised the court officials, Hoggatt, Corson, and all the Republicans who were campaigning against him. Pleased with his performance, he recorded the event in his diary:

> The meeting at the Auditorium theater was the largest ever held in Tanana valley and I was the only speaker. The stage was covered with my friends—the boxes and upper seats filled with ladies, and the house jammed to standing room only to the doors.
>
> I gave the Oklahoma bunch (Judge Reid's officials) the roasting of their lives. I realized that nothing which any of them would think about would be left undone to injure me—so I gave them the most vitriolic lashing that I could and the crowd cheered me to the echo. The meeting was a great success, and if it may be accepted as any criterion, I will carry a good plurality at least in Fairbanks.
>
> My friends made the town red until two in the morning. I am ready to go to Nome on the morning boat.[8]

Wickersham did not campaign in the panhandle, leaving that area for his friends to cover on his behalf. He felt it was more important to concentrate on the miners, and time and funds did not permit a complete coverage of the territory. En route from St. Michael to Nome, aboard the "Gussie Brown," which he described as "a small stub of a whiskey peddling steamer," he suffered his usual seasickness as the steamer rolled all the way. In a fit of anger and frustration over his discomfiture, he commented: "This damned little measly craft rolls twice for every foot ahead."[9]

When they reached the Nome harbor, his friends came out to meet him in a little steam launch with flags flying, to transport him ashore and escort him to his headquarters at the Golden Gate Hotel. He was agreeably surprised that the Cale forces were shouting and working for him.

His campaign manager Dan Sutherland had arranged a public meeting at the Eagle hall, and when they arrived, the hall was packed "from pit to dome." It was another rousing success in Wickersham's opinion:

> I kept them at a fever heat for over an hour and a half, as I roasted Corson and his platform. The meeting was a great success and my friends were elated and are thoroughly aroused to the fight! And FIGHT IT IS!

My efforts seem to have struck the people of Nome just right. The whole town is laughing and cheering yet, and my enemies are on the run. One portion of my speech was loudly cheered for so long a time as to surpise me. I said, speaking of my permanent residence in the Tanana, that I lived "in my own house and with my own wife!" It was a mere slip of the tongue, but for a few minutes the house roared - then roared again.

Today, I am informed that the people applied the statement to one of the leading politicians who is living in his own house - with a women who is not his wife! This afternoon he called on me at my headquarters and in the presence of my manager, suggested that he had heard that a personal campaign, etc., was to be indulged in and desired that it be avoided! I readily agreed and thus by happy accident, I am to be saved any reference to my own early accusations and other similar charges![10]

Wickersham had to rely on personal politicking in the Nome area as the local press was committed to his opponents - the *Nugget* and *Gold Digger* were for Corson, the *Pioneer Press* for Clum, and the *Industrial Worker* for Chilberg.

Corson's official Seattle residence was made much of throughout the campaign, with front-page reproductions of a page from Polk's Seattle business directory, showing his law office address as "room 323, Alaska Bldg." and his residence as the Butler Hotel.

Ronan's chances for victory were blasted by a Seattle *Times* story telling of his hiring 5,000 strike breakers in that city.

Wickersham's opponents re-hashed many of the old charges they had filed against him in the confirmation fight. Front page space was given to his letter to Hoggart expressing anti-territorial government sentiment and his letter to Steve Birch offering to serve as legal counsel for the Guggenheims. Frequent snide references were made to his "dishonorable past" while a Tacoma resident.

In Juneau Hoggatt's paper, the *Record*, ran a daily banner across the top of the front page reading: "A vote for Wickersham is a vote for capital removal." Informed of this allegation, Wickersham wired Mayor Emery Valentine, his campaign manager in Juneau: "Never have, never will advocate capital removal. Contrary statements political lies. Will use utmost endeavor to secure large appropriation for federal buildings at Juneau."[11]

Wickersham was in Nome on election day, awaiting a steamer for his return to Fairbanks. A stinging election eve editorial appeared in the *Nugget*:

> It is said that Wickersham is a man of pronounced individuality. He is. It is absurd pigheadedness that gives him a certain following. When he first came here a great future was predicted for him, but that he will ever be an important factor in Alaskan affairs is not likely, for, unlike wine and whiskey, he does not improve with age, and makes new friends only at the expense of tried and true ones.
>
> He has a penchant—almost a mania—for stabbling his best friends to the heart the very moment he imagines the idol of popularity demands such sacrifices. . . .
>
> But always he has a certain following. This is due to his magnetism, his persistent activity, his contempt for consistency, his utter unscrupulousness, his faculty of throwing down his old friends. . . .[12]

Wickersham and Ronan traveled on the same Yukon riverboat, the *Susie*, from St. Michael to Chena, enjoying many pleasant conversations about their early youth in the Midwest; they had come north about the same time. Ronan said he had spent $20,000 on his campaign, which was ten times what Wickersham spent.

The telegraph lines were down for days, so they remained innocently unaware of their respective election results. Wickersham had been assigned the bridal suite, which he enjoyed so much that he usually did not appear on deck much before noon.

At Kokrines, the station eighty miles below Fort Gibbon, Wickersham received a telegram from Chauncey Boyer in Fairbanks which read: "You carried every district southeastern landslide. Victorious over thousand. Your arrival here signal great demonstration. Keep us posted your movements."[13]

A couple of days later he got a letter from Dan Kain, a prospector at Valdez Creek, saying that he had received forty-seven out of fifty votes cast there and the miners were looking for the three who had disgraced the camp.

At Chena Wickersham found the steamer *Reliance* waiting for him with a group of friends aboard who had come downriver to escort him back to his hometown in the style of a conquering hero. They brought a band with them, and their banners and horns gave him a gala salute. At

Fairbanks citizens welcome Wickersham home, Aug. 23, 1908.

Fairbanks a still larger delegation was on hand to declare him the victorious hero; Debbie was there to add her quiet words of approval.

He was honored with a public reception the following evening at the Auditorium theatre; every seat in the house was taken and many were turned away at the door. The crowd consisted of miners and business-men, with the gallery filled with women seated demurely in their boxes watching their menfolk cavorting about on the main floor exchanging congratulations on the election returns. Although the final tally was still unknown, their candidate had such a head lead that only if the Guggs packed the ballot boxes in the coastal towns in the vicinity of their rail-road and copper mines could he possibly turn out the loser.

When Wickersham rose to speak, he was given a rousing ovation. A bevy of school girls dressed in white and occupying boxes overhead showered him with flowers. It was some time before he could make himself heard over the applause. He pledged himself to work for increased self-government and to oppose the Guggenheim-Morgan combine at every turn of the road. When he finished, the floor was cleared of the benches and dancing was enjoyed until the early morning hours.[14]

Despite the blatantly fraudulent voting of nonresident workers on the Guggenheim railroad out of Cordova where 925 votes were cast, Wickersham garnered 3,802 votes out of a total of 9,625. Chilberg, the Labor-Socialist, ran second with 2,383 votes; Corson, Republican, was third with 2,139; Ronan, Democrat, was fourth with 1,007; Clum, Independent, came in fifth with 283 votes, and there were eleven scattering votes.[15] In his hometown of Fairbanks Wickersham received 60 percent of the total vote and he carried every division.

Both Wickersham and his Fairbanks committee wired President Roosevelt to report the results. The committee boasted that "the people of Alaska had confirmed the president's high opinion of the judge and overthrown his detractors, giving him a splendid vindication."[16]

Wickersham stressed that his election as a Roosevelt Republican was "distinct approval of Roosevelt's administration and message on Alaskan affairs" and his own approval of a territorial legislature which the president had recommended.[17]

Press reaction to the election returns ranged from gloating to agonizing. Editor Thompson attributed Wickersham's victory to the voters' resentment at outside interests trying to run Alaska's political affairs:

> It wasn't a matter of person popularity - Wickersham isn't a good mixer; he isn't a demagogue, or popular idol; he's not a spellbinder. It was simply a crisis; a condition created by graft and treason—the MAN volunteered and the common people did the rest.
>
> Strangled in its infancy, the "Infant Republican Party" begun by Bi Dodge's renegade Fairbanks *Times* out of its graft and treasonable affinities, and wet-nursed by that he-prostitute, the Fairbanks *News,* is but an unmentionable scarlet letter throughout the northland, and the twin-consorts of treason and spoils are exposed before the whole north for just what they are![18]

Lamenting Wickersham's victory, the Fairbanks *Times* vowed to "fight any attempt on his part to build up a political machine. . .As to Wickersham the politician, we shall bury the hatchet only in his vitals."[19]

Chapter 23

Wickersham Goes to Washington

> *I am the sole and only representative elected from Alaska to go to Congress. No other man has the right to say he represents Alaska, and while I shall not interfere with the duties of any officer of Alaska, should any such officer undertake to interfere with me in the discharge of my duties, or seek to represent himself as representing Alaska, there will be war, and that war will be of the offensive kind and if I go down to defeat, my adversary will carry scars the remainder of his life. . . . (Speech at Seattle banquet, Seattle Post-Intelligencer, Feb.22,1909)*

Wickersham's decision to return to the federal payroll after six brief months as an independent private citizen, earning a more than adequate competence, conjures up multiple motivations. Had the wounds he had suffered during his years of fighting for senate confirmation of his judgeship healed so quickly that he was ready to re-enter the treacherous arena of politics? He had spoken repeatedly of his desire for a lucrative livelihood which would make possible a happier and less worrisome future for him and his wife. The measly delegate's salary was in sharp contrast to the potential of a private law practice. Did the prestige of being a member of Congress (though voteless) make up for the financial inadequacies? Was there an inner craving for recognition among his peers to offset the wounds inflicted upon him in private life? Whatever the answer, he chose to risk the pitfalls which a political career threatened.

He turned his law practice over to Heilig and Roden and rented his home. Debbie "went out over the ice" by herself in early January in order to be on hand to welcome Darrell aboard the U.S.S. *Louisiana*, when the United States fleet arrived in Norfolk, Virginia, culminating a year's round-the-world cruise.

When she arrived in Seattle, she gave one of her few newspaper interviews, telling a rollicking, good-humored story of her experiences along the trail. Accompanying the story was a picture of the pretty, but fragile-appearing, wife of the delegate-elect:

> Really I had one of the most pleasant trips of my life, coming over the trail from Fairbanks. The gentlemen who were on the sleigh were the jolliest lot I ever met and we just laughed all the way out. . . .
>
> It mattered not what we had for breakfast at the roadhouse, or whether we had to get up at five o'clock or two o'clock as we did when we crossed Thompson Pass, everyone got up good-natured.
>
> There are so many alarming things happening which turn out to be harmless. Just for instance, coming down the south side of Thompson Pass, the sleigh that I was bundled up in turned over several times. I was cold and the wind was blowing, yet after having my roll in the snow, it all appealed to me as being so funny that I laughed until I was warm.[1]

Debbie also told about the new townsite being named Wickersham in honor of her husband. It was located near the mouth of Grant Creek on the Yukon River, about twenty-four miles below Tanana.[2]

Wickersham hired Barney Goss, former editor of the Fairbanks *News*, as his private secretary to accompany him to Washington. This displeased the union miners because of the anti-union stories he had written during the miners' strike, when he was a reporter for the Tanana *Miner*. His fondness for the bottle forced Wickersham to let him go a year or so later.

President Roosevelt wrote Wickersham suggesting that he arrive in Washington a few days early so that they could have a visit before he relinquished the reins of the presidency to Taft, so Wickersham left Fairbanks in early February. He was tendered a farewell banquet before setting off on the trail for Valdez. The trail was in excellent driving condition for the horse-drawn sleds, with the temperatures forty and fifty below zero. He suffered some sleepless nights as the roadhouses let their fires go out during the night, and no amount of extra bedding could keep him warm.

As they approached Valdez, they had to pull their sleds to the side of the road to allow about two hundred sleds to pass on their way into the interior loaded with supplies for the mining camps.

Receptions were held in his honor at each of the towns where he stopped en route to Seattle. In a speech in Juneau he said he realized he would be "a very small potato" in Washington, but at the same time he would be repesenting:

> More coal than the two senators and thirty-six representatives from Pennsylvania. . .more gold than the two senators and thirteen congressmen from California; more copper than Montana's two senators and representatives. . .and greater fishing interests than all senators and congressmen combined along the Atlantic coast. In fact, though the small potato, he would represent the greatest empire of the country.[3]

In Seattle two hundred guests, including some of the most prominent Washington state officials, turned out for a testimonial banquet in his honor. After speeches by both Democrats and Republicans, Wickersham arose to acknowledge their accolades. His rising was the signal for a wild demonstration which the toastmaster could not stop for many minutes. When order was restored, the judge delivered a half-hour speech on home rule for Alaska, throwing down the gauntlet to Hoggatt, warning him not to interfere in his efforts to get a territorial legislature for Alaskans.

He also took the salmon packers to task for not paying taxes in Alaska in lieu of operating hatcheries and promised he would see that that legislation was changed, adding: "I want to see the fishing corporations who take millions of dollars worth of canned salmon from Alaska's waters, contribute some of that rich profit for the maintenance of her courts, her schools and other institutions."

He said he also favored getting capital invested in Alaska for the construction of new railroads. He was frequently interrupted by long-continued applause, and the demonstration at the close of the address was one of the most remarkable scenes ever witnessed. There was a din of shouting, stomping, clinking of glasses, and a cloud of napkins sailing through the air.[4]

The following day he was eastward bound. At Spokane he was joined by his old friend Judge Richard Achilles Ballinger, who was slated to be secretary of the interior in the Taft administration. The two of them had many long conversations about Alaska's future, during their long train ride. Ballinger urged the delegate not to become involved in open warfare with Hoggatt and Shackleford, assuring him that he would get a fair deal with the new administration despite any influence which those two political leaders could wield.

Upon arrival in Washington Wickersham found Debbie waiting for him at the Raleigh Hotel. She had enjoyed her visit with Darrell and he was scheduled to join his parents in Washington the following week, when he would come there to take his examination for promotion to a lieutenancy. The Wickershams took a suite at the Portland Hotel on Fourteenth and Thomas Circle.

Inauguration day (March 4) was ushered in with a heavy snowstorm which discouraged spectators for the parade. A foot of snow and slush covered the streets and made marching hazardous. Debbie watched the parade from a covered seat opposite the treasury building.

Contrary to the usual custom, the inaugural ceremonies took place in the Senate chambers, where Wickersham had a seat on the Senate floor. President Taft was sworn in and Roosevelt came forward and shook hands with him, then retired through an outer door, leaving immediately for his home in Oyster Bay.

The delegate succession from Cale to Wickersham was celebrated at an informal get-together of Alaskans for dinner at Hancock's Restaurant, 1234 Pennslyvania Avenue. It was a dutch-treat affair in order to avoid any personal or political priorities. At first it was proposed to give a farewell dinner for Cale, but that idea was rejected as Governor Hoggatt probably would refuse to attend.

Aiming at a surface show of political harmony, no speeches were given and the evening was devoted to nonpolitical conversation. Wickersham was seated to Hoggatt's right and Falcon Joslin sat to the governor's left. Wickersham proposed the governor's health, and the governor responded with a toast to the delegate's health.

Wickersham's practice in self-restraint at this gathering served him well in facing the next crisis to befall him.

Four days before he was to take his oath of office, James E. Snevely of Salt Lake City, Utah, distributed a petition to every member of the House protesting the seating of Wickersham on the ground that he was a convicted felon and that it was illegal for a felon to occupy a seat in Congress. Snevely alleged that the delegate-elect, while a resident of Tacoma, was accused of rape and convicted of the charge. This was the latest version of the Brantner-Wickersham case.

Snevely was angry over a legal opinion rendered by Judge Wickersham in Eagle in 1902 when Snevely lost his homestead to the townsite of Eagle, the judge ruling that the townsite had a superior right to the property. When Snevely learned of Wickersham's election as delegate, he wrote him threatening to expose his past in Tacoma unless he sent him a specified amount of money; Wickersham ignored the letter.

When Wickersham found that Snevely was making good his threat, he pondered what his response should be. Should he expose Snevely's letters demanding money and probably have him arrested for blackmail, or should he remain quiet and wait for the response from the congressmen? The time came when an explanation was asked of him and he gave it, his story being verified by other Alaskans in Washington, including Cale.[5]

A special session of Congress convened on March 15, and Wickersham was sworn in without incident. He was assigned seat number 300 on the Republican side, which had formerly been occupied by Wesley L. Jones of Washington state; he had moved up to the Senate.

Shackleford tried to have Wickersham disqualified as a Republican, filing objections against his acceptance on the grounds that he had been elected as an Independent. However, when Wickersham learned what was going on, he asked to attend a Republican caucus of House members and succeeded in having them vote to accept him and place his name on the "regular" roll.

Chapter 24

Fights For Recognition

> *Governor Hoggatt is a political misfit who would be a joke,*
> *did not his official position enable him to vitally harm the terri-*
> *tory as chief claquer for anything that bears the fleur de lis of*
> *the corporations.*
>
> *He sojourns in Washington. . .for the express purpose of*
> *burking every attempt made by Alaska's elected representative*
> *in Congress to secure something approximating a square deal.*
> *(Katalla Herald, Feb. 13,1909)*

Governor Hoggatt and Republican National Committeeman Shackleford traveled to Washington soon after Taft's election to lay the
groundwork for control of patronage under the new administration.
They knew they would have problems with the new delegate, who
would presume to have some say in such matters.

By the time Wickersham arrived in Washington, they had their
campaign well underway. As a first step in convincing Washington
officialdom that the delegate should be ignored, they filed a
communicaton with Postmaster General Hitchcock claiming that Wickersham was elected by the gambling and liquor machine, which
counted the Fairbanks Chamber of Commerce as an integral part. They
argued that a majority of Alaskans favored gambling and were
clamoring for wide-open towns and Wickersham was spokesman for
that element; for that reason his recommendations should not be
respected.[1]

Reaction in the Alaska press to this slanderous evaluation of Alaskans
and their elected delegate was immediate and vociferous; typical was
the Fairbanks *News-Miner's* comment:

It is the rottenest piece of slander an official ever put forth against his home country. Judged by his own story, Hoggatt is an unmitigated liar and a slanderer, and he is no more fit to be governor of Alaska than our people have ever believed him to be. . .The people of Alaska do not want open gambling, and have never so declared. . . .

The crux of Hoggatt's complaint is. . .an effort to throw more power into the hands of the carpetbaggers and to remove it from the hands of Alaskans. . .Alaskans will work their hardest to rid Alaska of Hoggatt as governor, a work which they will pursue uninterruptedly until they accomplish it.[2]

Wickersham wanted to follow Ballinger's advice not to declare open warfare on the Hoggatt-Shackleford forces, but he had no intention of tamely surrendering to their whims and fancies. He was a fighter by nature and feared no man. All his life he had had to fight to get what he wanted. He had fought to get an education; he had fought his way up the political ladder as a newcomer in Washington territory; he had fought to clear his name in the Brantner scandal; he had fought to stay on the federal bench and bring law and order to the Alaskan frontier. He had just finished a tough fight to become Alaska's elected delegate in Congress; he intended to continue to fight for the best interests of his fellow Americans who had chosen Alaska as their home.

The first patronage fight came over the three Alaskan judgeships. Wickersham won acceptance of two of his endoresements - Edward Cushman of Tacoma and Peter Overfield of Nome - but lost the third to Shackleford's law partner, Thomas R. Lyons. Wickersham objected to his appointment because of his long association with the Guggenheims as their counsel in Alaska.

Although a compromise was effected on patronage, Hoggatt and Shackleford remained in Washington to lobby against the delegate's program. Convinced that it was no longer necessary for Alaska's governor to be in Washington full-time as a lobbyist, with a delegate elected for that purpose, Wickersham complained to Secretary Ballinger about the governor's obstructive behavior and questioned his spending so much time away from his governor's desk in Alaska. Ballinger agreed that the governor's place was in Alaska and promised to issue an order to that effect.

He got the president to issue a general order requiring all territorial officers to remain at home and attend to their business until they had special authority from the secretary or president to leave their posts.[3]

The order came out on March 20 and Hoggatt submitted his resignation on that very same day. He made his resignation effective October first so that a successor could be found in the meantime. Wickersham did not learn of the governor's resignation for almost a month.

Secretary Ballinger took Wickersham to the White House to meet President Taft, and when the delegate invited the president to visit Alaska the coming summer, he replied that he would be happy to do so if Congress would appropriate the necessary funds for the trip, otherwise he could not afford to come as he had returned from the governorship of the Philippine Islands with only fifteen hundred dollars and he spent that on his presidential campaign.

When the subject of an elective legislature for Alaska was broached, Taft expressed vehement disapproval on the basis that Alaskans were not a settled people and they were given to turbulence. He cited the fact that he had had to order the movement of federal troops to maintain order during a strike at the Treadwell mine. When Wickersham reminded him that troop movements had been ordered in the various states from time to time, the president smiled and changed the subject. It was obvious that Hoggatt had prejudiced the president's mind against Alaskan home rule.

On their return to the secretary's office, Wickersham observed to Ballinger that it was evident that if Alaska was to get any attention it would have to come through his office. Ballinger confided that "what Alaska needs first is a governor of the right type - one who has a broad mind and can and will appreciate the needs of Alaska." He added that Hoggatt would not be a candidate for reappointment.[4]

About a month later, Wickersham got a telephone call at eleven o'clock at night from Secretary Ballinger asking him to come to his office at nine the next morning. When he arrived, the secretary told him that the president and secretary of state Knox were considering appointing Walter Eli Clark, a Washington newspaper correspondent, to the governorship of Alaska. Ballinger went on to say that he understood Wickersham and Clark were good friends so he assumed there would be no objection to the appointment.

When Wickersham got a chance to speak, he protested quietly but earnestly against the appointment, saying that Clark represented the Hoggatt-Shackleford-Guggenheim-Jarvis interests and had fought Wickersham in the recent delegate race through his press reports in the Seattle *Post-Intelligencer*. Much to the secretary's annoyance, Wickersham begged him not to make the appointment. The secretary suggested that the delegate go to see Secretary Knox and tell him how he felt about the appointment; Ballinger made an appointment for him to see Knox later in the day.

In voicing his objection to Clark as governor, Wickersham told Knox that his appointment would be a blow to the best interests of Alaska and in the interest of the fish, transportation, coal and copper trusts. Wickersham urged that the new governor have no affiliation with any Alaskan faction. But he saw that Knox was not impressed by his arguments and he went away depressed and convinced that Ballinger had let him down and that from then on he (Wickersham) would remain outside the pale as far as influence on the Taft administration.

Within two hours after being told of Clark's pending appointment to the governorship, Wickersham learned that he had actually been appointed and he still had not been told of Hoggatt's resignation.

Clark called on the delegate at his hotel rooms later that evening and they had a frank discussion during which Wickersham told him why he had opposed his appointment. It is to be recalled that when Wickersham first encountered Senate opposition to his reappointment to the bench, four of his staunchest supporters were Clark, Hoggatt, Jarvis and Steve Birch, the Guggenheim executive. Repeatedly his diary entries indicated how much he prized their friendship: "Walter Clark is a friend worth having and so is Jarvis" and again - "Jarvis and Clark have never ceased to work for me and I owe them much" and still again - "While I have had many good and energetic friends to assist me, one stands higher than the rest on any list, Walter E. Clark,"[5] How fragile friendships become in the ruthless political arena!

Not one to accept defeat gracefully, Wickersham sat down and wrote Secretary Ballinger, angrily:

> The purpose of this communication is to protest against the trick which was perpetrated upon me and the people of Alaska in the manner of Clark's appointment.
>
> When we had that conversation on Tuesday morning you knew that I had no knowledge that, at that moment, Governor Hoggatt's resignation was in your hands and that the office had been offered to Mr. Clark, who had accepted it, and that it was intended immediately and on that day to appoint him.
>
> You knew that I and the people of Alaska would protest against this appointment to the president, if we knew the facts. Mr. Shackleford said to me yesterday that he and Governor Hoggatt gave the "rush act" to this appointment so that I and my friends could not be heard.

Mr. Clark has long been the active Washington member of the Hoggatt faction, having fixed ideas of the legislative needs of the territory from that quarter and never tiring in opposing the delegate in his efforts to secure legislation which the people demanded.

Because the people of the territory know these facts, and know the influences which will control him, his appointment means the renewal of factional strife there. Yet you permitted this appointment to be made secretly, while looking me in the eye and talking about party harmony and good government there. . . .[6]

Ballinger explained to the delegate later that Clark was the choice of Secretary Knox and the president and there was little he could say in protest. He refrained from adding that Hoggatt also had recommended Clark to the president, just as Clark had endorsed Hoggatt four years before.[7]

Clark was confirmed in a night-time executive session of the Senate within forty-eight hours after his nomination was first mentioned to Wickersham.[8]

Clark had not sought the governorship and was surprised when the president called him into his office to tell him that his name had been approved that morning at a cabinet meeting. Considering the unbridgable chasm of personal antagonism existing between the Shackleford and Wickersham forces, the president concluded it would be impossible to find an Alaskan resident who would be acceptable to both factions. His alternative was to send a man to the territory in whom both he and the secretary of interior had confidence and hope that he could work in harmony with the two groups.

As Washington correspondent for the Seattle *Post-Intelligencer* for nine years, Clark was well acquainted with Alaskan affairs, but he knew he would be resented as a carpetbag appointment. His personal contacts with the territory were limited to two summers' mining in Nome and a four-month trip through the territory gathering material for a series of newspaper articles.

Clark disapproved of Wickersham's bitter attacks on the Guggenheims during his delegate campaign and indicated such in his news coverage for the *Post-Intelligencer*. His editorial bias earned him a reprimand from the editor[9] and so infuriated President Roosevelt that Clark was banned from the White House. Thus, when Taft chose him for the territory's governor, Roosevelt took it as a personal affront and it

was added to the list of incidents which created a permanent rift between the two longtime friends and contributed to the election of a
Democratic president - the first in twenty years.

Clark had been a close friend of the Taft family for years and was a
frequent visitor in the Taft home in Beverly, Massachusetts.[10]

The Alaska press generally echoed the delegate's objections to Clark's
appointment. The Katalla *Herald* predicted that "no federal official in
Alaska, who is tainted with the Hessianism and Toryism of the Hoggatt
political faction can have aught but a thorny road to travel in Alaska.[11]

The Nome *Gold Digger* vowed that "the people of Alaska will run
Clark through the sluice boxes and drown him if he endeavors to serve
as governor."[12]

W.F. Thompson of the *News-Miner* felt sorry for a fine fellow like
Clark to give up the exciting life of a Washington correspondent for the
pitiful Alaska governorship. As for the "factions" which Clark was
expected to harmonize, they exist among the corporate interests vying
with one another in finding ways to exploit the territory's natural
resources rather than among bona fide Alaska residents:

> The "factions" referred to in the excuse offered for Clark's
> appointment are. . .the rival railroad promoters, the rival min-
> ing companies, the land grabbers and the coal-lands sharks. . . .
>
> As for the governorship. . .it is really a step downward for
> him, taking him out of the living, breathing world, the world of
> wealth and fashion which he has been raised in and in which his
> way is pleasant and upward, and planting him in a held-back
> wilderness where he can never be himself, but always the tool of
> politicians or capitalists. . . .[13]

On June 7, 1909, Wickersham introduced his first bill to create a legislative assembly for Alaska (H.R.10418). In preparing the bill, he
consulted with President Taft. It provided for a legislature of twenty-
four members - eight in the Senate and sixteen in the House. Two
senators and four representatives were to be chosen from each of the
four judicial districts. It also stipulated that the legislature should not sit
longer than sixty days every two years and that all Russian-American
subjects residing in Alaska on March 30, 1867, be regarded as citizens of
Alaska.[14] Senator Knute Nelson was to introduce a similar bill in the
Senate the following day.

By introducing the bill before Congress adjourned for the summer,
the delegate could have copies to distribute to his constituents to secure

their criticism and suggestions preparatory to the big push for passage which he would make when Congress reconvened. He had 4,000 copies printed of the assembly bill.

Praising the delegate's efforts, the *Dispatch* urged the press of Alaska to support Alaskans' free-born rights as American citizens, predicting that once the illusion of Alaska being a wilderness populated by semicivilized people is dispelled, some day statehood may be conferred on the territory. It predicted also that those who wish to "milk the territory for eastern stockholders will oppose the measure."[15]

Instant opposition came from the corporate interests with large holdings in Alaskan transportation, coal, copper, fisheries, and other valuable undeveloped resources. So active and efficient was this opposition that it persuaded President Taft to denounce the plan repeatedly in his messages to Congress.

As an alternative Senator Albert J. Beveridge, Republican of Indiana, introduced a bill, prepared under Taft's supervision, providing for an appointed legislative commission of nine members, including the governor and one or more United States Army officers.

The evening before he was to depart for the West Coast, Wickersham invited Secretary Ballinger and Governor-elect Clark to have dinner with him at the Shoreham Hotel. An atmosphere of goodwill pervaded the evening's discussion.

With Congress in recess for six months, the Wickershams returned to their home in Fairbanks, where he resumed his law practice until he had to leave again for Washington to be on hand for opening day in January.

They received warm and enthusiastic welcomes at the ports of call as they sailed northward. Though it was seven o'clock in the morning when they arrived in Ketchikan, a crowd of friends was on the wharf, blowing whistles and waving flags, and a brass band played "Hail to the Chief." A banner "Welcome Wickersham" was stretched across the warehouse. The delegate was escorted uptown where he made a speech from a street corner before eating breakfast. It was a beautiful, sunny day and Wickersham was happy to be back home again.

At Wrangell a similar welcoming crowd was on the wharf with the Shakan Indian brass band of fifteen pieces. It was the Fourth of July, and he was invited to make an appropriate address at Redman's Hall, followed by Indian canoe races. He presented an American flag to the Indian band. The steamer departed at eight o'clock in the evening, and a patriotic program was held on board, with the delegate delivering a talk on Alaskan Indians for the audience of tourists.

There was no official welcoming party at Juneau, although the steamer was in port all day. Wickersham saw the governor at a distance on the street, but neither of them made an effort to greet one another. Juneau was a "corporation" town and Wickersham was viewed with suspicion by the prominent community leaders.

A committee was on hand to greet the Wickershams at Skagway even though they were in town just an hour before boarding the train for Whitehorse. They were pleasantly surprised to be invited to travel north as guests of the general manager in his private car. Skagway was a Wickersham town; the townsfolk named a waterfalls on Mount Dewey in his honor.

After a week's stopover in Dawson, during which they were honored at a round of parties hosted by the "government house" officials, they continued on to Chena, where a boatload of admirers from Fairbanks was on hand to escort them to their hometown, replete with brass band and flags flying. At Fairbanks a still larger crowd awaited their arrival, and a small cannon boomed a welcome. In the crowd were many miners who had come in from the creeks just to shake the hand of their delegate. It was midnight and though deeply moved by this display of friendship, the Wickershams were glad when the opportunity came for them to sneak away to their little home for a good night's rest. The next evening he addressed a public gathering, reviewing conditions in the nation's capital.

Governor-elect and Mrs. Clark accompanied President Taft to the West Coast in September, as the president was to speak at the Alaska-Yukon-Pacific Exposition in Seattle. When the presidential party arrived in San Francisco, both Taft and Clark told the newspaper reporters that their principal goal for Alaska was to encourage its economic development.[16]

The Clarks continued on their way to Alaska. In a dockside interview during their stop at Ketchikan, Clark said he recognized Delegate Wickersham was the elected representative of the people and he had no intention of interfering with his work.

They arrived in Juneau at midnight and were met by Governor Hoggatt, who escorted them to the governor's residence. Speaking briefly to the people assembled on the wharf, Clark tried to make his first words as diplomatic as possible. He said he appreciated that the Alaskans would have preferred the appointment of an Alaskan, which was an indication that the men of the north had good rich, red blood in their veins, but that they also should not consider the appointment of an outsider as a reflection upon their capabilities.

He went on to say that he had no intention of becoming a dictator to the sourdoughs who had been in the country for years. His appointment was unsolicited and carried with it a promise to try to run the office free from faction control and with a friendly disposition toward both the men investing and earning money in the territory.[17]

The following day he took his oath of office and delivered an inaugural speech; no reception was held, in accordance with his request. He said he hoped for a cessation of political strife and a pulling together toward the development of the resources and the encouragement of capital. He was opposed to capital becoming monopolistic and pushing out smaller workers and investors, but at the same time he did not think the individual should pursue a dog-in-the-manger policy and keep out capital from developing resources which the individual could not afford to do.

In an oblique reference to his stand on increased self-government, he remarked:

> What appears to me to be at the present time of most importance to the territory is the development of her natural resources. This I feel to be of far greater moment than questions of government.
>
> Alaska has been neglected by Congress, but the evils to which this neglect has given rise may be remedied simply and by methods safer than a reconstruction of the form of government. This would consume energies which are needed in full for the more immediate work of the pioneer. . . .[18]

While the new governor was trying to establish a friendly rapport with the Alaskans, the president was alienating them against his administration. In his Seattle speech, he said:

> It is too early for Alaska to talk of a territorial form of government. The population is too scant and is too widely scattered. Under a territorial form of government, the larger camps would dominate the entire territory. I should rather see Alaska under the supervision of a special bureau in Washington.[19]

His speech was received in stony silence, except for an occasional shout of "No, No," when he said the territory was not ready for self-government.[20]

Anticipating Taft's negative posture, Wickersham queried all Alaska's mayors and newspaper editors by wire, asking if he could use their names in asking Taft to support a territorial legislature in his next message to Congress. Nineteen papers and nine mayors replied in the affirmative. The only papers opposed were the Juneau *Record* (Hoggatt's paper) and the Wrangell *Sentinel*.[21] In turning a deaf ear to the appeal of such a wide cross-section of Alaskan opinion, the president displayed a legal mind with a military accent rather than that of a politician; politics was not his fare.

Taft's remarks piqued the Alaskans generally, and they rallied to support their delegate. A mass meeting of 500 people was held in Fairbanks, and a resolution was passed by unanimous vote asking Congress to allow them to have a local legislature.

The delegate urged Alaskans to write members of Congress and the president and send photographs that would illustrate the civilized conditions of the territory. He was optimistic that in time the president and Congress would be brought around to the Alaskan's viewpoint. The keynote of the meeting was - write, urge, persuade - flood Washington with letters demanding the territory's rights.[22]

Wickersham's confidence that some day Alaska would play a strategic role in world commerce appeared time and again in his speeches and writings. On one occasion when the New York *American* queried all members of Congress on their stand on government subsidy to American shipping, he responded in the affirmative. His argument was that Alaska lay midway between Seattle and Yokohoma, and one day it would be involved in a brisk trade with the Orient. In such case he believed American shipping needed protection in extending trade into the great undeveloped north Pacific Oriental market.

Wickersham left Fairbanks on November 9 planning to spend the holidays with his family before going on to Washington. Debbie had preceded him by six weeks, taking one of the last riverboats of the season via Dawson and Whitehorse. She wanted to visit Darrell at Vallejo before he left on a two-year naval cruise to the Orient.

En route south Wickersham spoke at a public meeting in the Guggenheim town of Cordova, giving the "grabbing trusts a hell of a roasting."[23] A committee composed of Mayor George Hazelet, Sam Blum, George Dooley, Dr. S. Hall Young and Dr. Will Chase met him when his boat docked and urged him not to discuss his bill for a territorial legislature because the Guggenheim officials strongly favored Taft's appointed commission.

Harry Steel was editing the Cordova *Alaskan*, which served as the official organ for the Copper River and Northwestern Railroad. He announced a day or two before Wickersham's arrival that the latter would not be a candidate for reelection and "roasted" the delegate for his anti-capital position.

The railroad officials extended him a courteous welcome, taking him in the general manager's car to the end of construction at mile forty-nine. Wickersham was impressed by what had been accomplished and expressed the hope that the track might eventually be pushed as far north as Fairbanks.

He attended several public functions in Seward and Valdez, and enjoyed Thanksgiving dinner at the home of Dr. and Mrs. Frank Boyle in Valdez; after dinner they went to the Tillicum Club where he played "500" until a late hour.

During his stopover in Juneau, he accepted the challenge of his political enemies to talk to the miners at the Treadwell mines. The Juneau *Record*, the Hoggatt-Treadwell organ, had been taunting him about being afraid to appear in a hall full of miners. The mine officials were mad at him on general principles for his anticorporation propaganda and specifically for his comments about the unsafe conditions for the working miners.

During his delegate campaign he called the Treadwell mines the worst death traps in the territory. He repeated those charges at this meeting and told the officials they could all go to hell.[24] Just a month later, sixty miners were killed in a dynamite blast and a large number of others were badly injured.[25]

The miners were hostile toward him because of his anti-strike position while serving on the Juneau bench when federal troops were brought in from Fort Seward to prevent rioting.

The stage was set for a hi-ho Wickersham bombardment! Shackleford, attorney for the mine, brought a delegation of corporation officials and A.R. O'Brien, editor of the *Record*, with him to the meeting hoping to embarrass the delegate by their unfriendly questions and comments. Wickersham had his retinue as well, including United States Marshal Sutherland and three deputies and Ed Russell, editor of the *Dispatch*, a Wickersham supporter. Wickersham recorded the evening's happenings in his diary:

O'Connor, the Irish mug mayor, the tool of Treadwell, opened the meeting by asking me a lot of questions to prejudice the crowd against me on local matters and then criticized and roasted me for half an hour and finally gave me an introduction and I went at the combination.

For two hours I roasted them and talked for an elective legislature and mine inspection laws for Alaska. Shackleford was on the stage and their scheme was to have him answer me; they posted O'Brien in the audience to ask me questions and Kennedy, the assistant superintendent of Treadwell, was also engaged in that same line and they went after me good and vicious, but they got it back as vigorous as it was sent though with more skill since they got mad and made it so bad that they thus admitted defeat.

I was greatly amused to be able to hold the crowd for two hours and then to see them break for the door and leave Shackleford sitting there without saying a word.

It was a conspiracy to break up my meeting and it failed and I got the best of them in the talk and rapid fire debate and my friends were pleased. Went back to Juneau on the ferry and had midnight lunch with Russell and Sutherland and my boat came at 2 a.m.[26]

At Seattle Wickersham was honored with a reception at the Arctic Club. In a speech he told his audience that Alaska was in bad straits being caught between the conservationists and the greedy corporations; it rested with the people to continue the fight for the rights of the individual Alaskan resident.

The Wickersham clan living around Tacoma gathered at his mother's home in Buckley for Christmas dinner. After dinner they drove to Enumclaw to visit his brother-in-law's family sawmill operation. The Hansons had their own steam railway which transported the logs from the forests to the mill. Beside Jennie's husband, Charlie, his brothers Lon, Axel, and Frank and his married sisters were associated in the family business.

Two days after Christmas, the Wickershams boarded the Northern Pacific train for Washington, arriving there Sunday evening, January 2. They took a suite at the New Varnum Hotel.

Chapter 25

Muckrakers Victimize Alaska

> If the development of Alaska has been retarded, it is those scandalmongers, who raise the cry of "fraud" and "grab" whenever any action is taken by the administration affecting Alaska, who are alone responsible. They must certainly be held accountable for the check to the activities of capital in Alaska and for the shaking of confidence in investments in Alaska. . . .
>
> (President Taft's special message to Congress, July 26,1911)

Wickersham's arrival on the Alaskan scene coincided with an era of social reform in the nation which was creating upheavals both economically and politically in which the territory of Alaska was to become a centrifugal force.

The economic depressions of the 1890s had stimulated the railroads and other large industrial enterprises to adopt various forms of cooperative combinations to assure their survival. Convinced that their strength was important to the nation's well-being, President McKinley did everything possible to help them, including sponsoring a high tariff on foreign imports.

With the upsurge in the economy came the criticism that large corporate enterprises were threatening the basic foundations of the democracy. Corporate greed was in danger of destroying the principles on which the nation had been founded. The McKinley administration was accused of being the tool of big business, when actually it was McKinley who came to view these expanding, interlocking commercial interests or "trusts" as "dangerous conspiracies against the public good."

When Vice President Theodore Roosevelt took over the presidency in the fall of 1901, following McKinley's assassination, the spirit of reform had taken hold and he was quick to reach for the torch and march forward with the boldness which was to characterize much of his future actions. Being dubbed a "socialist" by some of his corporate friends did not deter him in the slightest.

Proclaiming himself in favor of greater political democracy and economic justice, he promised individual citizens greater political participation by restricting corporate encroachments on their rights. Besides being industrial monopolists these trusts were in danger of wasting the national heritage of natural resources. Skillfully playing upon the power of public opinion, Roosevelt forced an unwilling Congress to give the people a "square deal" by curbing the barons of Wall Street. He urged Congress to establish suitable guidelines under the heading of a conservation policy.

He quietly instructed his attorney general to move against the Northern Securities Company, a giant railroad trust organized by J.P. Morgan, and got the Supreme Court to uphold the Sherman Anti-trust Act, causing the company to be dissolved.

Roosevelt toured the West in the spring of 1903, noting in many places how the uncontrolled exploitation of lands, forest, minerals, and water was threatening the natural resources. He camped in Yosemite Park with naturalists John Muir and John Burroughs and became converted to their view that the resources could best be preserved under federal control.

The president appointed a commission to study the best use of the resources and prepare a report with its recommendations. Placing conservation second only to trust-busting as the most vital internal issue for the country, he declared: "I recognize the right and duty of this generation to develop and use the natural resources of our land; but I do not recognize the right to waste them, or to rob, by wasteful use, the generations that come after us."

He set aside some 150 million acres of timberland for national use, establishing fifty game preserves, doubled the number of national parks, and founded sixteen national monuments. On the suggestion of Senator Robert M. LaFollette, Republican of Wisconsin, he withdrew from public entry an additional 85 million acres in Alaska and the Pacific Northwest pending a study of their mineral resources by the federal Geological Survey.

Included in the Alaskan withdrawal was all coal, timber, and oil lands on the public domain. The Alaskans and Westerners, keen for rapid economic development, resented the federal government's making such sweeping reservations.

The nation's metropolitan press attacked Roosevelt's program as socialistic and called him a reckless demagogue; the editor of the New York *Sun* even forbade the name Theodore Roosevelt to appear in his paper. His popularity with the people, however, continued to grow and he won reelection handily in 1904. That was the year he gave Wickersham the first of eight recess appointments in order to keep him on the federal bench despite a handful of hostile senators.

Alaska became entangled in the web of controversy between conservationists and developers when its gold creeks were worked out and miners started looking about for other means of livelihood. They found copper, tin, oil, and most important of all at that time, coal. Gold-mining operations could be extended by use of a local fuel supply to thaw the frozen ground; coal would fire the engines of the riverboats and railroad locomotives. Railway routes were being planned from the coast into the interior to develop the newly discovered minerals.

The civil code of 1900 extended the coal-mining laws of the United States to Alaska but did not provide for public surveys. Four years later, Congress amended the law to allow private individuals to make surveys, but each claim was limited to 160 acres; this made coal mining unviable in Alaska.

On November 12, 1906, President Roosevelt withdrew all coal lands from entry by executive order, thus cancelling any claims which had been staked by private individuals; this was to be a temporary action while Congress decided on appropriate protective measures. Two years later Congress permitted the consolidation of claims staked previous to the 1906 withdrawal date, in tracts of 2,560 acres, but forbade any individual or corporation to own an interest in more than one tract. Despite these limitations, approximately three hundred coal claims were staked; in many instances it meant the individual investing his life's savings.

In 1906 the international banking house of J. P. Morgan and Company, in association with the Guggenheim brothers, formed a partnership which came to be known as the Alaska Syndicate. As a result of a decision rendered by Judge Wickersham in the Bonanza case, this syndicate acquired the rich copper mines in the Chitina Valley and constructed a 200-mile railroad inland from Cordova at an approximate cost of $20 million.

At the same time the syndicate acquired controlling interest in the Northwestern Commercial Company which owned the Alaska Steamship Company and the Northwest Fisheries, the latter being an association of twelve of the largest salmon canning operations in Alaska.

Criticism of this corporate octopus made ready political fodder, and Wickersham did not hesitate to appropriate it for his political advantage; it served him well during his fourteen years in the delegateship.

Alaska became a cause celebre in the national controversy between those who were convinced that corporate greed would gobble up the natural resources which rightfully belonged to all Americans and those who believed that the American economy was based on private enterprise and that outlawing private investors was tantamount to socialism.

Muckraking articles began appearing to the effect that the Guggenheims were contriving to create a monopoly of Alaska's coal, as well as the territory's other natural resources.

The term *muckraking* was first used by President Roosevelt in 1906 in an attack on sweeping charges of corruption in business and politics. He was alluding to a character in Bunyan's *A Pilgrim's Progress* who was so intent upon raking muck that he could not look up to see a celestial crown held over him.

The term soon became almost a title of distinction. Muckrakers set themselves the task of saving political and economic democracy by writing exposés for popular magazines. A brilliant group of journalists, Lincoln Steffens, Ida Tarbell, and Upton Sinclair, were among the foremost. Tarbell's exposé of John D. Rockefeller's empire-building brought legal and social problems to that gentleman. Wickersham wrote articles for McClure's and Collier's magazines which were muckraking in that he accused the Morgan-Guggenheim interests of exploiting Alaska's natural resources for their own selfish interests, with no concern for the people's welfare. Rex Beach's novels and articles were also exposés of corruption in Alaskan courts and politics.

Such was the situation in Alaska when Wickersham first ran for delegate in Congress and Taft succeeded Roosevelt in the White House. Wickersham went into office on an anti-Guggenheim platform, and through the years as he fought the corporate interests, he enlisted the help of the professional conservationists, including Gifford Pinchot, under whose tutelage Teddy Roosevelt profited much in his political battles with the Republican conservatives.

The battle between the conservationists and the economic developers reached its zenith in the Ballinger-Pinchot controversy, which took place early in the Taft administration and split the Republican party into two great factions, defeating Taft for reelection and electing Woodrow Wilson president of the United States.

Rumors began spreading that a group of thirty-three holders of coal claims had hired Clarence Cunningham, a Seattle attorney, to help expedite their patents to their land so that they could be put into one package and sold to the Morgan-Guggenheim syndicate.

Special agents were sent north to investigate the Cunningham matter. Among them was Louis B. Glavis, an employee in the Interior Department. During his investigation he became convinced that his boss, Secretary of Interior Ballinger, favored validation of the transfer of the claims to the syndicate. He consulted with Pinchot, who advised him to submit his findings to the president, thus going over the head of his immediate superior. Taft was so angered at this display of insubordination that he ordered Ballinger to fire Glavis for "unjustly impeaching the integrity of his superior officer."

After his dismissal, Glavis wrote an article for Collier's magazine for the issue of November 13, 1909. It was entitled "The Whitewashing of Ballinger - Are the Guggenheims in Charge of the Department of Interior?" It created the sensation he desired.

On the first day that Congress reconvened in January, 1910, a joint resolution was introduced in the Senate and House providing for an investigation of the involvement of Secretary Ballinger and Forester Pinchot in the Alaska coal claims cases.

Ballinger had been commissioner of the General Land Office in Seattle (1907-08) when Cunningham first applied for patents on behalf of his clients. He resigned and returned to private practice in Seattle, during which time he advised the Cunningham group on the procedure to be followed in processing the claims.

In court hearings held in Spokane, Seattle, and Cleveland, Ohio in the fall of 1909 and the spring of 1910, Cunningham admitted that at one time the Guggenheims had an option to buy all of the claims. He charged that Glavis had used false pretenses in obtaining his evidence and that the signatures to the affidavits he procured were obtained by fraud. The original claimants were not in agreement in their testimony on what they had planned to do when they first staked their claims. No convictions resulted from the hearings, but neither were any of the claimants permitted to retain their staked property.[1]

After the joint congressional committee made its report, Pinchot was fired on charges of insubordination for writing a letter to Senator Dolliver highly critical of Taft's handling of the affair and of his support of Ballinger; the letter was read on the Senate floor. Ballinger was exonerated by the committee, but a year later he decided to resign from the cabinet for the sake of party harmony. In accepting the secretary's resignation, Taft wrote him: "I do not hesitate to say that you have been the object of one of the most unscrupulous conspiracies for the defamation of character that history can show."

The "insurgents" in the Republican party considered Taft's administration policies a betrayal of his promises to Roosevelt when he accepted the presidential nomination. Taft favored opening a tract of valuable coal land in Alaska for private sale—land which Roosevelt had previously withdrawn from the market—and this exposed him to the violent indignation of the conservation faction in his party. It hastened the rift between Taft and Roosevelt which led to Roosevelt's formation of the Progressive "Bull Moose" party in 1912.

Alaska was the innocent bystander, getting "clipped by every slanderous brickbat that was thrown." Development had come to a standstill; investments were not being made for fear they would be taken away by a government policy yet to be formulated. The national press began asking Congress to give Alaska a square deal.[2]

Though distressed over the stalemating of economic development in the territory, Wickersham did not hesitate to use muckraking devices to convince Congress that if Alaskans were accorded greater self-government they would be in a better position to control the exploitation of their resources by the Guggenheims; he found a ready ally in Gifford Pinchot.

To indicate how far-reaching the Ballinger-Pinchot feud was in national politics, when President Franklin Roosevelt took office in 1933, Glavis was reinstated as chief of the Division of Investigation in the Interior Department. Remedying what the Department of Interior characterized as "an injustice that has been allowed to stand for a quarter of a century," the president by executive order restored Glavis's civil service status.[3]

In due time, Glavis fell into disfavor with Secretary Harold Ickes and the president, the latter requesting his dismissal on a charge of having indulged in wiretapping as part of espionage of high government officials. Ickes related this in an article appearing in the *Saturday Evening Post*, May 22, 1940, in a series he wrote for the *Post*, in which he offered proof of Ballinger's innocence of any wrongdoing. Glavis's concern for his superiors' moral integrity apparently remained a lifetime compulsion!

Alaskans viewed Ballinger as their hero and Pinchot their enemy; Pinchotism was a dirty word in Alaska. The dire effect of the coal-land withdrawal was catastrophic to individual investors and to the country generally. Mining and railroad building came to a halt, for no investor would sink his money into industries dependent on cheap fuel when it was no longer available. Alaskans were obliged to buy expensive Canadian coal to heat their homes and businesses.

A typical example of the withdrawal's effect was that of 500 miners at Candle Creek, 300 miles north of Nome. An agent from the Interior Department notified the operators of a coal mine there that they must cease mining coal or criminal prosecution would result.

Owing to the isolated location of Candle Creek, Canadian coal would cost between thirty-five and forty dollars a ton, while the local coal cost four dollars a ton. Candle Creek's annual production of gold amounted to between seven hundred thousand and a million dollars. During the winter season a vast amount of coal was consumed in boilers, the steam thus generated being used for thawing auriferous gravels to be sluiced up in the spring.

Had the gold miners not been able to use local coal, they would have had to shut down their mines. Therefore, notwithstanding the ultimatum of the government official, they continued to mine coal for their needs and served notice on the agent in these words: "There's never a law of God or man runs north of 58; this is 66.2."[4]

Ballinger was succeeded by Walter L. Fisher as Secretary of Interior. He was vice president of the National Conservation Association, an organization headed by Gifford Pinchot. When Fisher visited Alaska in 1911, one of his stops was at Katalla, where he witnessed a deplorable example of how the withdrawal had affected Alaskan communities. Half the town's stores and dwellings were empty. The residents were in need and without hope. Business was at an absolute standstill. The people pleaded to be allowed to mine just enough coal to keep their bodies and houses warm; they were refused.

The small, struggling railroad operations already deep in debt in their efforts to build a road into the interior faced bankruptcy; the individual stockholders would stand the brunt of the financial failures. One such railroad spent more than $200,000 for coal used in construction work. Its tracks crossed a fifteen-foot blanket of coal of which, under the law, they could not, and did not, mine a single pound. They paid all the cost of transportation from British Columbia, the cost of lighterage and other incidental expenses, when there was an abundance of good coal situated squarely on their right of way.

The management of the Copper River and Northwestern Railroad Company, in constructing a road from Cordova to Kennecott, paid

$5,000 more for Canadian coal than they would have paid if they could have used Alaskan coal. When the Guggenheims started building their railroad from Cordova, they didn't own any coal claims, but they did try to make a contract with the owners of some of the nearby claims. They planned to build a smelter on Prince William Sound, where the ores from their copper mines would be smelted, and they needed the coal from the Bering River field for this purpose. They expected also to utilize the coal in the operation of their railroad. Instead, they were compelled to import Canadian coal, paying the United States government a duty, and they built their smelter in Tacoma, where the ore was reduced by Australian coke.

Jack Hellenthal, pioneer Juneau attorney, summarized the pathos and infamy of conservationist policies as they affected Alaska, in his book entitled *Alaska Melodrama*:

> We prospered before Pinchotism came; if we ditch Pinchotism, we shall prosper again. . . .Time was when Alaska was more prosperous than any other portion of the U.S. Why is it less prosperous now? Don't let them tell you that Alaska's early prosperity dwindled with the goldrush. Alaska was prosperous long after the goldrush was over. True, the lure of gold brought many to the territory—the gold-seekers became home-seekers. When gold mining became less active, they looked about for other sources of livelihood, and they found them.
>
> They found copper, tin, oil, coal. . . .they started building railroads. . . .then something happened. . . .These pioneers had committed an unpardonable blunder—they had located hundreds of coal claims. . . .coal very like the anthracite fields of Pennsylvania and West Virginia. . . .
>
> There was an organized group of reformers, who called themselves conservationists and their leader was Gifford Pinchot. . . . Charges of fraud were promptly made. . . .Richard Ballinger, secretary of interior, whose duty it was to pass on the patent applications. . . .didn't believe that pioneers were crooks. He had to be liquidated. . . .
>
> His successor denied all the patent applications, except two; in other words, he held that out of approximately six hundred Alaskan pioneers there were two honest Men—one third of one percent—less than the percent of alcohol allowed under prohibition. Immediately twenty thousand people left the territory. . . .

The national resources committee in 1937 concluded its report with this statement: "In the name of a balanced use of American resources, let's keep Alaska largely a wilderness. . . .Such is the attitude of the economic planners, the brain-trusters of conservation. . . ."[5]

Chapter 26

Alaskans Saved From Commission Rule

My, but I am tired and disgusted with the whole silly effort to get a lot of big boys to legislate for a great territory about which they have no information and which scares them as much as the "dark" does the average child. "Alaska" - boo - and they run. Ballinger-Pinchot scares them out. (Wickersham Diary, May 3, 1910)

Wickersham arrived in Washington like a lone horseman invading the enemy's camp, equipped with javelin and spear but with his supporting cohorts thousands of miles in the rear. He had received his orders from them but they were too impoverished to accompany him into the fray; he must go alone, planning his own strategy and return the victor.

He had accepted a formidable assignment when he promised the Alaskan voters that he would go to Washington to win permission for them to elect their own local legislature rather than continue under the dictatorship of a bureaucracy located thousands of miles away, unfamiliar with their needs.

To most men he was tackling the impossible. The president of the United States had spoken loud and clear that he did not think the Alaskans were capable of governing themselves. He had made the same judgment about the residents of the Philippine Islands when he was sent there as their governor. His solution then was rule by an appointed commission and he deemed the same would be appropriate for the Alaskans. That meant that Wickersham could not look to any member of the administration for help. Members of the president's political party in Congress were equally loathe to act contrary to his wishes.

Wickersham faced another equally formidable obstruction in his fight for home rule in the powerful lobby supported by the corporate interests with financial investments in the territory. He had succeeded in defeating their delegate candidates but they promised to follow him to the nation's capital and see to it that he was thwarted in his efforts to win any semblance of home rule.

In combination with these two powerful enemy forces, was the national mood of suspicion and ignorance regarding Alaska's future development which held the general public, including members of Congress, in a grip of fear and indecision, following the Ballinger-Pinchot exposé. What kind of people were these Alaskans who wanted to control their own land and way of life? Could they be trusted or would they betray the heritage belonging to all the American people?

What chance did a voteless delegate have to break these barricades? His predecessors had departed Washington frustrated and disappointed men because of their failure to accomplish anything of consequence. But Wickersham had special qualifications for the role he had chosen for himself and it took a lot to discourage him. The day before he was to make his first appearance before a congressional committee in connection with his legislative bill, he wrote in his diary:

> We begin the war for home rule tomorrow and I am delighted! Maybe not a victory at all, but as to that, one takes the chances in war, and I can no longer refuse the risk and will go armed with the spear and javelin for whatever enemy appears.[1]

He tried to make appointments with various officials, including the president, to discuss his bill, but found none of them willing to talk with him about it. The president's private secretary told him that the chief executive saw no purpose in discussing it as the administration had its own bill which Senator Albert J. Beveridge, Republican of Indiana, would handle in the Senate and Congressman E.L. Hamilton, Republican of Michigan, would pilot through the House. Major Wilds P. Richardson, chairman of the Alaska Road Commission, had joined the Taft-Hoggatt forces in support of rule by an appointive commission of which he was to be a member.

Ex-Governor Hoggatt was there, more hostile than ever, as a lobbyist for the corporate investors in Alaska, and so also was Shackleford, to add his testimony against the delegate's legislative bill.

The national conservationist organizations were ready to mount a major assault on the Taft administration and the members of Congress were fearful of taking any position which would prove embarrassing to them when these organized groups descended on Washington.

With the executive branch adamantly opposed, it was up to Wickersham to seek support from the legislative. He would tell his story to the congressional committees and hope to win a few converts.

To emphasize the importance of his legislative project, Wickersham used red ink to inscribe in his diary the strategy he had drafted to counterattack his enemies:

> The refusal of the president to permit me to talk to him about it and the determination of Senator Beveridge, chairman of the Senate committee on territories, to introduce the president's bill there and the intention of Hamilton, chairman of the committee on territories, to introduce it in the House—these are all parts of the administration plan to cary the matter over my head and protest.
>
> Today, however, a ray of hope comes from a visit which I received from Mr. Ben B. Hampton, owner and proprietor of *Hampton's* magazine. This is one of the great magazines of New York—a muckraker of the most virulent type—a fighter of Apacheland, and one which can reach millions of readers. . . .
>
> *Hampton's* will immediately enter upon a campaign of indictment, arraignment and trial of the administration's scheme of a Guggenheim commission government for Alaska.
>
> I see no other way to fight it—for myself, I shall be as discreet as I can—smile and be a still villain until the administration shall find out that I am furnishing the facts—evidence—and then I'll fight openly. We begin the war tomorrow and I am delighted. . . .[2]

On January 18 Senator Beveridge introduced a bill which would place Alaska under the control of the Bureau of Insular Affairs, with the War Department. The measure increased the prerogatives and emoluments of the chairman of the Alaska Road Commission. It established a military oligarchy with legislative and executive functions, with power to grant "franchises, concessions and privileges" in coal land, transportation, and government, and would have jurisdiction over the lives, property, and liberties of citizens, unlimited by the usual constitutional checks found in other organic laws for territories.[3]

The bill provided for the appointment by the president of a governor, an attorney general, a commissioner of the interior, a commissioner of education and health, and a commissioner of mines. These, together with four others also appointed by the president, one from each judicial division, would constitute a legislative council, one or more of the offices being filled by Army officers.

The administration planned to steer the bill through legislative channels without notifying the delegate but he learned of it quite by accident one morning when he dropped into Senator Nelson's office to see him about another matter. The senator, with a twinkle in his eye, said to him: "Have you seen the Alaska government bill which Senator Beveridge introduced yesterday?"

On receiving an answer in the negative, the senator continued: "Yes, it was introduced yesterday, and the Senate Committee on Territories is now in session considering it and the chairman hopes to report the bill favorably today and pass it soon."

The delegate hurriedly crossed the corridor to the door of the Senate committee room and finding it closed, knocked several times before it was opened by the Negro porter, who securely held it open about six inches, and said: "The committee is in session, suh, and you can't come in."

"But," the delegate answered, "I am the delegate from Alaska and I wish to see Senator Beveridge." "Yes, suh," the porter replied, "but he done tole me not to let you in."

Whereupon the delegate put his foot in the crack of the door, and with his shoulder quietly pushed it open and walked in. When he walked over to the committee table and sat down, Senator Beveridge said: "Mr. Delegate, the committee is in session and I cannot see you."

"But, Mr. Chairman," the delegate answered, "I am informed by a member of this committee that the Alaska government bill is now under consideration by the committee, and I wish to be heard before it is reported."

Then followed a heated colloquy during which Beveridge tried to compel the delegate to leave the room. Finally the other committee members insisted that the delegate should be given a hearing; Beveridge grudgingly gave him fifteen minutes.

The delegate asked for a copy of the bill, which he had not seen until then, and began to read and criticize its contents. So many objections were raised that the hearing was continued until the next day and for the remainder of the week. Other witnesses were called, including Steve Birch, managing director, and John Steele, corporation attorney, for the Alaska syndicate.

One day Wickersham and Hoggatt nearly got into a fistfight while testifying before the committee. Wickersham intimated that Hoggatt was there as an agent of the Guggenheims, whereupon Hoggatt sprang from his chair, calling Wickersham a liar and swearing loudly at him as he came closer. A couple of committee members moved in between the two embattled witnesses, and Beveridge called the committee into executive session, clearing the room of reporters; the rest of the performance remained unreported.[4]

Wickersham intimated that Presidents Roosevelt and Taft, because of the powerful influence of the Guggenheims, had encouraged Hoggatt to remain in Washington during the previous sessions of Congress to lobby for the Guggenheims. Beveridge reprimanded the delegate, stating that so long as he was chairman of the committee, no one would be permitted to impugn the integrity of the chief executive of the nation. Wickersham apologized and asked that the remark be stricken from the record; the request was granted.

Hoggatt testified that Wickersham was only humbugging because he was mad at Hoggatt ever since the latter had threatened to prefer charges against him if he did not resign from the judgeship. Beveridge asked Hoggatt to desist from any further personal acrimony.[5]

Wickersham also clashed with Major Richardson, who supported the commission bill. Their contradictory testimony wound up in highly emotional scenes when physical violence seemed threatened. They had previously been personal friends but from then on they were implacable enemies.

Richardson, as chairman of the Alaska Road Commission, was a man of considerable influence in the territory. He first came to Alaska in 1897, right out of West Point, to assist in the establishment of a series of army posts. He had been Alaska Road Commission chairman ever since its creation in 1905. He was in charge of the construction and maintenance of all the territorial roads, hence had a sizable payroll. Three United States Army officers constituted the Alaska Road Commission.

The Beveridge bill came up for debate on the Senate floor on February 16, and for two hours the senator from Indiana was bombarded with embarrassing questions. Senators Borah of Idaho and Crawford of South Dakota, both Republicans, led the fight against it. Crawford declared it was opposed by 90 percent of the Alaskans and it was an outrage for the federal government to impose upon American citizens a form of government which they resented.

Senator Borah declared it smacked too much of carpetbaggism and lack of self-government. He believed that the 40,000 good Americans in Alaska were competent to select their own officials by ballot, without having them appointed from a distance. Senator Nelson also spoke against it. When passage appeared unlikely, Senator Beveridge gave up the fight, pleading a case of laryngitis.[6]

Episcopal Bishop Peter Trimble Rowe of Alaska was invited by the president to come and discuss the bill with him, and after that interview, the president allegedly told Senator Beveridge that he considered additional pressure on behalf of the bill ill-advised. Bishop Rowe told the president the bill was an outrage against the people of Alaska.[7]

In the House, Congressman William Sulzer, Democrat of New York, caused a mild sensation when he took the floor and declared that the people of Alaska have every right to rebel and revolt, as did the original thirteen colonies, if the commission bill passed, and that he would do all in his power as a free American citizen to encourage them to do so. The colonies, he declared, started a successful rebellion when Great Britain insisted upon fastening upon them what was nothing more than a limited monarchy. The bill promoted by President Taft is nothing less than a provision for a limited monarchy within the boundaries of the United States, which is nothing less than treason to American freedom.[8]

The Beveridge bill was dead for the time being, which in itself was a victory for the delegate even though his fight for a legislative assembly was also at a standstill. He got a miners' labor lien bill through the House and also a bill providing for a territorial mine inspector. Shackleford tried to block the latter, but when the delegate forced him to admit that he was appearing as counsel for the Treadwell gold mine, from which he received a sizable retainer's fee, the congressmen were more convinced than ever that an inspector was needed.

Wickersham took a first step toward getting the federal government interested in promoting railroad construction in the territory by introducing a bill providing for an Alaska railway commission to consist of the governor and two members of the United States Army Corps of Engineers. They would have charge of locating the approximate routes of all railways projected from the coast to the interior and would receive propositions from railroad builders and determine which should be accepted and which rejected.[9]

Normally, Wickersham did not approve of the government's intrusion in private enterprise but in view of the hurdles imposed by the federal government on railroad construction in the territory, a commission seemed the best solution. Instead of helping the railroad ventures in Alaska as it did the transcontinental railroads in the late nineteenth century, the government was exacting a tax from them at a rate of $100 a mile, even before the line was in operation. Depriving them of the use of the coal lands along their right of way also worked a hardship.

In the debate on the House floor, Wickersham argued that a government guarantee of assistance was necessary to prevent a Guggenheim monopoly in transportation and the copper market; that the Guggenheim-Morgan interests already controlled three railroads. He warned that if such a monopoly was permitted, that combine would force up the price of copper so that the market would be demoralized.[10]

In announcing to the press that he would run for reelection to the delegate's seat in Congress, Wickersham said he felt it was his duty to do so in order to continue his unalterable opposition to the Beveridge bill and to Guggenheim domination. After making this announcement, he received a surprise visit from Steve Birch, who came to Washington to spend the day with him, taking him to lunch and dinner. The thrust of the day-long visit was to persuade Wickersham to quit his fight against the Guggenheims. Birch said his firm wanted a declaration of peace and stood ready to make whatever concessions Wickersham asked for, if only he would quit attacking them.

But Wickersham was not in a conciliatory mood and postured: "Can you stop a prairie fire when the whole great grassy plain is ablaze? And driven before a fifty-mile gale?"

The delegate went on to enumerate the many criminal practices to which the Guggenheims resorted to achieve their goals: stuffing of the Cordova ballot box in the delegate election; fixing the Valdez grand jury in the Keystone riot case and the bribery of the deputy district attorney and the witnesses in the Hasey case. He showed Birch photographic copies of correspondence which proved this to be a fact.

The visit was over when Wickersham said he would quit fighting the Guggs when they quit their criminal maneuverings and lent their support to his efforts to give a popular legislative government to Alaska; Birch went away unhappy.[11]

As Congress headed for adjournment and soon he would be again on the campaign trail, Wickersham decided to deliver a speech on the floor of the House delineating his reasons for wanting an elective legislature for the territory. Confident that he would be returning for the next session and hopeful that he would succeed in getting his bill through Congress, he wanted his colleagues to give some thought during the recess to the justice of treating Alaskans as other American citizens had been treated since the first colonists arrived from across the Atlantic Ocean. He was convinced that a lack of accurate information about Alaska lay at the root of congressional pessimism, so he would try to portray the character of resident Alaskans:

> It is a mistake to suppose that prospectors and miners are entirely transient, nomadic, or migratory. . .Wherever the prospector and miner in the west found the pot of gold in the wilderness he set his stake, brought his family to it, and became the foremost citizen of the camp, the town, the city, and the state.
>
> And of such is the prospector and miner in Alaska. His constant hope by day and his prayer by night is that he may find the "home-stake." With his pack on his back he trudges into the wilderness, bravely facing the rigors of the climate, the dangers of mountain and stream, and the hardships of a lonely life, ever seeking that golden store which will enable him to bring the faraway family to the land of his labors and success, which then becomes his haven of rest—his home.
>
> He is not a transient by nature nor a migrant by temperament. He is a laboring man whose long trail ends at hope and whose successes have built the cities of the west and added millions of wealth to the general capital of the nation. Those who taunt him with being transient and migratory are ignorant of his character and the history of the west, and know nothing of the best type of men who made it.
>
> They do not appreciate the pioneer work which the prospector and miner did there, the schools, churches, homes, colleges, towns, cities, and states he has built. . .Instead of denouncing him as. . .unworthy to intrust with the duty of pioneer work in nation-building, Congress ought to emulate his civic virtues, applaud his work in Alaska, and give him sympathetic aid and encouragement. (Applause)
>
> If Washington will "stop, look, and listen" to the real facts about the worth and character of the brave pioneers of Alaska . . .both Washington and Alaska would be benefitted by it. . . .[12]

Wickersham also prepared a thousand-word article for *Collier's* magazine, at the request of its editor, who was preparing an entire issue on Alaska and wanted Wickersham's article to be the principal focus; the title chosen by the editors was: "Alaska, 49th Star" and it appeared in the August 6, 1910, issue.[13]

In this article, Wickersham wrote:

> Nothing less than the dissolution of the nation will prevent the organization of the State of Alaska. In 1850 when California was admitted into the union, she had no lines of railway, telegraph, trades, or business connecting her with the other states, and was thought to be only valuable for placer gold. Her agriculture and trade, her railroads and present grandeur, have all grown since her admission.
>
> Alaska is a greater country and richer in all its natural resources than California was in 1850. . .Her output of gold and fish for last year amounted to nearly thirty-two million dollars and had increased from fifteen million in 1900.
>
> Her total cash trade with the rest of the United States for 1909 amounted to more than fifty-two million dollars, while that between China and the United States amounted to only forty-eight million. . . .

Chapter 27

1910 Delegate Race

> *By the reelection of Wickersham, the Independent Republican candidate for delegate to Congress, the people of Alaska have emphatically protested against the system of government by executive commission which Mr. Taft considered adequate for them.*
>
> *It is significant that the Guggenheim interests figured openly on the losing side with the administration. That they should have been identified in the popular view with the executive commission project is unfortunate for Mr. Taft. Their influence was exerted in Alaska at the expense of his prestige. . . . (Skagway* Alaskan, *Oct.3,1910, editorial quote from the New York* World)

While Wickersham was winding up his affairs in Washington preparatory to returning north to campaign for reelection, the Alaskan politicos were scurrying about trying to find candidates to defeat him. The Democrats gave up after being turned down by Major Strong and Falcon Joslin. Strong was preoccupied with starting a new paper in Iditarod, the site of the latest gold strike, and Joslin's business ventures required his full-time attention.

The Republicans were also having difficulty finding someone who could defeat the incumbent. With National Committeeman Shackleford back in Washington busy lobbying for his clients, he had neglected issuing a call for a territorial convention until he learned that Wickersham's friend, Emery Valentine, had issued a call for one in Juneau on June 28. Thereupon, Shackleford issued a call for one at Douglas on the same day, labeling Valentine's call "unauthorized."

Shackleford was determined to keep Wickersham from getting the Republican nomination by branding him a renegade Republican. He ignored the fact that the Republican members of Congress had accepted him and also that Wickersham had secured more Republican votes in the last election than any other candidate despite the large amount of money spent to defeat him.

Sid Charles, veteran Alaskan newsman, cautioned the Shackleford Republicans that they were making a big mistake if they thought they could "bamboozle, mislead or dictate to" the people of Alaska. The voters were not so blind they could not see that Shackleford's political machine was dominated by the monopolistic corporations who were their enemies. The fact that the machine happened to have the ear of the national administration would not carry any weight in the eyes of the voters.[1]

As usual, the Republicans held dual conventions. One hundred delegates attended the Valentine-called convention, which gave its unanimous endorsement to Wickersham. Across the Gastineau Channel in Douglas, Edward S. Orr, stagecoach operator at Fairbanks, was the unanimous choice of the one hundred and fifty-two delegates in attendance.[2]

Press reaction to Orr's nomination ranged from a muted silence to a quiet sigh of resignation. The Ketchikan *Miner* commented: "He is a nice, sociable gentleman and an able stage driver; Shackleford should have picked out a less useful citizen to slaughter. God knows there are enough among his following that can be spared.[3]

The Tanana Valley Labor party nominated William O'Connor, editor of the *Miners' Union Bulletin*, as that party's candidate for delegate. He had once worked as a blacksmith at the mines and was a member of the Western Federation of Miners. He had passed the Alaska bar the previous fall.[4]

The Wickershams were traveling across country enjoying the scenic vistas from their train windows while his political future was being pondered by friend and foe alike in the smoke-filled auditoriums of the Juneau and Douglas lodge rooms. During the four-day train trip, there was ample opportunity to evaluate what had and what had not been achieved during the past months in the nation's capital. He knew his enemies would say he had been a failure because he hadn't gotten more bills passed; keeping the Beveridge bill from becoming law probably would impress only a few voters.

His anti-Guggenheim crusade had lost him the support of the Seattle papers, as well as that of many of the major papers in the territory. He was sorry for this loss of support, but he was confident that he had no other choice.

It was just twenty-four hours after the dual Republican conventions had adjourned, when the Wickersham train pulled into King Street station in Seattle. He learned from his friends, who awaited his arrival at the depot, that Ed Orr, his old Tacoma friend, was his Republican opponent and the only other one was the Labor candidate, who had a serious drinking problem. It promised to be a relatively mild campaign although he conceded that Orr was probably "the most dangerous opponent they could have given me; he is big, strong, good-humored, silent, obedient - an ideal candidate for the "big interests."[5]

Orr was an unprepossessing, quiet-spoken man, standing a little over six feet tall. He had a grade school education and had been a laboring man all of his life. His admitted deficiency as a public speaker made him a striking contrast to the incumbent, whose oratorical talent was widely recognized. As one Wickersham supporter observed: "Ed Orr cannot even give a phonographic reproduction of what he is told to say."[6]

Orr went north with the Klondike gold stampeders in 1898, stopping in Skagway to build and operate a tramway over Chilkoot Pass for T.B. and Hugh C. Wallace, Tacoma capitalists, before the White Pass and Yukon Railroad was in operation. Then he went to Dawson, where he operated a freighting service and moved to Fairbanks in 1904. He inaugurated the first stagecoach operation over the Richardson trail from Fairbanks to Valdez.

Wickersham faced a bellicose press - Alaska's five largest dailies opposed him, and the mudslinging which these papers indulged in would have buried a less stalwart soul. Their news columns carried editorial comments expressing the editor's personal dislike for the delegate. Editor Thompson, now of the *News-Miner*, who had supported Wickersham two years before, was one of his chief attackers in this election. He wrote:

> Wickersham must be exposed for what we know him to be. He is absolutely unreliable, the acme of personal selfishness, and ingratitude, a character assassin, always seeking his personal advancement at the expense of his country, absolutely the greatest living menace Alaska has today. . . .[7]

Both the *News-Miner* and the Fairbanks *Times* published from one to ten editorials daily lambasting the delegate. According to the *Times*:

> Wickersham. . .is the stormy petrel of the north. With Wickersham in public office, there will never be peace at home or at Washington. He is a trouble-maker and an incessant quarreler. So long as he remains the representative of Alaska at Washington, just so long will it be impossible for Alaskans to unite upon any petition or demand at Washington and by just so much will the progress of Alaska be retarded.[8]

The Wickites, ignoring the personal insults hurled at their candidate, insisted that there was but one real issue for the voters to consider and that was whether or not they wanted home rule. They vowed that the "subsidized press" would be unable to blind the voters with irrelevant claims of fancied wrongs so that they would forget what they wanted most of all - the right to govern themselves. They were certain that he had won the people's love for his denunciation of the appointive council which the Taft administration had tried to foist upon them.

The banks and many of the businessmen in Fairbanks were displeased with Wickersham for having gotten the miners' lien law passed; this gave the laborer prior rights to other creditors.

A stellar event of the campaign was a public debate in Fairbanks between Wickersham and Shackleford, which the delegate proclaimed as "the greatest success I ever met with on the political platform." According to Wickersham, Shackleford was so bitterly insulting in his remarks and displayed such anger that the audience felt sympathetic toward the delegate. When Wickersham got up to speak and asked the audience: "Did you ever see such a bottle of the milk of human kindness before?" the people roared with laughter and cheered for minutes on end.[9]

Resorting to the old political trick of disseminating false press releases, the Shackleford press bureau at Juneau flooded the Fairbanks and Nome newspaper offices with dispatches claiming that Orr was sweeping the first division, when in fact the campaign for Orr had been abandoned in that division because his friends publicly proclaimed that "Wickersham could be elected as Jesus Christ in the first division if Shackleford and Hoggatt would oppose him before the voters."[10]

Wickersham and Orr traveled together over much of the campaign trails as they were obliged to use the same means of transportation and visit the same communities. Along the Yukon River stops, Orr was entertained by the Northern Commercial Company officials while Wickersham had to mount a platform made from packing boxes on a street corner, to deliver his political message.

Governor and Mrs. Clark traveled the length of the territory, spending sixty days along the way, right in the midst of the delegate race, calling Wickersham an obstructionist and endorsing Orr. They were wined and dined wherever they stopped.

Wickersham criticized the absentee-owned fisheries for not paying their share of taxes to the territory. As president and general manager of the Northwestern Fisheries Company, Captain Jarvis was sent to Washington by the canned salmon industry to get its federal taxes reduced; he accomplished this through a subterfuge of their promise to liberate salmon fry in lieu of taxes. By this means, the canneries succeeded in reducing their taxes from $80,000 to between $1,000 and $2,000 annually, which meant a substantial cut in Alaska's available funds for the construction and maintenance of roads and trails.[11]

In Juneau the delegate's supporters sold campaign buttons in miniature likeness of a flannel shirt, with the inscription: "I am a roughneck; so is Wickersham." That irked his opponents, who contended that Wickersham had never been anything but a government official while Orr had worked with his hands during all of the thirteen years he had been in Alaska.[12]

Finally August 9 arrived, and the people had their say and the newspapers had to accept the verdict willy-nilly. Wickersham won reelection overwhelmingly even though there were so many voting irregularities and illegal voting by nonresident railroad and cannery workers in the Cordova and Seward areas that the canvassing board issued two sets of totals. Even when counting the illegal votes of the nonresidents, Wickersham received 48.3 percent of the total vote.

The total was nearly 9,300, of which the approximate distribution was Wickersham 4,500, Orr 3,200, and O'Connor 1,400. Of the irregular vote, Wickersham had about 1,200, Orr 750 and O'Connor 350. Fraud was also prevalent at Fairbanks and Treadwell and was recognized by the governor's office. The only reason the contest was not brought before the House was that Wickersham's total vote, regular and irregular, showed that nearly one-half the electorate had voted for him.[13]

The excessive irregularities in the delegate elections of 1908 and 1910 were reported in House committee hearings. The irregularities were credited to the machinations of small politicians working hand in glove with the Alaska syndicate in their efforts to defeat Wickersham.[14]

Orr was promised all construction crews on the Copper River and Northwestern Railroad, which numbered close to four thousand men. Also all cannery crews in western Alaska, numbering approximately

eight thousand men, mostly aliens, had been promised. The C.R. & N.
vote was delivered as promised, but the insurance companies refused to
allow cannery vessels to remain in northern waters awaiting election
day.[15]

On election night in Fairbanks, when it was determined that Wickersham was the winner, his boosters paraded the streets with a band
heading the procession, and broom torches furnished the illumination.
There was great enthusiasm and loud cheering. They visited the Tanana
Club, Shackleford's office, and the *Times* office, the funeral march was
played and chanted at each place.

Commenting on the results, the Fairbanks press, which had tried
frantically to defeat him, admitted that though different causes swayed
the people to vote for Wickersham in different localities, "in all districts
alike, personality counted for most. Reasonable and logical objections
were overlooked in the magnetic and pugnacious personality of the delegate, and such a thing as party can be said not to have entered into consideration to any great extent."[16]

The night after the election, Wickersham encountered John McGinn,
one of his severest critics, in one of the big saloons. A thousand men
were on hand to witness the exchange between the two antagonists:

> McGinn, mounting a chair and throwing a hundred dollar
> bill on the bar, asked everyone present to drink to the success of
> Wickersham. But Wickersham instantly mounted a chair and
> said: "Gentlemen, you all have heard me express my opinion of
> John McGinn before election and I wish to assure you that I
> have the same opinion of him after the election."
>
> Then turning to McGinn, he said: "I thank you, Mr. Mc-
> Ginn, I do not care to have a drink this evening." And there was
> not a man in the house who would drink with McGinn, and he
> had to put his hundred dollar bill back in his pocket.
>
> Then Wickersham placed a bill on the bar and every man in
> the house walked up and took a drink. If there is one thing that
> Wickersham despises more than another it is a fawning political
> hypocrite.[17]

In evaluating the election results, veteran newsman John Strong
suggested that the "Morganheims" should recognize the futility of their
mixing in Alaskan politics. Their money might be able to buy a seat in
the Senate for a member of the family, but did not secure results in
Alaska. As he put it: "They spend their money and some people get it in

their pockets but the Gugg candidate invariably gets it in the neck." His concluding advice to the Morganheims was:

It was an unlucky day for the Morganheims when they burgeoned as political dictators of Alaska. Their eclipse has been total. They would better muzzle Steve Birch, abolish their bureau of misinformation and mendacity and attend strictly to building and operating railroads, and mining copper and coal. Alaska needs their money, but it does not need their brand of political domination. Alaskans will have none of it.[18]

Wickersham's own analysis of the election came at a victory rally held in Gordon's Hall in Fairbanks. He said:

I have been reelected by a large majority. I received a few votes at Juneau (he won eighty percent of the southeastern vote) and Valdez notwithstanding that they declared they had me obliterated, and I won out in Nome in spite of the message sent there that I had no show. Whenever the people had a free vote they gave us a majority and only where the corporations had the power were the others victorious.

Don't think all you have to do is to elect a delegate and get a bill introduced in Congress. He'll meet the strong opposition of the grasping corporations with the same conditions he had met heretofore. I'm going to be maligned and blackguarded as I was before, and we've got to stand shoulder to shoulder in this fight. I am simply your agent. However much we have disagreed in the past, now is the time for you to help me. . . .

A campaign fund of fifty thousand dollars, with every corporation against me, yet the people asserted themselves and the victory was won, not by any great effort, but by the little white ballot of the laboring man. . . .[19]

When word arrived that Senator Beveridge had lost his bid for reelection, a group of Alaskans headed by George Baldwin of Valdez, sent the ex-senator a telegram rejoicing in his political defeat, reminding him that he had tried to establish an Oriental despotism in Alaska, refusing its citizens a democratic form of government.[20]

Relaxing after the election, Wickersham went grouse hunting, a sport he had enjoyed since early youth. Then he began preparations for his vacation in the states before returning to Washington. He reorganized his law firm, retaining Roden and dismissing Heilig. He and Heilig had been having some differences and he wanted to do business "in peace." George Jeffery was kept on as the firm's stenographer.

He arranged for the management of his mining property during his absence; some of it was beginning to look valuable. He paid his campaign bills and was pleasantly surprised to learn they were so small, his friends having been generous in their financial assistance.[21]

The Wickershams boarded the river steamer *Tana* for Dawson in the latter part of September. They stopped for an afternoon's visit at Ft. Gibbon, where they visited with the commanding officer and his wife, whom they had known in 1900 at Ft. Egbert. The delegate inspected a building under construction near the military reserve, which he owned and rented out as store space.

Later they stopped at Carshe's cabin to take on wood. It reminded the delegate of the first time he visited Carshe in the spring of 1901:

> I found Carshe and his partner living - one in each end of the cabin - neither would speak to the other - each had his own stove, bed, etc., and each cooked only for himself. It was a "silent" partnership for they refused to speak to each other. Carshe is still cutting wood - but now alone.[22]

Wickersham had a thirty-five-pound cabbage with him from Fairbanks, which he planned to show to his colleagues in Washington as proof of Alaska's great agricultural potential. Shortly after boarding the steamer at Fairbanks, he told his friend, Chris Harrington, old-time Alaska mining man, about the cabbage he had in his luggage.

Feigning doubt about its size, Harrington asked to see the cabbage. Whenever a new passenger boarded the steamer, Wickersham would boast about his cabbage until Harrington grew bored by it. One night he stole the cabbage and took it down into the engine room. Pushing back the leaves, he drilled a hole in the center and poured in about five pounds of buckshot. The next morning the cabbage was again put on the scales to prove its weight to a sourdough friend of Wickersham's. The overweight pleased rather than alarmed the delegate.

That night Harrington repeated the lead dose. Wickersham grew doubtful of the accuracy of the scales, but continued to display the cabbage. Harrington continued to add shot. When the boat docked at Whitehorse, the cabbage weighed fifty-three pounds. The deception was discovered when the plug came out as Wickersham boarded the train at Whitehorse for Skagway. Buckshot rolled the full length of the floor of

the coach, whereupon Wickersham carried the cabbage to the rear platform and kicked it off. He did not speak to anyone for five miles. He
was brooding over what Congress had missed in not seeing a heavier
cabbage than had ever been grown east of the Mississippi River.[23]

At Skagway the Wickershams were honored at a public reception.
Skagwayites liked Wickersham—they always treated him well at the
polls - this time he received 160 votes to Orr's 28, and O'Connor did not
get a single vote. During the reception at the Elks Hall, Wickersham explained why he was anticorporation:

> I am in favor of that kind of conservation for Alaska that al-
> lows the people of Alaska what they need of its great natural re-
> sources for their own use. I am opposed to that form of govern-
> ment for Alaska that will allow a few large corporations to skim
> off the cream of our natural wealth for the purpose of taking
> that wealth out of the territory to build palaces and add to the
> millions of the Alaska syndicate, the Alaska fisheries syndicate
> and allied interests, in New York, San Francisco and Seattle. . . .
>
> Alaska was purchased of Russia in 1867 and the same year the
> Alaska seal fisheries were turned over to a corporate interest.
> These fisheries were the greatest the world has ever known.
> They have produced $150,000,000 and there is not one person in
> this audience who can point to a single schoolhouse, a single
> church, or a single home that all that great wealth built in
> Alaska.
>
> During the past season the Alaska salmon canneries have pro-
> duced $11,000,000 and all of that wealth has gone out of Alaska.
> Now these great interests are reaching out for our coal. . . .
>
> I am returning to Washington as your representative to do the
> best I can to carry out your will, to stand between you and the
> great lobby maintained there by the Alaska syndicate and allies
> and try to secure such legislation for Alaska, as will give the
> people of Alaska a fair share of the resources of the terri-
> tory. . . .[24]

In a speech at a public reception at Juneau, Wickersham declared
himself to be a "Roosevelt Insurgent Republican" and added that he was
proud of being one. He said he had always voted for the Republican
presidential candidate but he was an American before he was a Republican. When any branch of the party sided with corporate interests

against the best welfare of the people, he would cease to be affiliated with that branch.

He recited the history of how the seal and salmon had been taken from the territory without any reimbursement; now the same could happen to the copper and coal, he said, if Alaskans did not watch out for their interests. He said Alaska was getting about the same deal as "Windy Bill's dog." Out in a blizzard and starving, "Windy Bill" cut off the dog's tail and made soup. The dog was rewarded by getting the bone from the end of the tail used for soup. That's how Alaskans would fare if the Morgan syndicate did not face laws checking their greed.

The Wickershams spent a month on the West Coast before going on to Washington. Half of the time was spent in San Francisco, where the Ferdinand de Journals extended them warm hospitality. They had a dinner party given for them at their Burlingame home on the Wickersham's thirtieth wedding anniversary. That evening Wickersham wrote in his diary: "God bless my good wife. I hope we can live together for thirty years more!"

De Journal took him to lunch at the exclusive Bohemian Club, and he arranged for his admission to practice in the United States Circuit Court of Appeals.

The Wickershams stayed at the Palace Hotel and had numerous visitors, mostly ex-Alaskans, as a result of newspaper interviews in the *Call* and the *Examiner*. Even a long-lost cousin showed up and they had a pleasant visit reminiscing about their youth in Patoka. The cousin lived in Vallejo. He recalled having attended church meetings at which he heard Wickersham's grandfather preach; the Reverend James Wickersham was a Campbellite preacher.[25]

Chapter 28

Defeats Coal Leasing Scheme

James Wickersham is no saint. . . .A man as impulsive, hot-tempered and combative as he, is sure to make mistakes. . . But his faults are of that sturdy, rugged character that rather endear him to an Alaskan.

Although a minister of the gospel of peace, I must myself confess to more liking for a strong sinner than for a weak saint. A man like Wickersham will always make warm enemies and warm friends.   (Letter from Dr.S.Hall Young to Dr.L.S.Keller, Skagway Alaskan, *May 31,1911)*

Wickersham was returning to Washington for his second term at the same time that his idol, Theodore Roosevelt, was flexing his muscles for a new role in American politics. While Wickersham was on the campaign trail in Alaska preaching the gospel of the people's welfare superceding the selfish exploitation by large corporations, Roosevelt was on a speaking tour in the West enunciating a "new nationalism"—a new concept of social justice—the reconstruction of society by political action.

Conservative Republicans shuddered at this new philosophy, and when the Democrats took over the United States House that fall, the old guard knew that Taft was in trouble and his reelection in serious doubt. To Wickersham the possible coalition of "insurgents" and Democrats inspired hope for passage of his home rule legislation. If Congress would pass it, it was unlikely that the president would veto it.

En route to Washington the Wickershams stopped for a few days' visit in Springfield, where they had Thanksgiving dinner with Debbie's sister, Emma, and her husband, John Kenney. They also visited friends dating back to their newlywed days, including Mrs. John Palmer and her daughter, Mrs. Jessie Webber; the governor had died.

In Washington they took a suite at the new Congress Hall Hotel for the winter. It was the home of several other House members and their wives; the common dining hall brought the congressmen and their wives together in the evenings for a social exchange of the day's events. Debbie joined the wives during the day in card parties.

When Wickersham learned that Rudolph Spreckles, the proprietor, and Fremont Older, the editor, of the San Francisco *Bulletin*, were at the New Willard Hotel, he sought them out to give them an interview on his future legislation for Alaska. Since the Seattle papers tended to be pro-Guggenheim, it would be helpful if he could get the San Francisco papers on his side. The *Bulletin* men shared Wickersham's denunciation of Taft and his commission form of government for Alaska, and they promised to help him get a boost from *McClure's* magazine, similar to the one in *Collier's*.

Thanks to Older, the Wickershams were invited to dinner at the home of Miss Elizabeth Marbury in New York City. Other guests included: Governor and Mrs. Hiram Johnson of California; Miss Anne Morgan, daughter of J.P. Morgan; Cosgraves, editor of *Everybody's* magazine. Wickersham was asked to escort Miss Morgan to the table as his dinner partner. Charmed as he was with this unexpected privilege, Wickersham chuckled to think of the political sensation this morsel of gossip would create in Alaskan political circles—he, the archcritic of the Morgan-Guggenheims, escorted the daughter of J. Pierpont Morgan, the head of the Alaska syndicate, to dinner!!

Wickersham was deeply impressed by this group of intellectuals who were bent on bringing radical social reforms to the American society. His diary got the benefit of his thoughts when he returned home that evening:

> Miss Marbury is fat, fair and forty - or fifty! She is a woman of keen intellect and strong mind and having tired of all the pleasures that society and wealth can give has now "gone in for radicalism" in politics. . .is evidently seeking to know the radical leaders in political thought and declares with Rooseveltian energy that things radical are "bully."
>
> Miss Morgan is a worthy daughter of the greatest financier the world has ever known. She is 28 or 30 years old, rather tall and of a heavy mold, but a woman of vigorous and clear mind. Miss

Marbury and college professors of radical views have planted thoughts concerning the reorganization of society and business in her mind which have no place in the rules of business in Mr. Morgan's banks or business.

Miss Morgan is a handsome, Junoesque and clear-eyed goddess who wishes to aid Pinchot and ideas from the safety of the Morgan fortune. She ought to say "yes" to some strong and vigorous man in her own walk of life. However, she is an admirable character and will do much before she dies to undo the mighty things her father has done—wrongly.

They urged me to talk of conditions in Alaska and I am free to confess that it required all my skill to describe with the proper show of respect the criminal things the Alaska syndicate—Morgan and Guggenheim—is doing there, without being guilty of rudeness. . . .

The dinner was elegant in all its appointments and the few bites I took between periods were excellent, but they kept me talking.

After dinner a Mr. Garrison, connected subrosa with a new radical newspaper scheme - the establishment of the *National Post*, intended to represent radical views and to be controlled by the Progressives with no one to have more than two hundred dollars interest—gave his report upon that subject. . . .[1]

Wickersham made more of an effort to cultivate contacts outside of congressional circles than he had during his first term, when he felt obliged to concentrate on legislation coming before committees under the sponsorship of the administration. He refused to attend receptions at the White House because of his animosity toward its occupant; Debbie attended with other congressional wives.

Gifford Pinchot proved to be a stalwart ally, especially in fighting the coal-leasing scheme being proposed by the administration. He offered Wickersham free access to the columns of the *National Conservation* magazine. The Wickershams were frequent dinner guests at the Pinchots' home, where strategy was planned to fight legislation deemed unfavorable to Alaska's best interests. Other dinner guests included senators and congressmen among the "insurgents."

In his message to Congress on December 6, 1910, President Taft repeated his lack of confidence in the ability of Alaskans to make their own laws, stressing the migratory character of the population.

The administration's major Alaskan legislative effort was the development of its coalfields. It proposed to open the lands to leasing by the federal government—no one could own the land but they would mine the claims under government lease. Representative Frank W. Mondell, Republican of Wyoming, introduced a leasing bill in the House and Senator Nelson introduced a similar bill in the Senate. An individual coal claim was not to exceed 2,560 acres, and the lease rental would be on a royalty basis of from three to ten cents a ton.

Convinced that the individual Alaskan coal miner would become a vassal in a huge feudal kingdom and that it would enable the big interests to get a monopoly of the coal lands in Alaska, Wickersham opposed the idea with all the energy he could muster. He argued for private ownership of Alaska's coal lands.

Wickersham worked long and hard on his arguments against the Mondell leasing bill. One day he met Mondell on the floor of the House and asked him when he expected to bring it up; he said he didn't know as he had made no arrangements for it. About two hours later, without any notice to the delegate, Mondell called up the bill under the gag law suspension rule, allowing only forty minutes for debate, and without opportunity to amend, and started to steamroller it through.

Madison of Kansas, James of Kentucky, Lenroot of Pennsylvania, and a dozen others joined in the fight against it. Wickersham was given an opportunity to speak against it. While in the midst of his argument, Mondell, sitting not ten feet away, just in front of the delegate, called him a liar, and a free-for-all ensued.

A variety of versions of the fracas appeared in the national and Alaska press, but the write-up in the Washington *Post* perhaps was as reliable as any:

> Delegate Wickersham of Alaska, shouting, "You are a liar if you say that," rushed upon Representative Mondell of Wyoming . . .and clutched him by the throat. . .Members who closed in upon the struggling men declared that no blows were struck. From the galleries, however, it was plain that this was not due to any disinclination on the part of either of the belligerents.
>
> Wickersham, his fingers around Mondell's neck, was seized in similar fashion by Representative Foster of Vermont. And all the time the Wyoming representative was wriggling to get himself free, and making futile efforts to use the chair, from which he had arisen, as a weapon against his assailant.

The crowd around the two men grew. Representative Longworth of Ohio and other members. . .attempted to pull Mondell from the tenacious grasp of the infuriated delegate. Wickersham, in spite of the grip which Foster had secured on his throat, was still able to express his sentiments in vigorous, if not parliamentary, language. Foster, as peacemaker, seemed to be the target for his characterizations, rather than the man he had started after, Mr. Mondell.

Finally, the Republican whip, Representative Dwight of New York, who would weigh in at the ringside at about 250 pounds, interposed his bulk between Wickersham and Mondell, and the delegate was forced to release his hold on his opponent's throat. . . .

Representative Olmsted of Pennsylvania, who was in the Speaker's chair, was making about as much disturbance with his gavel as the contestants on the floor. At his order, the sergeant-at-arms took down from its resting place the mace of the House, surmounted with its silver eagle, and, gingerly holding it at arm's length, bore down on the congested crowd of hostiles and mediators. But, whether he walked as fast as he could, or whether his progress was delayed by his sense of the dignity of his mission, by the time he reached the combatants and their friends, the actual trouble was over.

Wickersham, still panting and feeling his collar, which had been pulled somewhat awry by the enthusiastic efforts of the pacific Foster, was back in his place, and Mondell, his throat relieved from the Alaskan's grip, was again seated and drawing in grateful breaths.

Wickersham was the first to take advantage of the calm which had been restored by such strenuous methods, Olmsted quickly accorded him recognition.

"I want the Record to show that I apologize to the House," he cried, "but I also want it to show that I was called a liar. . .I apologize. I lost my temper."

Mondell made somewhat of a "Scotch apology." "I made no statement, such as has been reported, in debate," he explained. "I turned to the gentleman from South Dakota and said: "Then he must be a liar." My remark was not directed toward the gentleman from Alaska, and it was not uttered in debate, but to a gentleman who sat beside me. I realize, however, that I should not have uttered the word here, or anywhere, for that matter, and I apologize to the House."

Representative Tawney. . .attempted to secure an adjournment. . .but the opponents of the Alaska leasing bill demanded a roll call, and the House stayed on the job. The bill was then defeated by a vote of 151 to 32. It would have required a two-thirds vote to pass the measure. The Democrats and the insurgent Republicans made up the force in opposition to the bill. . .[2]

Wickersham regretted having been involved in such an unseemly row, "but when a man calls another a liar, without smiling, it means a blow."[3] He was particularly worried about the effect the row would have on Debbie, and that evening when they entered the dining room at Congress Hall and they were greeted with an applause and every evidence of approval, Wickersham was greatly relieved. Several congressmen came over to their table to assure him that they thought he had done right and approved of his action.

After he had an opportunity to weigh the matter in his mind, he concluded that probably more good than bad would come out of it. It taught the members of Congress that the delegate from Alaska could not be snubbed or abused without fear of the consequences.

The delegate's resort to fisticuffs was praised and denounced in the Alaska press, depending on how the editor felt toward the delegate in the first place. A mass meeting in Valdez denounced the interference of Mondell in Alaska affairs and passed a resolution praising Wickersham for defeating the Mondell bill.[4]

James F. Callbreath, secretary of the American Mining Congress, visited the Alaska coalfields the following summer and came to the same conclusion as Wickersham, namely, that the leasing system would forever bar the small individual miner from receiving the fruits of his labor as a prospector. There would be no incentive for the miner to prospect and develop coal veins or leads, for the minute he would perfect title the man with the money could demand his own terms and deprive the poor miner of his just due.[5]

When it became obvious in the spring of 1911 that President Taft was intent upon keeping the coal fields under lock and key, a group of Cordova citizens decided to stage a demonstration to tell the nation that they were fed up with the government's dilatory tactics in not allowing the coal claims of bona fide entrymen to be released.

Cordova, the natural outlet to one of the richest copper districts in the world and to the rich Bering River coal fields, had slid in population from 6,000 in 1908 to 1,779 in 1910. The Morgan-Guggenheim combine spent $20 million in the construction of a railroad to develop the nearby Bonanza Copper Mine; the payroll of the railroad amounted to $25,000 a day, and the town's general merchandise business ran to $101,000 in 1909. Then came the slump when the federal government decided to lock up all the coal lands.

On the evening of May 3, 1911, a group of Cordovans began stockpiling shovels in the rear of the Alaska Transfer Company, owned by Mayor Austin E. Lathrop. At a given signal at three o'clock the following day, approximately three hundred men and at least one woman marched to the dock, armed with shovels, and proceeded to dump several hundred tons of British Columbia coal into the bay. Alaska Steamship Company agent Richard J. Barry tried to dissuade the demonstrators, pointing out that the coal belonged to his company and it wasn't the company's fault that the Alaska coal was not available; the crowd was unimpressed and continued their shoveling.

It so happened that the deputy marshal was out of town, so the United States commissioner swore in Mayor Lathrop and Chief of Police George Dooley as deputy marshals and armed them with warrants for the arrest of the shovelers. The officials ordered the crowd dispersed in the name of the United States, but they were ignored and the heaving of coal continued. The woman declared that the spirit of the Revolution was not dead and that Alaskans needed to be courageous enough to no longer tolerate injustice.

When the shovel brigade decided they had made their point, they marched back up town to their respective homes. No arrests were made. The national press heralded the incident as a modern-day "Boston Tea Party."

The night before, a group of coal miners on the beach at Katalla built a big bonfire and burned Gifford Pinchot in effigy and also burned a copy of President Roosevelt's proclamation withdrawing the coal lands from entry.[6]

Washington officialdom was in accord that Alaska's coal should be mined, but could not agree on the proper system. Fear of muckraking critics frightened away potential capital investors, and it was much safer for the Washington politicians to scream at the "grasping Guggenheims" and let Alaska die on the economic vine. After all, there were no constituents' votes to worry about in that faraway land.

All of the claims in the Cunningham case were summarily canceled by Secretary of Interior Fisher, and the locators lost thousands of dollars expended on the staking of the properties.[7]

A front-page banner story in the Seattle *Times* quoted W.B. Vanderlip of Tanana Valley to the effect that "the people of interior Alaska are on the verge of revolt and will secede from the Union before the snow flies, unless relief is provided by the federal government before that time. . .they are tired of being throttled and they will either annex themselves to Canada or hoist a flag of their own."[8]

The government's experience in the state of Colorado did not help in solving Alaska's coal problem. The coal lands had first been withdrawn just as in Alaska, and later released under political pressure, only to discover that they were gobbled up by "the band of commercial buccaneers who sail under the Guggenheim flag." The government was suing the American Smelting and Refining Company, owned by the Guggenheims, to recover $25 million in damages for alleged swindling in the acquisition of these coal lands.[9]

Having successfully defeated the coal leasing bill, Wickersham shifted his attention to another coal-related situation with which he hoped to embarrass the administration. He introduced a resolution in the House calling upon the attorney general and the secretary of war to inform the House what had been done regarding irregularities in the letting of coal contracts at Fort Davis and Fort Liscum in 1909. He claimed that he had documentary evidence to the effect that Captain Jarvis, as treasurer of the Guggenheim corporation, robbed the government of several thousand dollars in connection with those contracts and United States Attorney General George Wickersham had deliberately allowed the statute of limitations to expire against the defrauders. The Democratic majority in the House was happy to cooperate in embarrassing the cabinet officer. The attorney general was ordered to produce all pertinent papers to a special Democratic investigating committee.[10]

The following morning the Seattle papers carried two front-page stories - one about Wickersham's resolution and the other about Jarvis's suicide! That morning Captain Jarvis's body, fully dressed, was found in a bedroom of the Seattle Athletic Club, with a bullet hole through his brain and a revolver still clasped in his hand. On the dresser lay a note: "Tired and worn out. That's all."

Jarvis lived in a fine home on Capitol Hill with his wife and two children. He had come downtown a day or two previous and taken a room at the club. He was vice president and active manager of the northwestern branch of the Booth Fisheries Company.

Friends of Jarvis declared he was hounded to death by H.J. Douglas, who up to three years previous was auditor of the Northwestern Commercial Company, a Guggenheim corporation of which Jarvis was treasurer. While still in the employ of the company, Douglas took photographs of vouchers which showed that Jarvis, on behalf of the company, had spent considerable sums of money in the defense of Ed Hasey in his murder trial held in Juneau in 1908. Some of these payments made by Jarvis were of doubtful legality, and Douglas continually worried Jarvis with the implied liability to prosecution.

The photographs of the vouchers figured prominently in the delegate campaign in the summer of 1910. Douglas sold his ill-gotten photographs to the Wickersham workers, and copies were circulated freely throughout the territory and printed in the pro-Wickersham newspapers. As a countermove, Jarvis gave out the facsimile of the telegram sent him by Wickersham, showing that Wickersham had sought financial backing from the Guggenheims in his 1908 delegate campaign.

Other friends attributed his depression to his failure to get the presidency of the Alaska Steamship Company after the resignation of Peabody; J.H. Young had been appointed instead. When he did not get the presidency, he resigned as treasurer and assumed the presidency of Booth Fisheries, which later was taken over by Northwestern Fisheries, a subsidiary of the Alaska Steamship Company.[11]

Jarvis never defended Hasey's shooting. He held Hasey to blame for having taken matters into his own hands, but he believed it was the duty of the company to defend a man who had acted in loyalty to his employers.[12]

Wickersham's filing such serious charges of malfeasance against a senior cabinet officer can be viewed either as courageous or foolhardy, considering the effect on his own political future. But, characteristically, he was willing to take the gamble. He saw it as a possible means of breaking the stranglehold which the Guggenheims had on Alaskan affairs. If successful in proving his charges, he should receive reenforcement in his fight for a territorial legislature. He was certain that he had a foolproof case based on documentary evidence.

The War Department had advertised for bids to supply coal to the two military posts and the John J. Sessnon Company and the Northwestern Commercial Company had been awarded the contracts. The delegate had a sworn affidavit from Douglas, the discharged auditor of the Northwestern Commercial Company, to the effect that the two companies had conspired with each other to defraud the government by charging an excessive price for the coal. The delegate had forwarded this information to the attorney general but he had done nothing about it, allowing the three-year statute of limitations to run out, making the criminals exempt from prosecution after that time.

The delegate, however, erred in his three-year calculation as the contractors continued to deliver coal over a year's time, thus extending the statute of limitations for an extra year. The attorney general testified that he had sent an investigating committee to Alaska and it had found strong indications of collusion between the bidders and the price of coal was extortionate. He had made plans to prosecute the contractors. Thereupon all charges against the attorney general were dismissed.[13] It was an embarrassing incident for the delegate and his enemies in the Alaskan press emphasized that fact.

But he was not one to remain down for long. With the help of the muckraking national press and the insurgents within the Republican party, he was able to explore new ways to embarrass the Taft administration.

The next revelation of secret intrigue between the administration and the Guggenheims had to do with the Cordova harbor, known as Controller Bay. It was discovered that President Taft signed a secret order withdrawing 12,800 acres of land from the Chugach forest reserve, including Controller Bay and the following day Dick Ryan, as secret agent for the Morgan-Guggenheim syndicate filed soldiers' script on the waterfront. In ordinary procedure a proclamation would have been issued and sent to land offices all over the country and thus would have gained wide publicity.[14]

Some weeks later Senator Clark of Wyoming introduced a bill giving the Copper River and Northwestern Railroad an exclusive monopoly of the wharf and waterfront at Cordova, and all the adjoining tidelands. It was at this point that Wickersham got into the picture. He presented his objections before the Senate Committee on Commerce, describing the Clark bill as "the daintiest piece of legislative gum-shoeing I ever saw."[15] This would give the Guggenheims a monopoly of right-of-way and transportation of the Copper River Valley and the Katalla coal fields.

Wickersham mailed copies of his objections to Senator Jones of Washington and to Gifford Pinchot. He also alerted Angus McSween, a reporter for the Baltimore *North American* newspaper, who developed a national "graft" exposé out of it.[16] The Clark bill was defeated and the executive order was cancelled.

With the Guggenheim bugaboo ever before them, the members of Congress hesitated to give serious consideration to allowing the Alaskans to elect their own lawmakers, even though the delegate argued that such a body would serve as an effective tool against corporate monopolies.

In testifying on behalf of his home rule bill before the House Committee on Territories, he argued that a legislature would be a means of "organizing" the Alaskan people so they could protect and help themselves. A legislature would enable the people to develop the resources and at the same time reserve effective control over the big interests who sought to create a monopoly. He pleaded:

> Give us the beginning of a legislature. . .a method by which we can have a policeman on the ground to keep the public property, for which you are trustees, from being stolen until Congress can make up its mind what finally to do with it.
>
> I say this earnestly because I feel earnestly about it. It is a shame and a disgrace to postpone the creation of an elective legislature in Alaska from year to year, while the big interests are permitted from day to day to gather to themselves the advantages and undeveloped resources of the land.[17]

Adjournment came on August 4 and Wickersham visited his son Darrell in St. Louis on his way to the West Coast. Darrell was becoming disenchanted with navy life and was thinking about resigning. He had bought himself an automobile and took his father riding about the city. "Automobiling" was a favorite recreation of the Wickershams in Washington on Sunday afternoons. They would rent an automobile and drive through the parks just to enjoy the fresh air and listen to the birds singing in the trees.

It had been a hard four months for the delegate; there had been more unpleasantness than usual. Hence, it was doubly gratifying to find a letter awaiting him in Tacoma from his newspaper friend, Dr. L.S. Keller of Skagway. Enclosed was a clipping from his paper of "An Appreciation of Wickersham" written by their mutual friend, Dr. S. Hall Young, which read:

> From my observation of his conduct as a judge, I am prepared to endorse the opinions of two judges of the circuit court of appeals. . .who both told me this winter that Judge Wickersham was the best judge Alaska has ever had. . . .
>
> As a man, he has been growing steadily in my esteem. Both in and out of office, he has never missed a chance to do a kindness

and I have never made a request of him that he has not done all in his power to fulfill.

I like his record especially his remarkable work in defeating the iniquitous, un-American and insulting Beveridge bill. . . That the credit of defeating this bill belongs almost entirely to Delegate Wickersham nobody conversant with the facts will attempt to deny. The odds against him were tremendous, the whole power and influence of the adminsitration, the Guggenheim millions, the Hoggatt-Shackleford political machine, all the self-seeking politicians hoping for fat offices in Alaska, the "stand-patters" in Congress, the Army, the Navy, all these and other forces which wished to exploit Alaska for their own interests combined to pass that Tory bill. . . .

Wickersham has won his fight for recognition. One of his fellow congressmen told me that he was acknowledged to be one of the most forceful members of the House. When he speaks Congress listens. . . .[18]

Chapter 29

Wins Elected Legislature

> *The representative in Congress from Alaska who can have
> his name identified with legislation conferring upon the people
> of this district the right of self-government will be the longest
> remembered official the district will ever have.*
>
> *His will be the name of the patron saint of the future com-
> monwealth of the north.* (Skagway Daily Alaskan, Oct. 5, 1906)

> *When I die, all I ask is that on my tombstone be placed the
> inscription that I was the patron and secured the passage of
> home rule for Alaska. That will be all that I want.* (Wickersham
> speech, Fairbanks, Sept. 28, 1912)

Wickersham's dejected mood when leaving Washington inspired a reporter to write that he would not be a candidate for reelection but
would instead support Major Strong as his successor. The story even
suggested that he had confided to friends that he planned to leave
Alaska and would become associated with a corporation in the Pacific
Northwest: the story appeared in the Seattle and Alaska press.[1]
Actually, Wickersham was having private thoughts about not running
but took care not to say so publicly for fear it would weaken his
influence when he returned to Washington to push his home rule legislation in Congress.[2]

Interviewed in Dawson, Wickersham labeled as false any reports that
he would not be a candidate for reelection. "I believe that a year from
now, the polls will show me to be as popular as the last election showed
me to be," the delegate predicted.[3]

247

He was optimistic about favorable action on his legislative bill at the next congressional session because both Speaker Champ Clark and Congressman Oscar Underwood, Democratic floor leader, had assured him that the House would give it special attention.

Wickersham was pleasantly surprised with the changed attitude of the Northern Commercial Company agent towards him. When he boarded the *Susie* at Dawson, he found he was assigned the "blue room," the best on the boat, and there were two bottles of liquor and two boxes of cigars in his room, compliments of the company. The year before he was given a small room on the upper deck near the cooks and pantrymen. "Fighting the big interests brings it to their notice that you are in the ring," he confided to his diary.[4]

Inasmuch as he would be in Alaska less than two months and would be traveling much of the time, Debbie remained in Tacoma. Hence, rather than disturb the tenants in his home, he fitted up a bedroom and living room across the hall from his law office in Fairbanks, as his living quarters. His law partner, Henry Roden, decided to move to Iditarod to open a branch office there as law work in Fairbanks was slow while the town of Iditarod was booming, with new gold strikes reported daily.

Wickersham's Fairbanks friends staged a political rally in his honor, and in reporting the rally, the *Times*, a sharp critic of the delegate, said he delivered a forceful and often dramatic address which was repeatedly interrupted by audience applause; the speech lasted two hours.

In introducing him, Frank Gorden, a local merchant, recalled the previous delegate race in which three candidates participated and observed that the gentleman who came out the winner had performed his responsibilities in a satisfactory manner. He observed further that the other two contenders were filling their respective roles in an equally suitable manner—one was engaged in the worthy pursuit of pitching hay in the neighborhood of Tacoma (Orr) and the other was languishing in jail in Cordova (O'Connor).[5]

In his speech, Wickersham criticized Major Richardson's handling of road funds, claiming a criminal waste of public monies and demanding a congressional investigation of the road commission. He had brought an engineer and a transportation expert north with him, and the three planned to travel on the trail from Fairbanks to Valdez to check on the road's condition. He planned to continue his criticism of Richardson when he returned to Washington and wanted to be equipped with expert testimony to fortify his charges of malfeasance.

Out of a nearly $2 million appropriation, Richardson admitted spending three-quarters of a million on the Valdez road (370 miles), but

Wickersham thought it was closer to a million and a quarter, and still it was not fit for automobile travel. He compared that with a 340-mile automobile road from Dawson to Whitehorse which cost $140,000 to build and $10,000 a year to maintain.[6]

Senator Miles Poindexter, Republican of Washington, and Gifford Pinchot visited Alaska that fall in order to gather antiadministration propaganda for the coming session. Wickersham helped arrange their visits to Controller Bay and to the site of the Cunningham coal claims. They urged the delegate to run for reelection and promised their support. They wanted an Alaskan "insurgent" delegation to the national convention to assist in the nomination of Senator Bob LaFollette for president.[7]

Sensing that he was losing the support of westerners in his opposition to an elected legislature for Alaska, President Taft modified his position in an address in the Seattle armory. He promised he would support such legislation at the next session of Congress, which brought a tremendous applause from the audience. He did not favor dispensing with all federal appointees, however.[8]

During his stopover at Cordova, the Guggenheim headquarters, Wickersham was treated to some colorful journalistic jibes from the pen of his old editor friend, Will Steel, whom he first knew when he served on the Nome bench. Through the years, Steel had been an off-again, on-again critic and supporter of the delegate. As publisher of the Guggenheim's town journal, Steel welcomed Wickersham in his choicest satirical style as follows:

> Beat the drums, sound the cymbals, and sing hallelujahs, for lo, out of the valley of the Tanana will come today the great prophet and pooh-bah. The Right Honorable James Wickersham, minister plenipotentiary who deigns to represent his humble minions of the wilds of Alaska at the great court of political jurisprudence in the capital city of Washington, will take up his line of mush over his own beloved land, to push on until he reaches the very citadel of his political enemies.
>
> With the courage of a warrior bold, the marvelous seer and wordy Goliath of this northland will traverse the despised thorny paths that lead him into that thriving little city of enterprise, Chitina, where the rails of the monstrous railroad constructors, Morgan-Guggenheim, will convey him to the sea coast. . . .

The great monarch of all Alaska may even condescend to linger a few hours in the humble little village of Cordova, where the residents had the temerity to raise a few thousand dollars to assist in building the trail from Chitina to Willow Creek, after the fighting statesman had wired them to "go to."[9]

Wickersham found a cool reception awaiting him in Seattle. The *Times* and *Post-Intelligencer* disapproved of him so vehemently that they wouldn't even mention that he was in town! There was a general feeling among the Seattle-Alaskans that he should be told to sit down and cool his outbursts and allow quieter and saner voices to be heard. Four or five different groups had organized themselves for the specific purpose of going to Washington to lobby for legislation which they deemed beneficial for Alaska. Though he resented this interference in his assigned responsibilities, he tried to appear appreciative.

One such group called itself the "Alaska Square Deal League" and had William Pigott as its president. Its principal goal was to promote self-government for the territory. They had launched a letter-writing campaign, enclosing a circular entitled "Why Alaska Should Have Territorial Government." The group sponsored a public meeting at the Colliseum Theatre, inviting Wickersham to speak. Mayor Dilling presided and Dr. Mark A. Matthews, minister of the First Presbyterian Church, and Professor Edmund S. Meany, history professor at the University of Washington, were the other speakers.

Wickersham promised he would do everything possible to avoid controversy when he returned to Washington and would work harmoniously with other Alaskans there to get favorable legislation for the territory, especially an elected legislature. The *Times* quoted him as saying: "I am willing to be good. I don't want to fight. Let us get what we want by standing together and let us fight afterwards if we want to. Let's quit our petty quarreling, get together and accomplish some results."

Governor Clark questioned the propriety of residents of Puget Sound setting themselves up as authorities on what was good for Alaska. He wrote Pigott that "there are a good many people in Alaska who do not believe at all it would be a 'square deal' to give this territory an elected legislature at present." Pigott replied that Alaskans had been holding meetings ever since 1900 at which resolutions were passed asking for self-government. In short, the people of Alaska had used every available avenue to make their position plain on that proposition.[10]

The Alaska bureau of the Seattle Chamber of Commerce was opposed to an elected legislature and worked hand in glove with Governor Clark sending lobbyists to Washington to work against it.

By the time Wickersham arrived in St. Paul and Minneapolis, en route to Washington, his promise "to be a good Indian" had been forgotten. In speeches in both cities he condemned the Gugg-Morgan combine which was trying to monopolize the territory, concluding with the exhortation: "Come up and help fight the Guggenheims!"[11]

When reports of his Midwest speeches reached Seattle, his enemies called it "an act of perfidy that only the cheapest political trickster would try," adding that "the Guggenheim bugaboo provided such savory muckraking morsels for sensational speeches" that Wickersham could not resist its inclusion.[12]

When Congress convened in January, Wickersham threw a sheaf of bills into the hopper, chief among them being one providing for an elected territorial legislature. It was introduced on January 16, 1912, and given the number 18034. Senator Jones of Washington introduced a similar bill in the Senate. This was Wickersham's third such bill, the first one having been introduced on June 7, 1909, and the second on April 4, 1911.

Governor Clark spent the winter in Washington at the request of Secretary Fisher, leaving Juneau on Janury 5 and returning on May 15. He testified before committees in opposition to the delegate's legislative bill, arguing that self-government would mean self-support and the territory was not financially capable of supporting itself. He urged that no change be made in Alaska's present government until it was more fully developed. He complained that he was doing his utmost to secure passage of measures upon which all Alaskans were agreed but found himself constantly obstructed by the delegate, who did not offer anything better but who interposed with the mere objection that he was the elected representative of Alaskans.[13]

The home rule bill reached the House floor on April 17, and debate continued until April 24, when it was passed by a unanimous vote. Wickersham delivered a masterful presentation of the arguments in its favor on the last day. He dealt separately with the four major objections offered by the bill's opponents: the migratory character of the population; the impermanence of the population; its being too small a population to support its own government; and the territory being too large in area.

Committee Chairman Henry D. Flood, Democrat of Virginia, piloted the bill through the House, speaking glowingly of the wealth Alaska had contributed to the national coffers. He said in part:

> Including the purchase price of $7,200,000, we (the nation) have spent $35,700,000 on Alaska during the forty-five years since the purchase. . . .
>
> During that period the people of this country have received in money for the products they have brought out of that territory and in cash collected in taxes the vast sum of $444,000,000, thus showing a net balance in favor of Alaska of over $408,000,000, which has gone into the channels of trade in this country, enriching many of our citizens and adding to the prosperity and wealth of the Pacific Coast states, even at times saving that section from bankruptcy. . . .[14]

The bill provided for a Senate of eight members and a House of sixteen members. The legislature had no authority to create any territorial or municipal indebtedness or to amend laws concerning the sale or manufacture of game or fish.

The Senate Committee on Territories took the bill at once and began holding hearings. One major difference in the versions favored by the two houses was the Senate's preference for a unicameral legislature, dispensing with the Senate and having only a House of Representatives of sixteen members.

After House passage the Alaska press showered the delegate with praise. Even his historic critic, the Juneau Chamber of Commerce, passed a resolution commending him on his speech and on his victory.[15]

In his hometown of Fairbanks, his old friend, Bill McPhee, proprietor of the Washington Saloon, rigged up an illuminated oil portrait of Wickersham and hung it outside his place of business. The portrait was encircled with a frame of sixteen-candlepower electric light bulbs. When darkness fell, the picture blazed forth in all its splendor to celebrate "Our Jim's getting the home rule passed in the House."[16]

The Skagway *Alaskan* hailed the bill's passage as "the beginning of the end of a regime of exploitation unparalleled in modern days except perhaps in the government of the Belgian Congo. . . ."

> For the past twenty years, each administration has paled its predecessor in brazen schemes of concerted corruption. Each

school of political sharks that has preyed upon the district has been more ravenous for graft than the preceding sharks.

Wickersham entered the struggle for the American rights of Alaskans at the darkest hour. Speaker Cannon had complete control of the House; the doors of the Senate were as the gates of hell for popular legislation and a president dominated by predatory wealth was in the White House. . .But Wickersham was just the right man in just the right place.

He tore away the mask that concealed the shriveled littleness of a willing president and laid bare a conspiracy that startled the nation and all so circumstantially and irrefutably as to draw to his aid Senators Borah and LaFollette. . . .

The people of Alaska have watched the career of their delegate with intense interest and sympathy during the long, trying years he has borne their banner of forlorn hope; they have burned with indignation at the insults and villifications that have been heaped upon him by the collar-bearers of the Alaska syndicate machine. They have glowed with pleasure at the deft ease with which their champion has nailed the falsehoods of the cabal, refuted the arguments of its attorneys and answered the misstatements of its reporter-governor and press bureau. . . .[17]

During the testimony before the Senate committee, Wickersham's old adversary, Senator Nelson, took a verbal swing at the delegate, depicting him as the real stumbling block in the path of Alaska's progress and vowing that nothing would ever be accomplished for the territory as long as Wickersham represented it in Congress. He said further:

The attitude of the delegate, throughout his career in Congress, has been that he must receive all the praise for securing legislation for the territory. If his vanity in this respect is not satisfied, then he condemns me, Governor Clark, and everyone else interested in the territory's welfare, to the people of Alaska.[18]

Senator Nelson tried to keep the bill buried in committee until after the delegate election in Alaska, but Chairman William Alden Smith, Republican of Michigan, refused to play petty politics with a piece of legislation so important to the territory. Finding an opening on the Senate calendar on July 24, Smith called up the bill and then sent out a page for Nelson.

When Nelson arrived, Smith said: "I sent for you, senator, because I have called the Alaska bill up and I know you will want to help put it through." Nelson replied: "I am sorry you called it up. I shan't do anything to help," and he did not! Wickersham figured that Nelson had promised Governor Clark that no action would be taken on the bill at that session of Congress.[19]

Several amendments were offered, and one which did not pass was moving the capital either to Fairbanks or Valdez. When the bill finally passed the Senate on July 24, there were so many amendments that it had to go to a conference for final drafting.

When the time approached for Wickersham to announce whether or not he would run for reelection, he found himself in the customary quandary on whether he should quit the poor-paying political job and devote himself to becoming financially secure. His vacillation this time was more prolonged than before. Debbie wanted him to quit politics as she hated to see him suffer such continuous mental and physical misery. She had opposed his running in the two previous races. The continuous criticism of the Seattle and Alaska press depressed him, and his ostracism by the regular Republican organization in the territory, under the dictatorship of Shackleford, was a frustrating situation.

His friends began writing him in January begging him to make up his mind. One such friend was Bill Gilmore, mayor of Nome, who had been Wickersham's campaign manager on the Seward Peninsula two years previous. Their mutual friends were urging Gilmore to run if the delegate chose to retire. Gilmore was a strong vote-getter having received 90 percent of the total vote in the mayoralty race. On January 13, Wickersham wrote a friend in Nome that he would gladly support Gilmore were he to become a candidate.[20]

Gilmore delayed making any commitment, writing and telegraphing Wickersham to know his plans, but the latter decided on a "wait and see" attitude and did not respond to Gilmore's queries.

On March 9 Wickersham wrote Dr. Frank Boyle and Elmer Ritchie in Valdez and Dr. Will Chase in Cordova, and others, that in case the Republicans should endorse Taft and his Alaskan policies at their convention in Cordova, he did not want the nomination even if it was offered to him. In that case, he suggested that his friends might consider bolting the convention and making their own nominations in a separate meeting.

Two weeks later he wrote in his diary: "I am longing for March 4, 1913, when I can go home and settle down to developing my mining property and begin the accumulation of a small fortune for old age and Darrell."

In the primaries for the selection of delegates to the territorial convention, the Republican party bosses promulgated a ruling that only those who had voted for the "regular" Republican candidate for delegate in 1910 would be eligible to vote in the present party primaries; this automatically ruled out those who had voted for Wickersham. Thus, in each major community, two separate primaries were held, one being held for Wickersham supporters.

The Shackleford steamroller was in complete control of the territorial meeting in Cordova, achieving near unanimity on all votes. William Gilmore was nominated for delegate; Charlie Herron, Nome miner, was elected chairman of the central committee; Shackleford and Jafet Lindeberg were elected delegates to the national convention and were committed to vote for Taft as president.

Deploring the tactics of the Shackleford machine, Editor Ritchie of the Valdez *Miner* said that Shackleford, corporation lawyer who couldn't be elected dogcatcher in his hometown of Juneau, controlled the convention by use of "wads of vest-pocket proxies collected from star chamber caucuses, or forged, having turned over control to three or four persons and one man pressed the button."[21]

Queried by the *Daily Industrial Worker* of Nome regarding his reaction to the convention's nominations, Wickersham telegraphed: "Same old trap with different bait. Water cannot rise higher than source, which, in this case is Guggenheim, Northern Commercial Company and Pioneer Mining Company. I am not in harmony with the efforts of Shackleford and Herron to deliver Alaska to their employers and do not endorse Taft's policy of appointive military legislation for Alaska."[22]

These harsh words came as a shock to Gilmore and his supporters, most of whom had been Wickites for years. Having given him his blessing in January, why did the delegate condemn him so mercilessly? Wickersham and Gilmore had been personal friends for years when both were residents of Tacoma.

The Cordova *Alaskan* lamented that Wickersham was unwilling to contribute to that party harmony for which his followers had longed for so many years. He had repeatedly indicated his desire to retire from politics, and when his opponents went so far as to name one of his followers as his successor, the Wickites had it within their grasp to gracefully become part of a harmonious Republican party. But, no,

Wickersham must completely dominate politics of all Alaska, municipal as well as territorial.[23]

A week after Gilmore's nomination, Wickersham wired Ritchie that he had decided to be a candidate for reelection. Shortly thereafter he wired his friends urging them to support Dan Sutherland as his successor in the delegateship. They began to wonder what kind of a game he was playing. Was it the old politician's trick of flushing out his possible rivals before committing himself? But on May 7 Wickersham received a telegram from Sutherland stating that he could not make the race as he did not have the necessary finances; furthermore, the people wanted Wickersham and his reelection was a cinch.[24]

Wickersham's supporters decided to call a convention of their own and nominate him for delegate, leaving it up to him then to accept or reject the nomination. Emery Valentine as chairman and Ritchie as secretary issued a call for an "independent" Republican convention May 29 in Valdez. Caucuses were held in various towns equally as "starchamber" in character as those of the "regular" or "stand-pat" Republicans.

Captain George Baldwin, Alaskan miner and riverboat skipper since 1894, served as convention chairman. In his keynote address, he spoke of the many difficulties which the delegate had to contend with and which would have driven an ordinary man to despair:

> But we are represented by no ordinary man. Patiently where he could be patient, vehemently where necessary, but always vigorously and forcefully he has fought the battles of the pioneers of Alaska in Washington almost solitarily and alone.

Wickersham received the unanimous endorsement to run for reelection, and Valentine was nominated as national committeeman. Delegates to the national convention were instructed to support Teddy Roosevelt for president.[25]

It was Decoration (Memorial) Day and Wickersham was home enjoying a holiday from the office when he received the telegram informing him of his nomination. Flushed with a warm glow of satisfaction, the old warrior readily assented to carrying the banner of the people against big business for the third time. He worried that his delegation might not be seated at the national convention and knew it would be possible only if Roosevelt won the nomination for president.

He received more good news from his business agent, Henry Ray, who wired that his Eva Creek property had produced a spring clean-up worth approximately $16,000; that meant he would be receiving several checks during the summer, which would help with his campaign expenses.

The Democrats held their usual zestful gathering, which required the summons of the United States marshal and two deputies to prevent rioting. Dual sets of delegates arrived from the different sections of the territory posing difficult decisions for the credentials committee. It was basically a sectional contest between Tanana Valley and the Juneau-Seattle faction in the coastal area. Control of patronage was of paramount concern since a national Democratic administration appeared a possibility. The battle developed over whether proxies or personal attendance was to be counted.

The press hailed Harry Bishop, pioneer Juneau mining engineer, as the hero of the fracas when he saved Chairman Zina Cheney from being struck with a chair by William O'Connor of Cordova. The galleries howled and hooted as they approved or disapproved of what was happening on the floor. Relative peace was restored when the two groups met separately, one group nominating Martin Harrais, a pioneer Fairbanks miner, as a candidate for delegate, and the other nominating Robert Jennings, a Juneau attorney. Both groups charged the other with having manufactured forged proxies.

The Socialists held a convention in Fairbanks at which Ketchikan attorney Kazis Krauczunas was nominated for delegate. National organizers John C. Chase and Mrs. Lena Morrow Lewis attended the meeting and promised to campaign through the territory for the nominee.

In Washington Wickersham's attention shifted temporarily from the delegate race when word arrived telling of the volcanic eruption of Mt. Katmai burying six villages — Cold Bay, Katmai, Kanatuk, Douglas, Savoonsky and Kamgamute—under twenty feet of ash and that at least one half of their 430 inhabitants had perished. He rushed through legislation providing for a $50,000 appropriation for relief of the hundreds of homeless villagers.

Once aid was assured to the disaster victims, Wickersham attended the Republican convention in Chicago to plead for the seating of his delegates. Their credentials were thrown out on a technicality - they had not been filed early enough; no attention was given to the merits of their case.

Shackleford and Hoggatt were accorded seats as the official delegates from the territory. Lindeberg had been elected just as a blind as he had no intention of attending and his proxy was given to Hoggatt, who could attend from his home in Indiana. To have elected Hoggatt in the first place "would have been more than the subservient conventioneers would stand."[27]

Wickersham attended the big rally at which both Senator Borah and Roosevelt spoke. The latter gave notice that if he and his supporters were not given control of the convention, they would bolt and hold their own convention.

The conservatives, by electing Elihu Root temporary chairman, obtained control of the convention machinery and awarded almost every contested seat to a Taft man. That meant Shackleford and Hoggatt were recognized over Wickersham and O.P. Hubbard. Roosevelt instructed his followers to walk out and Taft was easily renominated.

The Roosevelt supporters, including Wickersham, met in Orchestra Hall, where Governor Hiram Johnson of California nominated Roosevelt for the presidency. About fifteen thousand cheering enthusiasts greeted the nominee as he made his acceptance speech. The Republican party was rent in twain.[28]

The Democrats met a week later in Baltimore. The two leading candidates for the presidency were Woodrow Wilson, governor of New Jersey, and Champ Clark of Missouri, Speaker of the House of Representatives. When the convention opened, Clark had twice as many delegates pledged to him as had Wilson, although he did not have the necessary 726 votes needed to secure the nomination.

The convention remained deadlocked between these two candidates for five days; finally on the forty-sixth ballot, Wilson won the nomination. Throughout the nerve-racking days and nights of voting, Wilson firmly refused to let his managers make any political deals or promise any political offices in order to get the nomination.

Wickersham returned to Washington to make himself available to the conferees as they worked on a final version of the legislature bill.

He knew he would be criticized for not going to Alaska to campaign, but he felt it would be a brighter feather in his cap eventually if he were successful in getting a satisfactory bill passed. Hence, he decided to campaign by telegram and postcard.

On June 26 he received word from Valdez that rumors were being circulated that he had withdrawn from the race, whereupon he telegraphed: HAVE NOT WITHDRAWN. SHALL NOT WITHDRAW. WILL BE CANDIDATE UNTIL LAST BALLOT CAST AUGUST 13.[29]

He sent out 6,000 postcards with the following message:

My dear Sir: The people of Alaska again nominated me for delegate to Congress, at Valdez on May 29. However, the home rule bill and other important Alaskan legislation now pending in Congress will keep me from making an early or an extended speaking trip through the territory. As soon as the interests of Alaska will permit it, I will come, via Ketchikan, Juneau and Skagway, to Seward, Cordova and Valdez, and thence go via Chitina and Copper Center, overland to Fairbanks.

If there is time before the election on August 13, my trip will extend to Ruby, Iditarod and Nome, but while I remain here attending to your interests, I appeal to those Alaskans who favor home rule and progressive legislation for Alaska to give me their active support, promising in return to faithfully continue my efforts for Alaska in line with the platform pledges adopted by the Valdez convention which nominated me. Very truly yours, JAMES WICKERSHAM, delegate from Alaska.[30]

He also sent copies of bills he had introduced and other documents which would help convince them that their delegate was hard at work on their behalf.

He slipped away to Chicago the weekend that Roosevelt's new Progressive Party met in convention and was accorded an official badge. It was an inspiring experience for the delegate to see his political idol accorded such heartfelt recognition. With the fervor of an old-fashioned revival meeting, the conventioneers paraded around the hall singing "Onward, Christian Soldiers" and other stirring melodies.

"We stand at Armageddon, and we battle for the Lord!" shouted Roosevelt to enraptured followers. Another remark, "I am feeling like a bull moose" developed into the party label, alongside the Republican elephant and the Democratic donkey. Hiram Johnson, former governor of California, was the new party's candidate for vice president.

As soon as Wickersham arrived at the convention, he contacted Gifford Pinchot and Senator Poindexter and got their assurance that the party platform would include a plank endorsing home rule for Alaska and the appointment of bona fide residents to federal jobs in the territory.

The plank, as drafted by Wickersham, read: "We promise the people of the territory of Alaska the same measure of local self-government that was given to other American territories, and that federal officials appointed there shall be qualified by previous bona fide residence in the territory."[31]

Chapter 30

1912 Delegate Race

> *The nation went Democratic and the Territory went Wicker-sham. That is the story in a nutshell. . . .*
>
> *It is no secret that the Wickites will always be able to carry Alaska and perpetuate Wickershamism here, so long as the other politicians are fighting among themselves and for politi-cal gain.*
>
> *All parties help the Wickites - when the grafters of any party obtain control of that party and seek to use it for their own profit, the other and honest men of that party put in with the Wickites. . . .* (*Fairbanks* News-Miner, *Nov. 6, 1912*)

Five candidates ran for delegate to Congress in 1912—a "regular" Republican, a "Bull Moose" progressive Republican, two Democrats, and a Socialist. All were seasoned, longtime Alaskan residents.

William Addison Gilmore, the "regular" Republican had enjoyed a lucrative law practice in Nome since 1900. Robert William Jennings, one of the Democrats, had been practicing law in the southeastern region since 1898. His Democratic colleague, Martin Luther Harrais, came north in the Klondike stampede and later moved to the Tanana Valley district as a prospector and miner. Kazis Kay Krauczunas, the Socialist, came to Ketchikan in 1906 as head of the United States Immi-gration Service for Alaska, but he too, turned to the practice of law in that community.

All five candidates had similar platforms. They all declared for home rule with a territorial legislature; demanded the opening of the coal fields; favored construction of railroads by the federal government;

favored conservation against waste but not against development; asked for the conservation of the fish supply and a direct tax on the fisheries; demanded doing away with the hatchery rebate; asked for liberal appropriations for roads, including construction of an automobile road from Fairbanks to tidewater.[1]

Gilmore tried to woo Wickites to his support by stressing that never would he have been a candidate had Wickersham indicated a desire to run for reelection. Gilmore called himself a compromise candidate in the interests of party harmony.

"Judge Wickersham never had a better, more earnest and more zealous advocate of his cause than I have been," Gilmore declared. "I supported him in both of his campaigns and managed his campaign in Nome and the Seward Peninsula two years ago. I spent over a thousand dollars out of my own pocket without hope of reward or expectation of reward from him and I made six speeches for him," Gilmore continued. "I introduced him to the Nome public and urged them to support him; his friends in Nome were my friends," he concluded.

Gilmore's sincerity won many converts, including Elmer Ritchie, Valdez editor. This group circulated a petition requesting Wickersham to withdraw in Gilmore's favor. Ritchie was also disenchanted with the delegate when he showed up at the Bull Moose convention as a supporter of Roosevelt, the man who had saddled Pinchotism on Alaska.

Ritchie excoriated the delegate in long, verbose editorials almost daily throughout the campaign. In an effort to dissuade anyone in Valdez from voting for him, Ritchie argued that Wickersham was trying to take the bread and butter from the mouths of the residents of Valdez by favoring the removal of the offices of the court, road commission and telegraph communication from Valdez to Cordova. As proof of this dastardly intention, he pointed to the delegate's bill appropriating $100,000 for a federal building in Cordova; also, he had been seen in close conversation with Steve Birch and George Baldwin aboard a steamer bound for Cordova.

The worst accusation to be hurled at Gilmore was that he was a Taft-Guggenheim candidate and affiliated with the Hoggatt-Shackleford-Lindeberg crowd, thus being pro-corporation by association. In reply Gilmore asked how he could be a Guggenheim man when for ten years he had been defending workingmen against corporations who were prosecuting them. Furthermore, if he were the candidate of the corporate interests, why did the miners in Nome reelect him as mayor with an overwhelming vote? He vowed that he had not given a single pledge to anyone and wouldn't even know Shackleford if he came into the same room.

Gilmore attacked Wickersham for his quarrelsomeness, which had become so flagrant that he had rendered himself worthless to the territory. "You can't get anything by calling the congressmen names," Gilmore declared. "If you do, one half of them won't speak to you and the other half won't for fear that they will be seen talking to him."

As for corporations investing in Alaska, he said he hoped and prayed that the capitalists would bring a hundred billion dollars to Alaska to build railroads, factories, and to develop mines. He did not approve of their involving themselves in the territory's politics, however.[3]

Governor and Mrs. Clark made their biennial tour of the territory during the campaign, just as they had two years before. The governor campaigned vigorously for Gilmore, but his opposition to an elected legislature lost him his former popularity among the voters. The usual welcoming committees were conspicuous by their absence; at some towns he was not only ignored but was met with open hostility. Fairbanksans were angry with him for refusing to approve the construction of a detention hospital there.

Jennings' campaign theme was a blend of "it's time for a change" and "Alaskans should elect a Democrat because the new national administration is going to be Democratic." In support of choosing a Democrat who would be privy to the inner party councils of the national administration, he suggested that "Gilmore would be an outcast; Wickersham would be unaffiliated and unattached; Krauczunas would be out of his element."[4]

Party lines became increasingly blurred as the campaign progressed; Wickersham became notably the target of attack by the combined Republican-Democratic forces. There was nothing new about this, however, as the conservative elements in the two parties had worked hand in glove with one another ever since Wickersham entered the political arena as that was their only hope of defeating him.

Harrais received strong support from the *Alaska Citizen* in Fairbanks on the grounds that it would show "those dirty Juneau-Seattle politicians that they could not dictate to the citizens of the Tanana." Harrais was portrayed as an honest and honorable pioneer who deserved the votes of his fellow Alaskans. He stood for everything the territory needed and was under no obligation to any trust or corporation.

Wickersham was portrayed as a "dictator" perched high on a pedestal and looking down upon the people of Alaska, convinced that he knew what was best for them better than they did themselves.

Discounting the delegate's rivals as unworthy of consideration at the polls, the Wickite ads read: "Gilmore owes his candidacy to the hated Shackleford-Guggenheim forces; Jennings and Harrais obtained their nominations by means of perjured affidavits and forged proxies, according to their own party reports; Krauczunas has no qualifications and has been repudiated by his party both in Valdez and Juneau.[5]

The Skagway *Alaskan* prophesied early in the campaign that Wickersham would get support from the same groups which had elected him in the past—"the common people, the miners, the fishermen, the loggers and the workers everywhere. He gets no support from the officeholders, the grafters and the politicians."[6]

Wickersham won 40.5 percent of the total vote. The vote totals, as certified by the canvassing board, were as follows: Wickersham, 3,335; Gilmore, 1,726; Krauczunas, 1,688; Jennings, 1,174; Harrais, 281; scattering, 16, making a total of 8,220.

Editor Thompson of the *News-Miner* offered a characteristically cogent analysis of the returns:

> The patent fact demonstrated by the election in Alaska is that Alaskans are entirely dissatisfied with the way Alaska's affairs are being handled by the government, and they evince their dissatisfaction by returning to Washington the Alaskan who is most distasteful to the present administration.
>
> That Alaskans should return defi for defi, insult for insult and abuse for abuse is characteristic of a people who have always been and always will be able to look every damn man in the face and tell him to go to.[7]

When the Republicans suffered defeat nationally, Thompson said that Wickersham's victory fitted into the picture perfectly. Noting that when conditions become unbearable, the people blame the men who have the reins of government in their hands, it was to be expected that Wickersham, as one of the administration's severest critics, would be selected by Alaskans as their spokesman in Washington. He continued:

> In the territory the Republicans have mismanaged things so badly that almost all of its resources are tied up. As a protest Alaskans send a man to Congress who works to embarrass the government in every way, just as the people of Alaska wish him to do - the effort ends there, however, for he also works with the conservationists to keep our resources tied up. . . .

He has quite a number of followers in Alaska who will not believe their own eyes or ears when the delegate goes wrong, and
they are well organized. Being the only body of politicians in
Alaska who are at all well organized, they can carry Alaska. . . .[8]

Wickersham made the national headlines as the first "Bull Mooser" to
win in a statewide election. . .To all intents and purposes he had been
reelected as a Roosevelt Republican." The New York *Times* heralded his
victory with this heading: *Bull Moose Elects Alaska Delegate.*[9]

With Wickersham reelected, the conferees on the Alaska bill had no
further reason to stall their confabulation, so they met to iron out the
differences between the House and Senate versions. Wickersham was
invited to attend and give his views; he objected to a unicameral legislature. Senator Nelson stood strong for a single house, but the majority
voted for a two-house assembly. With that basic difference resolved, the
bill went to the president for his signature.

Wickersham was aboard the Northern Pacific traveling through
Wyoming when he received word at Huntley Junction that President
Taft had chosen his (Wickersham's) fifty-fifth birthday on which to sign
the elected legislature bill—the best birthday present he had ever
received!

Wickersham knew he would be criticized for the numerous limitations
under which the legislature would have to function, but he was
convinced it was the best he could get, in view of the strong opposition
from corporate interests, which feared excessive taxation by a local
legislature. Wickersham's bill was carefully drawn to quiet their
concern. Expenditures were to be limited to current income; territorial
taxes were limited to one percent of the assessed valuation of property,
and municipal taxes to two percent. Nonresidents were to be taxed no
higher than residents; county organization was prohibited, and indebtedness was carefully hedged about to preclude extravagance.

Other limitations recalled earlier events in the territory's history: no
territorial funds were to be expended on religious education, which
harked back to the days of the Jackson-Brady hierarchy; no stock could
be purchased in private corporations in recollection of the
Reynolds-Brady Development Company. No gambling or liquor laws
were to be passed except by Congress, in order to keep those interests
from controlling the local lawmakers; the delegate's enemies had
charged that he owed his election to these interests.

The nonresident cannery interests had watched the progress of the bill
carefully and had gotten a clause inserted during the debate on the

House floor forbidding the legislature to legislate on game and fish. But in the conference committee, the House conferees put through a clause which neutralized the above prohibition which read: "Provided that this provision shall not operate to prevent the legislature from imposing other and additional taxes or licenses," thus giving the legislature the right to tax the fisheries, just what they had tried to avoid.

Though jubilant over the bill's passage, Wickersham felt that his long fight against Taft and his big business allies had destroyed his political future—he would never be forgiven for coming out victorious over their best efforts.[10]

Chapter 31

Lobbies For Government Railroad

> *I take this opportunity of expressing to you my appreciation for the great work which you have performed since you have represented this territory in Congress and particularly the masterful way in which you handled yourself during the last session. . .which resulted in the U.S. government pledging itself to spend $35,000,000 in the building of a railroad across Alaska. . .You have placed your name in the Alaska Hall of Fame forever. . . . (Letter to Wickersham from James J. Godfrey, Mother Lode, Copper Mines Co., Kennecott, Alaska, May 8,1914)*

Now that the Alaskans were allowed to elect their own lawmakers, the main topic of conversation was how to choose them. They would have until November to make their selection as the legislative bill changed Alaska's election day from August to November, for the convenience of the miners and fishermen who would have completed their summer's work and the winter trails would be in good condition for travel.

Wickersham had two recommendations to make: choose only those who were supporters of home rule while the legislation was pending in Congress as otherwise they would not be sincere in wanting to see it work for the people's benefit. Secondly, choose year-round residents - home-builders who love Alaska enough to live there and raise their families. One of the provisions of the bill required a two-year residence for a legislator; that eliminated the carpetbagger aspirant.[1]

The delegate promised he would take no part in either the selection or in any individual's campaign for election. He would leave it up to the people to use good common sense in making their choices.

The unfriendly Alaska press warned against letting the Wickite machine's one-man rule of Alaska encompass the new legislature and tended to be editorially supportive of corporate-oriented candidates. The primary goal of the corporate interests was a Senate majority. In the eight-member house only four senators were required as a four-to-four tie vote would kill an undesirable piece of legislation.

The Alaska syndicate came out the winner in Alaska's first Senate, which included: two corporation attorneys, a part-owner in a Guggenheim mining operation, and the local manager of a mine owned by another absentee corporation. In addition, Wickersham's former law partner, Henry Roden, won a seat and he had become sympathetic to the Guggenheim interests through serving as their legal counsel on several occasions while Wickersham was in Washington. Dan Sutherland of Ruby was the only dependable Wickite in the lot.

The Wickershams left for Washington right after the election. Debbie had been ailing and dreaded the trip over the Valdez trail. A domestic episode along the trail made the headlines of the Fairbanks papers. While crossing the Tanana River at Little Delta in a rowboat, the delegate pulled out a handkerchief from his pocket and in so doing, flipped a roll of some two hundred dollars in paper bills into the fast-flowing river. Irked by such carelessness, Mrs. Wickersham suggested that he hand over the rest of the money roll to her for safekeeping.

All went well with this arrangement until the last day when they stopped overnight at Tonsina Jake's place at Lower Tonsina. The room assigned to the Wickershams was warm and stuffy, so Mrs. Wickersham decided an open window would bring them relief. There was no catch to keep the window open, so she propped it open with her purse.

The next morning when the call came to move on, they tumbled out of bed, dressed, and, after a hurried breakfast, proceeded on their way, leaving the purse containing drafts, travelers checks, currency, and gold still on the window sill. Jake found the purse soon after their departure and came running after the stage and handed it to the delegate. Silence reigned between husband and wife as the former retrieved the valuables and placed them in his pocket.[2]

By the time they reached Seattle, Debbie was worn out. They spent a week in the Puget Sound area, during which the delegate packed his Tacoma library for shipment to Washington. His mother accompanied them to the nation's capital and remained there until the following

February, when Wickersham was to go to Juneau to address the legislature. Debbie remained in Washington while Wickersham and his mother visited the haunts of their early youth en route to the West Coast.

They first visited Sandoval, a coal-mining community in southern Illinois where the Alexander Wickershams once lived; there they renewed old friendships. Then they rented a horse-drawn carriage to go to Patoka. On the way they passed their old home where his mother came as a nineteen-year-old bride and where James was born. Four large silver-leaf maple trees were still standing, and his mother recalled that James had transplanted them fifty years ago, bringing them from Grandpa McHaney's homestead.

They drove through Fairman, which looked old and gray. With the discovery of oil the beauty of the farming countryside disappeared. Passing along the East Fork River, where James used to go fishing, was also disappointing as it had been stripped of its heavy forest, which had lined the riverbank when he helped his father in their sawmill operation.

Patoka had grown to twice the size it was when the Wickershams lived there, and now there were fine concrete sidewalks and many new buildings. But again they were saddened to see that all the trees were gone from streams and valleys. They visited Deer Creek, James's old swimming hole, and they looked up his grade school teacher, Jennie Wheeler. They also visited Aunt Becky Carter and Cousin Ben Wickersham, a mechanic and the father of five children. After a week's reminiscing on the olden days, they boarded the train for Seattle and Buckley.

The legislature had convened the day before the delegate's arrival in Juneau, and its opening session was made notable by two speeches delivered before a joint session of the two houses; one by Representative Charles Ingersoll, Ketchikan attorney and hotelman, and the other by Governor Clark. Both spoke disparagingly of the scope of the virgin lawmaking assembly.

Ingersoll called the enabling act a paradox of hopeless inconsistencies:

> Resplendent in promises, we find from one end to the other an inocuous dearth of hoped for privileges. Looking for the substance, we find the shadow. Asking for bread, we get a stone. In the words of the immortal bard, it may best be characterized as "a madness most discreet, a choking gall and a sickening sweet."

Why the reluctance of Congress to extend to us those rights and privileges that long established precedent has made our due? What in the world are we here for?[3]

Governor Clark also lamented that it was "unfortunate" that "a rather large scope of authority" had not been granted to the legislators. He urged that they give early attention to the matter of taxes and suggested that two likely sources would be the canned salmon industry and foreign corporations doing business in the territory. "The salmon cannery business does not now bear its full share of taxation," the governor said.

When Wickersham's friends told him about the two demeaning speeches, he was disappointed as he felt sure it was "as good a bill as the people of any territory have had and gave Alaska home rule without the expenditure of a nickel."[4]

He concluded that powerful influences were at work to demoralize these first legislators in order to nullify the potential of the lawmaking body. This was their means of continuing their opposition to home rule and of embarrasing Wickersham. He decided that he would not mince words in his own speech in pointing an accusing finger at the perpetrators of these negative forces. In defending the legislative limitations, he said, in part:

Ordinarily, a legislator who has succeeded in enacting an important law should treat criticism of the law with patience and silence waiting until time and fair trial shall vindicate his judgment or show that he erred therein. When, however, before any time or experience has demonstrated that the enactment is either good or bad, the representatives chosen to act under the law put forward a keynote speaker to denounce the act with unmeasured and hostile criticism, a different situation is presented.

When the effect of that harsh and hostile criticism tends to prevent the people from having relief from burdens which have long oppressed them, and comes with official weight and dignity, it must be fair and well sustained, else the critic is himself open to inquiry touching his motive and purpose.

When the gentleman from Ketchikan, a lawyer of wide repute and various attainments. . .in forceful phrase, condemned the act of Congress creating the legislative body. . .(one must wonder at his motive). . . .

At this point, the delegate was interrupted by Senator Bruner, the corporation attorney from Nome, who was presiding. Bruner called him to order and said the legislators had not invited him to lecture them or to hear one of their members criticized so severely. Considerable excitement ensued with half of the members trying to get the floor at the same time; some wanted the delegate to terminate his remarks while others wanted him to be allowed to continue uninterrupted.

Bruner called for a vote of the Senate to determine whether or not to allow Wickersham to proceed with his speech; the vote was four to four, whereupon Bruner arose from his chair and stalked out of the hall, muttering under his breath. He was joined by Senators Freeding, his colleague from Nome, a Swedish immigrant who struck it rich on the famous Anvil number 4, and Herman Tripp, superintendent of the Sumdum gold mine near Juneau, and Representative William Stubbins of Douglas.

When quiet settled over the gathering, Wickersham continued his remarks, telling how Ingersoll had supported him and his efforts to get an elected legislature, and wondering why he had such a radical change of mind:

> Why do gentlemen now neglect their duty to enact laws needed in the development of the territory and expend their energies in seeking how not to do it? Is it because the Alaska Fish Trust is afraid that some legislation may be enacted to protect the fishermen and fisheries of Alaska from long continued, unlimited and wicked exploitation?[6]

Editor John Frame of *The Commoner* was a spectator in the hall when the delegate was chastised by Senator Bruner, and he related a human interest detail of what happened after Bruner exited:

> Getting out in the open air, Bruner's wrath blazed even more fiercely. In a short time a fire alarm was turned in and a large number of those in attendance at the Wickersham meeting rushed out and the meeting was virtually broken up.
>
> The fire was in one of the outhouses near Governor Clark's residence. Bruner formerly lived in Frisco and there are a number of people in Valdez who knew him there. He has a record of doing things.[7]

Later that evening at a businessmen's smoker at the Elks Hall, Wickersham heard his former law partner Roden boast of being an attorney and agent for the Guggenheims and say that he considered them a good influence in the territory. Wickersham was shocked to hear him express such allegiance and considered his action a betrayal of the people and a declaration of loyalty to big business. It left the Senate in no doubtful position - Bruner, Roden, Millard, Ray, and Tripp were with the interests. No progressive legislation could be passed; it was the same old trick of buying the Senate and thus blocking all legislation in aid of the people.[8]

Back in Washington after his session with the Alaska legislators, Wickersham found his counsel being sought by the new Democratic administration in patronage matters. The new secretary of interior, Franklin K. Lane, was an old friend from his Tacoma days. Lane had been part owner and managing editor of the Tacoma *Daily News*.

The delegate was optimistic about seeing some progress for his railroad bill. When he had seen that it would not come to a vote in the previous session, he had added a clause to his legislative bill, providing for the creation of a railroad commission to study possible routes for a government-built railroad from the coast into the interior. As a result a commission was appointed by the president and the members visited Alaska that fall.

Lane was not an extreme conservationist. He wanted to see Alaska unlocked and its resources developed and believed the key would be the government's building a railroad in the territory. "The whole problem of civilization, as I view it, is to make nature serve us instead of allowing nature to run us," Lane observed. "Caesar made wagon roads, we build railroads," he added.[10]

Wickersham was invited to Lane's home one evening to discuss Alaskan affairs. The delegate got the impression that Lane had been forewarned that he would have difficulty working with him; that he was "a sort of bull in the political and legislative china shop and must be handled with care."[11]

A bitter fight was being waged between Major Strong and Thomas Riggs for the Alaska governorship. Wickersham told both Secretary Lane and Attorney General McReynolds that he favored Strong. He told them that Alaskans considered Riggs a rank outsider and a puppet of the big interests. Wickersham considered him "a miniature Hoggatt."

The day the White House announced the appointment of Strong, the Wickershams entertained the Strongs and Dr. S. Hall Young at dinner at the Driscoll Hotel, where they had taken a suite for the winter.

Later the Alaskans in Washington hosted a dinner at the National Press Club honoring editors Ira E. Bennett and Thomas F. Logan of the

Washington *Post*, in recognition of their support of Alaskan legislation; Wickersham served as toastmaster. Correspondents of all the principal papers in the country were in attendance.[12]

Wickersham reintroduced his railroad bill on April 7, the first day of a special session of the Sixty-third Congress, and Senator George Chamberlain, Democrat of Oregon, introduced a similar one in the Senate.

Wickersham's conversion to government ownership of public utilities did not come easily to him. His pioneer spirit of independence urged him in the opposite direction, in fact. It was only when he became convinced that big business interests were out to take advantage of their weaker competition did he change. That was the position he took as Tacoma's city attorney when he fought the private utilities who had negotiated a corrupt deal with the city.

Even as late as January, 1912, just two years before making his historic railroad speech on the floor of the House, he wrote a friend in Valdez that he could not agree with his recommendation that the federal government should take over both the ownership and operation of Alaska's coal mines and railroads. To him that was a socialistic tenet and one that he abhorred. He wrote that he could not agree "that a government official in a big, soft chair, in an elegant business office in Washington, was more competent to manage a business in Alaska than an Alaskan citizen."

But when he became aware of how the monopolistic power of the Guggenheims' interlocking corporations could put small businessmen out of business and raise the cost of living of individual Alaskans, he felt compelled to accept government ownership as the only alternative powerful enough to remedy the evils of private greed.

In his railroad speech he cited numerous instances of how the White Pass and Yukon Railroad, together with the Alaska Steamship Company, the Pacific Steamship Company, the Northern Navigation Company, and Northern Commercial Company, through contract agreements, in violation of the Sherman Anti-trust Law, forced the people of the interior to pay enormously excessive freight rates and reduced the small businessman to profitless competition with the Northern Commercial stores which lined the Yukon River.

Wickersham's sponsorship of a railroad into the interior raised his stock with his hometown press as Fairbanks had slipped into the economic doldrums; the placer claims were mined out and the people were leaving. Unless a railroad was built connecting interior Alaska with the coastal areas, Fairbanks' future looked bleak, and no one was quicker to recognize it than the newspaper editors who were operating on a shoestring and never knew when they might be putting out their final edition.

As committee hearings began on the railroad bill, opposition forces began showing up. Chief among them were representatives of private railroad ventures already invested in the territory. Joining them were the steamship companies and other Guggenheim subsidiaries. This combination brought about a surprise move by the Alaska Senate. Seven of the eight senators, Sutherland being the lone exception, signed a letter of protest addressed to the secretary of interior, denouncing the principle of government competition with private enterprise and stating that they spoke for the majority of Alaskans. In addition, four of the senators traveled to Washington to testify against the bill.[13]

Though the letter of protest was dated April, 1913, it took until the following February to become general knowledge in the territory. Reaction by Alaskans was immediate and violent. Tempers flared particularly in Cordova where it was a known fact that the Guggenheims had no intention of extending their railroad to the interior, so a government railroad appeared to be the most likely alternative. Cordova residents hoped the federal government would buy the C.R. & N. and extend it from Chitina to Fairbanks and perhaps beyond.

George Dooley, proprietor of the Rainier Grand Hotel, strung a rope across the street in front of his hotel and soon seven effigies were "hanged." They were labeled "traitors to Alaska," and each carried the name of one of the senators who had signed the letter.[14]

Editor Thompson of the *News-Miner* castigated the senators in an editorial entitled "Kill the Senate!" in these words:

> Under the leadership of Roden and Ray, the Senate treacherously and secretly attempted to sell and deliver Alaska to the syndicate and the Guggs. . . .
>
> No parallel case is known in American history. It remained for the senators chosen by sourdough Alaskans to perpetrate the greatest territorial crime in history. . . .
>
> Steps should be taken to impeach every damned traitor of the bunch, or compel them to resign. No square Alaskan will ever feel safe so long as such traitors and liars constitute our governing body. . .Hanging is too good for such traitors. They should be treated like mad dogs in the streets. Human snakes such as

they are a living menace to freedom and safety of property. . . .[15]

Wickersham took the senators to task in a speech on the floor of the United States House in which he pointed out that though Ray had signed himself as president of the territorial Senate and the other six had signed as senators, the document did not represent an official act of the legislature; they had connived privately to subvert the delegate's efforts.

Wickersham was cheered by President Wilson's reference to Alaska in his message to Congress as it represented a complete reversal of Taft's Alaskan policy. Wilson favored Alaska as a storehouse to be unlocked by a system of railways. "These the government should itself build and administer," the president said. The government should also own the ports and terminals so that they would be available for all who wish to use them for the service and development of the country and its people.

The bills authorizing the president to locate, construct, and operate railroads in Alaska came up for debate simultaneously in both houses in mid-January, 1914. On January 14 Wickersham delivered a five-and-a-half-hour speech on the floor of the House describing all the attributes of Alaska and the reasons why the government should build a railroad there.

It was the longest speech on record in Congress, Wickersham remaining on his feet continuously for the entire length of the speech. After two hours, the delegate asked Chairman Houston of the Committee on Territories if he should quit, but he replied: "No, go on till the audience wants you to quit."

His voice maintained a good tenor, but the following day he felt sore and worn out. When asked by Congressman Zeke Cauler, Democrat of Mississippi, how he felt, the delegate replied: "I feel like a woman who has had a baby - very proud, but damned sore."[16]

The speech was printed in its entirety in the Congressional Record, and Wickersham ordered 10,000 copies printed for distribution in Alaska; this cost him $283.

At the conclusion of the speech, Congressman Victor Murdock of Kansas, Progressive leader in the House, complimented him generously, bringing applause from his colleagues:

> Mr. Chairman, to my mind the most remarkable part of the remarkable speech which we have just heard, carrying the abundant information it did, was that until now it has not been possible for any man to give us more information about Alaska

. . .and I think there is no one on earth who could have given us this information with the completeness that marked the address of the gentleman from Alaska.

The bill passed the Senate on January 24 by a vote of 46 to 16. With the delegate's consent and that of the special Rules Commitee, it was substituted for the Wickersham bill in the House in order to obtain quicker action toward ultimate passage. The bill passed the House on February 18 by a vote of 230 to 87. Since the original bill had been amended in the House, it was returned to the Senate, where it was passed on March 10 without any changes by a vote of 41 to 29.

The Washington *Times* editorialized glowingly on Wickersham's efforts on behalf of Alaska, complimenting him particularly on his recent speech in the House:

> It was a model of its kind. He demonstrated an encyclopedic knowledge of Alaska in every phase. . .seldom has one man's exposition of a big subject in a single speech, been so convincing and conclusive with either house of Congress.
>
> It is to be hoped that the people of Alaska will continue to demonstrate their good sense and appreciation by keeping him in Congress. It is not a question whether Wickersham wants to stay in Congress. There have been intimations that he thinks his work is finished with the passage of the federal railroad bill and will seek to retire. He shouldn't be permitted to do so. Alaska needs him, Congress needs him, the country needs him. . . .[17]

When news of the railway bill's passage reached Seattle, the *Times* announced it by a salute of twenty-four bombs. A parade and bonfire was staged the following weekend. A special feature of the parade was a locomotive pulling two flatcars loaded with Alaska products from Yesler Way up Second Avenue to the Washington Hotel, where a big bonfire was built on a vacant square to the rear of the hotel.

The improvised train had Governor Lister as engineer, Banker J.E. Chilberg as fireman, and Mayor Gill as conductor. Mayor Gill, in the regulation blue and gold of the ticket puncher, gave the Governor the "high ball," then the Governor pulled out the throttle a few notches; Chilberg threw a shovelful of coal into the firebox, and the "first federal Alaska train" was on its way.

On the flatcars, acting as trainmen, were two businessmen dressed as President Wilson and Delegate Wickersham.[18]

Wickersham gave a dinner party for twenty-two guests to express his gratitude to Congressman William C. Houston, Democrat of Tennessee, chairman of the House Committee on Territories, for his efforts on behalf of the railway bill. The delegate presented his honored guest with a large caribou head in the name of all Alaskans who would benefit from the legislation.[19]

Chapter 32

1914 Delegate Race

I am and long have been a Woodrow Wilson Progressive and I intend to give him my support. He has supported me and the things I want for Alaska. He represents principles and ideas which I distinctly approve and I intend to stand with him in the future. . . . (Letter from Wickersham to Bill McPhee, Feb. 7,1914,Alaska Citizen,Mar.9,1914)

The Alaska political pot began boiling furiously in the spring of 1914 when word came from Washington that Wickersham was calling himself a "Woodrow Wilson Progressive." Did that mean he planned to be a candidate for delegate on the Democratic ticket? This did not set well with the simon-pure Democrats who had looked forward for years to the time when there would be a national Democratic administration and they would be appointed to positions of influence in the territory, which all too long had been reserved for their Republican friends and neighbors.

Wickersham wrote his friend, Bill McPhee, in Fairbanks, that he felt deeply grateful to President Wilson for his enlightened policy toward Alaska. He stressed that had it not been for the president's support and that of Secretary Lane, the opposition to the railroad bill could not have been overcome. He said that Wilson's administration was working earnestly to open Alaska in such a way that it would not be monopolized by the Alaska syndicate or any other big interest but would be kept free for the people who came to the territory to make their homes and build their businesses. He thought all Alaskans should give the president encouragement.[1]

John Cobb, Juneau attorney and secretary of the Juneau Democratic Club, returned from the nation's capital with a glowing report of the delegate's popularity with the Democratic administration. He told of having had a long talk with an old friend and classmate who was a member of President Wilson's cabinet. The friend said that the administration considered Alaska's Democratic national committeeman, Z.R. Cheney, a Juneau attorney, a tool of the old Republican "stand-pat" ring, rather than as someone working for the interests of the territory. This left the administration without a responsible adviser in territorial political matters.

He said the administration favored the nomination and election of the present delegate on a straight Democratic ticket. Cobb wrote a fellow Alaskan Democrat accordingly:

> Mr. Wickersham is now an avowed Democrat and is so recognized in Washington, though he has yet to have the brand placed upon him. Both Mr. Houston, chairman of the committee on territories, and Speaker Champ Clark, spoke of him to me as one of the strongest men in our national legislature. Mr. Clark said that Wickersham's speech on the Alaska railway bill, in his opinion, saved the measure from defeat. . . .
>
> Of course, you are fully aware that it has been largely Democratic votes that have elected Mr. Wickersham in the three preceding elections, and his bitterest enemies cannot deny his ability or the public service he has rendered to the people of this territory. . . .[2]

Alaskans were inured to the delegate's mugwumpism so it came as no surprise to have him assume a new party label for the coming delegate race; it was only the hard-core partisans who were concerned. The Democratic clubs in Juneau and Fairbanks passed rules prohibiting any but simon-pure Democrats from becoming party candidates.

The *Alaska Citizen*, a recognized Democratic organ, however, editorialized that it welcomed Wickersham into the Democratic party, saying that it was not necessary for him to prove himself a simon-pure Democrat to enroll as a member of the Tanana Valley Democratic Club. Declaring him to be the strongest candidate for the delegateship, the paper suggested that accepting him into the party ranks would be the Democrats' only chance to have a winner. It was even suggested that Wickersham's Democratic leanings might be considered a boon to the party inasmuch as there had been no other alternate on the horizon for some time.[3]

Importuned by some of his friends to run for reelection as a Democrat, Wickersham said he preferred to "let his fortunes stand with the statement that he was a Woodrow Wilson Progressive." Whether that made him a Democrat or a Wilson Progressive was immaterial as long as both worked together for the upbuilding of Alaska.

Thus, on June 4 he sent telegrams to the Alaska press and to his friends saying: "I shall be a candidate for reelection. The announcement is made upon the request of many people in Alaska, and because my duties as your representative in Congress prevents me from coming home at an early date to make it in person, I am taking this means of announcing it."[4]

In publishing the announcement, the *Dispatch* also quoted from a letter the delegate wrote Henry Ray, his business agent in Fairbanks:

> You and Bill McPhee seem to have transferred me bodily to the Democratic party, without consulting me about it. . . .
>
> I believe that Mr. Wilson is truly a great president and that he has only the good of Alaska at heart. He is intensely interested in settling the Alaska question and developing the territory free from monopoly.
>
> That is a platform broad enough for all of the people of Alaska to stand upon and I am determined to stand in the middle of it myself. . . .
>
> I think much more of the development of Alaska than I do of the name given to any brand of politics. The development of Alaska is political enough for me and I know that my friends there will stand by me in that determination.

Fearing that his alleged alignment with the Democrats would prove embarrassing to Governor Strong, he was greatly relieved and pleased when Strong called on him in Washington and assured him that he wished to aid him in every way possible in securing the passage of bills beneficial to Alaska's development. He was the first governor of Alaska to call on Wickersham; Hoggatt and Clark made a point of ignoring him and did everything they could to oppose any bill the delegate sponsored.

Governor Strong's friendly assurances portended a new day for Alaska, with cooperation rather than dissension the keynote. The governor said that Postmaster General Burleson and other administration officials advised him to support Wickersham for reelection as delegate, and he intended to return to Alaska and follow their advice.[5]

With Wickersham committed to running for reelection, it was once more Wickersham against the field, as Editor Thompson put it:

> Come on boys, trot out the best horses you have, the Wickershamites will give them a run. . .Democrats, Socialists, Republicans, Progressives or Mugwumps, they all look alike to the Wickersham followers. . . .
>
> Let the opposition prepare their arguments and criticisms - Wickersham has grown fat upon that kind of stuff, and he eats it alive as fast as they can throw it at him. . . .[6]

The Alaskan Republicans remained ominously silent and disinterested. Since their party organization was fractured beyond repair, the best for them to do was to join their Democratic friends. There were no convention calls issued and no candidate nominated on the Republican ticket.

The Democrats were surging with new life; rival factions were maneuvering for party control. The central committee called a convention for August 3 in Skagway and the Democrats backing Wickersham called one for July 30 in Valdez.

Delegates to the Skagway meeting had one common goal in mind - to find a candidate who could beat Wickersham. Each community had its favorite son: Tom Donohoe, Guggenheim attorney in Valdez, was conspiring to get control of the Democratic party; in order to accomplish this, he agreed to bury the hatchet to form a coalition with an opposing faction headed by Charles E. Bunnell, a young Valdez attorney and businessman. Both were elected as delegates to the Skagway convention with Mrs. Albert White of Valdez heading the delegation.[7]

Cordova Democrats nominated Falcon Joslin, president of the Tanana Valley Railroad, as their unanimous choice for delegate. The Cordova *Alaskan* described him as "towering in stature, of kindly and pleasing personality, with honesty of purpose a life-long characteristic, possessed of a keen and exceptionally bright intellect, with a fearlessness and utter unselfishness that is as exceptional as it is pleasing."[8]

Nome Democrats endorsed George Grigsby, former United States district attorney under the Republicans and recently elected Nome mayor as an Independent. Fairbanks Democrats chose William T.

Burns, a miner at Cleary City and member of the first territorial legislature.

Juneau Democrats tried to persuade Governor Strong to be a candidate, but he "gracefully and smilingly waved away the honor that was sought to be thrust upon him."[9]

While the delegates were en route to the Skagway gathering, John Frame, editor-publisher of *The Commoner* in Valdez, quietly took charge of the convention of insurgent Democrats meeting in Valdez; they designated themselves as Wilson Progressives or Progressive Democrats. Wickersham was nominated unanimously for delegate. When notified of his nomination, Wickersham issued a statement for the press as follows:

> President Wilson's progressive and constructive Alaskan policy promises to bring long-deferred prosperity to Alaska, and to open its natural resources to development without monopoly.
>
> It is my purpose to aid him in that effort and I am glad to have the endorsement and support of the Progressive Democrats of Alaska.[10]

Some of Wickersham's zealous supporters wanted to place his name in nomination at the Skagway convention as well but he begged them "to be shrewd enough not to stick his head in his enemies' mouth just to see if they would bite."[11]

Charles Bunnell of Valdez was chosen permanent chairman of the Skagway convention, and by the time the delegates were ready to nominate a candidate for delegate, they chose him by acclamation. Rhinehart F. Roth of Fairbanks, chairman of the platform committee, placed Bunnell's name in nomination and John Cobb made the seconding speech.

His nomination was as much a surprise to Bunnell as it was to the rest of Alaskans, as he had not sought the office. It was understood that he had agreed to run only after being promised a judgeship in case he was defeated. Outside of the convention hall, his nomination was greeted with derision. How did he win out over much better known nominees? Was it because they knew Wickersham could not be beaten and Bunnell was chosen as the party's sacrificial goat?

According to the *Dispatch*, "when the names of men like Falcon Joslin and William Burns, and other battle-scarred veterans, are passed up for an unknown, outsiders may be pardoned for indulging in speculation." It is a well-known fact that Bunnell was the last forlorn choice after

"CASEY" WICKERSHAM

Left: Campaign picture in 1914 delegate race. *Right:* Charles E. Bunnell, president of University of Alaska, 1921-49.

every prominent Democrat in Alaska had been solicited by telegram and had refused the "honor" before Bunnell was swallowed. The *Dispatch* feels sorry for Bunnell.[12]

The Petersburg *Progressive* chortled editorially:

> And so it came to pass that the Alaska Democratic machine in meeting assembled at Skagway, on the third day of the present month, after long, serious and deep cogitation and minute consideration, resolved that a goat had to be offered, and while the sacrifice is extremely painful it was accepted cheerfully.[13]

Wickersham was delighted with the Democrats' choice as Joslin, Burns, or Grigsby would have been much stronger opponents. Bunnell had been a Wickersham supporter for many years. He was a good man but did not have a forceful personality. Wickersham wondered what appointment Bunnell wanted, to agree to run; he was not aware of the judgeship promise.

Charles Ernest Bunnell's first job out of college was teaching school at Wood Island, five miles from Kodiak, in 1900. He continued to teach school in various towns for the next seven years. Then he resigned to become assistant cashier in the Reynolds-Alaska Bank in Valdez; nine days later the bank was discovered to be insolvent and its doors were closed. Bunnell then took over the management of the Phoenix Hotel. He studied law on the side and passed the Alaska bar. He practiced law and had some business interests as well.

The Socialists met in Fairbanks and nominated John M. "Jack" Brooks, a miner from Jack Wade Creek, as their candidate for delegate. Brooks came to Juneau in 1897 as a prospector and thereafter moved from one gold strike to the other.

Wickersham had more press support this time than ever before. Thompson of the *News-Miner* was his supporter this time but Ritchie of the Valdez *Prospector*, a former supporter, was opposing him. Other Wickersham supporters included: the *Dispatch* in Juneau, Skagway *Alaskan*, Wrangell *Sentinel*, Petersburg *Progressive*, Ketchikan *Mail*, *The Commoner* in Valdez, and the Douglas *News*. The Bunnell supporters were: the *Empire* in Juneau, Cordova *Times* and *Alaskan*, Chitina *Leader*, Fairbanks *Citizen* and *Times*, and the Nome *Nugget*.

The Socialists had two organs promoting their candidate—the *Alaska Sunday Morning Post* in Juneau and the Alaska *Socialist* in Fairbanks.

The Wickershams were given a gala send-off as they boarded the S.S. *Mariposa* at Seattle to embark on his fourth race for delegate. Although the steamer was not to leave until evening, they were urged to come aboard at 3:30 in the afternoon. When they arrived at the pier, they were escorted to the top deck, where twenty-five old-timers, dressed in the regalia of the Yukon Order of Pioneers, awaited them.

George Snow, actor and theater operator who mushed over the Chilkoot Pass with wife and baby daughter in 1898, was the master of ceremonies. He presented the delegate with a seven-foot-high floral horseshoe to bring him good luck in the coming campaign. All the old-timers assured Wickersham of their all-out support. A movie was taken of the presentation and it was to be shown in various towns during the campaign.[14]

This bon voyage celebration was the beginning of a series of enthusiastic greetings as the Wickershams moved northward. At Ketchikan they were met by a band and a cheering crowd. Cheer after cheer went up as the steamer was being tied to the wharf. As the delegate and Mrs. Wickersham walked down the gangplank, the band struck up "Hail, the Conquering Hero Comes."

In the evening he spoke to a capacity crowd in Redmen Hall. He read letters of congratulations received by him from bigwig Democrats like Bob Jennings and John Troy for his successful performance in Washington. He created a minor sensation when he produced copies of letters from Bunnell received during the years, signing himself as a Republican. In one, he wrote: "I have supported you in the past and have always been satisfied that you were the right man in the right place."[15]

Debbie went as far as Valdez and then returned to Seattle while the delegate went on to Fairbanks over the trail from Chitina in one of Bobby Sheldon's automobiles; the road was still frozen, so they made the trip in good time.

At Nine-Mile roadhouse he found 150 of his friends waiting to greet him. It was a Sunday afternoon and they had enlisted seventeen automobiles to form a caravan to escort him into Fairbanks; they had the usual brass band to give the festivities an uproarious note. When the procession arrived in town, there was another crowd waiting to welcome him and escort him to his home.

Even though Debbie was not with him, he felt he had come home - how he loved beautiful Tanana Valley! He had a telephone put into his home for the first time, and he used his home as his campaign headquarters. He hired John Conna, a Negro whom he had known in Tacoma, as his chef and general housekeeper. He remained in the Fairbanks area through election day, visiting the creeks and attending to his private business affairs along with his campaigning.

Speaking before an audience at Fox, Wickersham described his close friendship with President Wilson and Secretary Lane and his admiration of Teddy Roosevelt. He boasted of having helped get rid of President Taft. He praised the Socialists, declaring that Roosevelt, Lane, and he were all partly socialists at heart. He characterized Bunnell as "a perfectly lady-like gentleman" and insisted he had always been a Republican.[16]

The campaign brought out the usual slogans and nicknames. Bunnell was dubbed "Stovepipe Charlie" and Wickersham "Flickering Wick" and "Flypaper Wick." The Wickites warned against "changing horses in midstream" while Bunnell's advocates urged the election of a Democratic delegate to work with a Democratic national administration.

Even a quotation from the Holy Scriptures was used as an argument for voting for Wickersham. The first epistle of Paul, the apostle, to the Thessalonians, fifth chapter, twenty-first verse, says: "Prove all things, and hold fast that which is good." That referred to the years of trials and disappointments which the delegate had suffered in his devotion to the territory's interests while Bunnell's fitness for the job was unproven.[17]

Bunnell worked long and hard as a candidate, hand-shaking and visiting as many of the major towns as possible, but the odds were stacked against him. Even at his own political rallies, his workers could not refrain from complimenting the incumbent on his ability and achievements. At one such rally in Fairbanks at which Falcon Joslin presided, Rhinehart Roth, who had just been appointed district attorney for the fourth division, was the principal speaker. In a ringing speech, he declared that Wickersham was the smartest man in Alaska today, probably the greatest politician in the United States, and a delegate who had done the territory a world of good. In conclusion, he observed: "If I had had his brains and his opportunities, I would today be worth ten million dollars instead of what I am."[18] A surprising endorsement from the enemy's camp!

Wickersham's supporters called Bunnell a Prohibitionist and said he was hostile to the liquor interests, which the candidate denied vehemently. Bunnell was quoted as saying that it was a damn lie that he did not frequent the Valdez saloons, nor was it true that he did not drink, calling upon three former residents to testify to his having drunk hard liquor. He even apologized for never having been drunk, much to the surprise of his audience, which was made up of men who never became intoxicated themselves but neither did they think they should apologize for their sobriety.[19]

Cognizant of Alaskans' proclivity to consume hard liquor and their contempt for efforts to deprive them of that privilege, Bunnell attended a barkeepers' union meeting while in Juneau and the *Dispatch* ran a front-page story with the heading: "Bunnell Talks To Barkeepers; Grape Juice Not For Dickie Bird." The occasion was reported in the following humorous vein:

> Sunday afternoon, as the twilight was deepening and the setting sun was calling the moral and the highly virtuous to prayerful reflection and prayer, three representatives of the Wilsonian Democracy and the Bryan grape juice program, knocked at the outer gates of the barkeepers' union and asked for admittance; they were admitted.
>
> Charles the First. . .was asked to speak. . .He told the voters, brothers, companions and fellow citizens, that he was not a

member of any temperance organization. In fact, he proceeded to prove it and he proved it to the satisfaction of the most doubting. . .He said his Democracy was not of the grape juice but rather of the Bourbon brand.

So convincing were Bunnell's arguments to the barkeepers that he was one of them, that it is said the union is to adopt the first syllable of his name, "bun," as the password to the Sunday meetings of the union.[20]

A few days before election day, the Democratic papers carried a telegram from President Wilson addressed to Bunnell, expressing his hope that the people of the territory would send him to Washington. Wickersham felt hurt to think the president would stoop to such "a last-ditch political gimmick."[21]

On election night a crowd of cheering friends gathered in front of Wickersham's home and he went outdoors to thank them in a five-minute talk. Later in the evening he went to his downtown headquarters, which was filled with noisy merrymakers as if on the midway of a country fairgrounds. Out of a total Fairbanks vote of 933, Wickersham got 614 votes, Bunnell 233 and Brooks 62, with 24 scattering votes.

The delegate's supporters were raring to cut loose and launch a torchlight parade to celebrate his victory but he urged them to hold back until the Valdez vote came in, as that would be a good barometer of the territorial trend. That vote came in about one o'clock in the morning - 362 for Wickersham, 263 for Bunnell, and 104 for Brooks - pandemonium broke loose, and a rush was made for the doors to the street. A great blazing torch had already been lighted and a bagpipe was playing. Rapidly men fell into line, more torches were sent aloft; horns began blowing and the weird parade started down Front Street with unholy glee. From various street entrances men came out, saw the jollification, and joined the crowd. They all howled with joy over the fourth election of Wickersham. The delegate himself remained at headquarters, receiving congratulations.[22]

The total vote for the territory showed Wickersham receiving 59 percent and Bunnell 31.6 percent, with Brooks trailing with a little more than 1 percent. Wickersham was winner in all four divisions. Out of a total territorial vote of 10,808, Wickersham received 6,283 votes, Bunnell 3,416, and Brooks 1,109.

The Wickites fared well in the territorial legislative races, winning three Senate seats and eight House seats. Only one of his opponents re-

mained in the Senate from the first session—Millard, who was a hold-
over. Bruner had died, Freeding, Ray, and Roden did not run for
reelection and Tripp ran for a House seat. That meant the delegate
could control the legislature during the coming session.

Chapter 33

University of Alaska— Wickersham's Dream Child

> As we looked out to the north over a valley of varying shades of green through which wound the Tanana, we beheld the Alaska range, snow-capped and gleaming white and, towering above all, Mount McKinley, majestic and inspiring. . . Surely this was a wonderful place for our college! (Farthest North Collegian, *June 1925*)

When Wickersham returned to his Washington office in December, 1914, world events threatened to obliterate Alaska's chances for getting any major legislation passed on its behalf. The United States was having trouble with Mexico, and war had broken out in Europe. Although President Wilson had issued a proclamation of neutrality, Germany's surprise occupation of Belgium led to groups in the United States advocating preparedness for possible involvement.

Opposition was being voiced among congressmen to appropriate the $35,000,000 authorized for construction of a government railroad in the territory. Survey parties had spent the summer in Alaska examining possible routes for the proposed railroad. The Alaska Engineering Commission, appointed by the secretary of interior, made its report to the president without recommending any specific route, and now it was up to the president to choose the route.

Wickersham's disregard for party label injured him little in Alaska, but it was a handicap and bafflement to both his friends and his enemies in Washington. Having run as a Wilson Progressive in the recent delegate race, South Trimble, the clerk of the House, was at a loss to know what party affiliation should be placed after his name in the congressional directory. "Just put me down as a Progressive Democrat," said Wickersham. The directory came out with "Progressive" after his name, which still left unanswered whether he was a Republican or a Democrat, although he still retained his seat on the House floor on the Republican side of the aisle.[1]

To his supporters, Wickersham was an Alaskan and they saw no need for his having to adhere to any party label. He wanted to represent all Alaskans and not be tied to any party. This freewheeling attitude irked the leaders in both parties and contributed to the intensity of their dislike for him.

Appearing before the House Ways and Means Committee in January, 1915, he proudly proclaimed himself a Wilson supporter. He boasted he had been elected as a Progressive Democrat and had probably delivered more pro-Wilson speeches than any member of Congress and made them willingly and earnestly.[2] Four months later he announced in Fairbanks that he planned to support the Republican nominee for president in 1916. He had become disillusioned with Wilson's failure to maintain his interest in Alaskan affairs. The delegate also found himself shut out of patronage matters, the Strong-Troy-Jennings crowd being accorded sole recognition.

The Democrats and nonpartisans who had supported Wickersham through the years were disturbed when rumor had it that he was contemplating accepting nomination by the Republican organization in the territory. That group had never supported him, and it was doubtful that it ever would unless he was willing to make a deal with Shackleford, which would indeed be disenchanting.

Referring to him as the political acrobat of Alaska, a socialist viewpoint was that "Jimmie has been on both sides of the political fence, under the fence and on top of the fence, but is always working for Mr. Wickersham alone."[3]

Charles Wulff, editor of the Valdez *Prospector and Miner*, was amused by the delegate's chameleon antics:

> The delegate has been edging toward the elephant ever since pole and canvas of the bull moose side-show fell on that noisy animal and broke its back. On a steamer from Seward last October, he said to John Lyons and Al White, "We Republicans ought to get together."
>
> The Republican party looks now like a winner in the next heat and Wickersham is not bad at picking winners. He slipped

a cog in 1912 when he grabbed a tail-hold on the bull moose. . . .
When Democracy fell on the moose and smashed the critter's
slate, the Judge took a long breath and offered to become a
"Progressive Democrat." Failing to get encouragement from
anybody of consequence in the Democratic party he said no
more about it, and now he makes another try for a seat on the
Republican bandwagon.

The little thing that will bother the judge most in this Republican business is that, outside of the Tanana district, Alaska
Republicans are nearly all against him. The vote that elects him
is mostly Democrats and half-socialist. . . .[4]

Wulff noted further that Wickersham was equally changeable in his
stands on issues. In a speech on the House floor in February, 1911, he
roasted conservation fads being tried on Alaska, and three years later,
he went out of his way to eulogize Gifford Pinchot, the perpetrator of
these conservation fads.

The delegate's first weeks back in Washington were devoted to
opposing the creation of a new bureau to regulate Alaska's fur-bearing
animals being proposed by the bureau of fisheries. Alaskans were
already fretting under the multibureaucratic rule of Wahsington
agencies.

Wickersham and the deputy commissioner of fisheries, E. Lester
Jones, had spirited clashes before the House Ways and Means
Committee over the Palmer bill, which would give Secretary of
Commerce Redfield greater authority in regulating Alaska's game and
fisheries. The delegate argued that the territorial legislature should be
given more authority, and he was joined by Governor Strong in that
proposal.

Warming to his subject, the delegate declared that "under the Palmer
bill a citizen who disturbed a harmless jackrabbit, or frightened it from
repose, would subject himself to a term in the penitentiary." He
expressed the fear also that unless the legislature was given jurisdiction
of the fisheries, the fishing industry would be destroyed by the Seattle-
Alaska fish trust.

Of highest priority was getting his school land bill approved by the
House Committee on Territories. His bill provided for the withdrawal of
public lands in Alaska for school purposes and giving the legislature
authority to establish a uniform school system. Sections sixteen and
thirty-six in every township would be reserved for the support of
common schools, and four sections adjoining the agricultural experiment

station near Fairbanks would be withdrawn for an agricultural college and school of mines; section thirty-three in each township in the Tanana Valley would be reserved for the support of the college.

The idea of getting a college for Alaska came to Wickersham originally quite by accident. One day he picked up from the floor, an old law book which was being used to prop open his office door during the hot summer weather. Thumbing through it, he discovered a law which entitled every agricultural college and school of mines to an annual subsidy of $50,000 from the federal government. His immediate reaction was that with such a subsidy, even Alaska could afford a college.

When he first introduced the bill, his colleagues joked with him about how ridiculous it was to have a college in such a faraway place where there were so few people. His fellow Alaskans were equally unimpressed with the idea and had to be cajoled into giving it serious consideration.

A chief opponent to his school bill was John Ballaine, a Seattle resident who had bought real estate in what later became the townsite of Seward when he was promoting construction of the Alaska Central Railroad. His railway project having gone into bankruptcy, he was anxious to recoup on his real estate investment by having the proposed college established in Seward rather than in Fairbanks. He had sold lots to Congressmen Falconer of Washington and Norton of North Dakota, so they were ready allies in opposing the delegate's bill.

Wickersham had known Ballaine in Tacoma when he was a reporter for the Tacoma *Ledger*. He went to Alaska in 1902 to promote the construction of the Alaska Central Railroad, which was to connect interior Alaska with the coast. He and his brother Frank bought a large portion of the Seward townsite. The railroad company went into bankruptcy in 1907 and was taken over by a group of Canadian banks and later sold to a syndicate associated with the Morgan Guggenheim interests. [5]

When the federal government decided to construct the Alaska Railroad and chose Seward as its coastal terminus, Ballaine thought he had struck a bonanza and would become a multimillionaire selling lots in Seward. Unfortunately, his greed and bellicose attitude toward the government officials in charge of building the railroad led them to abandon Seward as the railroad's headquarters; they chose Anchorage instead.

Ballaine became an embittered man who spent much of his time in Washington, D.C., opposing legislation sought on behalf of the government railroad. He was constantly accusing officials of the Alaska Engineering Commission of squandering federal funds and performing their duties improperly. His animosity toward Anchorage and its civic leaders bordered on fanaticism.

He tried to block appropriations for the completion of the railroad, and the Anchorage Chamber of Commerce was obliged to send letters and telegrams to Washington assuring the officials that the AEC work was continuing efficiently and in a businesslike manner and that Ballaine was a disgruntled non-Alaskan who was not acquainted with the true facts.

Noting the difficulties he was facing in the House, Wickersham maneuvered to get his school bill before the Senate, hoping to save it during the final days before Congress adjourned. He secured the assistance of Senator Thomas Sterling of South Dakota, with whom he had studied law in Springfield.

Sterling was a member of the Committee on Public Lands and agreed to introduce the bill. Wickersham was permitted to testify on its behalf. Senator Smoot of Utah chastised the delegate for taking up the committee's time with legislation which had no chance of passage before Congress adjourned, but Wickersham persisted and succeeded in getting a favorable committee report. Sterling was instructed to make the report and take charge of the bill on the Senate floor.

It was twelve o'clock noon on February 17, and the Senate was just convening in regular session. Five minutes later Sterling stood on the floor of the Senate and asked leave to report the bill. He moved that the rules be suspended and the bill passed. Senator Smoot came in a moment later only to learn that what he had termed an impossibility had become a reality. The bill was on its way to the House for passage.

Had it not been for Speaker Champ Clark's friendly feeling toward the delegate, the bill's opponents would have been able to kill it, but Clark came to his rescue. The sequence of events leading to the bill's enactment into law was graphically described by the delegate in his Fourth of July address at the laying of the cornerstone of the college the following summer:

> Under House rules the Speaker could recognize any member during the last six days of the session to move to suspend the rules and pass a bill when it had been favorably reported, and was on the waiting calendar. The Speaker promised to recognize the delegate. . . .
>
> I waited for my turn and as the hours passed and the last chance began to fade away and the Speaker's eye failed to see

me in the throng of earnest and excited men struggling for rec-
cognition and the passage of bills so important to their constituents, it began to look like failure.

When the House met on the morning of the third it was
known there would be neither recess nor adjournment until
twelve o'clock noon. . .All day and all night I sat there waiting
and watching for recognition.

About three o'clock on the morning of the fourth, the Speaker's clerk came along with the encouraging remark that I would
be recognized soon. An hour went by before the Speaker looked
my way and nodded - what a relief that nod gave me!

The opposition argued that it was unfair and unprecedented
for Congress to locate the site of an agricultural college as it
should be left to the legislature. . .In answer to that argument,
which I had anticipated, I read a telegram signed by all members of the legislature and the governor. . .that turned the tide
and the bill passed by a viva voce vote largely in our favor. It
was the last bill passed by the House of the Sixty-third Congress. . .The bill was signed by President Wilson before noon on
March 4, the day of adjournment.[6]

The Wickershams were en route to the West Coast at 5:15 o'clock that
evening; they looked forward to a summer in their Fairbanks home
instead of sweltering in the Washington heat as they had had to do for
several summers in a row. They went via California so they could visit
the Panama-California Exposition in San Diego and the Panama-Pa-
cific International Exposition in San Francisco.

In San Diego thirty members of the Alaska Club honored them with a
reception in one of the hotel parlors. In Los Angeles, the delegate told a
newspaper reporter that he planned to introduce a bill at the next
session of Congress to make Alaska a state of the union. He said it was a
dream he had had ever since his arrival in Alaska as a judge in 1900. He
believed that once the government railroad was completed and a public
school system inaugurated, there would be such an influx of settlers that
soon the population would warrant statehood:

When the railroad begins operation, the world will learn of
Alaska's great mineral wealth, its fishing industry and farming
possibilities. . .Why, when we get the railroad, we'll supply the
entire Pacific Coast with potatoes, probably at prices lower than
the prevailing quotations!

> When the schools are opened, thousands of parents will be
> lured into the territory who otherwise would not have come,
> owing to the lack of facilities for the education of their chil-
> dren. . . .[7]

Wickersham told a Seattle reporter that he thought the Alaska Railroad was only the beginning of a whole system of government-owned
railroads to be built in the territory. He was still optimistic about what
the Wilson administration would do to develop Alaska.

After a week's stopover in Seattle-Tacoma, the Wickershams set sail
for Juneau, where he would confer with the legislators. Debbie would
remain there until the Yukon River opened for navigation and then she
would join him in Fairbanks; he would go in over the Valdez trail.

On board ship were the Harry Bishops returning to their Juneau
home. He was a former United States marshal, and he had suffered a
paralytic stroke, and had gone south for medical treatment. In his
diary, Wickersham described the Bishops as "kind, modest and sensible
folk." (Thirteen years later Mrs. Bishop became the second Mrs.
Wickersham.)

At Juneau the delegate found that the Democratic federally appointed
officeholders, under the leadership of Judge Jennings, were intent on
organizing an anti-Wickersham effort. John Troy was working with
them and through the colums of the *Empire*, was espousing what he
chose to label a "full territorial form" of government and accusing the
delegate of being opposed to it. The fact that Wickersham had been
working for home rule ever since he became Alaska's delegate in
Congress in 1908 was irrelevant. By a subtle change in nomenclature,
they hoped to confuse the people into thinking the delegate stood for
something other than what they wanted.

As a counter thrust, Wickersham and his followers decided to come
out for statehood as that would be the ultimate of "full territorial government." The two Juneau newspapers—the *Empire* and the *Dispatch*—
took up the battle cry, and their fighting editorials amused Wickersham
since he was for both in their proper sequence.

Troy and Wickersham had known one another when they lived in the
Puget Sound area. Troy was editor-publisher of the *Democratic Leader*, a weekly published in Port Angeles, Washington, and served
simultaneously as county auditor of Clallam County. He went to Skagway to cover the Klondike gold rush for a Seattle paper. He served as
editor of the Skagway *Daily Alaskan* until 1907 when he returned to

Seattle. Six years later he was hired as editor of the *Alaska Daily Empire*, which Major J.F.A. Strong had established in Juneau the previous year. When Strong was appointed Alaska's governor, he asked Troy to come north and run the paper for him; they had known each other in Port Angeles and Seattle. Arrangements were made for Troy to buy the paper later on.

Troy soon became recognized as the unofficial spokesman for Alaska's Democratic party. He made no pretense of being bipartisan in his editorials, but socially he cultivated Republicans as well as Democrats, so long as they held important government jobs. A fellow journalist called Troy "a fawning sycophant of Governor Walter Clark, the tool of Taft and Dick Ballinger, the notorious."[8]

Wickersham found Fairbanks in the doldrums. A long winter of unemployment, with no immediate prospect of railroad work, had left its residents pessimistic about their future. There had been an exodus to the new gold strike at Tolovana.

With little legal work to do in the office, Wickersham went on hunting trips and on hikes into the countryside. He decided to buy up a series of claims on Cleary Creek as an investment, hoping to sell them to some large corporation. The entire creek was valued at $20 million; it was considered the richest gold stream in Alaska. When Wickersham and Luther Hess visited the creek to pick up options on claims, they found it almost deserted. At Cleary City, for example, where once there were 2,000 residents, now there were only 20 people. By the time Wickersham was ready to return south in October, he had options on half of Cleary Creek, with Hess owning one-fourth and Henry Ray the other fourth.[9]

Another project which occupied Wickersham's attention that summer was the selection of a site for the agricultural college. He appointed a committee of three to make the selection—Frank Gordon, Tony Nordale, and Andrew Nerland. They made many treks into the surrounding wilderness before finding just what they wanted. Writing from his home in Santa Barbara, California years later, Gordon recalled the inspiration which was theirs on the day that the present site of the University of Alaska was chosen. Joining the trio on the morning of Sunday, June 22, were the Wickershams, Mrs. Luther Hess, the Reverend Hope Lumpkin of St. Matthews Episcopal church, and J.H. Groves. They set out in the Groves' automobile for the experiment station and from there they walked through the woods, finally coming upon a little knoll. Recalling that moment, Gordon wrote:

We beheld in the distance Mt. McKinley in all her majestic glory—the decision was made quickly, knowing what an asset this beautiful view, fine valley lands and nearness to Fairbanks would mean to students for many years to come. . . .

When all agreed that no place could be better, Delegate Wickersham said, "Mrs. Hess, mark the exact spot where the Alaska Agricultural College will be located." She tied a handkerchief to a small tree to mark the spot![10]

Wickersham decided that there should be a formal cornerstone laying ceremony held on Sunday, July 4, and so during the ensuing weeks, he and his friends spent part of each day cutting brush to make a trail and a cleared area for the construction of a cornerstone. Wickersham was to make the principal address, and with his strong sense of history, he had his remarks printed in pamphlet form for distribution on the day of their delivery.

Hundreds of visitors came to Fairbanks to celebrate the Fourth. Excursion trains brought them from the mining camps and the government steamer *General Jacobs* brought a band, baseball, and rifle teams from Fort Gibbon. It was a hot, sunny day. About three hundred people left the Tanana Valley Railway station for the site of the cornerstone laying; it took ten minutes to make the trip, and the army band was aboard to add to the festivities. The ceremony was in charge of the Fairbanks Masonic Lodge.

Wickersham traced the history of his efforts in Washington to get congressional action on behalf of the college-to-be. Besides the 2,500-acre campus, one section in each township in the Tanana Valley—some two hundred thousand acres—had been granted. Lease money from this acreage would provide a substantial source of support for the institution.

While Congress made this generous grant of public land, it was up to the territorial legislature to provide ways and means for constructing buildings, employing teachers, and organizing the work of the college. Wickersham named a committee of public-spirited citizens to lobby the legislature for the necessary funds.

The final sentence in Wickersham's speech is today inscribed on a bronze tablet marking the cornerstone in memorial plaza at the university; it reads: "And we who are gathered here today do most ardently dedicate these grounds and this cornerstone to the everlasting support of the principles of free government, free speech and free schools for which our forefathers fought."

Wickersham with council of Indian chiefs, Fairbanks, July 1915.

The 1917 legislature appropriated $60,000 to start construction of a college building. Governor Strong signed the bill reluctantly contending that the measure was premature, primarily because "building materials such as cement and brick" were unavailable because of World War I, which was in progress.

The original $60,000 proved insufficient to build and equip a college building and efforts to get additional funds in 1919 proved futile. But two years later a $41,000 appropriation made it possible to complete the building and equip it minimally, hire a staff, and begin instruction. The first six students enrolled on September 18, 1922, and the future University of Alaska was on its way; Wickersham's dream had become a reality.[11]

Wickersham's ethnological interest in Indians led him to a concern for their political well-being. He was the first political leader to develop an environmental impact statement on behalf of Alaskans, anteceding the national environmental protection agency of 1973 by almost sixty years.

On July 5, 1915, the day after the college cornerstone laying, Wickersham invited the seven Indian chiefs of the Tanana Valley to meet with him in the library of the Episcopal church in Fairbanks to discuss what impact the construction of the Alaska Railroad and the homestead law would have on their way of life.

The chiefs represented some 1,200 to 1,500 Indians from Salchaket down the Tanana River to Eagle on the Yukon. Wickersham told the chiefs he had invited them to come together to discuss what would happen to their good land and fishing sites when white men arrived and took over the land for other use, such as building the railroad and permitting newcomers to take up homesteads. As their congressional representative, he wanted to help protect their interests. He helped them organize the first Indian council in the interior so they could present a unified front in protection of their rights. He received frequent communications from the individual chiefs thereafter, asking for his assistance.

Debbie went south on one of the last riverboats of the season while the delegate remained in Fairbanks until the latter part of October. On his way Outside he visited the new town of Anchorage. It was only six months old and had 2,500 residents, living in well-built houses. The streets were cleared and graded and a schoolhouse was completed. The Anchorage Chamber of Commerce provided him with a hospitality committee which served as his official escort during his two-day visit.[12] He left Anchorage at five o'clock one evening, pushing through the ice of Knik Arm, arriving at Seward at two o'clock the following morning.

Chapter 34

Shuns Peace Offer of Republican Organization

> *"Will you walk into my parlor," said Shack to Wick, "and*
> *you may be the delegate while I'm the 'big stick.' The way into*
> *my parlor is up a combination stair, and I've many political*
> *suckers to show you when you're there."*
>
> *"Thank you," replied the old Wick fly, "I'd rather be politi-*
> *cally free. I've heard what's in your damned old parlor. I do*
> *not wish to see."* (*Wickersham Diary, May 5, 1916*)

Another election was approaching for both national and territorial offices and, as usual, Wickersham was being queried on whether he planned to run for reelection. And, as usual, the delegate chose to maintain the silence of the proverbial wooden Indian, waiting to see who the other aspirants would be.

Uppermost in the minds of the professionals in both parties was who could be groomed to defeat Wickersham. They were certain that he would run again, but on which ticket? Several prominent Republicans believed Wickersham would be willing to relinquish his hold on the delegateship if assured by the Republican leaders that he would be backed by the organization for the gubernatorial berth.

Wickersham himself would have liked to have the endoresement of the Republican party in Alaska, if he could retain an adequate degree of independence and could share in dispensing patronage. He had come to appreciate the advantages of party affiliation, when making the rounds in Washington. It would make the path of a voteless delegate much smoother. Also, he realized that he could never build a stable, dependable political base for himself if he were not in a position to

299

reward his faithful, hardworking supporters; otherwise he could not expect continued personal devotion.

Thus he was pleasantly surprised when William E. Bayless, Alaska's Republican national committeeman, called on him in Washington. He asked if Wickersham wanted the Republican nomination for delegate. He showed the delegate a telegram from Shackleford assuring him of his friendly disposition.

Wickersham assured him that he desired a reorganization of the Alaskan Republican party, a full and fair primary, and an un-bossed convention. Under those conditions, the delegate would gladly support the party's nominee. Bayless said that both he and Shackleford subscribed to the same tenets of party harmony and fair play.

Wickersham had expressed the same sentiment to his friends the previous fall while traveling through the territory. To prove that he was sincere about wanting to see the Republican party united, he offered to stop off in Juneau to see if he could reconcile his differences with Shackleford. But the latter was in the states so he could only talk with his law partner, Bill Bayless. While in Juneau, Wickersham learned that his friend, Ed Russell, editor-publisher of the *Dispatch*, had offered his services as mediator between the delegate and Shackleford.

The breach between the two political leaders stemmed from a mutual unwillingness to surrender control of patronage. In 1909 a truce was struck between them which Shack afterward accused Wick of violating. Shack controlled all patronage until late in the Taft administration, when he fell out with Governor Clark, who outranked him with the president. Following that breach, the governor dictated practically every federal appointment in Alaska until Taft went out of office. In the meantime, Wickersham was being reelected independent of political party and found himself ignored by both Republicans and Democrats when it came to making appointments to territorial offices.

Wickersham was wary of making any kind of a deal with his old adversary, as he did not trust him. When Russell wrote asking that the delegate meet with him and Shackleford in Seattle to conclude a political treaty of peace, Wickersham refused as he had decided that Shackleford would be more of a political handicap than an asset.[1]

In Alaska a spirit of optimism pervaded the Republican ranks; Al White of Valdez was traveling about the territory organizing new clubs. Charlie Herron, new owner of the Anchorage *Times-Cook Inlet Pioneer*, was chairman of the central committee. Shackleford indicated he would not take an active role in the coming election. Herron issued a call for a central committee meeting in Seward at which plans would be laid for the party primaries. The primaries were to take the place of the old system of smoke-filled backroom political wheeling and dealing.

A golden opportunity appeared to be at hand for Alaska's Republicans to wrest the control of the party from the Seattle-dominated carpetbaggers of the Shackleford era. The rank and file had had very little voice in party affairs, and their alternative had been to vote for Wickersham, the independent candidate. Inasmuch as Wickersham had announced his support of the Republican nominee for president, it appeared that he wanted the Republican nomination for delegate.

As Editor Thompson of the *News-Miner* observed, "it would be greatly to the advantage of the party to nominate a candidate that could be elected, for a change." Several Republican leaders in the first division who had fought the delegate in previous years indicated a willingness to give him their support this year; among these were Bob Heckman of Ketchikan and Mike O'Connor of Douglas.[2]

A harmonious central committee meeting decided to hold primaries in each of the four divisions at which delegates and alternates to the national convention in Chicago would be nominated, also candidates for delegate and territorial attorney general, as well as delegates to the territorial convention in Seward.

Rumors were widespread that a deal had been made between Wickersham and Shackleford. Shackleford affirmed its existence, but the delegate denied it. According to Shack, the delegate would be nominated on the Republican ticket at the coming territorial convention and Shack would be in charge of patronage, in case a Republican president was elected.

Bernard Stone, editor-publisher of the Seward *Gateway* and a veteran student of Alaska politics, observed that the world had surely gone topsy-turvy if it was true that Wick and Shack had gotten into the same political bed together.

Harry Thirsted, leader of the "Stick to Wick" forces in Fairbanks, wired the delegate: "Reported here that you have made combination with Shackleford. Such an alliance objectionable to local supporters and Republicans" whereupon Wickersham replied: "I have not and will not make any combination, political or otherwise with Shackleford."

Editor Thompson suggested that "one would as soon look for an agreement between St. Peter and Lucifer; a truce maybe, but a combination, never."

Referring to this strange amalgamation of oil and water, the Valdez *Miner* called it a "queer political deformity given birth in Seattle after much travail during the past winter." Five Alaskan politicians were named as midwives: Shack and four Nomeites yearning for office - Jafet Lindeberg, who wanted to be governor, and William Gilmore, George Schofield, and Cornelius Murane, who all wanted judgeships. Shack didn't want an office but merely wanted to run everything political.

Pressure was being applied on the delegate from all directions to set aside his stubbornness and cooperate with party leaders in their effort to build a new and harmonious party organization. Falcon Joslin called on Wickersham in Washington, saying he had come as an emissary from Steve Birch. Birch had told him that the delegate and Shackleford were cooperating amicably, and Joslin wondered what he could do to help the situation. Wickersham assured him that no such combination or friendship existed between him and Shackleford. As he saw it, Shackleford was having trouble keeping control of the party organization and was seeking Wickersham's help. The latter had no intention of extending that help as he knew that once Shackleford got control, he would turn against the delegate and work to defeat him just as he had in past years.

Wickersham was surprised to think that either Joslin or Birch would expect to have his confidence in view of their past actions against him; he did not trust them either. He suggested that they would do well to stay out of the fight.[3]

Wickersham received a telegram from Ed Russell chiding him for not cooperating, but the delegate remained adamant. He was convinced that he did not need Shackleford's endorsement in order to win reelection.

For several days preceding the convention, Shackleford publicly proclaimed that Wickersham could not have the nomination unless he would sign and deliver the patronage stipulation.

Convinced that his friends were being "used" by party leaders whose sole interest was to nominate a winning candidate regardless of the price to be paid by his supporters, Wickersham composed an open letter to the convention delegates reiterating that he would not enter into any deal for the control of his actions as the people's representative in Washington.

After the delegates gathered in Seward, Wickersham continued to be bombarded with telegrams, some urging him to give in to Shack and others telling him to stand his ground. All this was very frustrating to the delegate, and in the end he wired his friends to put their minds together and act unitedly. He hoped that if they joined together of their own free wills and "slit Shackleford's political throat, I will view the remains with interest though I may not shed a damn tear!"[4]

When it became obvious that Wickersham had no intention of acceding to his proposal, Shackleford supported a motion to appoint a committee charged with the choosing of a delegate nominee at a later date, thus taking it out of the hands of the convention delegates. The committee appointed was predominantly anti-Wickersham; it included H.L. Faulkner of Juneau, William Gilmore of Nome, Harvey Sullivan of Valdez, and Thomas Lloyd of Fairbanks. The committee decided not to make a nomination, preferring to have the Republicans join with the Democrats in trying to defeat Wickersham.[5]

Thus, the alleged "golden opportunity" for party unity came to naught; the Republican organization continued under the tutelage of a handful of Seattle-Alaskans, and their corporate agents in the territory.

Learning that the committee did not intend to nominate a Republican candidate for delegate, groups of Republicans got together in Fairbanks, Anchorage, and Juneau and nominated Wickersham for delegate. The Seward convention was repudiated for not having done so. A group in Cordova calling themselves Progressive Democrats offered him its nomination, but he declined. In the end, Wickersham decided to run as an Independent although he referred to himself as a Republican when asked about his party affiliations. He would rather represent those citizens who were free from corrupt boss rule, even if it meant his defeat, as he would at least have preserved his own self-respect.[6]

One time when Wickersham disembarked at Juneau, a group of friends greeted him with the question: "Tell us, Jim, what did you accomplish for Alaska in this last session of Congress?" He thought a moment and then said: "It isn't what I accomplished! It's what I prevented from happening! That's what you boys have got to be grateful for."

The need to be constantly on the alert to detect subversive legislative efforts placed Wickersham in an offensive role when appearing before congressional committees. One such situation came to light as soon as he returned for the 1916 session. Congressman Joshua W. Alexander, Democrat of Missouri, chairman of the Committee on Merchant Marine and Fisheries, had introduced a bill which would have given the Department of Commerce exclusive control of Alaska's fisheries and a companion bill which would take from the territorial legislature all authority over the fisheries, including the right to levy taxes on them.

The bills were an obvious continued effort on the part of the "fish trust" to get out from under any jurisdiction by the territorial legislature; they preferred to have federal officials in complete charge.

It was practically a redraft of the Calin bill which Wickersham had opposed so vigorously that it died in committee.

The most objectionable feature of both bills was a proviso whereby holders of a cannery or trapsite could obtain absolute and practically permanent title to the same. The bill was shown to be such a palpable attempt by the salmon canners to monopolize the fishing business that the committee refused to report on the measure.

One way in which the government bureau of fisheries and the private, Seattle-based fish companies maintained a close relationship was the hiring of bureau officials by the private firms at handsome salaries. This close alliance was noted in 1906 when David Jarvis, a longtime government bureaucrat, resigned to become president of the Northwest Fisheries Companies and lobbied a bill through Congress by which the packers got rid of all the cannery taxes, depleting the Alaska road fund about one-third thereby.[7]

On the surface, the law may have appeared as a conservation measure, but in practical operation, it was a monstrosity as it affected the territory and ethically questionable as far as the fish companies were concerned. In lieu of taxes, the fish companies were required to liberate salmon fry in their own private hatcheries. They received a tax credit of forty cents for each thousand salmon fry liberated, but the law required no proof that such an operation had taken place; the clerk of the district court was obliged to take the companies' agents' word for it.

The iniquity of the law became apparent to the Alaskans as they saw their fisheries being robbed by the alien fish trust and their tax coffers empty. The third division grand jury took occasion to expose and criticize the way in which the law operated, quoting the following statistics:

> Last year (1907) the Alaska Packers Association alone took over 800,000 cases of salmon from the waters of the third judicial division. They paid into the clerk's office the sum of thirty-two cents, in currency, and certificates in the amount of $32,272 for an alleged amount of fry liberated, for which no adequate proof was made that any court would admit as sufficient evidence of the fact.

In commenting on the grand jury's findings, Major Strong, who was then editor-publisher of the Katalla *Herald*, said that it was inconceivable that such a spoilation of the fisheries could have been permitted by Congress, "except through the densest ignorance, grossest misrepresentation, or on the hypothesis of venality in high places."[8]

Alaska's first legislature passed a memorial denouncing any congressional legislation giving canneries permanent trapsites. Still the Pacific Coast fish industry continued lobbying for control of Alaska's fisheries, and the Alexander bill was the latest. Secretary of Commerce William C. Redfield spoke in support of the bill and also recommended that section three of the 1912 Organic Act permitting the legislature to levy license taxes on the fishing industry be repealed.

Appearing in opposition to the bill Wickersham testified that it "would give the Libby McNeil Company, the Alaska Packers' Association and the Booth Fisheries Company, a monopoly of the Alaska fisheries and would represent a gift of $99,000 annually".[9] It placed no limitation on the number of trapsites which one person or corporation could own with an exclusive title in perpetuity. It would give the fish trust a complete monopoly of an industry worth $400 million.

The gross fishery products taken from Alaska from 1867 to 1916, according to official statistics, amounted to $247,363,828. Wickersham testified, in conclusion:

> I have been trying for seven years to get some laws passed here in order that we might have a fishing population in the territory; that we might have fishing hamlets and towns; that we might get something out of these fisheries with which to build homes, churches, schools, and establish a civilization there.
>
> But, on the contrary, the whole policy of these big fish trusts is to take everything out of the territory and not permit anything to come into it. They do not want to pay any taxes; they have never built a schoolhouse in the territory; they have never built a church or a home. They are robbing the territory. They have robbed the territory for thirty years of all of its fisheries. . . .[10]

Alaska's second legislature passed a law taxing cases of canned salmon processed in Alaska, whereupon the industry carried their protest up to the United States Supreme Court, which upheld Alaska's right to charge fisheries and mining companies a license tax.[11]

Wickersham succeeded in getting the Alexander bill killed for that session of Congress, but it was expected that the canneries would get it revived in the next session and Alaska's delegate would have to start the fight all over again.

On March 30, 1916, the forty-ninth anniversary of the signing of the treaty of the purchase of Alaska, Wickersham introduced the first bill asking Congress to accord Alaska full-fledged statehood in the family of states. Though not expecting its passage in the immediate future, he felt a start should be made.

In drafting his bill, he followed the enabling act of 1906 for the State of Oklahoma because it was a Democratic state and hence should appeal to the Democratic majority in Congress and because it was liberal in grants of money and in legal autonomy.[12]

In introducing the bill, Wickersham told his congressional colleagues on the House floor that "if the iron bands of government repression could be broken and population invited to settle her. . .valleys. . .they would in another decade erect there the forty-ninth sovereign American state. . .the richest and greatest of them all, the empire State of Alaska."

Statehood for the territory had been a longtime dream of Wickersham's. In a speech to the Seward Society of the Juneau high school on March 30 (Seward Day), 1907, he predicted that one day four sovereign states would be carved out of the territory - the state of Sitka, with its capital at Juneau; the state of Alaska, with its capital at Valdez; the state of Seward, with its capital at Nome; and the state of Tanana, with its capital at Fairbanks.[13]

Editor Troy poked fun at the delegate's delusions of grandeur in thinking that Alaska could ever become one or more sovereign states, but he continued to advocate "full territorial government." When Wickersham asked Troy publicly to explain the difference between his "full territorial government" and the "home rule" legislation on which the delegate had been working for years, the answer was vague. Hence, in order to take the thunder out of Troy's accusations, Wickersham introduced a bill providing for "a full territorial form of government," including in the bill everything he ever read in Troy's editorials. If and when it came before the Committee on Territories and was denounced, "then the boot would be on the Democratic foot!"[14]

Chapter 35

1916 Delegate Race

> *Alaska appears to have the usual factionalism in its politics this campaign year. . . .Alaska is mighty well represented in Congress by Delegate James Wickersham and in this period of development and construction, his services are needed at Washington more than ever before. To lose his services at this juncture would be a serious mistake. The territory cannot afford it. He is an encyclopedia of Alaska information. . . .* (Seattle Post-Intelligencer,*editorial, Sept.1,1916*)

Wickersham had two opponents in his fifth race for the delegateship—Charles Sulzer, a copper mine opperator on Prince of Wales Island, was the Democrats' nominee, and Mrs. Lena Morrow Lewis, a professional party organizer and lecturer, was the Socialists' choice. For a second time, the Republicans chose not to put a candidate in the field.

Charles August Sulzer came to Alaska in 1902 to be general manager of family-owned mining properties at Sulzer, including the Jumbo copper mine on Prince of Wales Island, forty miles west of Ketchikan. The copper mine had produced $1,250,000 and was continuing to produce at a rate of 5,000 tons a month.

Sulzer had been elected to the territorial Senate two years before, without campaigning. His brother William was a congressman for sixteen years and later governor of New York state. He visited Alaska frequently and supported home rule legislation for the territory.

Mrs. Lewis had traveled extensively in the territory organizing Socialist clubs. Before coming north she had been a professional lecturer, working out of the Socialist headquarters in Chicago.[1]

Wickersham faced the toughest race of his career. His aggressive independence was beginning to irk some of his most faithful disciples. A well-organized Democratic machine working in cooperation with the Shackleford machine posed a powerful opposition. However, he was fortunate in having more favorable press support than ever before. Four influential dailies were for him—the *Dispatch* in Juneau, the Anchorage *Times*, the Fairbanks *Times*, and the Nome *Nugget*. Even the Seattle *Post-Intelligencer* was strong for him this time. It attributed passage of the railroad bill to "his persistent, tenacious and intelligent effort, more than to any other agency or medium."

The anti-Wickersham press agreed unanimously that the delegate thrived on newspaper abuse as it made the people feel sorry for him and made them want to vote for him. The more the papers decried him, the more votes he got. As a consequence, the Ketchikan *Progressive Miner* vowed it would refrain from even mentioning his name so it would not feel it had helped him win another victory.

An advertisement ran almost daily in the pro-Wickersham press listing twenty-four separate accomplishments accredited to his legislative efforts, to counteract the Democrats' contention that all legislation beneficial to the territory had come through Democratic channels.

Wickersham's conspicuous disillusionment with the Wilson administration lost him votes as the general feeling among the people was that they were better off than they were during the Taft administration. His embitterment came primarily from the administration's support of the Alexander fish bill which sought to withdraw from Alaskans the few legislative powers captured from the Taft administration and transfer them to irresponsible bureau chiefs in Washington.

Sulzer's supporters touted him as "a friend of the laboring man" and exhibited a written statement to that effect signed by the president and secretary of the American Federation of Miners' branch union at Sulzer. In controversion, the Wickites produced an affidavit signed by a former mine employee who described the poor living accommodations at Sulzer's mine as the worst he had experienced in his thirty years as a miner; the ten-year-old, one-room bunkhouse accommodated fifty-one men - it was without windows and was bug-ridden.[2]

Wickersham distributed 2,500 copies of an endorsement by the Washington State Federation of Labor to balance Sulzer's endorsement by the Western Federation of Miners.

One of Sulzer's most vigorous campaigners was George Grigsby, the Democratic candidate for territorial attorney general. Both Wickersham and Grigsby employed the same brand of revivalist, crusading style of oratory and pulled no punches when attacking an adversary. Both had been Alaskan residents about the same length of time and both had been very active in territorial politics; both had crossed party lines in their quest for office.

Grigsby first came to Nome in 1902 as an assistant to his father, Colonel Melvin Grigsby, the United States district attorney for the second division. Colonel Grigsby allegedly spent only four months in Nome out of the two years he held the office, spending the remainder of his time in Washington answering charges of bribery and jury fixing. He was finally asked to resign because of his absence in direct countervention of orders from the United States attorney general.[3]

George served as acting district attorney during his father's extended absences and was constantly accused of misconduct in the performance of his duties as a law enforcement officer; he was eventually removed from office by presidential order. This angered him so that he renounced his Republican affiliation and vowed that henceforth he would be a Democrat. But when he made a bid for a judgeship under the Democrats, he was turned down on the grounds that he had served and been removed during the Taft administration.[4]

A significant factor in the 1916 delegate race was the plebescite or straw vote on prohibition authorized by the 1915 legislature. Although the Organic Act of 1912 did not convey to the legislature the power to control the liquor traffic, the dry referendum was designed to provide Congress with some indication of how Alaskans felt about the liquor issue.

The control of intoxicating liquor had been a troublesome problem ever since the arrival of white men in the territory, particularly because of the debauching effect on the native population. Municipal ordinances developed licensing systems to support local facilities, including schools. Soon local institutions depended largely on monies collected from illegal operations such as sale of liquor, gambling, and prostitution. Towns were split between those residents who abhored such vices under any circumstances and those who argued they were necessary to support schools and other programs essential to civilization.

To prepare for the referendum, the national Women's Christian Temperance Union organized a campaign; they sent several workers to the territory, headed by Mrs. Cornelia Templeton Hatcher, a handsome, talented speaker and organizer. She organized WCTU chapters throughout the territory and distributed literature supporting prohibition.

Inclusion of the prohibition referendum on the same ballot as the delegate, attorney general, and members of the legislature forced these candidates to take a public stand on the issue. Wickersham promised to introduce the necessary legislation in Congress should the Alaskan voters indicate their desire to have Alaska made a "dry" district, intimating at the same time that his opponent was a servant of the liquor interests. Sulzer, too, promised to carry out the will of the people but his campaign manager in the first division was attorney William Holzheimer, secretary of the Juneau Liquor Association. He was accused of spending extravagant amounts of money promoting Sulzer's candidacy, with the major portion allegedly coming from the California Liquor Dealers' Association.

Alaskans voted almost two to one in favor of making Alaska "dry." Governor Strong said that he thought the vote demonstrated quite plainly that a substantial majority of the people of Alaska stood for civic righteousness and that they had come to a lively realization of the menace of the liquor traffic.[5]

An interesting sidelight to the vote was that the mining camps voted universally in favor of prohibition; this disproved the campaign argument that the roughneck and freedom-loving workmen could not be procured to take out the gold in interior Alaska mines if "the lid was on."

There were so many irregularities discovered in the voting process that an accurate final tally could not be made for months. Military personnel stationed in the territory were not eligible to vote, yet they did; Eskimos and Indians who were not American citizens had voted; second division voters were not required to register, as they were elsewhere; individuals voted in districts where they did not have legal residence; technically, hundreds of ballots could be declared void, depending on who made the determination; if wholesale voiding of ballots was resorted to, it could be anyone's race.

At Ouzinki the natives used Democratic sample ballots instead of official ballots and their names appeared in the registry in the same handwriting. At Tanana, a small trading post at the confluence of the Yukon and Tanana Rivers, 145 votes were cast, which was proof that the soldiers at Fort Gibbon had voted, though ineligible to do so. At Utica, where Wickersham won a plurality, the Democratic officials claimed the election was illegal because official ballots were not used. At Susitna, where Wickersham got every vote, the United States commissioner was replaced eight weeks later.[6]

As the election results remained in doubt and there seemed a possibility that Wickersham had been defeated, he received a letter from Debbie, who was in the East visiting with Darrell. He treasured it so much that he tucked it into his diary, where it remains until this day. Her political awareness, her confidence in and devotion to her husband made him proud of her and deeply grateful that she was his wife. She wrote:

My dear husband:

Some people may think you are to be pitied and want to sympathize with you but as far as I am concerned, I think you are to be congratulated. You have worked long enough for other people and got nothing but kicks for it, now we will try it for ourselves awhile and I want you to decide for yourself what you want to do.

I would just as soon go to Alaska as to remain in Seattle, and if I ever get back to you I don't care where we are—so we are together. I felt dreadfully over Hughes's defeat at first, but everything has its compensations and to see George W. Wickersham throw up his hands and "holler" comforts me greatly.

The Progressives took their spite out on Wall Street and I can't say I blame them—only it was too bad to make a fine man like Hughes the "goat"—but if he had been elected I don't think you and Dan would have had much show with him.

I had a lovely trip with Darrell from New York to Buffalo in his auto—spent a month with him and would have stayed longer . . .but I wanted to get where I could see the Alaska papers.

When George (Jeffery) got your telegram saying you would not be here (Washington) before the middle of December I could have wept—it seemed so long. I try not to feel blue but when I think of your having to start all over again at your age—and how helpless I am, I certainly have to whistle hard to keep up my courage—but I guess that is more homesickness than anything else. . . .

I am at Mrs. Morton's in our old room and will stay here until you come—then we must go back to Congress Hall and finish in a blaze of glory. I have to laugh when I think of our side of the dining room—beginning with the first table—Davenport was defeated—then. . . .

After reading and thinking about his wife's letter, Wickersham wrote in his diary:

The above letter from Debbie is so typical of her clean, solid and lovable character that I have pasted it here hoping to retain it as long as I live. I almost hope now—quite so—that I am elected for her sake, but if not I'll certainly see to it that she loses nothing in comfort or happiness by the change.

Personally I have felt a sense of relief that I may be free from the heavy burden of duty to Alaska which she, equally with me, has so aided me to carry for nearly sixteen years. God bless her![7]

Chapter 36

Contested Election Case of Wickersham vs. Sulzer

> *Bully for the governor and Davidson. Evidently they think better of themselves and their party than to be parties to a ballot box robbery. Grigsby, of course, will not hesitate. . .like Troy, he thinks nothing of doing partisan politics.*
>
> *But, the Democratic organization will have much internecine trouble for the governor and others know that when a candidate has received a majority of the votes at a free and honest election, it is a dangerous and a revolutionary act to attempt to throw out the votes and to reverse the result.* (*Wickersham Diary, Mar. 8, 1917*)

Returning to Washington for the lame duck session, Wickersham was depressed and puzzled about his political future. As he sat looking out the window of his train compartment, he tried to analyze the situation. Had the people turned against him or was there political skulduggery going on, as reflected in fraudulent voting? If so, how could he hope for a fair hearing with all of the offices filled with Democrats? Maybe he should quit politics? Perhaps he had taken on too powerful an enemy in his fight against the corporate interests who were exploiting Alaska's natural resources?

No doubt the liquor referendum affected the election returns because much of the money sent to the territory to defeat the referendum was used to buy anti-Wickersham advertisements.

In accordance with the people's wishes as expressed in the liquor referendum, Wickersham introduced a bill which would make it unlaw-ful for anyone to sell, manufacture, or dispense any intoxicating liquor

313

or alcohol in the territory, or have it in his possession, except for medicinal or scientific purposes, for which a permit had to be gotten from the clerk of court, to be effective January 1, 1918.

The bill further provided that anyone might swear out a search warrant to search any premises for liquor; and no property rights in alcoholic beverages were recognized. The maximum penalty for violation was one year in jail and a fine of $1,000.

Mrs. Hatcher came to Washington to lobby for the bill's passage. She and the delegate had never met before but the two got along very well, she interviewing practically every member of Congress while he prepared his testimony for committee hearings and on the floor of the House.

During the House debate, Wickersham admitted that he was not a prohibitionist himself but he was acting on behalf of the good and clean people of Alaska, who voted to make their country a "dry" district.

Some opponents argued that it was a God-given right to have a bottle of whiskey in one's possession! Others said that prohibition legislation drove people to strong drink and recalled that the first law that was ever violated by man was a prohibition law for Adam and Eve! As soon as God was out of sight they broke the law and they ate of the forbidden fruit. Then, like a liar, a sneak, and a shypocrite, Adam blamed it on the woman.

The bill sailed through Congress without the formality of a roll call. The Washington papers gave Mrs. Hatcher major credit for its speedy passage. All the papers ran pictures of her on the front page the day the president signed the bill.[1]

Wickersham had other legislation which he was anxious to get through Congress before his possible demise as Alaska's delegate. He wanted to settle his old score with Colonel Richardson by defeating a half a million dollar appropriation for the Alaska Road Commission, of which Richardson was chairman. If successful, hopefully the commission would go out of existence. The personal hatred between the two men overshadowed the benefits which might revert to the territory in having half a million for its road programs. The appropriation was killed.

With this accomplished, he next turned his attention to a bill authorizing the territorial legislature to establish and maintain a school system, drawing its support from the "Alaska Fund" from which Richardson had been drawing his road funds. This power was withheld from the legislature by an amendment to the Organic Act by

Senator Nelson to protect Richardson's road funds. The school bill passed two days before the session ended.[2]

Wickersham also saw his bill for the establishment of Mt. McKinley national park enacted into law. He had first introduced the bill the previous June at the urging of the Boone and Crockett Club of New York City. Charles Sheldon, hunter-naturalist and Belmore Browne, mountain climber-artist, both of whom had spent considerable time in the proposed park area, were the chief instigators of the idea, in order to preserve its wildlife environment.

The bill set aside approximately twenty-two hundred square miles around Mt. McKinley as a national park. Originally it was proposed to be called Denali national park, but the name got changed during the legislative process. President Wilson signed the bill into law on February 26, 1917.

The Boone and Crockett Club passed a resolution expressing appreciation to Wickersham for his efforts in getting the bill passed. It read, in part: "It is particularly fitting that Mr. Wickersham, who was the first man to attempt to climb Mt. McKinley, in 1903, should have introduced the bill. . .and it is fitting also that the bill should bear his name." It was signed by W.A. Wadsworth, president, and Kermit Roosevelt, secretary.[3]

Wickersham kept busy attending to his legislative duties, but he was depressed in spirit. Word from Alaska was not encouraging as it appeared that his political enemies were intent on getting the canvassing board to throw out certain precincts which would assure victory to Sulzer. Also, he was worried that he was losing his eyesight; his oculist told him he had only 25 percent vision in his right eye.

On March 1, 1917, the official canvassing board, by a vote of two to one, declared Wickersham the winner by 31 votes, the final tally being: Wickersham, 6,490; Sulzer, 6,459; Mrs. Lewis, 1,346. The canvassing board consisted of Governor Strong, Surveyor General Charles Davidson, and John Pugh, Collector of Customs and brother-in-law of Judge Jennings, the district judge for the first division; all three were registered Democrats.

In announcing the board's decision, Governor Strong issued a statement disavowing any partisanship on the part of the individual board members. He said that "the question of partisan politics had not entered into their deliberations" as they had been actuated solely by a desire to perform their duty in accordance with the expressed will of the voters. They did not enter into the legal technicalities of the vote as they considered themselves a ministerial body rather than a judicial tribunal.

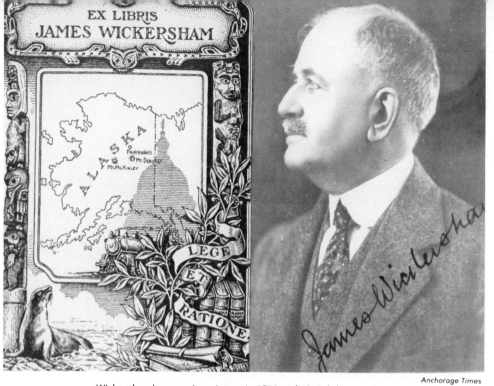

Anchorage Times

Wickersham's campaign picture in 1916 and 1918 delegate races.

Anchorage Times

Left: Governor J. F. A. Strong, 1913-18. *Right:* Governor John W. Troy, 1933-39.

The board had decided to count all returns from all precincts, irrespective of irregularities that might be on the face of the returns, and to issue a certificate of election to the one receiving the highest number of votes. Strong and Davidson voted for that course of procedure and Pugh against it.

In arriving at this decision, the majority of the board disregarded Attorney General Grigsby's opinion that the precincts of Utica, Choggiung, Nushagak, and Bonnifield should not be counted. These precincts gave Wickersham fifty-one votes and Sulzer eleven; with them omitted Sulzer would have had a plurality of nine.[4]

On Grigsby's solicitation, the board agreed to give Sulzer's attorneys opportunity to secure any legal writ they considered necessary, up until ten o'clock the following day, before it issued a certificate of election to Wickersham. Sulzer's attorneys, John Winn and Jack Hollenthal, petitioned Judge Jennings to have a writ of mandamus served on each of the three board members, individually, setting aside their decision of Wickersham's election and instead declaring that Sulzer was the winner.

The board was directed to show cause why the precincts of Choggiung, Deering, Nizina, Nushagak, Utica, Bonnifield and Vault should not be thrown out of the official count because official ballots had not been used. Grigsby had told the canvassing board that the Australian ballot was clearly mandatory in Alaska and that only those precincts could be counted where the Australian official ballots were used or where proper certificates as to their nonuse had been made.

Telegrams had been sent to the board explaining that the official ballots had not arrived in time to be used on election day, but the telegrams allegedly had not been received before the board had completed its tally. If all the suggested precincts were thrown out, it meant Wickersham lost 69 votes to Sulzer's 19, making the final vote Wickersham 6,421 and Sulzer 6,440.

Immediately on being served with the writ, the board convened and on motion Grigsby was disqualified as legal counsel for the board on the basis that it was a federal board and Grigsby was a territorial official.

Judge Jennings insisted the law had been violated since the election judges had failed to certify that they had used unofficial ballots through failure of the official ballots to arrive, and he issued a peremptory writ of mandamus on the board, ordering it to issue a certificate of election to Sulzer without holding any hearings where witnesses could be heard.

Pugh agreed with the judge's order immediately, but Strong and Davidson remonstrated with the judge, inasmuch as they had received a communication from Emery Valentine of Juneau, to the effect that irregularities existed in returns from forty-seven other precincts, which if declared "false, spurious and illegal," Wickersham would come out the winner. Strong and Davidson acknowledged that there were technical irregularities but took the position that no fraudulent intent was involved, hence the irregularities should be overlooked.

Valentine said that if the votes of all the forty-seven which he protested were thrown out as the votes of the precincts brought into court previously were thrown out, it would reduce the vote of Sulzer by 1,000 votes.

Violations of the election code included: forwarded no register of voters; election judges not sworn in; discrepancies between the certificate of vote tallies and ballots cast; no certificate of results forwarded with the returns; no registration of voters.

Right in Juneau's first precinct there was no certificate of result of the election forwarded and there was no election register. In Loring there was no certificate of result forwarded with the returns but one was filed separately and subsequently sent to the canvassing board after the final tally had been made. Election returns were not sworn to, and the judges were not sworn in.

It was learned from other sources that the votes in the Bristol Bay precincts, which were some of those forming the grounds for the Sulzer writ of mandamus, were counted if they favored Sulzer and thrown out if they favored Wickersham. At both Naknek and Nushagak, only Democratic sample ballots were used; in Naknek, Wickersham and Lewis got no votes, but in Nushagak, the name of Wickersham was written in in ink and he got the majority.

It should be noted that prior to the 1916 general election, official ballots had never been used. The only form of transportation to remote villages was by boat, and there was only monthly service. Many places did not have registration books, and many election judges never bothered going through the ritual of oath-taking, all of which was well known to Jennings, Grigsby, Winn, and Hellenthal, who had been Alaskan residents since 1900.

As Wickersham was being kept informed by his friends of what was happening in Juneau, it became crystal clear that Grigsby and Jennings had undertaken to advise the canvassing board to steal the election. Thereupon, Wickersham decided to institute a suit in contest before the House of Representatives. He felt duty bound to do so on behalf of the voters who had elected him and to Strong and Davidson, who had incurred the ill-will of the party bosses by doing their duty fearlessly and according to law.

John Rustgard, former United States district attorney for the first division, prepared a brief as amicus curiae, holding that the board was entirely within the law in its canvassing procedure and was not subject to court control.

The canvassing board, however, complied with the judge's order and issued a certificate of election to Sulzer, whereupon he left for Washington and was sworn in and took his seat.

Wickersham filed his official protest with the House giving a series of reasons why Sulzer should not be recognized as Alaska's delegate in Congress. Both men began taking depositions in Washington, D.C., Seattle, and throughout the territory. Both also were busy lining up congressmen on their side for the time when the case would be heard. Some interesting human interest stories developed from the depositions.

In some villages, natives were handed ballots covered by a paper frame with apertures over the names which were to be marked with an X; this mechanical means would guide them to the right candidate's name. In Seldova the United States deputy marshal entertained the natives at a cake and coffee party, handing each a Sulzer-marked ballot and instructing them how to mark it. Going directly from the party to the polling place, the natives double-crossed the marshal by voting for Wickersham, even though there were no Wickersham sample ballots in the precinct. Sulzer received only thirteen votes out of a total of eighty-two.

At Kodiak the Russian priest admitted he preached a Sulzer sermon, displayed Sulzer's picture with the holy pictures on the church walls, and personally solicited native votes while acting as an election judge.[5]

Interminable delays prevented a decision in the case until after Wickersham and Sulzer had run a second delegate race in November, 1918. The elections committee had voted unanimously in July of that year that Wickersham had been elected delegate by a plurality of forty-seven votes but waited until the following January to bring it to the House floor.

The committee upheld the canvassing board's counting the returns from the six contested precincts on the grounds that though they had technical defects, they clearly showed the intent of the voter. It also held that the provisions of the Alaska law, in this regard, were directorial and not mandatory, thus reversing Judge Jennings' opinion. The soldier vote was thrown out.

Alaska's Tammany leaders persuaded the committee chairman, Riley Wilson, Democrat of Louisiana, to keep the report secret until after the second delegate race, for fear it might affect the voters' attitude.

Wickersham was obliged to practice the difficult art of patience. He delayed his departure from Washington, hoping daily that the House would take some action. He and Debbie were living in one large room on the second floor of a rooming house. Since he was not receiving a salary, they had to economize. The government provided him with office space while preparing his contest case. During his spare time, he completed his fifth Alaska judicial report and sent it to the printer.

When the matter was finally brought to the House floor, the committee's report was adopted by a vote of 229 to 64, thus ousting Sulzer from the delegate's seat and turning it over to Wickersham to occupy until March 4. As soon as the vote was announced, Wickersham was sworn in and assumed his duties.

Both Sulzer and Wickersham were paid full salaries for the two years during which their contest remained undecided. Wickersham received approximately $20,000 back pay and mileage; his salary was $15,000 for two years and he was entitled to two round-trips from Fairbanks to Washington. An additional $4,000 was allowed him for the preparation of his case.[6]

Things did not go as well for Governor Strong, however. His first four-year term was about to expire and the party bosses were determined to block his reappointment because of his refusal to join in their fraudulent plot to "terminate the Wickersham dynasty."

The Tammany bosses realized it would be difficult to discredit the governor in the eyes of Washington officialdom so they started delving into his past, hoping to find something they could use. They discovered that he was born in Canada and had never become a naturalized American citizen. When this was determined as a fact, Secretary of Interior Lane requested his resignation.

Chapter 37

A Frustrated Delegate Fights For Survival

> Politically and personally Wickersham is the best personal advertiser who ever came north. He knows no rule of fairness or political honor which he will observe a minute longer than it serves his interests to do so. . .(there is) no length he will not go in the effort to obtain credit or hurt an opponent. . . .
>
> This is probably the reason he has worn out his welcome and his "pull" in Alaska. He has the ability which would enable a kinder man to remain delegate of Alaska forever, but. . .his political Machiavellianism makes him the menace he always will be in Alaska and has finally reduced his voting strength until it is no longer formidable - hoisted by his own petard!
> (*Fairbanks* News-Miner, *Mar.28,1919*)

The third territorial legislature passed an open primary law aimed at doing away with the proxy system and party convention nominations. Those favoring the open primary contended that the proxy system kept the people from having any voice and generated fraud. Opponents contended it destroyed party responsibility as officeholders were not beholden to platform or program. Alaska's first open primary was held on April 30, 1918.

Wickersham had to change his traditional method for announcing his candidacy for reelection. No longer could he sit back and wait for his adversaries to declare their candidacy, not knowing what the incumbent planned to do. The deadline for declaration of candidacy was two months before the election. Wickersham filed as a Republican, the first time he had done so since he started running for the delegateship; he had no opposition in the primary.

Sulzer was renominated by the Democratic machine, and he was opposed in the primary by William Maloney, territorial mine inspector. It was generally believed that Governor Strong and a combination of labor unions were supporting Maloney in an effort to defeat Sulzer. Strong insisted that he had tried to discourage Maloney from running but his counsel was ignored.

Maloney came to Nome from Colorado in 1900 and had mined on the Seward Peninsula for twelve years. He and Strong became friends while both were living in Nome. When the office of mine inspector was created in 1913, Governor Strong appointed Maloney to the office.

National Committeeman Tom Donohoe urged Maloney to withdraw, threatening that the Democratic organization would refuse to recognize him even if he defeated Sulzer in the primary and would put up another candidate in the general election to run against him. When Maloney refused to withdraw, Donohoe promised him "the fight of his life."[1]

Mrs. Cornelia Hatcher took to the stump on behalf of Maloney, declaring that Sulzer and his cohorts had tried to destroy Alaska's prohibition law. Sulzer's "full territorial government" bill provided for another liquor referendum, giving the people an opportunity to reverse their former decision and vote to legalize the manufacture and sale of intoxicating liquor.

Attorney General Grigsby campaigned on Sulzer's behalf and he and Mrs. Hatcher often exchanged uncomplimentary observations about one another. She frequently referred to his bibulousness and he called her "a fine old lady with a 60-horsepower tongue and a mule-power brain."[2]

Sulzer defeated Maloney easily, receiving 3,450 votes to Maloney's 1,430. Immediately following the primary, Governor Riggs asked for Maloney's resignation as mine inspector, stating that he did so at the request of the Democratic organization.

Wickersham launched his campaign in Nome the first week in August. He delivered one of his "hell and brimstone" speeches "roasting" those "penurious peanut politicians" who tried to steal an election from him. He said they might have thought they could scare one who was easily frightened and easily bluffed, but he was neither, so he went to Washington and "sat by the rat hole until it came out and I swatted it with a club."[3] He referred to Sulzer as the "court ordered delegate" and stressed his inept performance in Washington, while usurping the delegate's seat.

Wickersham placed himself squarely on record in favor of an eight-hour day and ridiculed Judge Bunnell's opinion that it was unconstitutional, calling it "the silliest rot" he had ever read in a judicial decision. He also said he favored continued prohibition for the territory. Sulzer had nimbly sidestepped both of these issues in his campaign speeches.[4]

The new town of Anchorage was on the delegate's campaign itinerary; he traveled there by ship from Seward. Southbound he traveled on the first through train to carry passengers and freight between the two towns, leaving Anchorage nine o'clock one morning and arriving in Seward at seven o'clock the following morning. Their train jumped the tracks half a dozen times, and the passengers were crowded into a small freight caboose halfway to Seward. What irked the delegate most of all was that the division superintendent hooked on his private car fifty-four miles out of Seward and didn't even invite any of the passengers to share his deluxe accommodations, leaving them to stand up all night while the chairs in his car were unoccupied.[5]

Campaigning in southeastern in a motor launch, they ran into such foul weather that they had to heave-to in little inland bays while the storm slackened its ferocity. They were in Taku harbor the night the *Princess Sophia* was driven onto Vanderbilt reef in Lynn Canal and sank with 346 passengers aboard. It had left Skagway with a full load as many interior residents had been stranded in Skagway for days on account of a shipping strike against the American steamship companies. Several prominent Alaskans lost their lives in this tragedy, including John Pugh, collector of customs.

When the campaigners eventually arrived in Juneau, their political efforts were curtailed because the town was under quarantine due to an influenza epidemic and all public gatherings were banned. The town was also in mourning over the *Sophia* wreck and in no mood to think about politics.

Election day came and went, with the final results as confusing and uncertain as they were two years before. There were the same irregularities in voting procedures as in 1916 and the same determination by the Democratic machine to topple Wickersham by whatever means necessary.

The Wickershams returned to Washington where he resumed his work as delegate, for the brief interval remaining in his term. He did so with little fervor as it seemed obvious that another contested case loomed on the horizon. Moved by bitterness and frustration, Wickersham resorted to personal revenge, lashing out against any and all whom he considered his enemy. The first to feel his wrath was Secretary of Interior Lane, whom he held responsible for Governor Riggs' active campaigning against him in the recent delegate race.

The day after he was reinstated as delegate, Wickersham wrote an open letter to Lane demanding his immediate resignation and accusing him of knowing that Riggs was "hopelessly incompetent" when he appointed him to the railway commission and later to the governorship. Wickersham distributed copies of his letter to the press and to members of Congress simultaneous to his mailing a copy to Lane.

Holding Lane responsible for Riggs' incompetence in constructing the railroad and for his participation in "the most corrupt political machine we have ever seen in Alaska," he wrote:

> Drunkenness, Mr. Secretary, in the headquarters building at Nenana was publicly flaunted in Mr. Riggs' face, and cost the government one million dollars and years of loss of time. . . .
>
> Mrs. Riggs and Mrs. Cramer, wife of the disbursing officer, voted illegally at the Nenana election in November 1916. . . Since the husbands encouraged their wives to vote, all four were guilty of a criminal act and ought to be punished as if they were plain common people, instead of securing immunity because they were high officials. . . .
>
> Poor Ballinger was a "piker" compared to you. When Riggs had become a menace to the completion of the Alaska government railroad through his incompetency, you appointed him governor of Alaska, notwithstanding his record at Nenana. . . .
>
> Your partisan influence as secretary of interior and as administrator of the government railroad was such that it was directly responsible for many criminal violations of the election laws there. . . .
>
> It was your bad example which made the ARC (Alaska Road Commission) the head and front of a corrupt political machine . . .that undertook to steal the election for delegate.[6]

Wickersham concluded his harangue by listing ten reasons why Lane should withdraw from the management of the government railroad.

When Congress adjourned without making an appropriation for continued construction of the railroad, Wickersham was blamed by the majority of Alaskans because of his scathing criticism of Lane's management. A group of Republican senators filibustered the bill to death, arguing that an investigation should be launched before additional funds were approved.[7]

Whether Wickersham's widely publicized letter to Lane was responsible or not, both Lane and William Edes, one of the three commission executives, handed in their resignations within a year.

In the same spirit of angry retaliation, Wickersham launched an attack on Judge Bunnell and District Attorney Roth to prevent their Senate confirmation, as both had campaigned actively against him. It was they allegedly who advised the soldiers at Fort Gibbon and Fort Liscum to cast ballots, even though they were well aware of their illegality. Though Wickersham succeeded in keeping the two officials from being confirmed, they stayed in office through recess appointments until 1921, when they were replaced by Republicans appointed by President Harding. Wickersham thereby deepened Bunnell's hatred for him beyond redemption.

Two weeks after Bunnell was relieved of the judgeship, the board of trustees of the Alaska Agricultural College and School of Mines offered him the presidency of the college, which he accepted.

While Wickersham was busy in Washington dealing out punishment to his adversaries, the Tammany machine was busy in Juneau counselling the canvassing board on how to handle the election returns in the delegate race. Grigsby delivered a twenty-page ruling to the board to the effect that the board was merely a counting machine and must accept any returns which a local precinct official had certified. This opinion was diametrically opposed to the one he rendered two years before and also was opposite to Judge Jennings' ruling rendered at the same time when he ordered the board to give the certificate of election to Sulzer instead of to Wickersham. Both officials had abrogated the canvassing board's original decision to restrict itself to a counting role when Wickersham was declared the winner by thirty-one votes.

Governor Riggs and Acting Collector of Customs Garfield voted to accede to the attorney general's ruling, but Surveyor General Davidson cast a dissenting vote, reading a statement into the board's minutes pointing out the inconsistency in the attorney general's legal opinions. Wickersham's attorneys were on hand to protest the board's action.[8]

When Congress adjourned, the Wickershams left for the West Coast, traveling via Los Angeles and San Francisco, in order to visit the delegate's sister, Jennie Hanson, and his brother Edgar. The Hansons were living in Los Angeles as Charlie was convalescing from a serious illness, and Edgar and Lizzie were living in Pasadena. In San Francisco the Wickershams stayed at the Palace Hotel. At a private dinner sponsored by the chamber of commerce, Wickersham talked about Alaska coal being shipped south to San Francisco. He said he was working on legislation permitting the leasing of coal lands in Alaska so that cheaper fuel costs would accrue to the local residents. In his audience was Captain Robert Dollar, president of the Dollar Steamship Company and he expressed great interest in the idea of having Alaskan coal available on the West Coast.

In a newspaper interview, Wickersham advocated the construction of a tunnel under the Bering Straits like that under the English Channel; it would connect Alaska with Siberia, which would contribute to a railway trade between Asia and North America.

While at the Frye Hotel in Seattle, the delegate told a reporter from the Seattle *Union Record* that he planned to sail north to Juneau in a few days "to study the latest improvements in the art of stealing elections. I haven't heard that the canvassing board intends to issue a certificate to Sulzer," Wickersham continued, "but it is a cinch that they will, no matter what the returns are. The tricks that Johnnie Troy and Governor Riggs won't be able to think of will not be worth mentioning."[9]

While still in Seattle awaiting his steamer's departure, Wickersham received word from his Juneau attorneys, Messrs. Rustgard and Marshall, that the canvassing board had reported unofficially a vote tally giving Sulzer 4,487 votes to Wickersham's 4,454 and Connally (Socialist) 2,329 votes; no final official report or certificate of election had been issued. His attorneys indicated there were ample grounds to contest the election results as there was evidence of illegal voting, intimidation, coercion, creation of illegal voting precincts, destruction of ballots, and several missing precincts.

When Wickersham got to Juneau and began preparing his petition in contest against Sulzer, he soon concluded that there was very much more fraud in 1918 than in 1916, and for that reason he was confident he could defeat Sulzer's claim to election before the House of Representatives.

Both sides were quietly planning their strategy when the news came over the wire that Sulzer had died. He was aboard his launch, the *Taku II*, en route to Ketchikan from his home in Sulzer to seek medical treatment for a stomach ailment when death claimed him.

Without precedent in Alaska's political history, the moot question was —who would be delegate under those circumstances? The Democratic canvassing board moved quickly; it concluded its compilation and issued a certificate of election in the name of Sulzer, even though they knew he had died two days previous. They forwarded it to the clerk of the House of Representatives. The ballots had been in the hands of the three board members for months, and only when they heard Sulzer had died did they hurriedly complete their canvass and issue a certificate in the name of a dead man.

The Tammany machine decided a special election should be held to fill the vacancy created by Sulzer's death. The legislature happened to be in session, and so, at the request of the governor, passed a bill providing for such an election. Both parties held meetings to prepare for the election. The Republicans voted unanimously not to place a candidate in the field, agreeing with Wickersham's contention that he was the true winner in the November election when he ran against Sulzer, hence there was no vacancy requiring another election. His fellow party members voted to support him in his contest for the seat.

The Democrats nominated Grigsby to run for delegate. The Ketchikan labor union nominated L.J. Jones of Ketchikan to run against Grigsby. It was hoped that a coalition of workingmen, anti-machine Democrats, and independent voters would unite behind Jones.

Ignoring the special election set for June 3, Wickersham hurried back to Washington to file his notice of contest based on the November election, in hopes that this action would stop Grigsby from being seated when he arrived with his certificate of election from the special election. Wickersham did not get the support he hoped for from his Republican colleagues; this was a great disappointment to him. Representative Mondell, with whom he had the fisticuff encounter years before, headed the opposition against Wickersham.

Grigsby won the special election with a plurality of 980 votes over Jones, carrying the first, third and fourth divisions, but losing the second, where he had made his home for many years.[10]

The canvassing board issued a certificate of election to Grigsby and he left immediately for Washington to present his credentials and was permitted to take his oath of office without question. The Republican majority in the House refused to grant Wickersham's request to postpone Grigsby's seating until the contest case was decided.[11]

Just before adjournment, the House passed a resolution giving legal recognition to Wickersham's election contest, naming Grigsby as his opponent in the place of Sulzer. The two contestants were given ninety days in which to take testimony to support their claims to the delegateship. The resolution also gave Wickersham authority to examine forty soldiers and signal corps officers, who were to be assembled in Valdez for that purpose; it did not require the men to disclose for whom they voted.

It was a strenuous three months for Wickersham taking depositions throughout the territory and in Seattle. It was an agonizing ordeal reaching its climax in Valdez. After having interviewed a group of soldiers at Fort Liscum, he was walking along the main street of Valdez,

on his way to his hotel room, when he was assaulted by Hal and Tom
Selby, the father and son proprietors of the *Prospector-Miner*. The
ferocity of the attack made it a banner line story in all of the major
newspapers in the territory, with varying interpretations, depending on
the editor's feeling toward the delegate.

Wickersham gave a blow by blow description of the assault in his
diary:

> Aug. 23. Took depositions of Donald H. Tyer and his wife this
> forenoon. Tyer swore that he voted for me on last Nov. 5 - in
> which I am satisfied he committed perjury. Mrs. Tyer refused to
> say whether she had voted for Sulzer or me and I requested
> them to remain for further hearing next Thurs., hoping to get
> the evidence.
>
> After the hearings were ended I started to my rooms - two
> blocks away. As I came to the S.E. corner of McKinley and
> Reservation st., I saw some men there, and when I got close
> enough, I recognized Dimond, Grigsby's lawyer, as one of them.
> He moved away as one of the men blocked my way and said to
> me: "You insulted my sister in your examination—she is over
> there crying."
>
> I answered as soon as my surprise would permit, "Who, no I
> did not insult your sister," and he answered, "Yes, you did and
> she is over there crying now, and I am going to beat you up." I
> am not sure about this last expression—it may have been "smash
> your face," or some such form, but it meant an assault.
>
> Immediately he struck at me but as I have a square view with
> my good eye, I parried it, but he kept coming. The man by his
> side, at my right and blind side, said to him, "Hit him—kill
> him" and as the fight progressed, repeated, "kill the son of a
> bitch" and the young pugilist did his best.
>
> I was on the outside edge of the sidewalk and either one of
> them pushed me off or I stepped off backwards and stumbled -
> my right, blind side coming toward them, when the young man
> sprang at me quickly and struck me two or more heavy smash-
> ing blows on the right side of my face, breaking out one of my
> back molar teeth and badly bruising my face on that side.
>
> The last heavy blow knocked me down, but I soon got up. A
> man with a black coat, whom I since learned was Cassler, depu-
> ty marshal, stood between us and waved his hand to my assail-
> ants saying, "That will do."

While the scrap was on, and after I got up, the elder of my assailants kept encouraging the younger with the cry of "kill him —kill the son of a bitch." I was so blind that I could not tell who he was—he was on my right side. I am totally blind in my right eye. . .I was later told that the men were the Selbys, father and son; father and brother of Mrs. Tyer, whom I had so recently examined.

I went up to Ritchie's office—no one came near me—no one said a word. Ritchie soon heard of it and came in and we went down to my hotel and I called in Dr. Silverman. I was not hurt except on my right side—and on my head. My molar tooth was broken square off and my face badly mauled up. My blind eye was black and the ear and jaw made very sore.

I am informed that Selby is a much younger man than I - that his son is twenty-two and an athlete and has just had a year's training in the army. Dimond, who was with them, is mayor of Valdez. Well, it took three of them on my blind side to knock me out anyway. I feel sure I can lick them one at a time notwithstanding my sixty-two years and blind eye—but I did not.

Aug. 24. My 62nd birthday. Sick and sore—a black eye—the blind one—and a smashed jaw—not a pleasant anniversary. Of course I cannot chew and can hardly swallow liquids.

My friends have urged me to have my assailants arrested but after a night of painful consideration I think I can use the incident to a better advantage, for every official here is either a partisan opponent ready to violate the law of homicide to injure me, or so far under the control of those as to be unwilling to assist in enforcing the law.

The signal corps men are also pleased at my humiliation and publicly express their feelings. I am satisfied beyond any doubt that Tyer—Selby's son-in-law—swore falsely and that others will do so in saying he and they voted for me instead of Sulzer.

I think it is a deliberate plan of their lawyer leaders to do me all the injury they can—they are now frightened at the thought of being prosecuted for illegal voting—a felony—and think to bulldoze me to quit.[12]

Wickersham remained a week in Valdez, remaining in his hotel room and keeping a hot water bottle on his jaw to relieve him of a severe neuralgic pain. He could not chew his food so was obliged to subsist on a liquid diet. Many of his friends visited him to express their sense of humiliation at the outrage heaped on him "by the mayor of this town and his mob of waylaymen."

Continuing on to Seward and Anchorage, he was unable to take any depositions personally, having to minister to his painful neuralgia, while his lawyer friends took charge of the depositions. When he arrived in Seattle the latter part of October, he had his broken tooth extracted and his jaw repaired. The doctor told him that he barely escaped a general paralysis of the right side of his face and head as the nerves had almost been destroyed.

Debbie accompanied him to Washington, where they spent the next several months while he prepared his brief and presented testimony in connection with his contest case.

Darrell joined them for the Christmas holidays. On Christmas night, Wickersham noted in his diary that his little family had "little to grumble about." Debbie's health was quite good considering the "ravages made on her lungs by tuberculosis years ago."

He wished they could settle down in their own home and he could have his library at hand. Except for a few months in Fairbanks, the Wickershams had lived in hotel rooms throughout his twelve years as delegate, eating their meals at boarding houses or in hotel dining rooms. He wished, too, that Darrell would marry and settle down as he was sure his son would be happier, even though he did not realize it himself.

Wickersham had decided he would not run for reelection but would throw his support to his longtime friend, Dan Sutherland, who had agreed to run.

While waiting for his contest case to be heard, Wickersham worked on his bibliography of Alaskan literature, his Alaska Law Reports, and wrote articles for various national magazines. He spent most of his time in his home office where his library was located.

PART V

WICKERSHAM RETIRES FROM DELEGATESHIP

Chapter 38

Wickersham Seeks Governorship

> *The secretary of interior asked Sutherland: "Have you endorsed Judge Wickersham for governor, Mr. Sutherland? Dan answered - "No, I have not endorsed anyone, but the people of Alaska are behind Judge Wickersham. . . ."*
>
> THAT *is the trouble. Dan won't stand up and endorse me or the other fellow either. He is frittering away his influence and is looked upon by all parties now as afraid to take a stand.*
> (*Wickersham Diary, Mar.21,1921*)

After running six delegate races Wickersham was ready to shift the arduous task to someone else as long as his successor was willing to fight for the same basic policies that he had fought for these many years. Of all his loyal followers he thought Dan Sutherland, the miner-fisherman, stood the best chance of being elected and Wickersham had every reason to think that between the two of them, they could control Alaska's political affairs.

Prospects for a national victory for the Republicans looked promising and in view of his long tenure as a federal official he should be considered as a likely candidate for some top office like the governorship. How happy and proud he would be to cap his career with that prestigious office!

He wrote Sutherland that he did not want to run again for delegate and wanted him to take his place. To make sure that the succession was certain, he wrote:

> Of course, you must understand that my determination not to be a candidate is because I expect you to be a candidate. Either you or I must be a candidate without fail in the next election and it is up to you to do it, so roll up your sleeves and go at it hard. . . .[1]

Fearful that Wickersham might change his mind, as he had on previous occasions, Sutherland filed his nomination early and the two agreed that he should begin a low-key campaign during the winter months visiting mining camps in the interior, traveling mostly by foot, as he lacked the funds to do otherwise. The miners were impressed to see a candidate for high office tramping through the wilderness.

Sutherland's Democratic opponent was none other than the perennial office-seeker, George Grigsby. Neither he nor Sutherland had any opposition in the primary but there was a stiff fight among the Republicans for the national committeemanship between the pro- and anti-Wickersham forces. Charlie Herron, publisher of the Anchorage *Times* and a Wickersham man, lost to Jack McBride, a Juneau hardware merchant and a longtime Wickersham foe. McBride's victory was a serious blow to the Wickersham camp.

Wickersham warned Sutherland that if the Republicans got back into the White House, the Shackleford-Faulkner crowd would try to control patronage just as they had in the past. He also cautioned Sutherland against making any deals with McBride as he could get elected without the national committeeman's help.

When the campaign got underway in earnest, John Troy ran daily editorials on how a vote for Sutherland would mean a continuation of the bitter strife which had existed for years under Wickersham. He called Sutherland a puppet of Wickersham's and ridiculed his abject subservience to the delegate. Troy's craftiness was aimed at offending Sutherland's pride to such a degree that he would feel compelled to assert his independence of Wickersham. The latter had only to hope that Sutherland would not fall into the trap being set for him.

However, Wickersham's worst fears were realized a couple of weeks before election day when he learned that Sutherland had both verbally and by signed written contract agreed to turn over patronage to McBride. He promised he would make no recommendations for federal

Robert DeArmond

Delegate Dan Sutherland, 1920-30.

appointments without first getting the approval of McBride's central committee.[2]

When election day rolled around, the voters trooped to the polls in Alaska and throughout the nation, returning the Republicans to office in landslide proportions. Sutherland won a plurality of 2,195 votes over Grigsby, defeating him in each of the four judicial districts. It was the most decisive victory since Wickersham beat Bunnell in 1914 with a plurality of 2,867. Sutherland received 5,914 votes to Grigsby's 3,719.

Wickersham's health problems played a role in his decision to modify his political activities. His loss of eyesight was a constant worry and he suffered frequent bouts with an upset stomach and arthritic pain. Debbie also suffered severely from arthritis.

For two and a half months before leaving Washington, Wickersham was in and out of the Episcopal Eye, Ear and Throat hospital undergoing operations for cataracts on both eyes. The right eye required removal of the lens. In between operations, he returned to his hotel room and was obliged to lie flat on his back, with his eyes blindfolded. Finally his oculist said he was sufficiently recovered that he could wear glasses, and the Wickershams departed for the West Coast.

During a month's stay in the Puget Sound area, the Wickershams came to the decision that he would go into private law practice in Alaska rather than in the Tacoma-Seattle area. He rejected returning to Fairbanks on account of Debbie's health and also because business was slow there. Their final choice was Juneau as he figured that some of the old-timers in the local bar would be leaving soon, including Judge Jennings and the rest of the judiciary, with a change in administration in Washington.

He rented rooms in the Valentine building for his office and a corner suite on the top floor of Lockie McKinnon's Zynda Hotel for his living quarters. They would have a grand view of Gastineau Channel, the cities of Juneau and Douglas, as well as the mountain range. They would take their meals at Mrs. M.P. Berry's boardinghouse.

Glowing over the election returns, Alaska's Republicans started choosing who they wanted for their top political posts. A groundswell of endorsements of clubs and individuals began surfacing in favor of Wickersham for governor. Approximately fifty-five hundred individuals signed petitions asking the president to appoint Wickersham.

Cordova businessman and Guggenheim associate, George Hazelet, announced himself as an active aspirant for the office and received the endorsement of National Committeeman McBride, the territorial central committee, and local clubs in the third division.

Hazelet came to Valdez in 1898 to prospect for gold. Later he became associated with the Guggenheims in their prospecting for copper and he helped organize the Copper River and Northwestern Railroad. He mapped Cordova's original townsite and served as its first mayor and as townsite trustee.

In true Alaska style, streams of letters and telegrams began flowing to Washington both for and against the two aspirants. Hazelet was denounced for his ownership of houses of prostitution and for his Guggenheim association, while Wickersham's enemies declared that he was of too quarrelsome a temperament for the job.

Both men, together with their friends, traveled to Washington to present their applications in person. Despite Hazelet's strong party endorsement, his name was dropped at an early stage, leaving Wickersham the top candidate.

Wickersham was in Seattle sitting eating lunch at the Frye Hotel when a telegram was handed to him from Representative Richard Elliott, Republican of Indiana, saying that the Committee on Elections had decided the contest case in his favor.

After studying various irregularities in the 1918 voting, such as voting outside home precincts and foreign aliens' voting, etc., the majority concluded Wickersham won by a plurality of thirty-seven votes.

When the matter finally came to a vote on the House floor, the vote was: yeas, 177, nays, 163, answered "present," 9, not voting, 79. The case had grown into an 840-page document and had become a bitter partisan fight.[3]

Immediately after the vote was tallied, Wickersham was summoned to the clerk's desk and sworn in. He had three days to serve before a new Congress took over. He received $21,500, $15,000 of which was back salary, $4,500 in mileage and $2,000 for expenses incurred in his preparation of the case. His expenses had actually amounted to $6,000.

Besides paying both Wickersham and Grigsby full salaries and mileage expenses, Congress appropriated $7,500, a delegate's salary for one year, to Sulzer's widow.[4]

With the delegate contest out of the way, Wickersham could concentrate on his campaign for the governorship. He had several interesting conversations with Sutherland which convinced him that he could look for absolutely no help from him. Sutherland told him frankly that he had agreed with the Hazelet forces he would not interfere in the governorship contest; that he would not endorse either Wickersham or Hazelet.

As his political foes continued their attacks on him, he found that both the president and Secretary of Interior Fall were pulling away from their support of him. In his interview with President Harding, he found the president friendly but very much impressed with the accusation that he was not a good Republican. He asked him squarely, "Did you run for office in Alaska on the Democratic ticket?" and Wickersham answered him just as squarely - while looking him directly in the eyes—"No, never!"

Wickersham learned from his friends who had talked with the president and the secretary of interior that they were hesitant in supporting him because they had been told he was not of the right "temperament" to be governor; that he was the head of one faction and Hazelet another and his appointment would destroy the Republican party organization; that he was a "disturber"; and that he was not friendly to capital.

McBride and Hazelet even filed the old Brantner charges of 1888 against him with Secretary Fall.[5] In other words, all his old chickens came home to roost!

Senator Willis told Wickersham that if Sutherland had been for him from the beginning it would have assured his appointment, but Sutherland's refusal to support him left Wickersham without "organization" support, which gave strength to the report that for a long time he had not been a good Republican - that he was independent politically and inclined to support the Wilson administration.

It was hard for Wickersham to understand how Sutherland, who had been his strong supporter for so many years, would refuse either to endorse him or to go to the secretary or president to speak on his behalf. As he put it, "Sutherland has lain down like a whipped dog!"[6]

For three months Alaska's governorship received top-priority attention from both the president and secretary as both wanted to appoint a bona fide Alaskan resident, if they could find someone on whom both McBride and Sutherland agreed. Secretary Fall recommended Wickersham in the beginning, and this dimmed Hazelet's chances. Other aspirants' names appeared on the horizon for brief intervals only to be shot down when a deluge of telegrams, letters, and personal interviews showed sharp dissatisfaction among Alaskan residents.

The president offered the post to Sutherland but he absolutely refused to be considered.[7]

In the meantime, friends of Scott Cordell Bone, former editor-in-chief of the Seattle *Post-Intelligencer*, were urging that he be considered. He had many influential friends in Washington, having been managing editor of the Washington *Post*, and editor and principal owner of the Washington *Herald*. While editor of the Seattle *Post-Intelligencer*, he served as chairman of the Alaska bureau of the Seattle chamber of commerce and visited the territory on a chamber tour. He was presently publicity director for the Republican National Committee, with headquarters in New York City.

After concluding that no Alaskan resident could be appointed because of the bitter factionalism which existed in the territory, President Harding nominated Bone for the governorship and he received Senate confirmation without any difficulty.

Chapter 39

"Keeping His Powder Dry"
As A Private Citizen

We greet today, my friends, men of the North
One who has proved his excellence and worth.
In welcoming salutation we extend to him our hand,
Wishing him the gladness and the fullness of the Land;
This Land for which he labored long and many years,
Though ofttimes o'er a path beset with doubts and fears.
Disappointment and illusion have often been his lot,
But never has he backward turned, one tithe or jot
On the high road that leads to the success
Of making an empire out of a wilderness.
So with glad hearts, without pretense or sham,
We welcome your return, James Wickersham!

(First stanza of a poem by Dan Noonan, entitled "Greetings to
Judge James Wickersham," Aug.27,1921)

Wickersham's failure in his quest for the governorship appeared to have closed the doors to further public service and his future seemed limited to a role of private citizen. Yet he promised his friends and admirers that he intended to "keep his powder dry," and he warned his enemies that he intended to "step on the tail" of any undesirable political schemes they might hatch.

The Wickershams spent three weeks in Tacoma before returning to their home in Juneau. During that interval, he celebrated his sixty-fourth birthday, enjoying his favorite dinner of fried chicken and

337

strawberry shortcake, prepared by his eighty-four-year-old mother in her home in Buckley. Visiting with his mother was Maggie McNichols, a seventy-eight-year-old Scotch woman who had been their family seamstress back in Patoka fifty years ago!

He spent part of his birthday composing a financial statement, as he stood on the threshold of a new career. He was pleasantly surprised to note that all his assets had not been swallowed up during twenty years of politicking. He listed $20,500 in stocks and bonds and $12,897 cash in bank accounts. His real estate holdings included ninety-five acres of farmland in the Puyallup Indian reservation; twenty-five residential lots in Buckley, a house and two lots in Tacoma, as well as a house and lot each in Valdez, Fairbanks, and Fort Gibbon; and two mining claims on Cleary and Ester Creeks near Fairbanks.

A warm welcome awaited them in Juneau where their friends had arranged a public dinner in their honor at the Moose Hall. About two hundred and fifty people showed up to express their appreciation for what he had done for the territory. Attorney John Marshall presided and speeches were delivered by a number of prominent local citizens, including Governor Bone.

In his responding speech after dinner, Wickersham talked about his library of twenty thousand titles which he had been building for twenty years and of how he hoped someday he could give it to an institution in the territory. It was being stored with the Washington State Historical Society in Tacoma until he found safekeeping for it in Alaska. It contained several foreign language books which he had had photographed page by page, translated, and placed in the collection, among them being four Russian books describing life in Alaska during the Russian occupation.

Dan Noonan, the genial chief steward of the S.S. *City of Seattle*, had composed a poem for the occasion, reviewing Wickersham's Alaskan career:

> Twenty years and more have passed in time
> Since first the Judge came to this Northern clime.
> But more than twenty years it means to those
> Who still are numbered among the Sourdoughs.
> The history of those twenty years is writ
> In terms of courage, fortitude and grit.
> What hopes, what griefs, what joy and what despair
> For those that pioneered have been the share.

Ah me, those twenty years have been a span
Unequalled since the world began.

The "mad stampedes, the toil beyond all measure,"
The lust of greed, the scrambling after treasure!
The noble deeds, the heroism unfeigned
Of those who ventured where only silence reigned!
The happy days when gold at last was found,
The wild delirium when the lucky staked their ground!
The torch of anarchy, the flame of sin,
The strife, the turmoil, before the law came in!
All this the Judge has seen and been a part
Of bringing order out of chaos at the start.
Wise in council, and in counsel grave,
The rugged miners heeded the advice he gave.
In time chosen as Alaska's Delegate,
Devotedly he gave his talents to affairs of state.
What a chronicle of pep and zeal and scrap
As he struggled congressional red-tap to unwrap!
What a record of accomplishment he made
In all things that would give Alaska aid!
I fain would laud the number of his acts,
But the Judge is modest and I only state the facts.

The Home Rule that we enjoy today
Was won by Judge Wickersham after years of fray;
The railroad that will soon haul Alaska's freight
Was possible because of his eloquent debate;
Our coal, our timber, that the plunderers would rob,
Were saved to use because the Judge was on the job;
Our mails were sent to us with fast dispatch,
And not shipped as common freight beneath the hatch;
He didn't camouflage and ask for more police,
Nor did he cater to a clique's caprice,
But we noticed in his speeches beneath the Capitol Dome
He always spoke in reverence of Alaska as his home,
He didn't libel and traduce our body politic
By calling them a bunch of rough-necks or Bolshevik,
But as men who labor in their sphere and give
Their love and loyalty to the Land in which they live.

Such the man who returns to us and tells the world
That Alaska is Home, here his standard is unfurled;
That this is not a Land in which to earn one's bread
And then to go and live Outside instead.
How beautiful is this Land, how bright it gleams,
How it keeps one buoyant with its aspirations, dreams,
Land of Beginnings, its history's page but scratched,
Embryo States, fledglings of the Eagle, waiting to be hatched.
The Land of Youth, yet a Land that will engage
And reward the ripened wisdom of Old Age.
The Judge says he'll retire now and practice law,
Which sounds peace-like as when savage takes a squaw.
What then? Shall we find no other work that he might do
Except our litigation when we stew?
Big things remain to do in this Land of Do and Dare,
Even for retired folk of silver hair.
The Judge, we hope, will no exception prove
That the man of action will ever find his groove.
Alaska now as ever is in need
Of strong, resolute, men of the Judge's breed.
Scholar, statesman, friend so tried and true,
James Wickersham, we shake your hand and welcome you![1]

The first "step on the tail" of a political scheme which he deemed offensive to the territory's best interests came when he tried to keep Charles Bunnell from becoming president of the Agricultural College and School of Mines, which, as delegate in Congress, he had "fathered" into existence. He had no use for Bunnell in the first place, considering him wholly incompetent for the job. Equally distasteful to him was the fact that a group of Democratic trustees were putting something over on the people of the territory without consulting the Republican citizenry. Wickersham devised a plan for undoing the Democratic scheme of "fastening Bunnell upon the college as president."

With the cooperation of the new Republican governor, the plan got underway in a hurry. Two trustees had resigned so the governor could make two new appointments. He offered Wickersham one of the places, but the latter declined, contending that the board should consist of Fairbanks residents so that they could consult together more readily. However, Wickersham recommended two staunch Republicans - Robert Lavery and Robert Bloom, two Fairbanks merchants.

Of the original eight trustees appointed by Democratic Governor Strong, only two were Republicans; they lived outside of Fairbanks and soon resigned when they realized how difficult it would be for them to attend board meetings. Later, as vacancies occurred, three more Republicans were appointed because a Republican majority controlled the legislature and appointments had to be confirmed by that body. Thus, when Wickersham's strategy was to go into action, the Republicans had a majority of five out of the eight trustees.

The grounds for ousting Bunnell was based on a clause in the Organic Act prohibiting a person to hold two government offices at the same time, and Bunnell was still serving as a district judge. The Republicans were prepared to elect Milton Snodgrass, a Republican trustee, to the presidency. Snodgrass had been an applicant when the original selection was made by the trustees. He was not a member of the board at that time but had since been appointed. He was superintendent of the agricultural experiment station located on the site of the college.[2]

When the board met, Lavery introduced a resolution stating that "it is for the best interests of the college to remove from office Charles E. Bunnell, president." After some discussion, a vote was taken and only Lavery, Bloom and Snodgrass voted in favor of the resolution. Republicans Rickert and Stevens voted with the opposition, thus defeating the Wickersham plan.[3]

The Wickershams lived a quiet social life in Juneau, not being "given to frivolity or social silliness." They were frequent guests at the governor's house and they entertained members of the legislature when they came to town for the biennial sessions. On Sundays Wickersham spent a few hours at his office, just as he used to do in Washington. They slept late and then had an eleven o'clock breakfast at Mrs. Berry's boardinghouse and a five o'clock dinner. They were not churchgoers.

Wickersham enjoyed attending weekly meetings of the Moose, the Pioneers, the Elks, and the bar association. He did not like it when legislators were invited to join the attorneys as they were inclined to turn the meetings into political debates; he preferred having the luncheon meetings restricted to members of the bar so they could discuss their professional problems.

Wickersham's law practice grew so fast that he took Joe Kehoe in as a partner. Joe was a young Irishman, formerly of Portland, Oregon, who had been practicing law in Haines after mustering out of the United State Army following the armistice. Mrs. Kehoe was acceptable to Debbie because she was "a good industrious worker and not given to frivolity." Kehoe was a Democrat and later served as a district judge in Nome and then as Secretary of Alaska.

Wickersham's legal work required him to travel to other parts of the territory as well as to Seattle and San Francisco. His clients ranged from the territorial government to Outside fisheries; private individuals also came to him with their problems. At first he accepted all kinds of cases - divorces, murders, rapes, etc., but he looked forward to the time when he could afford to devote his whole time to civil cases. Besides his law practice, he took a few fliers in mining claims which netted him more worry and disappointment than financial returns. His long years of exposure to the gambling spirit of grubstaking miners with a "sure thing" in the interior had made him vulnerable to taking a chance. He was also a "soft touch" for the old prospector who stopped by his office "just to talk" but who usually left with a hundred dollars in his pocket to buy supplies for another foray into the mountains to search out a fortune.

Wickersham had occasion to revisit his former hometown of Fairbanks during the summer of 1922, traveling on the Alaska Railroad from Seward. An overnight stop was made at Curry, originally called "Deadhorse." "Alaska Nellie" (Neal) was the roadhouse cook, and Wickersham enjoyed both her cooking and her stories about her hunting escapades. The walls of the dining room were covered with moose and caribou horns, skins of bear, wolf, and wolverine, even a tiger, as proof of her prowess as a huntress.

Arriving at Fairbanks, he was disappointed at how small and deserted the town looked; a recent fire had destroyed the best block in town, and the buildings stood gutted, waiting to be rebuilt. Still, it brought back many happy memories. Except for his first summer in Eagle, this was the only home the Wickershams ever had in Alaska and he had built a goodly portion of it with his own hands and he had tended the flower and vegetable gardens surrounding it. His present tenants, the Walter Rynersons, wished to buy the home and he agreed to sell it for $1,500.

He took an evening's drive out to the site of the agricultural college and was thrilled to see the fine farms being cleared in the wilderness; it was a dream coming true as he had always dreamt of great agricultural development for the Tanana Valley in the vicinity of Fairbanks.

Wickersham was in Anchorage for the Fourth of July celebration and was invited to give the principal patriotic address. The festivities started with the parade marshal riding a big, white horse, followed by a military band of the Fifty-ninth Infantry; then came the organizational floats, dogteams, and decorated bicycles. The formal program was held in the baseball park and was followed by games and races.

He participated in a dinner party honoring C.H. Huston, assistant secretary of commerce, who was making a round-the-world cruise aboard a United States Coast Guard vessel. From Anchorage the party went to Nome, Siberia, Japan, then through the Indian Ocean, the Mediterranean, and across the Atlantic to New York—a luxury cruise for a minor bureaucrat!

One evening he went for a five-mile hike to Lake Otis, watched a nighttime baseball game, then, upon returning to his hotel room, he began writing a letter to Debbie. Being in a playful mood, he proceeded to attach the papers one to the other until it measured ten feet long!

Sailing down Cook Inlet aboard the *Admiral Watson*, stops were made at a clam cannery at Snug Harbor, salmon and herring canneries at Seldovia, Uganik Bay, Ouzinkie, and Kodiak. On their return to Seward, they passed close to the sea lion rocks outside of Ressurection Bay, where they saw 200 lions sunning themselves on the rocks.

Wickersham took no part in Sutherland's reelection race. His Democratic challenger was E.J. "Stroller" White, editor-publisher of *Stroller's Weekly* in Juneau. It was a relatively quiet campaign, with Sutherland defeating White in a vote of 6,125 to 1,733.

Wickersham sat on the sidelines enjoying what he described as "one hell of a fight" going on in the Juneau Republican circles with Sutherland pitted against Governor Bone and Thomas Reed, the district judge. Wickersham said he felt like the old woman when her husband and the bear were fighting, "I don't care which one wins—let 'em fight."[4]

Debbie's health became a serious problem; she was bedridden much of the time. Her right lung had been badly damaged in her first bout with tuberculosis, and now her left lung was affected. She spent the winters in Southern California and Wickersham visited her when he came south on business trips.

Excitement reigned supreme when word came that President Harding would visit the territory, in the summer of 1923; it would be the first time that a United States president had visited the territory. The towns started planning elaborate welcoming parties for the presidential party. Accompanying the president would be his own wife and three cabinet members and their wives. The cabinet officers included: Secretary of Interior Hubert Work, a physician from Pennsylvania; Secretary of Agriculture Henry Wallace, an Iowa magazine editor; Secretary of Commerce Herbert Hoover, a civil engineer from California.

As plans materialized for the president's Juneau visit, Wickersham's friends told him that Chairman Bob Robertson, a local attorney, and his committee members had decided that Wickersham was to be excluded from welcoming the chief executive, even though he was one of the few local residents who had met the president personally. According to the report, this was their way of punishing Wickersham for having "talked politics" when he had been permitted to speak at a recent banquet honoring a group of visiting congressmen!

Although he was shocked and disappointed at first, Wickersham rationalized that it should not be surprising since Robertson and Bert Faulkner, another attorney on the committee, were corporation attorneys, who had fought him for years because of his exposures of the corporate exploitation that was raping the territory.

Apparently the committee suffered too much criticism for its plans to seclude the presidential party to their own elite circle of friends, because three days before the president's arrival, Mayor Izzy Goldstein appointed a new reception committee of one hundred members and invited Wickersham to be a member.[5]

As the army transport *Henderson*, escorted by two destroyers, the *Corry* and the *Hull*, approached the Juneau dock, it was greeted with a twenty-one-gun presidential salute by a detachment from Chilkoot barracks near Haines. The party arrived at ten o'clock in the morning and remained in port all day.

As soon as the party was deposited at the governor's house, the president's press representative, Judson C. Welliver, went to Wickersham's office together with Delegate Sutherland; Wickersham knew him well from his delegate days in Washington. Welliver asked Wickersham to help him prepare a brief urging statehood for southeastern Alaska, and all that part of southern Alaska west of 141st meridian, south of the 66th degree and east of the 154th degree and including Kodiak Island. He wanted the material so that he could take it with him when the boat left Juneau during the night. Wickersham went immediately to work preparing a map, computing boundaries, and composing a statement of the resources involved. By foregoing attendance at any of the social functions scheduled for the party, he had the assignment completed by six o'clock.

Just before he finished, a special messenger arrived with an invitation from Governor Bone to attend a reception for the president at 9:30 that evening. Wickersham surmised that the governor had just learned that Robertson's committee had not included the Wickershams in the guest list. They accepted the invitation and were cordially received by the president, who recalled meeting him in Washington.[6]

In a public address in Seattle following his Alaskan tour, President Harding predicted that "in a very few years" the panhandle of Alaska would be ready for statehood. He described that section as containing easily 90 percent of the white population and of the developed resources of the territory.[7]

Those comments set aflame a long-smoldering controversy between that section of Alaska and the western and interior regions. For years there had been a sentiment in the panhandle favoring splitting away from the rest of the territory. Encouraged by Harding's remarks, a meeting was held in Juneau that fall which authorized Bob Robertson to go to Washington to lobby for an early separation. Sutherland resented this intrusion on his jurisdiction as delegate, contending that the citizens of Juneau were in fact being assessed to pay Robertson's expenses to lobby for his cannory clients, who were the principal advocates of separation.

Wickersham was engaged to file an injunction suit constraining the city council from spending taxpayers' money on the lobbying trip. He won a circuit court ruling that it was an illegal disbursement by the city council and must be returned to the city treasury. When Robertson returned, he repaid to the city $500 of the $1,500 he received originally.[8]

Robertson met with ridicule from the congressmen he contacted as the general feeling was that Alaska as a single territory was already too expensive for the federal government and it was preposterous to think that the United States was going to bear the expense of a two-territory government.[9]

One day when he was on a little launch going from Ketchikan to Hyder, Wickersham's ethnological interest in early Indian lore compelled him to commandeer the captain to stop at the deserted Tongass Island, where there once had been a thriving Indian village. He recalled being told by an Indian in Ketchikan that in the forest of abandoned totem poles in this old village, there was a life-sized statue of Abraham Lincoln.

Wickersham and his fellow passengers went ashore and tramping through the high brush and weeds which had overgrown the abandoned village site, came upon a high pole amidst a group of smaller totems, with a statue of Lincoln on its top. The pole stood thirty feet high and Lincoln stood six feet tall at the top. He was dressed in Civil War attire, including a long-tailed dress coat, with his famous stovepipe hat on his head, and breeches covering his legs. His whiskers were carefully carved, and altogether it was a startling likeness of the great president, standing there above the hundred carvings on dozens of totems.

When the group returned to their boat they organized the "Lincoln Association of Alaska," electing Wickersham as its president. The purpose of the organization was to see that the Lincoln statue was protected and preserved. [10]

When President Harding visited Alaska, Wickersham wrote a petition to the president and a letter to the secretary of interior, asking for the reservation of Tongass Island as the "Lincoln Park National Monument," for the purpose of preserving the totems, especially the one of Lincoln. [11]

Wickersham wrote a story of the Lincoln totem pole for the *Sunset* magazine issue of February, 1924 and he continued to crusade for its preservation through the years. Though he did not succeed in getting the area set aside as a national monument, the Lincoln totem stands today in the state museum in Juneau and a replica stands in the totem park of Saxman, near Ketchikan.

The breach between Wickersham and Sutherland gradually healed through the years as the latter came to recognize his need for his old mentor's counsel. Though he tried to work through party channels, Sutherland found himself ignored in patronage decisions, being superseded by that same little coterie of Juneau politicians with whom Wickersham had had to struggle during his delegate days.

Regardless of which party was in office in Washington, this group composed of Democrats and Republicans, managed to find ways to influence the dispensing of political rewards or to punish those they deemed unworthy. An editor once referred to them as "bipartisanship in perfidy." The nucleus of the group was the governor, the district judge, John Troy, editor of the Empire, and H.L. Faulkner, a corporation lawyer.

One reason for the bitter feuding between Wickersham and Faulkner was that the delegate discovered Faulkner had held office and voted in elections while still a Canadian citizen. Wickersham filed charges with the Bureau of Naturalization in Washington. Faulkner had lived in Alaska for 22 years without becoming an American citizen, during which time he had served as deputy United States marshal and United States marshal for the first division and voted regularly in municipal and territorial elections. He was admitted to the Alaska bar, taking an oath that he was a United States citizen. He was one of the foremost condemners of Governor Strong for his having concealed his Canadian citizenship when he was appointed governor.

When Faulkner finally petitioned to become a citizen in 1925, he admitted that he had long "erroneously exercised the rights and performed the duties of a citizen of the United States in good faith because of 'misinformation' regarding his citizenship status." In Wickersham's opinion it was not "misinformation" but perjury and fraud on the part of an educated, practicing lawyer. Stories of Faulkner's Canadian citizenship appeared in both the *Empire* and the Ketchikan *Chronicle.*[12]

In 1929 when a vacancy occurred in the district judgeship in Juneau, Wickersham applied for the post and Sutherland tried to help him get the appointment. It soon became known that Faulkner and his cohorts had written maligning letters to the Justice Department in an effort to block Wickersham's nomination. Faulkner stressed Wickersham's blindness as disqualifying him for the judgeship. The fact that Wickersham was conducting an active law practice apparently was irrelevant.[13]

As further proof of his unworthiness for the judgeship, was the submission of a photostatic copy of a cancelled check, filched from Wickersham's personal files, showing that he made a fifty dollar campaign contribution to Bob LaFollette for his presidential campaign.[14] Wickersham did not get the appointment.

Chapter 40

Wickersham Becomes A Widower And Then Remarries

We have been married more than forty-six years. During our whole married life I never knew her to do an immodest act, nor to utter a vulgar sentence. She was clean in mind and body and always acted from a sense of justice and cleanliness.

She was fearless in the defense of what she thought was right. Whatever I may be credited with doing that is good or worthy, the greater part was her.   (*Wickersham Diary, Nov. 23, 1926*)

Wickersham served as Sutherland's southeastern campaign manager in the delegate's fourth race for reelection. Sutherland faced a stiff battle in that section because of his widespread exposé of the corruption which he described as rampant due to the law enforcement officials' failure to perform their duties. He had a pamphlet printed and distributed in the states describing the flagrant violation of the liquor laws and of gambling and prostitution which went unpunished. The Hearst papers carried a series of stories about the vice conditions in Alaska. Though the residents of Ketchikan, which was the hotbed of these vices, acknowledged that they were bad, they were embarrassed to have their congressional representative broadcast them. Actually it was the delegate's means of embarrassing the governor and the judiciary, with whom he was feuding over patronage favors!

Also, Sutherland's attacks on the fisheries and transportation interests, which operated primarily in southeastern Alaska, inspired these Seattle-based corporations to raise a "slush fund" with which to "buy" newspaper support in an effort to defeat him.

348

Sutherland's Democratic challenger was Tom Marquam, a Fairbanks attorney who had been prominent in Republican party affairs for years. He was a stereotype of a rather common variety of early-day Alaskan politician—glib of tongue and amoral in personal conduct. He was "tall and handsome, dressed stylishly and wore a well-trimmed black Vandyke beard and was an able and eloquent trial lawyer."[1]

In his campaign speeches, Wickersham denounced the newspapers for their support of Marquam with "cannery corruption funds." Henry Roden was Marquam's southeastern campaign manager. No official tally was kept of the election returns but newspaper accounts on the day following the election, with 90 percent of the vote reported, gave Sutherland 6,960 votes to Marquam's 4,242.[2]

On election day, Wickersham received word that Debbie was critically ill in a Seattle hospital. He turned over his law office to Roden and went south to be with her. Upon his arrival at the hospital, he found her in a semi-coma from which she rarely awakened. She lingered on until November 23, when she became unconscious and finally ceased to breath. In his diary that evening he noted that she had been an invalid ever since Howard's death in 1901—for twenty-five years. Yet "she was the most courageous, uncomplaining and loyal woman I have ever known."

Darrell came north from his home in San Francisco to help his father in making the funeral plans. In accordance with her repeated requests, her body was cremated. The graves of her two sons, Arthur and Howard in the Tacoma cemetery, were excavated and their urns placed beside their mother's so that they could have a common tombstone. Bishop Trimble Rowe, pioneer Alaskan Episcopal bishop, conducted the funeral service.[3]

Loneliness was not a new experience for Wickersham as his wife's poor health had kept them apart for years, but as he stood on the ship's deck northward bound, at age seventy, his aloneness bore down on him deeply. Never again would Debbie be standing there at his side as she had done so many times, since their first sailing on July 2, 1900, when little Howard was with them. He had no thought of remaining south, however, as he felt more surely than ever that Alaska would be his home until the end of his days.

The John Rustgards were on hand to greet him when he arrived in Juneau at the hour of midnight; they drove him to his hotel. The ground was covered with snow and the fir trees reminded him that Christmas was near. The Rustgards invited him to have Christmas Eve supper with them, and Dr. and Mrs. DeVigne and the Lockie McKinnons invited him to dinner on Christmas Day.[4]

Fortunately his law practice and mining investments helped divert his attention from his loneliness. When summer came he went on a two-week horse-packing trip into the Mill Creek area near Moose Pass, to inspect the quartz manganese iron claims he owned. He visited the Kachemak Bay region, which he envisioned as becoming a future metropolis. He had dreamt of someday building himself a home there and having a producing farm to enjoy in retirement. He also imagined it as an ideal site for a future state capital!

Back in 1921 he had tried to interest Secretary of the Navy Josephus Daniels and Secretary of Interior Albert Fall in the idea of building a major North Pacific naval base at Kachemak Bay. He wanted them to withdraw the Homer Spit and some lands on the north shore of the bay adjoining the sandspit and lay out a townsite, selling enough lots to pay for the necessary surveying. Secretary Daniels' preference for locating such a base in Hawaii instead led to the eventual construction of Pearl Harbor.

Wickersham also tried to interest General Gotwals and his New York friends in buying the Alaska Railroad and utilizing Kachemak Bay as a rail terminal, but this would have necessitated building 150 miles of additional track; they declined the project.

Wickersham bought two parcels of land from the John F. Mullen and J.H. Lamb homesteads, with soldiers' Civil War script.[5]

For years Alaskans resented the bureaucratic rule by federal officials and each succeeding legislature attempted to find a way for territorial officials to take over some of that authority. Repeatedly the attempts ended in failure because the vested interests preferred federal jurisdiction over territorial.

The need for Alaskans to reassert their independence of the stranglehold which federal bureaucracy was tightening around them reached a stage of urgency when Congress passed an act to bring the thirty federal bureaus engaged in Alaskan affairs under a single bureau, to be established in Alaska, with three members, one from each of the three major departments concerned with Alaska—Interior, Agriculture and Commerce—to control Alaskan activities.

As a counter attack to this federal take-over, an effort was made in the eighth legislature to pass a bill which would divest the federal officials of a large degree of authority, giving it to an elected territorial board; it was known as the Comptroller bill and Wickersham became its chief champion.

The bill would abolish the territorial boards of road commissioners, education, banking, trustees of the pioneer home, fisheries, directors of the historical library and museum, creating in their stead a governing triumvirate of comptroller, treasurer, and attorney general. The governor and secretary of Alaska would be stripped of all territorial administrative duties, making provision even for the removal of certain furniture and equipment from their offices.

Wickersham prepared a brief in support of the bill and had copies printed for distribution throughout the territory. In his "appeal to Alaskans" he warned against the steady drift toward greater federal control instead of toward local self-government; there was no serious effort being made to exercise the right of home rule which was promised in the Organic Act creating the legislature.

He pointed out that the proposed comptroller's department could be created and maintained without additional cost to the territory if the funds presently given to the governor and secretary were diverted to the new board. The seventh legislature had appropriated nearly $36,000 to enable the governor and secretary to carry on the territorial work assigned to them.

He warned also that unless such a step was taken, the newly-created federal board would grow in power and autocracy from year to year until it became the lawmaking and law-enforcing body in the territory in perpetuity and all thoughts of self-government leading to eventual statehood would disappear.

The bill's supporters met nightly in Wickersham's office to plan their next day's strategy. Senator Will Steel and Representative William Paul had successfully organized the two houses so that Wickites occupied most of the key positions, much to Wickersham's quiet satisfaction. The Wickites included four senators and nine representatives.

Chief opponents to the bill were Governor Parks, Secretary Karl Theile, and the bipartisan political machine of Faulkner and Troy. They warned that it was a trap to make Wickersham comptroller; he could then rule as Alaska's czar. The Anchorage *Times* called the bill "vicious, as it would completely revolutionize the present territorial government. . .and about all that would be left for the presidentially-appointed governor would be the right to live in the executive mansion, water the lawn during the summer and stoke the furnace in the winter."[6]

In a two-hour-long speech before a joint session of the legislature, Wickersham told the members that if they did not enact the law, "we will go out and ask the people to return a legislature next time that will." Just before the final vote was taken, Senator Steel told his colleagues that it was no idle jest when Wickersham promised that a test would be made in the courts of the legality of the acts of the governor and secretary in administering the territorial duties imposed on them by the legislature.

After a four hour debate, the bill was defeated in the Senate in a four to four vote. Senator Jensen argued that the measure was an insulting attack on federal bureaus that were expending approximately ten million dollars annually trying to open Alaska.[7]

The House passed a slightly modified version of the bill in a vote of nine to seven. Tom Gaffney of Nome made a masterful plea against it, warning against taking the unstaked trail of Wickersham and Sutherland, which would lead into shambles of over-taxation and would drive out industry; he urged instead following the well-staked, hard-beaten trail of Governor Parks that would slowly but surely lead to eventual statehood and would keep the axe of the tax collector from decapitating the few industries presently operating in Alaska.

Efforts to reintroduce the bill in the Senate were unsuccessful, and it died. Wickersham felt "his boys" had made a good fight, garnering thirteen affirmative votes to eleven negative. He rated the session as a whole as "the most disappointing legislature in our history as the private interests and their subsidized newspapers had controlled it in everything in which they were interested. . .the power of the cannery and transportation interests had been overpowering."[8]

The day after the legislature adjourned, Wickersham filed injunction proceedings against Walstein G. Smith, territorial treasurer, seeking to stop payment from territorial funds to the office of the governor and secretary for special legislative expenses involving compilation and printing of the House and Senate journals. The petition declared that the act of the legislature making the appropriation was ultra-vires and void and not within the powers of the legislature. For fourteen years territorial funds had been paid to federal employees which violated section seven of the Organic Act.

Governor Parks and Secretary Theile filed complaints in intervention against the issurance of a permanent restraining order. Judge Reed, in a decision of 140 pages, issued a temporary restraining order forbidding the treasurer to pay out the funds. For political reasons, the judge refused—or openly neglected—to enter final judgment in the case so

Wickersham was prevented from appealing the case to the circuit court of appeals, which he wanted to do.

Then Judge Reed died and the case remained in limbo until Wickersham had it dismissed but brought a second suit which caused the federal departments in Washington to take notice and Congress passed legislation supporting Wickersham's contention.

Wickersham was pleasantly surprised to have his son Darrell and Darrell's wife pay him a visit in Juneau; Darrell had never been in Alaska before. Wickersham arranged for them to occupy the corner room on the top floor of the Zynda Hotel where he and Debbie had lived in years past. They stayed only three days, but he was delighted to have them even for such a brief visit.

Wickersham took a case for D.E. Skinner, president and chief stockholder of the Alaska Steamship Company, which was to prove embarrassing to him in later years. For a fee of $7,500, Skinner wanted him to go to Washington and lobby for a bill giving the Bureau of Fisheries authority to lease trap sites to cannerymen for five years. Wickersham agreed to take on the assignment and hired William Paul to assist him.

When Wickersham wrote Sutherland asking him to introduce the bill which Skinner wanted, he received a long letter explaining why he had to refuse to do so. He said he was opposed to all trap fishing and blamed traps for the meager employment available to resident Alaskans. He admitted being prejudiced against the nonresident trap owners because of the way they had manipulated the territorial legislators through the years. In doing so they had prevented the enactment of many excellent laws.[9]

Curiously, there was no diary comment after Wickersham received that letter from his old friend, who expressed himself so clearly on the fish trap matter and who held a position identical to the position that Wickersham had taken during all the years he was delegate. Could there have been a slight twinge of conscience? But $7,500 legal fees were not that plentiful!

Wickersham liked to have company when he dined in the evenings so he usually invited a friend to join him and frequently it was a lady friend. When he was seen repeatedly with the same woman, the town gossips started rumors of possible romance; that disgusted him as he had no intention of remarrying at age seventy—that would be preposterous!

One day when he was in Winter and Pond's photographic shop, Mr. Pond rather hesitatingly said, "Judge, I suppose I can congratulate you - I hear you are to be married." Wickersham looked at him in astonishment and said, "No, you are mistaken. I have no intention to do anything of the kind. I am seventy years old."

That evening he wrote in his diary that apparently the report was being circulated that he was going to marry Mrs. Harry Bishop. He vowed he would stay at home and not see her so often because he did not want to be talked about in that way and did not want to bring that kind of talk upon Mrs. Bishop either.[10]

But as their mutual friends kept including them in their dinner parties, Wickersham began to find her more and more pleasant to be around. He discovered, too, that she was a good cook, when she invited him to have dinner in her apartment.

Mrs. Bishop was born Grace Elizabeth Vrooman in Michigan and her family moved to Washington Territory in 1878; her father was one of Seattle's first judges. She graduated from the University of Washington and in 1902 accepted a position as eighth grade teacher and principal of the newly established school in Juneau. She continued teaching school until her marriage to Harry A. Bishop, a pioneer Juneauite. When he died in 1920, she went back to teaching school in Juneau.

After two months of concentrated courtship, Wickersham wrote Darrell:

My dear Darrell: Mrs. Grace Elizabeth Bishop has resided in Juneau for twenty years; she is about forty-eight years old and was a particular and intimate friend of your mother's. She and Mrs. DeVigne and Mrs. Walstein G. Smith were her constant weekly bridge-playing friends.

Her husband was U.S. marshal here in Juneau until the time of his death about ten years ago; she taught school before her marriage as well as after, and is now teaching, but will quit with the end of this term. She is a woman of intelligence, refinement and fine character; a student and a reader of good books; she has the respect and confidence of the people of Juneau and mine likewise; she has many of those admirable womanly qualities which caused me to love your mother and my own mother above all other women.

I intend, as you know, to continue to reside in Alaska and I want a home of my own and I need it. I do not feel satisfied living like a traveler in a hotel, and I will not be content either

Left: Grace Wickersham, 2nd wife, 1930. *Right:* Wickersham's campaign portrait for 1930 delegate race.

to impose upon you and Jane. I must live my own life in my own way.

I am well and strong and my physician tells me that, barring accidents, I will continue to be so for many years yet, so I have determined to get a home of my own and to marry Mrs. Bishop, who has consented, early in the fall, probably upon my return from the Kansas City trip. . . .

I love you dearly, my son, and hope you will approve my determination to make my life more agreeable and happy in Alaska. Give my love to Jane. Your devoted father.[11]

Five days later the Wickersham-Bishop engagement announcement appeared in the *Empire* and they began house hunting before he left to attend the Republican national convention in Kansas City. Upon his arrival in Seattle, Wickersham found a beautiful letter from Darrell giving his wholehearted approval to his father's remarriage, which pleased Wickersham very much.

Wickersham and Mrs. Bishop were married at the bride's old family homestead at Des Moines on the new Tacoma-Seattle Boulevard midway between the two cities. Among the thirty guests were Alaska's former Governor Strong and his wife. The Wickershams returned to the Frye Hotel after the reception.[12]

At first the Wickershams planned to build a home, but when they returned to Juneau, they learned that the Alaska Gastineau Mining Company's big house at the top of "Chicken Ridge," on the corner of Seventh and Seward Streets, was for sale for $6,000. It was a three-story, wooden frame building with fourteen rooms built around 1900 by John Hays Hammond, noted mining engineer of the Hammond Gold Mining Company of Sheep Creek. It was one of the first large homes built in Alaska. It was occupied by mining executives of that company and later of the Alaska Gastineau Mining Company and by the H.L. Faulkners in the 1920s. It provided a beautiful view of the entire Gastineau Channel.

Wickersham was anxious to move out of Room 500 at the Zynda Hotel, where he had lived for seven years. They bought the hill-top home and spent an additional four thousand dollars remodeling it. They made a large library on the second floor so he could have a quiet and peaceful place away from the hustle and bustle on the first floor. He was impatient to get his books all together from their several depositories—a dream he had cherished all of his life. They moved into their new home in October and were busy for the next several weeks cleaning and polishing furniture and loving it.

Chapter 41

Wickersham's Seventh Race for Delegate

I will not be a candidate. . . .It goes without saying that if our friends decide that you shall run for the delegateship, I shall come to Alaska and do everything in my power to elect you. I would prefer seeing you in this office above any other man in Alaska. . . . (Sutherland Papers,letter from Sutherland to Wickersham,Oct.8,1929)

When the Hoover administration took over in Washington, Wickersham's friends tried again to get either a judgeship or the governorship for him, without avail. Telegrams were sent to the Department of Justice and Vice President-elect Charles Curtis asked President Hoover to make a recess judgeship appointment.[1]

The Wickites were especially interested in getting rid of George Parks as governor as they considered him a weakling and a supple tool in the hands of the cannery interests. The Marquam-McBride-Faulkner-Robertson crowd wanted to keep him governor and Parks himself was happy to remain in office.

Wickersham wrote Sutherland that he was not a candidate for governor but urged the delegate to suggest to the president that he appoint a (Henry L.) Stimson, a (Leonard) Wood, or a (William Howard) Taft (all governors of the Philippine Islands)—and not a Pollyanna! Alaska needed a man of high executive ability, experience, and eastern influence. In his words:

> Parks has no initiative, nor force of character, and is as soft as wet clay in the hands of the representatives of the interests who are pushing his reappointment. . . .

357

Why cannot Alaska have a man for governor equal in character and standing with those appointed for the Philippine Islands?. . .Why not give Alaska a real governor and not an
amiable clerk?

George Parks is a pleasant and honorable gentleman, and
made an excellent clerk in the interior department public lands
work in Alaska but he is hopelessly incompetent as a governor.
Why should this great American territory, which so much needs
an executive head of high executive character and influence, be
always cursed with a Pollyanna?[2]

Sutherland replied that he had gone to see Secretary of Interior Ray
Lyman Wilbur about selecting a strong governor for Alaska, telling him
that Alaskans were tired of the Bone-Parks type, but he was not
optimistic about bringing in a change as the cannery people were
lobbying to keep Parks in office. He added:

I know that the packers are making a h--l of a drive in the interest of Parks and it seems to me that about half of the members of Congress from California have told me of telegrams they
received from San Francisco packers urging the reappointment
of Parks.

Now naturally the question arises, what is their interest in the
governorship if Parks has not been running errands for them. In
a letter just received from Dave Williams he says that Lathrop
(national committeeman) told him that he was not enthusiastic
for Parks but the packers hounded the life out of him to endorse
Parks until he did so. . . .[3]

When Sutherland ran for a fifth term as delegate in 1928, he told
Wickersham that that was his last race as he wanted to retire and join
his sister in the operation of the Ogontz School for Girls in Philadelphia.
Wickersham expressed regret saying that Sutherland had become a fixed
habit with him and "since I am a creature of fixed habits it is quite a
shock to be compelled to change even one; but when that one is such a
satisfactory one as you have been the change becomes that much more
disturbing to me."[4]

For twenty-two years it had been a Wickersham-Sutherland team
representing the territory in Congress. Confidentially, Sutherland
expressed the wish that Wickersham might be his successor, but he
warned that campaigning had become an expensive operation and he

thought that Wickersham might not feel that he could afford it. If he had the backing of the reactionary element, he would receive contributions, otherwise he would have to use his own private funds. Sutherland suggested that maybe Attorney General John Rustgard could afford to make the race and he would represent the same political position as Wickersham and Sutherland had represented.

Apparently the urge to get back into the political harness was too strong a temptation for the old warhorse to reject because on the very day that the papers carried the announcement of Sutherland's retirement, there were also announcements by both Wickersham and Rustgard that they would be candidates for delegate on the Republican ticket.

Wickersham and Rustgard had been the closest of personal friends through the years and often discussed Alaska's political issues, but it is doubtful that the question of who should succeed Sutherland had been a recent topic of conversation, so that their simultaneous announcements came as a surprise to each of them.

The day following the newspaper announcements, Wickersham received a personally written note from Josephine Rustgard, the candidate's wife, reading: "Dear Judge: We find ourselves suddenly in the race for delegate and since I feel that Mr. Rustgard had you to thank for the inspiration, I am sure you wish us well. Sincerely, Josephine Rustgard."

On the outside of the envelope was printed three words: "Rustgard for Delegate." Wickersham assumed that Mrs. Rustgard had written similar notes to their friends throughout the territory and he was intrigued with this personalized style of campaigning and wondered how effective it might turn out to be.[5]

Rustgard was ten years younger than Wickersham. He was an immigrant from Norway, who left home at age fifteen to work as a cabin boy on a clipper ship. He earned his law degree at the University of Minnesota and practiced law in Minneapolis before going to Nome in 1900; he was practicing there when Wickersham was on the bench. He was a highly respected citizen having served as United States district attorney for the first division and was elected three times as territorial attorney general.

A practical political aspect to these two veterans racing against one another was that both had depended heavily on the Indian vote in the panhandle in their previous campaigns. How the Indians would vote would be a deciding factor in the outcome as there were between eight hundred and a thousand votes involved in the Indian bloc. The Indian leadership was split between the two Paul brothers, William and Louis, and the Peratrovich brothers, Frank and Bob. The Pauls supported Wickersham and the Peratrovichs supported Rustgard.

The campaign turned into as rough and tough a one as any Wickersham had experienced in his long political career. Rustgard brought up the matter of Wickersham's taking a handsome legal fee from the cannerymen to help get a fish trapsite leasing bill through Congress; he criticized him for falsely telling the Indians he would help them recover damages for the appropriation of their lands; he blamed Alaska's economic depression on Wickersham's demagogic assaults on big business.

He apologized for having been deceived into an innocent idolatry of his opponent, just as many other good Alaskans had been. He said:

> Many of us in Alaska have for years been burning candles before the picture of the candidate who heads the Paul ticket. A very few individuals have been blessed with the faculty of stirring public imagination with enthusiasm and devotion toward themselves. My opponent has been one of those favored few. Out of that enthusiasm and devotion the people of Alaska placed him in imagination upon a beautiful pedestal before which they performed their rites of patriotism, homage, and devotion. I confess to have myself performed priestly duties at those ceremonies.
>
> What has recently been exposed convinces many of us that our idol is made of ordinary clay—very ordinary, and we are wondering whether his enemies of old may not, after all, have been right in their contention. . . .[6]

Wickersham relied basically on reciting his past record of achievements in Washington. The remainder of the time he spent in answering his opponent's accusations.

He was fond of quoting frequently from a speech made by Rustgard in Anchorage in 1927 lauding Wickersham in extravagant terms. Weary of these repeated references, Rustgard decided to give his version of the circumstances which prompted those complimentary remarks.

After having been almost defeated in the 1916 and 1918 delegate races, Wickersham returned home vowing that he would never be a candidate again. This he emphasized frequently in private conversations with Rustgard. Then when the fight was being made in the legislature for more elected officials (the Comptroller bill), one of the arguments presented against the scheme was that Wickersham wanted one of the offices.

But Wickersham reiterated to Rustgard privately that he was through with seeking political office and would not be a candidate. Whereupon it was decided between them that Rustgard would go out and deliver a speech somewhere at a strategic point in support of the measure and try to convince the people that Wickersham was not an element to be considered because politically his life had come to an end many years before.

To thoroughly convince the public that he was politically dead, Rustgard proceeded to deliver such an eloquent funeral oration that before he had finished "the corpse commenced to stir and soon sat up, rubbing his eyes and looked around." Wickersham apparently concluded that a man possessed of such noble instincts and such superior qualities as a public official was indispensable to the public and was no doubt politically immortal.

"He now enjoys the singular distinction of being the first man to try to pass through the pearly gates of the national capital by means of his own funeral oration," Rustgard said. "But funeral orations are all designed to cover up or at least to palliate faults. The good that men do lives after them—not so their faults." he added.[7]

In a speech in Anchorage, Wickersham told of having helped frame a bill which the Alaska legislature passed, for the building of a road to Matanuska. It was not built, however, because Noel Smith, general manager of the Alaska Railroad, objected to a highway running parallel to the railroad. Influenced by Smith, Wickersham charged, Attorney General Rustgard issued "the rottenest legal opinion I have ever read" forbidding the highway commission to build such a road to the Matanuska Valley.[8]

Sutherland came out in support of Wickersham while National Committeeman Lathrop promoted Rustgard's candidacy, explaining that he could not support "a delegate who antagonizes and fights with those who are in a position to aid us" as he would be of little practical value to the territory.[9]

Lathrop owned the Fairbanks *News-Miner* and its editorial columns lambasted Wickersham mercilessly, depicting him as the lowest of scoundrels, stressing his racist tactics in creating false animosity between the Indians and the whites. The following was typical of its attacks:

> The dastardly effort on the part of Wickersham to incite the
> natives to hostility against the whites by proclaiming to them

that they have been ill-treated, abused and robbed by the government is having its effect on the white voters.

One of the most deplorable occurrences in Alaska since it came under American rule. . .is the effort of Wickersham and Paul to make the Indians believe that all the lands and waters of Alaska were their personal property and that of this they have been robbed by the government. . . .

After Wickersham announced his candidacy for delegate, he went to the Haines convention of the Alaska Native Brotherhood and unfolded his plan to make them all rich. Twenty millions of dollars, it was explained, was the minimum of which they were entitled to recover for southeastern. . .the lawyers (Wickersham and Paul) are to get five percent of the sum recovered, which will be a minimum of one million dollars, or $500,000 for each of them. . . .[10]

Actually, Wickersham had felt for years that the Tlingit and Haida Indians of the panhandle had a legitimate case to argue, that they were entitled to some remuneration for their fishing and hunting grounds which had been appropriated by the federal government without a treaty. The Indians themselves began discussing their land claim rights as early as the 1918 Native Brotherhood convention, and Wickersham included the concept in his public speeches during the early 1920s. Hence it was not a political gimmick which he had just thought up for the present campaign.

He was invited to be the feature speaker at the annual meeting of the ANB in Haines in November, 1929, at which he suggested the possibility of bringing suit in the court of claims to recover some compensation. He pointed out that permission to institute such a suit would have to be secured first from the Department of Interior. Preceding the meeting, Wickersham made a special trip to Ketchikan to enlist the interest and cooperation of William Paul, the ANB president, suggesting that they work together as a legal team.

He told the Indians that the United States government had assumed ownership of their lands and properties and either reserved them for sale in forest reserves or sold them to white settlers for salmon cannery sites, townsites, homesteads or mining claims, without consulting them in any way. It was not his idea, nor that of the Indian leaders with whom he discussed the matter, to try to recover these lands and property rights, but only to ask for just payment for them by the United States.

Wickersham secured unanimous approval from the conventioneers of a bill he had drafted asking permission from Congress to authorize their bringing suit in the court of claims. There were 90 official delegates present and another 200 Indians who took an active part in the discussion.

Wickersham sent a copy of his bill to Sutherland requesting him to introduce it in Congress and do what he could towards getting it enacted into law. Some months later Sutherland telegraphed Wickersham that he had learned the bill had been referred to Governor Parks by the Interior Department. Secretary Wilbur filed objections to allowing the Indians to bring suit; that brought the proposed legislation to a standstill.[11]

The Democrats were unable to find a prominent Democrat who would enter the delegate race so by default the nomination went to that perennial office-seeker, George Grigsby. He ran eight unsuccessful races for delegate! He ran unopposed in the primary.

Wickersham defeated Rustgard in a vote of 4,396 to 3,449, winning a plurality of 947 votes. He was gratified by this margin of victory, though small, in view of the strong fight made against him by the federal brigade in Juneau, who were all-out as supporters of Rustgard. In the first division only 230 votes were cast for Grigsby as the Democrats were herded into the Republican primary to vote for Rustgard. Wickersham calculated that his total campaign expenses amounted to $1,397.08, including printing, traveling, and every other chargeable item.[12]

Wickersham worried about the opposition he would have from members of his own party in the general election as he had heard rumors that many planned to "bolt" the ticket and vote for Grigsby. He wrote Will R. Wood, chairman of the Republican congressional campaign committee, about his concern and Wood replied that he would like to have the names of those Republican officials who were actively campaigning against Wickersham. He said it was an unwritten law that those holding office under a Republican administration were supposed to support the party nominees for Congress. Disloyalty to the party ticket would not be tolerated in the territories any more than in the states.

Wickersham wrote Wood that the threatened defection might be ironed out by a few persuasive letters from him to the following: Parks, Lathrop, Al White, J.C. McBride, collector of customs; Lynn Smith, U.S. marshal, Fairbanks; Charles E. Jones, marshal, Nome; Harvey

Sullivan, marshal, Valdez; Charles H. Flory, chief forester, and Rustgard.[13]

Sutherland came north to campaign for Wickersham in the westward and interior so that the latter could concentrate on the southeastern section, where the Indian vote could balance any Republican defections in the third and fourth divisions. Wickersham wrote approximately 2,000 personal letters to his friends outside the first division, asking for their support.

The Indian issue stressed in the primary continued to receive attention. The Eskimo vote had not been organized in those days, hence it was the white vote of the second, third and fourth divisions pitted against the first, where a fairly solid Indian vote could be delivered by their leaders to their favorite candidates.

The format for a political rally in those days entailed its being held in a movie theater, where the movie would be shown first, followed by a rousing pipe-organ concert or other live local entertainment; then the candidate was introduced by some popular local dignitary and then came the rivalist brand of oratory.

Grigsby was the "star" at one such affair in Anchorage. Following a tumultuous rendition of "The Sidewalks of New York" by Don Adler on the pipe organ at the Empress Theater, Grigsby swaggered onto the stage and let loose his assaults on Wickersham. He denounced the Organic Act which Wickersham had gotten through Congress as an insult to the people of Alaska as it deprived them of their basic sovereign rights, compelling them to seek permission from Congress for their every move. He promised all that would be changed if they sent him to Washington.

He assailed Wickersham for his betrayal of his supporters by reversing his stand on fish traps and accepting a large legal fee for drawing up a bill for the canneries he had formerly opposed. He said Wickersham received an $8,000 fee for a service any other lawyer would have performed for $1,000. He declared that the $8,000 had been paid in reality for the judge's political influence and the people of Alaska had Delegate Sutherland to thank for the bill not being introduced.

Grigsby held Wickersham responsible for enactment of the unpopular Bone Dry Law, which was at the root of so many evils in urban areas of the territory.

November 4, election day, arrived, and the voters returned Wickersham to the delegateship for the seventh time. he won with a plurality of 286 votes out of a total vote of 5,349, winning a majority in each of the four divisions.

In a postmortem analysis of the election results, Wickersham wrote Sutherland:

> Yes, I am elected but my majority is not up to your standard. However, these are stormy times, and the people had some reasons, they thought, to punish a supporter of Mr. Hoover. . .The visit of the Senate committee to the Alaska Railroad and the consequent discharge of two to three hundred employees, the threat of closing the road, and the slump of business along the line, was charged against the Hoover administration, and I was the only goat in sight, so I got the load of shot. I lost every precinct along the road, where I got fine support in April.
>
> Then, too, my opponent was able to organize the full bootleg and anti-prohibition vote against me, with the support of Judge Harding and the Republican court crowd. Ketchikan also was organized in a "boost-for-Ketchikan-candidates" against Juneau (Grigsby lived in Ketchikan). . .anyway the enemy nearly did us up, but we got over the fence with the chicken, as the fox did.
>
> Lathrop and the Marquam crowd at Fairbanks also left the reservation and went on the warpath, after promising on oath to be "good Injuns," but the old sourdoughs in the smaller precincts held the boat from tipping over, as they so often do. God bless 'em.[14]

Chapter 42

Wickersham's Final Tenure As Delegate

> On March 4 Judge James Wickersham of Juneau will be back
> in the national capital. . . . When he served as delegate in times
> past, Wickersham was in the prime of life, and was regarded,
> mentally and physically, as the peer of any member of that
> great legislative body. Now age has mellowed his fighting spirit,
> but he still retains his brilliant mind. (Alaska Weekly, Feb. 20,
> 1931, editorial)

Although delighted and flattered to be elected Alaska's delegate in
Congress for a seventh term, Wickersham regretted having to leave his
home, especially his library and, in his words, "become a tramp again."
He had spent so many years living in hotel rooms that he dreaded
returning to that routine.

They rented their home to Major Malcolm Elliott, head of the Alaska
Road Commission and he leased his law office to Frank Foster and
Clyde Ellis, Cordova attorneys.

Wickersham hired Will Steel, veteran Alaskan newsman, as his
private secretary and Mrs. Wickersham was to serve as his special
assistant. Steel worked on several Seattle papers before going north
with his brother Harry to establish the Dawson *Daily News*, together
with some other Washington state newsmen. Except for brief intervals,
Steel had been editing papers in Alaska ever since 1900, when he and his
brother published the Nome *Daily News*.

The Wickershams found an apartment at the George Washington
Inn, located across the street from the House office building. Mrs. Wickersham cooked their breakfasts and dinners as he preferred eating at
home rather than in restaurants.

One of the first issues to claim the delegate's attention was a controversy between the secretary of interior and the Lomen Commercial Company at Nome, over the reindeer industry. The Lomens had been charged with unfair encroachment on the Eskimos' grazing lands; the two groups operated a reindeer industry independent of one another.

In the 1890's the United States government had authorized the importation of 1,280 domesticated reindeer from Siberia and Lapland to give the Eskimos a food supply and furnish them with a means of livelihood. The deer were distributed to individual Eskimos, to their Lapp instructor, and to church missions working among the Eskimos. The herds thrived and increased in number so that the five to six thousand Eskimos on the Seward Peninsula owned approximately half a million reindeer—far more than they needed for food and clothing.

Seeing an opportunity to develop a profitable new industry by applying a modern processing and marketing system, the Lomens purchased a herd of twelve hundred deer from the Eskimos and organized the Lomen Reindeer Corporation at Nome.

The Lomens, together with New York financiers Leonard and Arthur Baldwin, invested over two million dollars in the organization of a reindeer industry. They were at the peak of their operations in 1931 when they found themselves the object of hostile criticism from various quarters. They were employing 600 Eskimos—the men in the herding, butchering, and processing operations, and the women in the manufacture of parkas, fur pants, mukluks, mittens, socks, caps, and sleeping bags. Fur clothing for the first two Byrd Antarctic expeditions, as well as for Byrd's North Pole flight, was supplied by the Lomen enterprises.

From 1928 to 1930 some thirty thousand carcasses of meat and thousands of reindeer hides for the manufacture of gloves were shipped to the states. The department of interior also marketed some carcasses from the Eskimo-owned herds at a much lower price. For example, the department brought a shipment south on its own ship, the *Boxer*, at a freight rate of five dollars a ton, while the tariff on private commercial vessels cost the Lomens forty-two dollars a ton.

Meat packers and livestock producers in the states objected to the competition. In Kansas and Nebraska they organized a boycott of chain stores buying Alaska reindeer meat. They complained to government agencies and finally succeeded in stopping the shipments on the grounds that the meat had not been properly inspected, as was required in the handling of meats in the states.

The Lomens also fell victim to a muckraking crusade by church and women's groups who had been persuaded that the poor Eskimos of Alaska were being robbed of their livelihood by this non-native monopolistic commercial firm. Clarence L. Andrews, a retired former schoolteacher for the Bureau of Indian Affairs in interior Alaska, was credited with having inspired the crusade.[1]

Hearings before congressional committees were in full swing when Wickersham arrived, and he testified for an hour and a half, contending that the department of interior had no authority to accept a plan offered by the Lomen-Baldwin interests to enter into a cooperative contract with the federal government. He argued that such a plan would afford the company a monopoly in the marketing of reindeer products, which would result in such great profit in stock selling that it would enable the stockholders to recoup their investment and the government would be left with the financial deficit.[2]

The Lomen-Baldwin interests offered to sell out to the government in 1934 for $950,000, but it took Secretary of Interior Harold L. Ickes six years to convince Congress that that was the best solution for the problem. Congress appropriated $720,000 to buy out all non-native reindeer owners, which included fifty in addition to the Lomens. That was supposedly payment for 82,442 deer, although there were over half a million deer involved. This final settlement barred non-natives from owning reindeer forevermore.

Thirteen years later, the Bureau of Indian Affairs reported an estimated total of 26,157 reindeer in the field. When the non-natives were ousted from the industry, most of the Eskimos quit also as they were no longer assured of a market for their products. They killed the animals for dog food and bait for fox traps. One village alone destroyed three thousand deer in a single year to provide food for their dogs. Unherded and uncontrolled, tens of thousands of deer traveled eastward and joined the caribou.

Another issue was what to do with Alaska's Bone Dry law inasmuch as the courts had held many of its provisions nullified by enactment of the Volstead Act, the national prohibition law. Wickersham introduced a bill to repeal the Alaska law but the national president of the WCTU appeared before the Committee on Territories to oppose his bill and succeeded in sidetracking it.

Though unsuccessful in getting his bill through Congress, Wickersham laid the groundwork which led to congressional legislation providing for territorial control of the liquor traffic within its boundaries and ratification of the legislature's act creating a liquor control board. It abrogated not only the Volstead Act as it applied to the territory but also the Bone Dry Law, which had been enacted by Congress specifically for Alaska.

Wickersham was in Seattle when the licensing system went into operation; when asked by a reporter how he felt about Alaskans being permitted to drink hard liquor for the first time since 1917, he replied: "It's about time. Alaskans have known for two decades that their prohibition laws were a failure. Dry laws never did work in Alaska and I don't think they ever will. It's high time we repealed them," he repeated, giving the floor a hearty thump with his cane.

Continuing, he said: "They tell me I can expect the saloons back any time now in Alaska, once the repeal movement gets underway. But what of it? Better have saloons than smuggling, bootlegging, and other evils of an unpopular, unenforced law."[3]

Wickersham called on President Hoover, hoping to establish a more friendly relationship than had existed between Sutherland and the president. Sutherland had a bitter personal quarrel with Hoover over his fishery policy when he was secretary of commerce, and Hoover had not forgotten it. He told Wickersham he would gladly accord him patronage recognition as long as Sutherland was not involved.[4]

With the friendly assurance from the president, Wickersham visited the department of justice to discuss judgeship appointments but soon learned that Lathrop had gotten ahead of him and the department was prepared to recognize his recommendations.

The Wickershams enjoyed two social affairs at the White House. One was a reception for the House members which he described as "a very spectacular and dressy function—Grace likes 'em that way!" The other was a small dinner party for twenty guests. Wickersham proclaimed the dinner good but not sumptuous and described the after-dinner routine:

> After the dinner the President and Mrs. Hoover rose and we followed them upstairs to a red room, where the ladies remained while we men followed the President to the Lincoln room. The gentlemen smoked—the President and I smoked cigars, the others cigarettes.
>
> They talked international matters—Japan and China difficulty, etc. I remained silent. After half an hour the President guided us down to the ladies—shook hands (as did Mrs. Hoover) and left us. We then took our carriages and went home. I enjoyed it—Grace was thrilled![6]

When reelection time rolled around, Wickersham was all for running again despite the fact that he was seventy-five years old and suffering from a variety of physical ailments. He had undergone a prostate gland operation while in Washington and his eyesight was deteriorating. He had no opposition in the primary so did not return to Alaska until it was time to campaign in the general election.

His Democratic opponent was Valdez attorney Anthony J. Dimond. Dimond defeated Grigsby and Adolph H. Ziegler, a Ketchikan attorney, in the primary. Dimond had been in Alaska since 1905, first as a prospector and later studied law and passed the Alaska bar. His law partner had been Tom Donohoe, the Democratic national committee-man. Donohoe retired to California on account of ill health and Dimond took over their law offices in Valdez and Cordova. Dimond served two terms in the territorial Senate.

The national economic depression made Hoover's chances for reelection look dim and the Democrats' hopes were high. A record turn-out of Democratic voters in the territorial primary was a little frightening to Wickersham. It was the first time since 1918 that the Democrats received the majority vote in a territorial election.

One of his last acts before leaving Washington to attend the Republican national convention in Chicago was to defeat a motion on the House floor eliminating the territories of Alaska and Hawaii from the benefits of a bill creating Federal Home Loan banks in the several states. He got permission to speak for three minutes against the motion, which was defeated. He was not sure what the benefits might be to Alaskans, but he was opposed to barring them from any program available to the rest of the nation.

When Wickersham arrived back in Juneau he arranged a meeting with the other Republicans running for the various territorial offices and the new national committeeman, Edward A. Rasmuson, Skagway banker. He knew he would need all the help he could get from his own party members to stave off the Democrats' onslaught.

They met in Grover Winn's law office - Winn was running for the House. In the group were the candidates for auditor, commissioner of education, attorney general and Al White, representing the central committee. But even with that small a group, harmonious planning proved futile. Cash Cole, the candidate for auditor, walked out mad, threatening to run as an independent. Rustgard, who was running for reelection to attorney general, refused to make the requested $250 campaign contribution, although he probably was the best off financial-ly of the candidates. Al White demanded a categorical promise from

Wickersham that he would permit the "organization" (meaning White) to control appointments. Wickersham agreed that no appointment would be made without full consultation, but he would not surrender his own freedom of choice.[6]

Al White read a letter from Louis Paul, Bill Paul's brother and editor of the Petersburg *Alaskan*, the official organ of the Alaska Native Brotherhood, making three demands of the Republican party: first, a cash donation of $1,500; second, suppression of the Petersburg *Press*, his opposition paper; third, the appointment of his brother Bill to some party office. The group voted to take no action.

Wickersham had received a similar letter while he was in Washington, demanding money in return for the Paul brothers' delivery of the Indian vote in the coming election. Then later when he arrived in Seattle, Mrs. Bill Paul asked him for $200 to pay her household bills so she could rejoin her husband in Ketchikan; she said her husband had told her to ask Wickersham to give her the money. At first he refused as he resented the insulting and threatening letters which he was receiving from the Paul brothers. But one evening he had dinner with Rasmuson and Edward W. Allen, the Seattle attorney for the Nakat Fisheries Company, and they advised him to give her the money for political reasons, which he did. Allen promised to see that Bill Paul got employment with his company, as Paul was without means of livelihood and had a family to support.

Wickersham continued to receive threatening letters from the Paul brothers throughout the campaign saying that unless they received a substantial donation from the Republican party, they would see to it that he and the other Republican candidates would not get the Indian vote. This was despite the fact that Wickersham had contributed nearly nine hundred dollars to the support of the ANB paper since the first of March of that year.

Later in the campaign, Bill Paul announced his candidacy for attorney general against Rustgard and James Truitt, the Democrat. Truitt won in the Democratic landslide and Paul came in third place.

Mrs. Wickersham accompanied her husband on his campaign trip to the westward. It was her first visit to that section of the territory during her thirty years residence in Juneau. They traveled by steamer to Valdez and then by car over the Richardson highway to Fairbanks.

Wickersham found campaigning a lot different from the olden days. Dimond was flying around the country in an airplane furnished him by W.E. Dunkle, Willow Creek mine operator and former Guggenheim mining engineer, at a cost of $100 a day. Wickersham had never flown a plane and was not anxious to do so; he wasn't convinced it was a safe means of travel.

Dimond was also using the radio in communicating with the voters, and that was a new experience for Wickersham. He tried it in Anchorage and reported that he felt cramped and awkward sitting in a little cubbyhole and talking to an invisible audience; he missed the audience response in the old-time rallies. [8]

He visited the old mining camps, which at one time were the bulwark of his voting strength and found them practically deserted. The diggings had played out and only a handful of workers were still living there; he met some of his old friends and passed out cigars along the highways.

In his campaign speeches Wickersham told of his pioneering struggles on behalf of the territory as judge and delegate, his legislative achievements in Congress and his continuous fight for the people's interests versus the corporations.

He criticized Dimond for "flying around the territory in a plane owned by a Guggenheim associate. "Who's putting up the $100 a day for that airplane and the broadcasting from Anchorage?" he asked. He said the law limited the campaign expenditures of a candidate for delegate to $2,500 and added that he was paying every cent of his own expenses, but expressed grave doubts that Dimond could say the same.

He also reminded his audiences that Dimond and his law partner, Tom Donohoe, had been attorneys for the "big interests" for twenty years - the Kennecott Corporation, the Copper River Railroad, the Alaska Steamship Company, and four or five big fisheries companies. "Is Tony working for you or the people who are putting up the money?" he asked. He pointed out that it was the fault of these corporations that the freight rates on the Alaska Railroad were so high, so excessive that the miners could not afford to prospect and operate their mines in the interior. [9]

Dimond told his audiences that he, too, was an old-timer, having lived in Alaska continuously for nearly twenty-eight years. "I did not come as a federal official; my trail-breaking was not done at the government's expense, carefully wrapped up in robes, with plenty of dogs to pull the sled," he added.

Dimond denied that the "big interests" were paying his campaign expenses, insisting that he was paying his own. As for using Dunkle's plane, he explained that Dunkle and he were old mining friends, and Dunkle was providing the plane at cost, and there was no Guggenheim connection. He drew a laugh when he pointed out that his opponent could well afford to travel around in a plane as the government allowed him $1,500 a year for mileage, from which he might easily hold out $2,000 in two years for campaign expenses, "but he won't spend the money or risk his skin." He thought his opponent should get out into the bush country, off the beaten trails, instead of confining his travel to a few of the larger communities.

Referring to his legal associations with the big corporations, he admitted doing legal work for them but contended that they always knew he would follow his own judgment and conscience in political matters. "My political influence, whatever it may be, has never been for sale and has never been sold," he said. He then spoke at length of Wickersham's accepting a fee from the fishing interests to help get legislation through Congress for the leasing of fish traps.

That Wickersham was in fact sympathetic to the canneries getting their trap leasing law through Congress is evident from his diary entry, which told of a visit from an emissary of Gil Skinner, a major cannery stockholder, to remind him that they expected Wickersham to support pending legislation. Wickersham promised to try to get the bill's sponsor, Senator Wesley Jones, to delay pushing it until after the elections were over—"Then I will not oppose it!"[10]

Wickersham received strong endorsements from the national legislative departments of the Brotherhood of Locomotive Engineers, the Order of Railway Conductors, the Brotherhood of Locomotive Firemen and Enginemen, Brotherhood of Railroad Trainmen, and the Brotherhood of Maintenance of Way Employees, all with offices in Washington, D.C. Their newspaper ads urged their Alaskan members to vote for Wickersham:

> We earnestly desire to assure you of the exceptional One Hundred Per Cent Record for ability, integrity and impartiality established and maintained throughout seven terms of splendid serivce by your present delegate in Congress, Honorable James Wickersham.
>
> With all due respect for the ambitions of other candidates, you cannot afford to take any chances of losing the services in Congress of such an able and influential legislator and outstanding friend of the workers. . . .[11]

On November 8, Alaska's Democrats swept their candidates into office with as overwhelming a victory as did their colleagues in the states. All of their territorial candidates were elected and they had full control of the legislature, with six of the eight senators and twelve of the sixteen

House members. Dimond defeated Wickersham by a plurality of 6,129 votes, the final tally being: Dimond 9,949 and Wickersham 3,820. In his own words, Wickersham was "licked to a frazzle."

The Wickershams returned to Washington for the "lame duck" session of Congress. Soon they were deluged by Alaska's Democrats importuning his assistance in getting them appointed to office. One of the first to show up was Bunnell, seeking the governorship. His official pretext for coming to Washington was to get Wickersham to introduce some legislation on behalf of the college, because as an alleged lobbyist for the college, he was eligible for an expense-paid round trip.

John Troy wrote Wickersham asking him to write letters to the president-elect and to James Farley, Democratic national committee chairman, recommending Troy for the governorship. After surviving the first shock of such effrontery, Wickersham concluded that inasmuch as some Democrat was bound to get the appointment, he would write the letters as he would rather see Troy in the office than any other Democratic aspirant.

Wickersham's spirit of brotherly love and forgiveness even extended to inviting Bert Faulkner and the Dimonds to dinner when they arrived in Washington.

Chapter 43.

Wickersham's Twilight Years

Alaska's "Wick" Burns Out, But His Light
Shines On

> *There will never be another man like Judge Wickersham*
> *because there will never be another setting like Alaska,1900-39,*
> *to bring out the particular qualities for which the world will*
> *remember him. . . .*
> *Alaska will not forget James Wickersham. His place in our*
> *history is secure. (Alaska Daily Empire,Oct.25,1939)*

The Wickershams were back in Juneau in time to attend the swearing-in ceremonies inducting veteran newsman John Weir Troy into the office of Alaska's twelfth American governor. Wickersham had his doubts about how good a governor he would make for three reasons: he was sixty-five and in ill health; he had been a bitter partisan Democrat all his life. But he was entitled to the governorship as a reward for years of devoted party service.

The ceremonies took place in the presence of the joint houses of the legislature and a large crowd of enthusiastic friends. There was no parade nor inaugural ball to celebrate the change in command.

Later in the evening the Juneau city band staged a surprise serenade under Troy's windows of his *Empire* apartment, playing marches and fox trots for thirty minutes. He acknowledged the greeting from his window, and when the musicians returned to their headquarters, they were soon treated to refreshments dispatched at the request of the new governor.[1]

One of Troy's first official acts was to offer Grace Wickersham an appointment to the newly created territorial board of education. Wickersham disapproved of the office of commissioner of education being made appointive rather than elective, as it had been for years, and he didn't want his wife to accept the appointment; she seemed amenable to his wishes.

But before she had an opportunity to say yes or no, Governor Troy called her to his office and offered her an appointment to the board of trustees of the Alaska Agricultural College and School of Mines instead. Later they learned that Troy had decided to appoint Bert Faulkner to the board of education.

Wickersham didn't want his wife on the college board either and went to see Troy to object, only to be told that the governor had already sent in his nominations to the legislature. Grace was pleased and cajoled her husband into withdrawing his objections.

Actually, Wickersham owed much to his wife in overcoming his feelings of hostility toward former political enemies. Juneau was full of them and were he to continue to foster these resentments, the Wickershams would be social loners. But Mrs. Wickersham was an extrovert and had many friends among Juneau's socially elite and was able to help her husband forget past grievances so they could enjoy a more relaxed social life in the small town.

They attended affairs at the governor's mansion, and Mrs. Wickersham usually was invited to be one of the hostesses, "pouring" together with the Democratic and socially acceptable Republican ladies of the town.

The Faulkners were their next-door neighbors, and the two wives had been longtime bridge partners so that it seemed awkward for the two husbands to keep up their feuding, now that Wickersham was no longer an aspirant for political office. The two couples began exchanging dinner parties.

Wickersham resumed attendance at the weekly luncheon meetings of the local bar association. The high degree of respect and admiration which he enjoyed in this group was shown when a resolution was passed proposing setting aside August 24, his birthday, each year as "Wickersham Day" in recognition of his long years of public service on behalf of the territory. The group urged that other civic and fraternal organizations send similar petitions to the territorial legislature urging enactment of legislation to that effect.

Wickersham was pleasantly surprised at the move and suggested that it was "very premature" and just a little embarrassing. It reminded him of the Negro mother who was being examined by a census taker. He said: "Why, Mandy, you report two children, one age four years and another two years and say your husband died six years ago, how do you explain that?"

"Dat needs no splanation," she replied, "for I ain't dead yet, if my husband is."[2]

In a letter to the bar association expressing his appreciation for the resolution, Wickersham wrote that although he was somewhat embarrassed at the suggestion that the people of Alaska should feel indebted to him to such an extent that they should repay him by giving his name "this great prominence in Alaskan history," he felt that the greater tribute, however, would be if the citizens of Alaska would always bravely defend those principles of constitutional government embodied in the Organic Act and "give their best efforts to prevent their destruction or abandonment."[3]

The legislature did not get around to according Wickersham this recognition until ten years after his death.

Wickersham accompanied his wife to Fairbanks when she attended her first trustees' meeting as he had been invited to deliver the commencement address. He also delivered the dedicatory address and turned the first shovelful of earth for the new Carl Ben Eielson Building. Eielson, a pioneer Alaskan bush pilot, lost his life in November, 1929, in a plane crash on Arctic ice off the Siberian coast while engaged in rescuing the crew of an ice-bound American fur trader vessel. He also made the first airmail flight within Alaska, going from Fairbanks to McGrath on February 21, 1924.

Wickersham's commencement address was printed in its entirety in the Fairbanks *News-Miner*; it covered twenty-one pages of the six-column paper. It was a scholarly treatise entitled "The Asia-American Migration Route: The Siberian-Alaska Land Bridge over which Man and Mammoth Reached America from Asia."

Later that summer Darrell and Jane visited the Wickershams for ten days, and in September Mrs. Wickersham's niece, Ruth Coffin, came to spend the winter with them while she taught art and music in the public school. Wickersham enjoyed having a young person around the house as her youthful exuberance brought a lightheartedness into his daily routine.

He insisted on going off to his office punctually every morning immediately after eating his breakfast. He used a cane to descend the steep stairway and hill from his home down to the Valentine Building. There wasn't much for him to do when he got to his office, but it was a form of self-discipline which he needed to impose upon himself in order not to feel that he was slipping into uselessness. He once described himself as "a creature of habits—chains which keep me in a groove but which seem good to me."[4]

His active mind continued to conjure up challenging projects to work on. For example, he spent months of research determining that the highly profitable Alaska-Juneau Gold Mining Company had been exempt from paying city taxes ever since it started operation thirty years ago (1913). No taxes had been levied either on its milling plant or its 29.06 acres of ground. Wickersham believed such an exemption was illegal and should be voided. It reminded him of his fights with the utility corporations when he was Tacoma's city attorney over thirty years earlier.

The city of Juneau had spent nearly twenty thousand dollars piping water to the mine. He planned to file a suit to put an end to the exemption and perhaps even to get the company to pay retroactive taxes. He discussed the case with Henry Roden and invited him to co-sponsor the case against the city to compel the officials to levy a tax on the mining company. Nothing was mentioned in his diary of subsequent action.

His eyes were a constant worry. He was troubled with dizzy spells and a low pain in the region of his sinuses, which he attributed partially to his cigar smoking. He knew he should quit smoking, but it gave him so much comfort that he refused to do so. He did not enjoy going to the movies anymore because the subjects on the screen had become blurred; that had been a favorite pastime all his life.

He was invited to be a speaker at a sourdough reunion in Los Angeles but he had to decline as he could not afford to make the trip. Instead, he wrote a whimsical greeting to be read at the meeting:

> It would be a pleasure to attend the festivities at that famous roadhouse, and sit with you, crowding near the round-bellied, red hot oil tank stove, stuffed with a roaring fire of spruce wood, while our felt shoes and wet socks hung steaming from the bailing wire stretched on the pole frame around the stove pipe, as we listen, open-mouthed to some gray-headed Yukon liar trying to outdo the last one.
>
> How often we have been happily entertained by Bill McPhee, "Waterfront" Brown, Dan Callahan, George Kilroy, Gordon Bettles, Bruce Slater and others of the numerous Yukon sons of

Wickersham standing in front of his home in Juneau, July 1934. Left to right: daughter-in-law, Jane Wickersham; son, Darrell; Wickersham; wife, Grace.

Wickersham and wife, with University regents and Governor Troy, Mar. 17, 1935. Standing, l. to r.: Wickersham, Charles Bunnell, Luther Hess, Andrew Nerland, Arthur Shonbeck, J. S. Hofman. Seated: Grace Wickersham, Governor Troy, Harriet Hess, George Lingo.

Ananias—and how we loved it, and them. May their kind never perish!

Memory calls up the picture, as I write, of the oldtime road-house table with its granite coffee pots, one at each end of the board, presided over by good old "Flatwheel" himself, flanked by cans of Eagle Brand milk, with nail holes ready for use, the can artistically ornamented with a picture of the contented cow; plates piled high with stacks of sourdough flapjacks, hunks of alleged fresh California butter just out of the brine barrel; platters overflowing with bacon and beans; a huge roast of caribou just off a nearby hillside; cans of Vermont maple syrup blended in a San Francisco warehouse, and jars of Alaska Commercial Co. pickles—a plentiful supply of grub, fit for any musher who straddled a gee-pole and cussed the dogs for a twenty-mile jaunt since he ate his breakfast at his morning campfire.

I would be happy to sit with you and drink a tin cup of hootch, Albert's best Circle City brew, or even take a swig from the bottle of Cyrus Noble—but it's a long wet trail from Alaska to your miners' meeting on the great outside, and I cannot come. . . .[5]

Wickersham received an honorary doctor of laws degree from the college at Fairbanks on May 20, 1935. He was the second recipient of an honorary degree from that institution, General James Gordon Steese, former head of the Alaska Road Commission and the Alaska Engineering Commission, being the first.

The institution's name was changed to the University of Alaska by the 1935 legislature, but it did not go into effect officially until six months after Wickersham received his degree. He was present in the governor's office when the bill was signed into law.

Wickersham began having serious financial troubles in 1935. Alaska was feeling the effects of the economic depression which had held the states in its grip for several years. Clients did not have money to pay him in the few cases that came his way. Although he owned property around Tacoma, he could not sell as there were no buyers. He felt bitter about being hard-up and blamed the New Deal policies of President Roosevelt for his condition. He received some temporary assistance from Darrell. He sold his mining property on Ester Creek to the Fairbanks Exploration Company which helped him pay his delinquent taxes.[6]

The Wickershams were put under further financial strain when Grace's Spanish sister-in-law and five-year-old son came to spend a year with them. Grace's brother, Henry Vrooman, an electrical engineer, had died in Barcelona, Spain. His widow and son escaped to the United States as refugees from the civil war which brought Francisco Franco to power.

The usual marital harmony in the Wickersham household underwent extreme strains during the winter of 1936 and 1937 when Grace's three relatives increased her household chores. She became tired and over-wrought and Wickersham became upset seeing her doing so much of the menial labor around the house; it emphasized his financial inadequacy.

Recognized as the Republicans' "elder statesman," Wickersham was privy to the internecine feuding going on within the party organization. There was nothing he enjoyed more than being party to a plot to flay an adversary. His role in a memorable party incident helped divert his attention from his private worries.

The Republicans' territorial convention met in Douglas in the spring of 1936, a national election year. The fight for control of patronage, in case the Republicans were victorious, inspired conspiratorial activities within the organization.

W.C. (Bill) Arnold, general counsel for the canned salmon industry in Seattle together with the canneries' Juneau legal counsel, Bert Faulkner, were scheming how to oust National Committeeman Rasmuson and Al White, the party counsel, so they could get control.

Wickersham's cooperation with the cannery interests in his later years, led Arnold to seek his support in the ouster move. He knew the former delegate was unhappy about the alleged lack of support which he received from the Rasmuson-White forces in his last race for delegate. Wickersham called Arnold "a cunning cuss" but in this matter he was on Arnold's side.

Arnold arrived at the convention with proxies from the second division and Andrew Nerland with those from the fourth division. Al White had been authorized to vote the 93 first division votes as a unit, which gave him control of the convention. Nerland was a member of the Rasmuson-White central committee, and the Arnold-Faulkner scheme was to try to alienate Nerland against his committee colleagues.

Knowing that Wickersham and Nerland were old-time Fairbanks friends, Arnold sought Wickersham's aid in trying to effect the alien-ation. At a conference in Wickersham's office, Nerland was proferred the nomination of national committeeman if he would swing his fourth division proxies to the anti-White side.

Wickersham told Nerland that the White crowd was plotting to unseat Bunnell as president of the university, knowing that Nerland was a staunch Bunnell supporter. The plot, as divulged by Wickersham, involved W.K. Keller, former commissioner of education under the Republicans, going to Fairbanks as superintendent of schools that fall. Then, in case of a Republican national victory and Rasmuson was appointed governor of Alaska, "he would fill the board of regents with friends of Keller, who would remove Bunnell and appoint Keller." This suggestion startled Nerland but he still refused to shift his affiliation.[8]

Later that evening when the convention recessed, Arnold forgot to take his personal briefcase with him. Rumors were about town that the disgruntled delegates had resorted to liquid palliatives to smooth their wounds and blur their sensibilities. A member of the White contingent took charge of the briefcase for safe-keeping. Its contents included political correspondence which constituted "a dynamite shock" in the wrong hands. Among the letters was one allegedly written by Faulkner claiming that he could control Wickersham and that Wickersham, in turn, could control Bob Bloom, Fairbanks merchant and prominent Republican. Other letters indicated that Arnold was involved in plans for the overthrow of Frank Burns, Republican national committeeman for the State of Washington.

When the delegates reconvened, the White and anti-White groups met separately and elected separate sets of national convention delegates and national committeeman and committeewoman. The national committee seated the White delegation after Committeeman Burns of Washington addressed the group in executive session, denouncing Faulkner as only interested in the Republican party in order to control patronage in Alaska, whether Republican or Democratic; all but three of the national committeemen voted affirmatively to seat the Rasmuson-White delegation.

Informed of the results, Wickersham observed: "This is a tough blow to the cannery interests! but will please Dan Sutherland, while Al White will be eight feet tall when he returns to Juneau.[9]

Wickersham was at sea en route to Anchorage on his eightieth birthday. Grace had alerted the ship's captain so as he sat eating dinner on the evening of August 24, the ship's musicians marched into the dining hall playing "Happy Birthday To You," and the chief steward brought in a large birthday cake and placed it before him.

One of the passengers served as master of ceremonies and delivered an oration on Wickersham's achievements as judge and member of Congress. The ladies crowded around asking for his autograph, all of which pleased the octogenarian no end.

He had granted an interview to the *Alaska Press*, on the occasion of his upcoming eightieth birthday, before he left Juneau. The paper introduced Wickersham to its readers in these words:

> High up on the hill, in a large, old-fashioned wooden home, lives one of Alaska's distinguished citizens, and a man whose hand in shaping the destiny of this great country was more powerful than most of its residents and beneficiaries realize.
>
> At eighty, Judge Wickersham's hair is whitening, but his mind and body are active and vigorous. His appearance belies his years and no stranger would dream that this stern-looking, kindly gentleman was born in 1857.
>
> When asked by *The Press* for a statement on his birthday anniversary, Wickersham obliged with a brief glimpse into the stormy days when the territory of Alaska was being born in the far-off halls of Congress. . . .

Wickersham's final years were spent in sporadic literary efforts. His law business had dwindled as, in his words, "people don't come to me for legal aid because they think I'm too old." His failing eyesight made it necessary for Grace to read to him in order that he could continue working on his research projects, which gave him so much satisfaction. They also worked together trying to establish a monetary value on his books and documents, in case they found a buyer for his library.

His crusading spirit and interest in government and politics continued to the end. One issue which aroused his vigorous opposition was a referendum on a unicameral legislature. Delegate Dimond had gotten a bill through Congress providing for such a referendum. Wickersham viewed it as an attempt to emasculate the legislature, which he had worked so hard to bring into being. He felt it was incumbent on him to register as strong a protest as possible, as he was suspicious of what the New Dealers might do to change the country's fundamental laws.

He drafted a ten-page pamphlet entitled: "An Appeal To The Voters of Alaska, To Defend Their Full Territorial Form of Government." On the first page was the following warning:

Stop, Look and Think before you vote on Sept.13,1938, to destroy the Alaska territorial senate. It is a **Block of Safety** found in every American form of government - in every constitution and organic act. Its presence there was and is intended to give additional protection to your **Personal Liberties and Civil Rights**.

The Dimond referendum which you are urged to adopt is the first step in an organized plan to create a **Full Centralized Bureaucratic Form of Government** in Alaska through a **Unicameral or One-House Legislature Without Check or Balance** - the Nazi-German type. **Vote Against It!**

James Wickersham

Wickersham's basic argument against a one-house legislature was that the framers of the American constitution instituted the two-house system as a safeguard against bad lawmaking. He contended that "good laws will not lose virility by a brief delay" while "bad laws ought never be allowed immunity from those obstacles. The senate has always been the conservative and safe body in the Alaska legislatures. It will be dangerous to allow unthinking or designing men to destroy it," he argued.

The referendum resulted in 4,975 votes in favor of the unicameral legislature and 6,639 against it.

While in Seattle on a visit to his oculist, Wickersham told a Seattle *Star* reporter that the federal government's "pump priming" money was ruining Alaska—"a country that had always paid its own way and supported its own citizens and always would. Put a beggar on horseback and he's going to run a race. With the government scattering this largess in our midst—money we don't need—we're going to grow too fast and not soundly," he maintained.[11]

Word came from Darrell that his doctor had ordered him to bed for three months as he was suffering from a lung infection bordering on tuberculosis. He could not longer aid his father financially and advised the sale of the real estate in Tacoma and in Puyallup Valley, even if it meant selling at a loss. Wickersham followed his son's advice and suffered severe losses. For example, his old home on C Street in Tacoma, for which he paid $10,000 in the 1880s, sold for $1,900.

Continued worry over finances and loss of eyesight finally broke him physically. Had the legislature consented to buy his Alaskan library, he would have been saved the mental torture which was wracking his mind and body. In May, 1939, he had to quit writing in his diary as he could no longer see to do so.

On May 12 he wrote: "I am so blind that I can hardly see and must quit my diary for the present. . .We leave for Seattle tomorrow for several weeks while I try to regain my sight." On the ship going south to Seattle, he stumbled and fell down the stairs leading to the dining salon, receiving numerous body bruises.

A new pair of glasses enabled him to resume his diary entries and by laborious effort, to continue working on his study of gold mining from Peru to Point Barrow. The renewed eyesight lasted only a few weeks, and on July 21 he wrote this mournful note in his diary:

> We need money very badly. Our taxes are due and unpaid. . .I am blind and busted. Grace is doing all she can to help. Our creditors are threatening to cut off our lights.
>
> I cannot see to practice law even if I had business which I cannot do. Cannot sell property.

On October 18, Alaska Day, Wickersham wrote his diary entry so poorly that it was scarcely legible, ending with these words: "Cannot see - blind!" The following day he tried again but all he managed to scrawl unevenly was: "Cannot see—blind!"

Grace then took over and wrote:

> I wonder if the first line of October 19 is to be the Judge's last written word. Such a tragedy for one who loved to read! Who has so many books he wanted to read! Who wanted to do so much more in preserving the records of men who had lived in Alaska in early days and had helped develop it! Pilz, Bremner, Franklin and many others the Judge thought were never given enough credit for their labor.

That evening Wickersham suffered a stroke paralyzing his right side. For two days he remained at home with a professional nurse caring for him, but as his condition worsened he was taken to St. Ann's Hospital. He lingered for two more days when the end came, with Grace at his bedside.

Leaving the hospital, Grace walked to her husband's office and sat down at his desk and made a final entry in his diary:

> October 24,1939. It is four minutes after 5 a.m. I am alone in the office. I have just left the hospital and all I hold most dear, my darling husband is gone!

> I cannot yet believe it—it seems impossible, I loved him so.
> He was so good, so kind, so forgiving, so unselfish. I cannot
> bear to think of life without him.

Alaska's press was generous in its tributes to the man who had been a favorite editorial target for decades. The *Empire* said that writing Wickersham's obituary was like putting lock and seal on an era in history. "God gave James Wickersham character and talents which fit like the proverbial paper on the wall the time and place in which he found himself when he came north at the turn of the century," it observed, predicting that Alaska would not forget him as his place in its history was secure forevermore.

The *Daily Press* commented that Wickersham came to Alaska during stormy times but in a few years he emerged as Alaska's dominant figure. So well did he build his reputation and character that for two decades whatever "Wick" said was tantamount to law, and this applied whether he was in official position or on the sidelines "pulling the strings."

Funeral services were held in Seattle with Bishop Peter Trimble Rowe conducting them. According to the *Alaska Weekly*, it was a difficult service for the bishop to perform as his own life had been so linked with the life of the deceased. He told of many meetings on the trails of the far north and many an old-timer in the audience could see the picture - Judge Wickersham out in front of his dogteam, parka open at the throat, fur cap in hand, and his graying hair touched with frost. One man was spreading the gospel of God, the other was spreading law and justice.

Chapter 44

Wickersham the Scholar

*If the money can be secured I would give my whole time. . .
to write the history of Alaska. . .and transfer my law office to
someone else. . . .*

*I am working in my leisure now on a series of biographies of
early day prominent Alaska characters. . .which work I greatly
enjoy. . .I will leave this material for the use of future scholars
and students of Alaska history, if it is not possible to get it in
type before I pass over the last great divide. I am now 78 years
old.(Wickersham Diary,Sept.26,27,1935)*

Wickersham the scholar was as dedicated in his literary efforts on
behalf of Alaska as he was a statesman and politician. His bibliography
of Alaska literature, 1724-1924; his book, *Old Yukon: Tales, Trials and
Trails;* and his Alaskana library comprise a priceless treasure trove for
students of Alaska's history.

Wickersham's impetus to developing a comprehensive Alaska library
was based on his ambition to present the University of Alaska with as
fine a library of Alaskan literature as could be found anyplace in the
world. By 1914 he had acquired 2,500 volumes and ten years later the
collection had increased to 10,380 titles.

He did not restrict his collection to books written in English but had
some in Russian, French, Japanese, German, and Spanish. In his search
for the earliest writings about Alaska, he found a *History of China* by
Father Jean-Baptiste DuHalder, a French Jesuit and geographer,
printed in France in 1735. It contained a map and descriptive narrative
of St. Lawrence Island brought back to Peter the Great by Captain

Wickersham in his law office, Juneau, 1930s.

Vitus Bering, following his first voyage to the Arctic Ocean. Bering had discovered and landed on St. Lawrence in August, 1728.

Wickersham was helped in securing much of his material on early Russian America by Dr. Frank A. Golder, who spent some time in Leningrad (St. Petersburg) and Moscow studying in the Russian archives. When Golder came across books and documents which he thought would interest Wickersham, he wrote him and the delegate sent him money to buy the material. When Golden returned to the United States, his "Guide to Materials for American History in Russian Archives" was published by the Carnegie Institution in 1917.

A valuable acquisition from Japan was the sixteen-volume set of "Kwaukai Ibun" written in 1793 in Japanese cursive, with colored pictures, relating the experiences of a group of Japanese sailors who were cast ashore on Unalaska Island and rescued by the Russians, who took them first to St. Petersburg and then around Cape Horn and the Hawaiian Islands, to Japan.

He had a copy of the charter given to the Russian-American Trading Company by the Russian czar in 1799.

Just moving his library from place to place was an expensive luxury. In 1912 he shipped it from Tacoma to Washington, D.C. and six years later, he shipped it back to Tacoma, placing it in the custody of the state historical society. When he bought a home in Juneau in 1928, he had all his books shipped north, where he could have them available for his research projects.

Wickersham was a self-educated scholar, his formal classroom education terminating with the eighth grade. He was an avid reader, especially of historical biography. Some of his favorites were: Beveridge's *Life of John Marshal*, Bishop's two-volume *Theodore Roosevelt and His Times*, Herndon's two-volume *Abraham Lincoln*, and Klebnikov's *Alexander Andreavitch Baranov*. He read everything he could find on Peter the Great and Catherine the Great. He was particularly fascinated with Catherine's background, as it was suspected that she was the illegitimate child of a Russian nobleman and a serf girl. He was fond of referring to her as the "godmother" of Alaska just as Queen Isabell of Spain was to America. He hoped to write a book about her someday.

To Wickersham, Catherine symbolized the vibrant spirit which brought the first settlers to Alaska and his sense of history linked the Russian explorers and furtraders with the American goldseekers and later the fishermen who came to love the land as did Wickersham.

Wickersham's interest in ethnological research developed concurrently with his law studies. As a teacher in the little town of Rochester,

Illinois, in Sangamon County, he became intrigued with the early Indian history of the region, and in 1884 he wrote a report for the Smithsonian Institute - "Mounds of Sangamon County, Illinois." It described the Indian relics unearthed in the archeological excavations in the area.

As assistant editor of the *American Antiquarian* magazine, he wrote numerous articles on ethnological subjects after he moved to Puget Sound, where he continued his interest in Indian lore.

None of the West Coast Indian tribes had a written language when Wickersham arrived in 1883, but by 1892, he had translated the Puyallup-Nesqually Indian language into written form, preserving many of their myths, traditions, and stories. His research led him to prepare a brief on why the famed mountain should be named Mt. Tacoma instead of Mt. Rainier. He had interviewed sixty Indian leaders before coming to that conclusion. He first presented his treatise at a meeting of the Tacoma Academy of Science, at Annie Wright Seminary on February 7, 1893.[1]

All of the Indians whom Wickersham interviewed regarding the name of the mountain and its definition, signed documents to the effect that "Tacoma" or "Tacobet" was the correct name, and they all desired "Rainier" to be dropped.

His brief was incorporated in a booklet prepared by the "Justice to the Mountain" committee of Tacoma, for a hearing held in May 1917, before the national geographic board of the United States in which the Tacoma group urged the board to change the name from Rainier to Tacoma, which was a modern version of the Indians' original name "Tahoma" or "Ta-ko-bet" or "Takoman."[2]

The hearing before the geographic board was in response to a memorial passed by the legislature of the State of Washington asking that the name be changed. When Wickersham testified he was introduced as "probably the highest authority on Indian names since Gibbs, lexicographer of the northwestern Indians." Supporting the Tacoma side were letters from Theodore Roosevelt, Secretary of Interior Franklin K. Lane, Professor Gregory of Yale, and Le Gorce, assistant editor of the *Geographic* magazine.

The Seattle advocates of retaining the name "Rainier" were supported by Professor Victor J. Farrar of the University of Washington, who argued that his historical research did not substantiate Wickersham's testimony. With these two conflicting "expert" opinions, the hearing was reduced to "a monkey and parrot" discourse, according to Wickersham. The geographic board took the matter under advisement.[3]

Wickersham presented a paper on the origin of languages used by West Coast Indians before the Washington State Philological Society on July 1, 1898. Mrs. Wickersham presented a paper on the nomenclature of the Northwest Coast at a meeting of the Washington Historical Society in 1892, giving the origins of the place names.

His reputation as an authority on Indian lore led the Tacoma *News* to comment: "If there is one man who knows more about the Coast and Puget Sound Indians than another, it is Judge James Wickersham of this city. His study in his home on C Street looks like an Indian curio store, while his books on Indian history are invaluable."

According to William Pierce Bonney, secretary-curator of the Washington State Historical Society, Wickersham had the most remarkable library on the history of the Pacific Northwest that he had ever seen.[4]

His interest in the Indians' social welfare led him to organize a Shaker church in Tacoma in 1895 for the Indians living in the Puget Sound area. When he was a delegate in Washington, D.C., he had visits from these Washington State Indians whom he had befriended. One came in 1916 to inquire about the church's history, and Wickersham was able to help him find out about its beginning in the annual report of the federal bureau of ethnology. He had a visit from another member four years later, telling him about the successful Shaker church in Klamath, Oregon; this was a branch of the Tacoma church; also a third was to be instituted in California.[5]

Wickersham was a proponent of the theory that the Chinese inhabited America and intermarried with the coastal Indians. He discussed this in a paper he delivered before the Washington Historical Society, in which he said: "There is no question but that the aboriginal people of America and the people of Asia are nearly related. . .The Indians of the Sound, known as "siwashes," according to investigations of government ethnologists for years back, show the Mongolian cast of features in the Indians from Alaska to Oregon so much so that the similarity is referred to as the Mongolian cast."

In support of this theory, he quoted from Bowen's "America Discovered by the Welsh," in which the author wrote: "In 1761 Degnignes, a French soldier, made known to the world that the Chinese discovered America in the fifth century. He derived the knowledge from Chinese official annals. . . ."[6]

Wickersham published a pamphlet entitled "Whence Came the American Indian?" This led to a study of China, and on July 20, 1898, he delivered a paper before the Washington State bar association convention in Spokane—"The Constitution of China."[7] Then when he came to Alaska, he carried his research forward to a study of the Asia-American migration route across the Bering Straits. His thesis that the earliest Alaskan natives came originally from Asia has gained acceptance among latter-day ethnologists.

Wickersham and his sister, Miss Nannie Wickersham, were among twenty-two citizens gathered at the Tacoma Hotel on the evening of July 2, 1891, for the purpose of organizing the Washington Historical Society. He was elected to the seven-member board of curators and was also a member of the first Ways and Means Committee.

He was vice president of the Alaska Geographical Society organized in Seattle in November, 1891; Arthur C. Jackson of Seattle was its first president.

As his Northwest collection grew and it became impractical for him to provide space for it, he stored it in the Tacoma headquarters of the Washington State Historical Society and at the University of Washington in Seattle. During his last year of life, he entered into negotiations for the sale of his whole Northwest library to Winlock Miller, Jr., a Seattle attorney, who planned to make it a gift to Yale University, his alma mater. Besides artifacts, the collection included over four hundred books on the early history of Washington, Oregon and California; the agreed price was $2,200. Wickersham had the books with him in Juneau at the time. He crated and shipped them to Seattle only to learn that Miller had died following an operation.[9]

Miller's brother wrote Wickersham that he would return the books, but Wickersham arranged for Ruth Coffin to take charge of the collection and try to find a new buyer. Miss Coffin arranged a public exhibit in hopes of attracting a buyer. In describing the exhibit, the Seattle *Times* mentioned the following unique items: the Gospel According to St. Matthew, printed in the old Oregon missions in 1845; a copy of Boulet's *Youth's Companion*, printed at Tulalip, Washington in 1882; and almanacs for Oregon, Washington, and Idaho from 1859 to 1871.[10]

No one buyer showed up so the collection was broken up and sold to various individuals, most going to the East Coast.

When Wickersham first visited the Library of Congress and discovered that there was no section on Alaska, he became inspired to develop the world's greatest Alaskana collection. As the collection grew, it became ever more exciting and he spent every leisure moment in reading, compiling, and cataloging the material. Hugh A. Morrison, assistant librarian in charge of the House of Representatives' reading room in the Library of Congress gave invaluable assistance. It took

Wickersham sixteen years to collect the material for his bibliography and another two years to classify and compile it. Upon its completion, it superseded the earlier bibliographies of Dall in 1879, Baker in 1884, and A.H. Brooks in 1906.

He was unsuccessful in his search for a publisher, so in March, 1927, the board of trustees of the Alaska Agricultural College and School of Mines voted to have it published as a project. The legislature appropriated $5,000 and it appeared as "Miscellaneous Publications,Vol.1" of the college. Sixteen hundred copies were printed, and Wickersham was given 400 as payment for his labor and expenditures. The college sold it for five dollars a copy and the money went to purchasing books for the college library.[11]

The book was printed in Seattle by Wickersham's old friend, Will Steel. Besides a listing of titles of Alaska literature appearing between 1724 and 1924, it contained a thirty-seven-page history of Alaskan literature written by Wickersham. He dedicated the book "To the pioneer mothers of Alaska, whose hearts are always deeply interested in the education of their children, and, as a typical example, to the mother of my own sons, Deborah Susan Wickersham."

He was to wait another ten years before seeing his second book in print - *Old Yukon: Tales, Trails and Trials*. It was a 514-page account of his experiences on the Alaska bench, 1900 to 1908. He labored for years on this narrative, rewriting and resubmitting it and having it rejected by publishers. He had about given up when West Publishing Company of St. Paul, Minnesota agreed to publish it. It was the company which had published his Alaska Law Reports. It was published from 1938 until 1960, when it was discontinued. In 1973 the company was persuaded to republish it, in view of the revived interest in Alaskan affairs. The latest edition in 1976 represented the eighth printing.[12]

Another monumental effort to preserve Alaska's history was Wickersham's collection and editing of judicial opinions of all Alaska's judges, beginning with Ward McAllister, the first territorial judge in 1884 up to 1937. There are eight volumes of these "Alaska Law Reports." He did all the work himself and paid to have them published.

One of his major literary efforts after he retired from the delegateship was a manuscript describing his attempt to climb Mt. McKinley. Although it remained unpublished, numerous excerpts were included in his *Old Yukon* book. When he completed his manuscript, he composed a dedication in verse, entitled: "To The Pioneers Of The Yukon: "

Who first explored the Kwikpak wide,
Who floated down wild Pilly's tide,
Who built fur posts for Indian trade,
And brought the Book to Yukon glade.

Who blazed the trail o'er Dyea divide,
Who built their rafts on Lindeman's side,
Who worked the Stewart's bars awhile,
And found the gold on the Forty Mile.

Who mined at Circle, and Klondike creeks,
Who camped at Nome 'neath Anvil's peaks,
Who founded Fairbanks, opened its mines,
And prospected where the Iditarod twines.

Who built its towns, its roads and trails,
Who planned its railroad and laid their rails,
Who guide in council, creating homes,
And in laying a State's foundation stones.

After completing his poetic effort, he wrote in his diary: "This may not be any fine poetry, but its good sentiment and that's the basis of all good poetry."[13]

Wickersham joined a group of Juneau businessmen in the fall of 1926 in publishing a monthly magazine called *The Alaska Magazine*. John E. Meals, former editor of the *Pathfinder* magazine, was the managing editor, and the Reverend A.P. Kashevaroff, curator of the territorial museum, was associate editor. Henry Roden was president of the firm. Wickersham agreed to provide a monthly article. Volume 1, number 1 came out in January, 1927, and the publication expired after six months.

A cherished dream of Wickersham's was to write a history of Alaska. In March, 1935, Wickersham discussed with Bunnell the possibility of securing a grant from one of the eastern foundations to underwrite his writing such a history. During the conversation, Wickersham told Bunnell that he planned to will his library to the university. Bunnell expressed interest in the idea of a foundation grant, but nothing further was heard from him.

The following September, Wickersham learned that Governor Troy was going to Fairbanks so he sent a telegram to Bunnell suggesting that he consult with Troy regarding the possibility of getting federal funds to enable Wickersham's writing the history in cooperation with Richard Geoghegan, a Russian scholar in Fairbanks. He received no response from either Troy or Bunnell.

On May 18, 1936, he picked up the *Empire* and read that the University of Alaska had secured a $17,000 grant from the Rockefeller Foundation for Alaska historical research and that it would be spent on cataloging and translating Wickersham's library. Three persons would be employed for two years, and they would spend most of their time in Juneau with Judge Wickersham.

Two weeks later he received a letter from Bunnell saying that he had employed a stenographer and research worker and placed the project under the direction of Professor Cecil F. Robe, who was an unknown to Wickersham. There was no mention of Wickersham's role in the project, just that these strangers were coming to work in his private library, which he had spent over thirty years in developing.

Wickersham was shocked at this twist in the research plan which he had originally proposed to Bunnell. Here he had made a gift of his bibliography to the university, and now his library was to be expropriated and he was to be completely shut out.

Robe, formerly an instructor at the University of Alaska, had been studying at Yale University for the past three years, on a leave of absence from Alaska. Bunnell had contacted him at Yale, offering him this opportunity to write a history of Alaska, with Wickersham's library his principal research facility. Further correspondence with Bunnell revealed that Robe would be arriving in June to go to work. In short, all of Wickersham's time, labor, expenditure, and acquired knowledge was to be placed at the disposal of Professor Robe to enhance his professional career. That was not Wickersham's idea of fairness, and he would have no part of it:

> They want me to donate all my work, library, etc., to a group of strangers for two years to prepare what they think is a history, from which I am to be excluded. These people utterly ignorant of the territory and its history, are to be paid big salaries for doing the work of arranging, subject to their use, while they take away two copies for the university and leave me one for my use. That is far from the promises made to me by Bunnell.
>
> I am greatly disappointed, but will not allow them to gain by it. I donated all my work, expense and the manuscript for the bibliography, gave the university the credit, though it did not

pay a cent, nor do an hour's work on the preparation of the work—now they demand I make this sacrifice—I won't do it.

Whereupon he sent the following telegram to Bunnell:

Your director has just informed me that my services and material for research and preparation as historical data must be entirely complimentary. Budget shown me today for first time is not satisfactory. Unfair to ask that my material be given exclusively to well-paid strangers having slight knowledge of Alaska history with my exclusion from participation in research.[14]

Later conferences with Bunnell brought no change in his plans, and when Wickersham refused to turn over his library, Bunnell arranged for Robe and his two assistants to do their research at the Library of Congress, paying them from the Rockefeller grant.

Subsequent correspondence with his son Darrell revealed that it was Darrell who first contacted Dr. David H. Stevens of the division of humanities of the Rockefeller Foundation regarding the underwriting of Wickersham's history of Alaska. Since the foundation had a policy of making grants only through institutions rather than to private individuals, Dr. Stevens had chosen the University of Alaska as an appropriate medium for the grant.

When Dr. Stevens learned of the difficulties which had arisen, he offered to seek a separate grant-in-aid for Wickersham for one year, if the university would agree to pay an equal amount to him for a second year. He stated clearly that he had made the original grant under the impression that Wickersham would be the central figure in the plan. Nothing came of this suggestion, so it can be assumed that Bunnell did not see fit to use university funds in that manner.

When Robe completed his two years' research at the Library of Congress, he returned to Alaska as a professor at the university to teach Alaska history, but no history of Alaska came from his pen.[15]

Wickersham wrote a manuscript on gold mining tracing the various gold stampedes which had taken place along the Rocky Mountains from Peru to Point Barrow. He paid to have Doroshin's 1867 report on the prospecting for gold in Russian America translated into English. He completed a ninety-eight-page manuscript on the gold strikes in the Juneau and Treadwell region; another chapter dealt with the discovery of gold on the Klondike by George Carmack and Kate.[16]

Wickersham was often called upon to settle an argument about an incident in Alaskan history. For example, a controversy developed over whether the United States paid Russia with one or two checks, when it purchased Alaska.

The two-check story stemmed from the "Letters of Franklin K. Lane," in which Lane said he attended a dinner party in Washington, D.C., at which he overheard Charles Glover, president of Riggs National Bank in Washington, relate how as a boy in the bank, he had been handed two warrants upon the United States Treasury—one for $1,400,000 and the other for $5,800,000. Glover said "those warrants were the payment to Russia for the territory of Alaska."

Determined to put an end to these rumors and determine the true facts, Wickersham applied to the Treasury Department to be permitted to enter the vault where the documents were kept and examine them himself. Permission was granted and in his presence the Treasury officials made full-size glass negatives of the warrant for $7,200,000 and the receipt for the $7,200,000 signed by Edward De Stoeckl, the envoy extraordinary representing the czar, who received the money.[17] Thus the two-check story was proven false.

As his fears and worries increased over impending blindness and lack of finances, Wickersham made it known that his library was for sale; no longer could he consider donating it as a gift to the territory. The Juneau Pioneers' Igloo and the bar association appointed committees to lobby the legislature to buy it to insure its remaining in Alaska.

Senator Henry Roden, at the request of the Pioneers, introduced a bill providing for an appropriation of $35,000 to buy the library and place it in the Alaska Historical Library and Museum. But despite his fervent pleas, together with those of Senators O.D. Cochran and LeRoy Sullivan of Nome, the Senate voted five to three to table the bill.

During the floor debate, Senator Sullivan made public for the first time the story of how the Rockefeller Foundation appropriated $17,000 to have the history of Alaska written by and with the active participation of Wickersham and his library, and of how the money was spent in Washington translating Russian documents which had already been translated and were part of the Wickersham library.[18]

Two years after Wickersham's death, the 1941 legislature appropriated $20,000 to purchase the library from his widow; she received $17,500 and the remaining $2,500 went to defray the cost of cataloging and preparing the material for library use.

Not included in the library purchase were forty-seven volumes of personal diaries which Wickersham had kept during his thirty-nine years in Alaska, plus other personal correspondence and scrapbooks. When Mrs. Wickersham passed away on June 9, 1963, her niece Ruth

Coffin Allman inherited the Wickersham home with the diaries and other personal effects. She developed the home into a summer tourist attraction, serving sourdough waffles while relating stories about Wickersham's life.

On March 29, 1960, the first state legislature passed a House resolution recommending the acquisition of the Wickersham home and its contents. The resolution concluded that the Wickersham collection of manuscripts, documents, books, maps, artifacts, and personal diaries and correspondence "comprise the most outstanding and valuable single holding of Alaskana now extant and the state would be remiss to the point of criminal negligence were it to allow this outstanding historical collection to be taken from it."

The resolution stated further: "The House of Wickersham, by virtue of its location, architecture, and furnishings is typical of early Alaska, and should, together with the Wickersham collection, be preserved for posterity, and would, as a shrine, be a great asset to the state as a tourist attraction as well as a research center for studies of historical significance.

The governor was directed to appoint a committee to enter into negotiations with the present owner, which Governor William A. Egan did on August 4, 1960. He appointed a three-member committee composed of Alaska Supreme Court Justice John H. Dimond, Richard Cooley, state research analyst, and Helen Dirtadian, state librarian. In discussions with Mrs. Allman, the committee members learned that she was opposed to selling the property to the state, preferring the creation of a private foundation which would operate and maintain it as an historic shrine.

In 1967 President William R. Wood, of the University of Alaska, and Theodore Ryberg, the university's director of libraries, tried to purchase the Wickersham manuscripts for the university, but again Mrs. Allman refused to sell them.

Shortly thereafter the Alaska Airlines obtained an option to buy the home and its contents, but that option was relinquished in 1972, with a change of management in the airlines, and the property reverted to Mrs. Allman. During the tenure of the option, the Airlines arranged for the microfilming of the diaries by the Alaska Historical Library in 1969. Three prints were made: one for the Historical Library in Juneau, one for the University of Alaska in Fairbanks, and the third for the Airlines, which copy reverted to Mrs. Allman at the termination of the option.

Epilogue

Some day they will set up a monument to Wickersham in the public square or the town hall of every Alaskan city. . .It is not beyond the possibilities that he may one day be a U.S. senator from the State of Alaska.

(*Washington* Times,*Mar.13,1914*)

He was the idol of thousands of Alaskans. . .He was the darling of the electorate for years and years and I now nominate him as Alaska's Foremost Citizen of the first half of the twentieth century.

(Empire,*Aug.24,1950,editorial by Henry Roden*)

His courageous and advanced stands on public issues earned him powerful enemies who did their best to destroy him as a public servant. . .He was the outstanding exponent of Alaska's cause in the first third of the century - the period which marked Alaska's emergence from an unknown wilderness.

(Empire,*Aug.25,1957,tribute by Ernest Gruening*)

For four decades Wickersham was the one Alaskan seen and heard in the flesh by more of his fellow Alaskans than any other. His straight-backed, five-foot-ten-inch stature, his firm, square jaw and well-groomed mustache were familiar to every man, woman, and child in the territory. His gray eyes surveyed his surroundings with a keen penetration. He had charisma; he was the object of a personality cult. He aroused strong emotional response whether it be in informal conversation or on a platform inveighing against his adversaries.

He appeard on the Alaskan scene at a point in time when he personified the unarticulated aspirations of its pioneers. Being plain-born, he reflected a provincial, solid, small-town quality. Though no ivory-tower intellectual, he came forth with a power both of thought and expression which moved his listeners. He was a surefooted realist rather than an ideologist. He believed that leaders must be guided by changing realities, not by political platforms, a notion that irked the party bosses.

399

As a trailblazer, Wickersham paid the price of ridicule, slander, scandal-mongering, revilement, and political assassination. A lesser man would have become embittered and retreated, but his versatility in temperament and interest saved him. At different times and under varying circumstances, he could seem predominantly tough or soft, aggressive or shy, adamant or flexible, frank or secretive, aloof or gregarious, autocratic or democratic. In many ways he was an inscrutable man, a complex mixture of antithetical traits which, to his supporters, could be baffling, exasperating, and endearing all at the same time.

A friend described him as having "a judicial poise that to some seemed austere and to others a seeming coldness, but that was not the case. He was tender-hearted and a responsive man, ever loyal to his friends and his principles.[1]

Barrett Willoughby, Alaskan novelist, recalled his warm personality, when she visited him in his Juneau home:

> When he met you as host at the door of his great, hospitable house on the slope of a Juneau hill, he clasped your hand warmly and welcomed you with a kindly look from remarkable hooded gray eyes that were deep with tolerant understanding of human nature, and bright with a sense of humor.
>
> A glow went through you and you thought, "Here is my friend.". . .He was the most spellbinding teller of Alaskan stories I've ever met. . . .[2]

There was evidence of his sincere desire to leave the sordid political world time and time again, but the pressure of the times, public sentiment, and a sense of mission impelled him to stay in the fray. Once in a fight, his indomitable courage, unflinching firmness of purpose, self reliance, and perseverance carried him through to the finish.

One of Wickersham's strongest attributes was his sensitivity to the mood of his constituents. He adapted readily to their thinking; he was not a stand-patter, hence his shifting political stances - Populist, Independent, Progressive, Republican. His genius for sensing public opinion helped him use it to achieve his political objectives. To him there was no inconsistency in shifting his allegiance from a Teddy Roosevelt to a Woodrow Wilson as both men represented that same spirit of reform to which he was committed.

Wickersham was shrewd and aggressive, and as the years wore on his intense combativeness antagonized one group after the other. His political hatreds biased his judgment to the point that he was handicapped in his efforts to reduce intraparty friction. He mistrusted politicians, always suspecting them of ulterior motives.

To the youth of today, however, Wickersham is a highly relevant figure. He was motivated by a sense of moral and social justice, and once convinced of the right course of action, he fought fearlessly and selflessly. Like all politicians, he wanted to be reelected, but he expected it as a reward for what he had achieved for his constituents, not just for his own glory. Had he not chosen to be an honest official, he might have left Alaska a millionaire and been lost to the state's history books - that choice took courage and stamina. He died poor in material goods but rich in his legacies to future Alaskans.

Sporadic gestures of commemoration have kept Wickersham's name alive even though the prophecy of "a monument to him in the public square. . .of every Alaskan city" has not come to pass.

The 1949 legislature designated August 24 as Wickersham Day, urging schools, civic groups, and the general public to sponsor programs on that day in gratitude for his years of service for Alaska. The bill was introduced by Republican Senator Anita Garnick of Juneau and was enacted into law on March 19, 1949.

His "fatherhood" of the state university has been memorialized by the naming of a students' residence hall on the Fairbanks campus "Wickersham Hall"; it was dedicated on January 12, 1958. A bronze plaque on the wall of the foyer recognizes Grace Wickersham's service on the university's board of regents; it reads:

> Judge Wickersham introduced in Congress the bill to establish the Alaska Agricultural College & School of Mines; laid its cornerstone; induced the territorial legislature to accept the land grant and appropriate funds for buildings and equipment.
>
> (And of Mrs. Wickersham:) Inspiring wife and helpmate to the Honorable James Wickersham and member of the board of trustees of the A.A.C. & S.M. and board of regents of the University of Alaska from 1933 to 1941.

When Alaska achieved statehood in 1958, the "Citizens for Statehood" committee of Fairbanks erected a stone monument on the bank of the Chena River where Wickersham landed from a river steamer after his first campaign for delegate to Congress in 1908. It has a pedestal of blue slate with a flaring white cement canopy and a bronze plaque listing his achievements while delegate.

Dedication ceremonies took place on the eve of Wickersham's birthday, with Secretary of Interior Fred A. Seaton making the principal speech, in which he lauded Wickersham as "a man who belongs in the company of great Americans of all times."[3]

In 1960, "Wickersham Day" was celebrated throughout the Forty-Ninth State, recalling his successful efforts in getting the Organic Act passed in 1912 and his introduction of the first Alaska statehood bill.[4]

In June, 1968, Republican Governor Walter J. Hickel gave the name "Wickersham" to the first ferry to inaugurate the state's marine highway along its coastal towns.

That same summer Wickersham's Fairbanks home was declared an historic monument and moved to Alaskaland, where it is preserved as one of the area's tourist attractions. Its original site on the corner of First Avenue and Noble Street is marked by a bronze plaque.

There are a number of mountains and streams named for Wickersham: Wickersham Wall on the west face of Mt. McKinley, named by Bradford Washburn about 1945; Mount Wick, thirty-nine miles northeast of Solomon on the Seward Peninsula; Mount Wickersham, forty-seven miles northeast of Palmer in the Chgach mountains, named in 1960 by United States Senator E.L. Bartlett and Secretary of Interior Fred Seaton; Wickersham Dome, twenty-seven miles northeast of Fairbanks; Wickersham Dome, four miles north of Wonder Lake in Mt. McKinley national park.

There are three Wickersham creeks: one is sixty-eight miles southeast of Healy in the Talkeetna Mountains; another is forty-eight miles north of Big Delta, at the junction of the Yukon and Tanana Rivers; the third is thirty-seven miles north of Fairbanks, where the Yukon and Tanana Rivers come together.

Wickersham was a joiner, being a member of six different fraternal organizations and being a fairly regular attendant at their semimonthly or monthly meetings. He joined the St. Paul Masonic lodge, number 500 in Springfield in 1882; he transferred to Tacoma lodge, number 22, on June 7, 1884, becoming a life member.

He joined the Elks lodge in Tacoma in 1898 and transferred to the lodge in Juneau on October 30, 1935. He became a member of the Arctic Brotherhood in Nome on November 17, 1901, the Order of the Moose in Valdez on January 29, 1903, and of the Eagles in Fairbanks, May 14, 1905. He was also a member of the Pioneers of Alaska, the Sons of the American Revolution (1925) and the Interlocked Moosehorn Club of Kenai (1909). He used a pair of interlocked moose horns as a hatrack for many years in his law office and later he presented them to the Juneau Moose lodge.

On June 9, 1963 Grace Wickersham died at St. Ann's Hospital in Juneau where she had received convalescent care for several years. Her remains were taken to Tacoma for cremation, and the ashes were placed beside those of her late husband.

BIOGRAPHICAL CHRONOLOGY

1857 (Aug.24)	Born on farm near Patoka,Illinois; son of Alexander and Mary Jane (McHaney) Wickersham.
1868	Lived a year in Wyandot County, Kansas, then returned to Illinois.
1874-77	Taught in rural schools in Illinois.
1877-83	Went to Springfield,Illinois, taught in nearby rural schools and studied law in Governor John Palmer's office;admitted to Illinois bar on Jan.14,1880; employed as law clerk,U.S.Census Bureau,Springfield.
1880 (Oct. 27)	Married Miss Deborah Susan Bell in Rochester,Illinois.
1882 (Apr.2)	Son Darrell Palmer born in Springfield,Illinois.
1883 (spring)	Migrated to Pierce County,Washington Territory, settling in Tacoma.
1884-88	Elected for two terms as probate judge of Pierce County (Tacoma).
1886 (Feb.21)	Son Arthur James born; died Feb.20, 1888.
1889 (Feb.-July)	Sadie Brantner seduction case.
1894-96	Appointed Tacoma city attorney.
1893 (Oct.19)	Son Howard Sullivan born; died Jan.11, 1902.
1898-1900	Elected to Washington State House of Representatives.
1900 (June 6)	Appointed U.S. district judge for third judicial district in Alaska;headquarters, Eagle City.

1901 (Aug.-Sept.)	Conducted first "floating court" in Aleutian Islands.
1901 (Sept.)- 1902 (July)	Served on Nome bench; returned to Eagle.
1903 (May-July)	Mt. McKinley expedition.
1904 (Dec.1)	Moved court headquarters to Fairbanks.
1904-07	Received recess appointments on following dates: Nov.16,Dec.24,1904;Mar.6, 21,Dec.5,1905; Mar.21,Je.30,1906; Mar. 4,1907.
1907 (Sept.27)	Submitted resignation from judgeship; retired from bench on Jan.4,1908 and opened law office in Fairbanks.
1908-20	Elected six times as Alaska's delegate in Congress:Aug.11,1908;Aug.9,1910;Aug. 14,1912; Nov.3,1914;Nov.7,1916;Nov.5, 1918.
1926 (Nov.23)	Wife Deborah died in Seattle hospital of tuberculosis.
1928 (Je.26)	Married Mrs.Harry (Grace) Bishop in Des Moines,Washington.
1930-32	Served a seventh term as delegate in Congress; defeated for reelection in Nov.,1932.
1935 (May)	Received an honorary degree of Doctor of Laws from the Alaska Agricultural College & School of Mines.
1939 (Oct.24)	Died in St.Ann's hospital,Juneau,following a stroke; remains taken to Tacoma for cremation; interred in family plot,Old Tacoma Cemetery, Nov.2,1939.

Appendix A

The Sadie Brantner Story as told in excerpts from the
Seattle and Tacoma press

Seattle *Daily Press*, Feb. 19, 1889   Eating Forbidden Fruit
Judge Wickersham on Trial for the Alleged
Seduction of Miss Brantner

Man's wiles and women's woes—that is the old story now being related in the trial of Probate Judge James Wickersham in progress in the district court today. It is a simple narration by Miss Sadie M. Brantner, a Tacoma book agent.

As a sensational trial of this character always attracts a large and morbidly curious crowd, the court room was almost jammed from the time Attorney Judson opened for the defense until the court adjourned.

Quite a number of the ladies of the W.C.T.U. present were as actively interested in the prosecution of the erring jurist from up the Sound.

Mr. James Hamilton Lewis of this city and Messrs. Judson and Sullivan of Tacoma are conducting the defense, and District Attorney Ronald is assisted by Messrs. Doolittle and Pritchard of Tacoma and Prosecuting Attorney Coiner of the Second judicial district in the prosecution.

In Mr. Judson's opening speech for the defense this morning, he alluded to the interestedness of Proprietor Radebaugh, of the Tacoma *Ledger*, in the prosecution, and intimated pretty plainly that the whole case was a put up job by Mr. Radebaugh to punish Judge Wickersham for giving the Pierce County printing to the Tacoma *News*.

Mr. Judson believes that he can produce threats made by Mr. Radebaugh which will bear out the proposition that Mr. Radebaugh is simply using the girl, the W.C.T.U., and the prosecution in a conspiracy to get even with Judge Wickersham.

The defense also promised to assail the character of Miss Brantner, and prove that it was not chaste, but that many other Tacoma celebrities, including "the power behind the throne," had carnal knowledge of her.

Furthermore, it would be able to prove that Judge Wickersham was quite innocent of the criminal intimacy charged.

Miss Brantner was placed upon the stand to testify as the complaining witness. She is a comely young woman, with light brown hair and blue eyes; is intelligent and of a positive nature, seems refined and of an affectionate disposition, states her answers tersely, and with certainty.

Sometimes her trying position overcame her and she was compelled to hesitate and nerve herself to bear the continuation of the ordeal, for the shame of her position was intensified by the curiosity of the very knowing audience that drink in eagerly every word of her answers to the prosecutor's carefully worded interrogations.

Her cloak and hat were laid aside as she gave her testimony, which seemed to be drawn painfully from her. She was quite candid in stating the state of her feelings for Judge Wickersham, whose nervousness was too apparent to be overlooked, although he tried hard to appear cool and possessed.

Miss Brantner's Story

. . .She first noticed Judge Wickersham in Chilberg's restaurant in Tacoma. He pretended to be reading a newspaper, but every time she looked at him she observed that he was looking at her, and seemed to be endeavoring to carry on quite a flirtation. Somehow or other he subsequently ascertained that she was canvassing for a book entitled "The Royal Path to Life," and he succeeded in addressing a note to her inviting her to call upon him at his office, informing her that he would be pleased to buy a book.

She went to a lady and inquired if the latter thought she should comply with the written request. The lady was of the opinion there would be no harm in it. She went one day at 5 p.m. and as the Judge was busy was asked to come again in the evening. He willingly purchased a book, and from that time his love-making began.

He told her to come next day and deliver the book. He said pleasant things to her and kissed her, and told her to come next day and he would pay her. The inference here was that the amorous Judge was manufacturing excuses so that he could see her quite often.

This led to buggy riding. The first time the judge took her to his own home. There didn't seem to be any harm in going out riding with a person who seemed such a gentleman. But the next time, alas! the judge's familiarity asserted itself and astonished Miss Brantner, although nothing serious ensued. He merely trifled with her clothing. She protested strongly and he gave her a nice little lecture, telling her to never let another man do anything like that.

He had supposed she was a girl of rather questionable character, and was pleasantly surprised to learn that she was a good girl. Indeed, she informed him that he was quite mistaken if he took her for a bad girl. They returned from their outing at nine o'clock at night and made an appointment that they would go out riding again two days later.

All this time she did not know the Judge was a married man and a father. It leaked out, however, the next time she visited him at his office. He attempted to kiss her, and she broke away, going around his desk to get away from him. Then she noticed a photograph and inquired, "Who is that?" His reply was, "Only a relative." But that was unsatisfactory, for the boy's face in the photo bore a striking resemblance to Judge Wickersham's.

Finally he came out with it: "That's my son," and immediately the truth flashed upon her. "Why, are you married?" He was and his wife was absent from the city - in the East.

Well, she went up the valley to canvass, and he kept track of her by telephone and train to Puyallup and Carbonado. When he met her he told her he loved her. "I thought a great deal of him," stated the witness. She told him she was going to Seattle, and he said he was well acquainted with the Queen City, and would take her around and introduce her.

She took the evening boat on Saturday, October 23, 1887, the fatal day, for Seattle, for he had told her that was the best boat, and to her astonishment, whether agreeable or not is a matter of conjecture, just when she had boarded the boat there was the infatuated Judge. She saw him as she was about to enter the ladies' cabin. He introduced her to a seat, and they sat there talking about the weather and her books, and after a while they went out on the deck and were there ten minutes - "talking about the water."

He accompanied her, of course, to Seattle. . .he took friendly charge of her, escorting her to the Brunswick restaurant, seated her in a box, and told her to wait until he found a room for her.

In about twenty minutes he returned, and, informing her he had secured a room for her, invited her to supper. After they had eaten, she arose to go to her room, and he picked up her satchel and went with her to show her the room. They went to the Eureka lodging house - to room 13, and when they were both inside the room he locked the door, put the key in his pocket and, seeing that she looked in a frightened way toward the window, he fastened that too.

All this time she didn't know what he intended to do. She said she had confidence in him, and thought him trustworthy as a gentleman, but as she testified her heart was already ensnared for "'I loved him."

When he locked her in the room, he told her it was no use for her to do anything or make any fuss or cry, as she couldn't help herself - they were in a house where nobody would come to her assistance - it wouldn't do any good for her to scream. He pulled her on his lap, kissed her, told her he loved her much more than his wife, tore her clothing from off her against her protests, put her in the bed, and against her weeping and entreaties, seduced her.

. . .She was about to testify that the illicit intercourse was repeated Sunday night, when Attorney Lewis objected with a brilliant series of reasons, based upon rulings in Michigan, New York and elsewhere. . . The court allowed the witness to testify as to what Judge Wickersham did Sunday and his subsequent acts so far as to show what his conduct was. . . .

Seattle *Daily Press*, Feb. 20, 1889   The Tables Seem Turned

. . .She accompanied Judge Wickersham to Tacoma on the Monday morning following the night of the alleged crime. She met the defendant on the street in Tacoma Wednesday afternoon, and he asked her to take a buggy ride with him at 7 p.m., and also invited her to go with him to Olympia on Saturday. . .They went on the *Fleetwood* and put up at Young's hotel. They went to Seattle on the *Fleetwood* on Sunday and stopped again at the Eureka lodging house.

Judge Wickersham was profuse in his protestations of love and proposed to her that she could file on a piece of land, and shortly afterwards he sent word to her. . .that he would like to confer with her about taking up some land.

She refused positively to swear that she was 21 years old, because she was only 19, but she was prevailed upon to represent herself as a widow named Mrs. Sadie Waterman, who had a crippled child back east.

The Judge made out the Land Office papers for her and she signed them here. This was in December. She saw him again on New Year's eve, and again about the end of February. Each time the land matter was discussed. Meanwhile Wickersham had been to Washington, D.C.

On March 1 she received a telegram from him asking her to "come to Seattle on the evening boat." She went, and again stayed at the Eureka lodging house. After fixing up matters at the Land Office, they returned to Tacoma. About six weeks later, at the Judge's instance, she drove out to the land, which was not far from Tacoma and saw the carpenter,

Mills, about arrangements for building the house. The Judge had given her $25 and a plan for a house, and she, representing herself as Mrs. Waterman, gave the money and plan to Mr. Mills.

Here the witness testified that the Judge gave her a book - Don Juan - with marked passages in it early in March. Also she stated that in May she discovered she was pregnant, and that the Judge was the cause of her condition. The Judge told her to see Drs. Miller and Brown about it, and by appointment she went, telling the doctors she was a married woman. She met the Judge there. A criminal operation, lasting about half an hour, was performed on her, while under the influence of chloroform.

Next morning one of the doctors, who had been with her all night, left with a bundle. . .In about a week she was able to get up.

Defendant had her come to Seattle to the Eureka lodging house. She was troubled with a continuous hemorrhage. . .at times she was delirious. . .At Dr. Miller's request, the defendant visited her, and he stayed with her all night, sleeping with her. . . .

It was at this time that fate seemed to be against Wickersham. Dr. Brown visited Miss Brantner and told her that a lady in Tacoma was making trouble and it would be necessary for Miss Brantner to go East. Judge Wickersham also urged her to go East and gave her $125 and paid her fare to her uncle's in Iowa.

She was induced to sign a relinquishment of her land claim in both the names of Waterman and Brantner. . . .

Seattle *Daily Press*, Feb.21,1889   Political Animosity

It did create a slight sensation when Prosecuting Attorney Coiner of Pierce county, was placed upon the stand for the prosecution. . .I told him I desired to have a conversation with him for about five minutes. He said he had an engagement with a young lady. I made some laughing remark about his wife being away. He explained that he was going out for a buggy ride with a young girl who had been up on the hill canvassing for a book entitled "The Royal Path of Life,". . .he said, in substance, that he had been familiar with the girl on the evening previous. . . .

The hot fire of cross-examination. . .witness denied that it was Judge Wickersham and his friends who had defeated him (for political office). . .or that he was. . .the bitter persecuting enemy of Wickersham for that reason.

Witness admitted that he was the president of the Lincoln Club, a Republican political organization. He said that no political enmity was felt toward Wickersham because of his leaving the Republican party, but he caustically informed Mr. Judson that Wickersham "was recognized in politics as a man who had no standing in any particular party except to get into office." He denied that he had been following and persecuting Mr. Wickersham ever since he joined the People's party. . . .

Seattle *Daily Press*, Feb. 22, 1889   Wickersham's Defense

Mr. Brown, of Miller and Brown, Tacoma surgeons, occupied the witness stand all day. He denied he had performed an operation on Miss Brantner but admitted being her doctor when she was "very ill from over-exertion and worry." She had spells of delirium and during one of these "spells" she told of having been married to Charles Waterman and she had had a child by him in Helena, Montana and it had been placed out for adoption. Dr. Brown said he had known Judge Wickersham only as Miss Brantner's attorney in a land deal.

Seattle *Daily Press*,Feb. 23, 1889   Her Character Assailed

Dr. Miller denied having performed any operation on Miss Brantner or of administering any kind of anaesthetic. He said she told him she had been married in Iowa when she was thirteen years old. Then followed several witnesses who testified that they knew Miss Brantner had spent nights with various men. The name of Steve Baker kept appearing in the testimony of the witnesses.

Seattle *Daily Press*, Feb. 25, 1889   Some Sensational Scenes

A series of witnesses brought forward by the defense tell salacious stories of Miss Brantner's bad conduct. Then she took the stand in rebuttal and denied everything that had been said against her.

Seattle *Daily Press*, Feb. 26, 1889   Guilty As Charged

The arguments of the respective counsel in the Wickersham trial yesterday will stand out prominent as among some of the best legal efforts. Mr. S.H. Piles made the first argument for the prosecution. He presumed the guilt of the defendant and criticized severely the action of a fellow member of the bar in perpetrating the crime alleged.

Mr. James Hamilton Lewis followed with a most brilliant masterpiece of eloquence, extremely dramatic, intensely effective. His defense of Judge Wickersham was sublime, his denunciation of the prosecution cutting, satirical, withering. . .How he contrasted the complaining witness of the stand "with cheek unblanched, not even a blush, not a tear shivering in her eye," to the ideal of maidenly modesty and virtue, that the prosecution had conjured! How he lashed the feminine friends of the prosecutrix, whose "womanly hearts had no kind sisterly feelings" toward the poor wife of the defendant, and whose natural emotions did not respond in tender words of sympathy for the infant boy of the accused!

It is saying but little to state that when Mr. Lewis had concluded, the sympathies of everyone present seemed to be with his client. . .Concluding, Mr. Lewis said: "To find the defendant guilty and consign him to the penitentiary, would be to take the lever of severest oppression and with it pry back the prison bars and then rivet their jagged edges about him with the broken law."

The judge's charge to the jury. . .The court instructs the jury that the defendant. . .is on trial for the crime of seduction. . .the woman must be unmarried and of previously chaste character. . . .

The jury found the defendant guilty as charged in the indictment. Judge Wickersham took the verdict with remarkable self possession.

The trial was given front-page daily coverage also in the Tacoma *Daily Ledger*, Feb. 20-27, 1889.
Seattle *Daily Press*, Feb. 27, 1889.

After the verdict. . .P.C. Sullivan, one of Mr. Wickersham's counsels, presented a motion for an extension of time to move for a new trial and also in arrest of judgment until such motion be heard. . . .

Immediately after the jury rendered its verdict. . .U.S. Attorney White had Wickersham arrested on a U.S. grand jury indictment for subornation of perjury in connection with the land transaction. . . .

Seattle *Post-Intelligencer*, May 3, 1889, pp.5.
A Sinful Plot: James Wickersham as a Conspirator
The celebrated Wickersham case has again been brought before the public by certain startling disclosures made by Miss Brantner to her attorneys and friends and by them given publicity. . . . These disclosures are to the effect that Wickersham had, through the assistance of a female detective and by his personal efforts, obtained two interviews with Miss Brantner; that in these interviews he had, through the influence of persuasion and threats of bodily harm, obtained from her a retraction of certain damaging evidence she had given in his trial. . . .

The Seattle *Daily Times* and the Seattle *Daily Press*, May 27, 1889,pp.5;) and the Seattle *Post-Intelligencer* and the Tacoma *Daily Ledger*, May 28, 1889 carried identical stories of Miss Brantner's new affidavit absolving Wickersham of guilt in the land case. In substance the affidavit said:

Seattle *Daily Press*, May 27, 1889,pp.5.

All portions of her testimony at the trial, charging Wickersham with inducing her to take up government land and call herself Mrs. Sadie E. Waterman and a widow, were untrue. Wickersham did not induce her to so represent herself, but the suggestions. . .were made by another, a certain Tacoma man, who sent her to Wickersham's office for that purpose; that affiant told Wickersham of her own volition that she had been married to one Charles E. Waterman in Iowa, was then a widow and had a living child - told him this prior to the land filings, and had a letter with her purporting to be from said Charles Waterman; also that she freely exhibited a marriage certificate, and in other ways induced Wickersham to believe that she had been a married woman. . . .

That she was induced. . .to make such representations. . .so that Wickersham would be accused of crime and destroy his influence, honor and credit; that affiant. . .now suffers remorse and sorrow. . . .

Seattle *Daily Times*, June 1, 1889, pp. 5 and Tacoma *Daily Ledger*, June 2, 1889, pp. 5:

This morning another chapter of the Wickersham case was opened by the filing by Ronald & Piles, the attorneys for Sadie Brantner, of affidavits in reply to the affidavits filed the first part of the week by Wickersham's lawyers. . . .

The affidavit fills some thirty pages of typewritten manuscript and reads like a chapter from a thrilling romance. If half the allegations made be true, there can be but one verdict in the public opinion as to Wickersham's guilt. . . .

Seattle *Daily Times*, June 17, 1889, pp. 3 and Seattle *Post-Intelligencer*, June 18, 1889, pp. 3:

This morning in the district court the attorneys for Wickersham filed three affidavits. One from Sadie Brantner, one from A.J. Lucas and one from Sadie Sevier, the female detective.

The affidavit of Miss Brantner is a startling one, and places her in a most peculiar light before the public. . .she swears that Wickersham did not induce her to swear falsely in the land cases and that she misled him. . . . Also that Wickersham is not guilty of her seduction. That she did know Steve Baker and frequently had intercourse with him during the year 1885. That she had had intercourse with other men before she saw Wickersham. . . .

Tacoma *Daily News*,July 9,1889,pp.4 and Tacoma *Daily Ledger,* July 10, 1889:

Wickersham Smiled: The Celebrated Case Nolle Prosed

At the conclusion of the arguments (for a new trial), Judge Allyn said he was prepared to render a decision in the case: that the complaining witness, Sadie Brantner, had, by her contradicting affidavits, proven herself utterly unreliable; that a doubt had thereby been thrown upon the case, and that he could only give the defendant the benefit of that doubt and grant a new trial, which he did.

Prosecuting Attorney Newlin then arose and said that, under the circumstances, he would move to dismiss the case. . .The case was dismissed. . . .

Appendix B

The decision, in part, as rendered by Judge Wickersham, in the case of McGinley v. Cleary, Fairbanks, August 8, 1904, quoted from the Alaska *Citizen*, April 20, 1914:

On the 29th of last November, the plaintiff was, and for some time previous thereto had been, one of the proprietors of that certain two-story log cabin described in the pleadings as the "Fairbanks Hotel," situated upon lot 1, Front street, in the town of Fairbanks, Alaska. The opening scene discovers him drunk but engaged on his regular night shift as barkeeper in dispensing whiskey by leave of this court on a territorial license, to those of his customers who had not been able, through undesire or the benumbing influence of the liquor, to retire to their cabins.

The defendant was his present customer. After a social evening session, the evidence is that at about three o'clock in the morning of the 30th they were mutually enjoying the hardships of Alaska by pouring into their respective interiors un-numbered four-bit drinks, recklessly expending un-dug pokes, and blowing in the next spring clean-up. While thus employed, between sticking tabs on the nail and catching their breath for the next glass, they began to tempt the fickle goddess of fortune by shaking plaintiff's dicebox. The defendant testifies that he had a five dollar bill, that he laid it on the bar, and that it constituted the visible means of support to the game and transfer of property which followed. That defendant had a five dollar bill so late in the evening may excite remark among his acquaintances.

Whether plaintiff and defendant then formed a mental design to gamble around the storm center of this bill is one of the matters in dispute in this case about which they do not agree. The proprietor is plaintively positive on his part that at that moment his brains were so benumbed by the fumes or the force of his own whiskey that he was actually not compos mentis; that his mental faculties were so far paralyzed thereby that they utterly failed to register or record impressions.

His customer, on the other hand, stoutly swears that the vigor and strength of his constitution enabled him to retain his memory, and he informed the court from the witness stand that while both were gazing at the bill, the proprietor produced his nearby dicebox, and they began to shake for its temporary ownership. Neither the memory which failed nor that which labored in spite of its load enabled either the proprietor or the customer to recall that any other money or its equivalent came upon the board. The usual custom of $500 millionaires grown from wildcat bonanzas was followed, and as aces and sixes alternated or blurringly tripped athwart their vision, the silent upthrust of the index finger served to make the balance of trade.

They were not alone. Tupper Thompson slept bibulously behind the oil tank stove. Whether his mental receiver was likewise so hardened by inebriation as to be incapable of catching impressions will never be certainly known to the court. He testified to a lingering remembrance of drinks which he enjoyed at this time upon the invitation of some one, and is authority for the statement that when he came to, the proprietor was so drunk that he hung limply and vine-like to the bar, though he played dice with the defendant, and later signed a bill of sale of the premises in dispute, which Tupper witnessed. Tupper also testified that the defendant was drunk, but according to his standard of intoxication he was not so entirely paralyzed as the proprietor, since he could stand without holding to the bar.

Not to be outdone either in memory or expert testimony, the defendant admitted that Tupper was present, that his resting place was behind the oil tank stove, where, defendant testified, he remained on the puncheon floor in slumberous repose during the gaming festivities with the dicebox, and until called to drink and sign a bill of sale, both of which he did according to his own testimony. One O'Neil also saw the parties, plaintiff and defendant, about this hour in the saloon, with defendant's arm around plaintiff's neck in maudlin embrace.

After the dice-shaking had ceased, and the finger-tip bookkeeping had been reduced to round numbers, the defendant testifies that the plaintiff was found to be indebted to him in the sum of $1,800. Whether these dice, which belonged to the bar and seem to have been in frequent use by the proprietor, were in the habit of playing such pranks on the house may well be doubted; nor is it shown that they, too, were loaded. It is just possible that mistakes may have occurred pending lapses of memory by which, in the absence of a lookout, the usual numbers thrown for the house were counted for the defendant, and this without any fault of the dice. However this may be, the defendant swears that he won the score, and passed up the table for payment.

According to the defendant's testimony, the proprietor was also playing a confidence game, whereupon, in the absence of money, the defendant suggested that he make him a bill of sale of the premises. Two were written out by defendant. The second was signed by plaintiff and witnessed by Tupper, and for a short time the defendant became a tenant in common with an unnamed person and an equitable owner of an interest in the saloon. The plaintiff testifies that during all this time, and until the final act of signing the deed in controversy, he was drunk, and suffering from a total loss of memory and intelligence. The evidence in support of intelligence is vague and unsatisfactory, and the court is unable to base any satisfactory conclusion upon it.

Above the mist of inebriety which befogged the mental landscape of the principals in this case at that time rise a few jagged peaks of fact which must guide the court notwithstanding their temporary intellectual eclipse. After the dice-throwing had ceased, the score calculated, and the bills of sale written, and the last one conveying a half interest in the premises signed by the plaintiff, he accompanied the defendant to the cabin of Commissioner Cowles, about a block away, on the banks of the frozen Chena, and requested that official to affix his official acknowledgment to the document.

Owing to their hilarious condition and the early hour at which they so rudely broke the judicial slumbers, the commissioner refused to do business with them, and thrust them from his chamber. He does not testify as to the status of their respective memories at that time, but he does say that their bodies were excessively drunk; that of the defendant being, according to the judicial eye, the most wobbly. He testified that the plaintiff was able to and did assist the defendant away from his office without any official acknowledgment being made to the bill of sale. The evidence then discloses that, in the light of the early morning, both principals retired to their bunks to rest; witness Sullivan going so far as to swear that the plaintiff's boots were removed before he got in bed.

The question of consideration is deemed to be an important one in this case. Defendant asserts that it consisted of the $1,800 won at the proprietor's own game of dice, but Tupper Thompson relapses into sobriety long enough to declare that the real consideration promised on the part of the defendant was to give a half-interest in his Cleary Creek placer mines for the half-interest in the saloon; that defendant said the plaintiff could go out and run the mines while he remained in the saloon and sold hootch to the sourdoughs, or words to that effect. Tupper's evidence lacks some of the earmarks; it is quite evident that he had a rock in his sluice box. The plaintiff, on the other hand, would not deny the gambling consideration; he forgot; it is much safer to forget, and it stands a better cross-examination.

The evidence discloses that, about three or four o'clock on the evening of the 30th, the defendant went to the apartment of the proprietor, and renewed his demand for payment or a transfer of the property in consideration of the gambling debt. After a meal and a shave, they again appeared, about five o'clock, before the commissioner; this time at his public office in the justice's court. Here there was much halting and whispering. The bill of sale written by Cleary was presented to the proprietor, who refused to acknowledge it before the commissioner. The commissioner was then requested by Cleary to draw another document to carry out the purpose of their visit there. The reason given for refusing to acknowledge the document then before the commissioner was that it conveyed a half interest, whereas the plaintiff refused then to convey more than a quarter interest. The commissioner wrote the document now contained in the record, the plaintiff signed it; it was witnessed, acknowledged, filed for record, and recorded in the book of deeds, according to the law.

The deed signed by McGinley purports to convey "an undivided one-fourth interest in the Fairbanks Hotel. . .The consideration mentioned is one dollar, but, in accordance with the fingertip custom, it was not paid; the real consideration was the $1,800 so miraculously won by the defendant the previous night by shaking the box. Plaintiff soon after brought this suit to set aside the conveyance upon the ground of fraud (1) because he was so drunk at the time he signed the deed as to be unable to comprehend the nature of the contract, and (2) for want of consideration.

It is currently believed that the Lord cares for and protects idiots and drunken men. A court of equity is supposed to have equal and concurrent jurisdiction, and this case seems to be brought under both branches. Before touching upon the law of the case, however, it is proper to decide the questions of fact upon which those principles must rest, and they will be considered in the order in which counsel for plaintiff has presented them.

Was McGinley so drunk when he signed the deed in controversy that he was not in his right mind, or capable of transacting any business, or entering into any contract? He was engaged, under the aegis of the law and the seal of this court, in selling whiskey to the miners of the Tanana for four bits a drink, and more regularly in taking his own medicine and playing dice with customers for a consideration. Who shall guide the court in determining how drunk he was at three o'clock in the morning, when the transaction opened? Tupper or the defendant?

How much credence must the court give to the testimony of one drunken man who testifies that another was also drunk? Is the court bound by the admission of the plaintiff that he was so paralyzed by his own whiskey that he cannot remember the events of nearly twenty-four hours in which he seems to have generally followed his usual calling? Upon what fact in this evidence can the court plant the scales of justice that they may not stagger.

Probably the most satisfactory determination of the matter may be made by coming at once to that point of time where the deed in question was prepared, signed, and acknowledged. Did the plaintiff exhibit intelligence at that time? He refused to acknowledge a deed which conveyed a half interest, and caused his creditor to procure one to be made by the officer which conveyed only a quarter interest; he protected his property to that extent. Upon presentation of the deed prepared by the officer, he refused to sign it until the words "and other valuable consideration" were stricken out; thus leaving the deed to rest on a stated consideration of "one dollar." Upon procuring the paper to read as he desired, he signed it in a public office, before several persons, and acknowledged it to be his act and deed.

Defendant says that the deed was given to pay a gambling debt lost by the plaintiff at his own game, and his counsel argues that for this reason equity will not examine into the consideration and grant relief, but will leave both parties to the rules of their game, and not intermingle these with the rules of law. He argues that they stand in pari delicto, and that, being engaged in a violation of the law, equity ought not to assist the proprietor of the game to recover his bank roll. It may be incidentally mentioned here, as it has been suggested to the court, that the phrase pari delicto does not mean a "delectable pair," and its use is not intended to reflect upon or characterize plaintiff and defendant.

There are cases where courts will assist in the recovery of money or property lost at gambling, but this is not one of these. The plaintiff was the proprietor of the saloon and the operator of the dice game in which he lost his property. He now asks a court of equity to assist him in recovering it, and this raises the question, may a gambler who runs a game and loses the bank roll come into a court of equity and recover it? He conducted the game in violation of law, conveying his premises to pay the winner's score, and now demands that the court assist him to regain it. Equity will not become a gambler's insurance company, to stand by while the gamester secures the winnings of the drunken, unsuspecting, or weak-minded in violation of the law, ready to stretch forth his arm to recapture his losses when another as unscrupulous or more lucky than he wins his money or property. Nor will the court in this case aid the defendant.

The case will be dismissed; each party to pay the costs incurred by him, and judgment accordingly.

Notes

PART ONE
Chapter 1
1. The Seattle Public Library has a copy of the "Second Reunion of the Wickersham Family," and there is a copy of the proceedings of the fourth reunion in Judge Wickersham's Papers, University of Alaska, Fairbanks.
2. Diary, Apr.26,1917.
3. Ibid, Dec.13,1914.
4. *Encyclopedia of Northwest Biography*,pp.291-95.
5. Diary,Feb.8,1925.

Chapter 2
1. Buck,Solon J.,*Illinois in 1818*, Springfield, 1918,pp.1-35.
2. Office of Sec.of State,Springfield,Ill.,Ill.State Archives.
3. Ibid.
4. Diary, May 30,1906.
5. Ibid, Aug.18,1908.
6. Patoka(Ill.)*Register*,May 1,1914.
7. Diary, Mar.11,12,13,1933.
8. Howard,Robert P.,*A History of the Prairie State*,Wm.P.Erdmans Pub.Co.,Grand Rapids,Mich.,1972,pp.327-403.
9. Diary, Dec.18,1910.
10. Ibid, June 19,1918;May 10,1920;Feb.28,1923;Feb.12,1927.

Chapter 3
1. Hunt,Herbert,*Tacoma,Its History and Its Builders*, S.J.Clarke Co.,Chicago,1916, vols.I,II,III.
2. Bonney,W.P.,*History of Pierce County*,vol.I,pp.496; Pierce Co. Auditor Annual Report,1910,pp.38.
3. Tacoma *Sunday Ledger-News Tribune*,Dec.12,1954,pp.3.
4. Hunt,vol.II,pp.356-83.
5. Archives, Washington Historical Society,Tacoma.
6. Bonney,vol.I,pp.420-21.
7. Ibid,pp.410-11.
8. Hunt,vol.I,pp.391;Diary,May 20,1913.
9. Pierce County auditor's annual report, 1909.
10. Goldwaite's Geographical Magazine,vol.V,nos.3-4,Mar. & Apr.,1893,pp.107-15.
11. Wickersham file,Wash.Hist.Soc.,Tacoma,letter from Darrell Wickersham to Robert Hitchman,Seattle,Nov.9,1947.
12. Tacoma *Daily News*,Aug.30,1889.
13. Hunt,vol.II,pp.108.
14. Ibid,vol.II,pp.180;Wickersham Diary,July 1,1926;a detailed description of the case is in the official record book of the city attorney's office,June 14,1894,to Mar.11,1896, archives Northwest Room,Tacoma Public Library.
15. Hunt,vol.II,pp.148.
16. Diary,Jan.28,1900.
17. Unpublished,handwritten manuscript,Wickersham House,Juneau.
18. Diary,Feb.27,28;Mar.1,1900.
19. Ibid,June 10,1900.
20. Hunt,vol.II,pp.75.

Chapter 4
1. Seattle*Daily Press*,Feb.19-27,1889; Tacoma *Daily Ledger*,Feb.20-27,1889; Seattle *Post-Intellegencer*,May 3,28,1889; Seattle *Daily Times* and Seattle *Daily Press*,May 27; June 1,2,17,1889; Seattle *Post-Intelligencer*,June 18,1889; Tacoma *Daily News*, July 9,1889; Tacoma *Daily Ledger*,July 10,1889.
2. Diary, Dec.14,1915.
3. Ibid, Feb.23,24; June 29,1928.

Chapter 5
1. Diary, Dec.26,1936.
2. Fairbanks *Times*, Mar.22,1914.
3. Diary, Oct.8,1931.
4. Fairbanks *News-Miner*, Aug.22,1931.
5. Diary, Aug.18,1927.
6. Ibid, Aug.20,1927.
7. Ibid,Mar.16,1926.
8. Letter from Jerry Geehan,managing director, Old Tacoma Cemetery, Mar.4,1975.

PART TWO
Chapter 6
1. Swineford,Alfred P.,*Alaska,Its History,Climate and Natural Resources*,Rand McNally & Co.,1899,pp.61-62.
2. *Alaska Times*, Oct.23,1869.
3. Delaney,Arthur K.,*Alaska Bar Assn.&Sketch of Judiciary*,Juneau,1901,pp.5-18.
4. Young,S.Hall,*Hall Young of Alaska,an autobiography*,Fleming H. Revell Co.,1927, pp.275.
5. *Daily Alaska Dispatch*,July 9,1900,quote from New York *Sun*.

Chapter 7
1. Young,S.Hall,*Hall Young of Alaska*,an autobiography,Fleming H. Revell Co.,1927, pp.275.
2. Hallock,Chas.,*Our New Alaska*,Forest and Stream Co.,N.Y.,1886,pp.188-189; Anchorage *Times*,June 29,1926,quote from Ketchikan *Chronicle*.
3. *McAllister* v *U.S.*,141 U.S.,174,by Act passed May 17,1884: 23 Stat.24,chap.58.
4. Hallock, pp.188.
5. Lazell,J.Arthur,*Alaskan Apostle*,Harper & Bros.,N.Y.,1960,pp.21.
6. Swineford, pp.120,224.
7. Young, pp.277-78.
8. Ibid, pp.279.
9. Sitka *Alaskan*, Apr.22,1893.
10. Juneau *City Mining Record*, May 23,1889; Dec.31,1891)
11. Ibid, July 7,1892.
12. *Pathfinder* Magazine, Feb.,1921,pp.12-13.

Chapter 8
1. Author's interview with sons John and Hugh Brady, in Seattle,Apr.14,1971. Brady discovered his birthdate recorded in a Catholic church in the New York City neighborhood where he lived as a child.
2. Fairbanks *Times*,Feb.26,1907,quote from New York *Sun*.
3. Harrison,E.S.,*Nome and Seward Peninsula*,Seattle,1905,pp.53-54.

PART THREE
Chapter 9
1. Hunt,vol.II,pp.185.
2. Wickersham,James,*Old Yukon: Tales,Trails and Trials*,Washington Law Book Co., Wash.,D.C.,1938,pp.4.
3. *Daily Alaska Empire*,Oct.18,1957.
4. Old Yukon, pp.26.
5. Ibid, pp.28.
6. Diary, July 15,1900.
7. Old Yukon, pp.36.
8. The U.S.Army in Alaska,pamphlet 360-5,July 1972,pp.66-77.
9. Diary, Oct.29,1900.
10. Old Yukon, pp.37.
11. Ibid, pp. 42-46.
12. Diary,Sept.29,1910.
13. Old Yukon, pp.49-50.
14. Diary,Nov.8,18;Dec.2,8,24,25,1900.

Chapter 10 '
1. Diary,Jan.21,Feb.9,14,19,Mar.1,22,1901.
2. Ibid,June 18,19,20,21,22,1901.
3. Nome *Nugget*,June 25,1902,letter from S.T.Jeffreys to Wickersham.
4. Diary,July 28,1901.
5. Old Yukon, pp.323.
6. Diary, Sept.9,1901.
7. U.S.Army pamphlet 360-5,July 1972,pp.46.

Chapter 11
1. Nome *News*, Sept.12,1900.
2. Ibid, Aug.25,Sept.12,14,Oct.20,1900; *Gold Digger*, Apr.13,1901.
3. Ibid, Mar.31,Dec.29,1908.
4. Washington *Post*, Feb.19,1901.
5. Nome *News*,Apr.13,1901.
6. Diary, May 3, 1924.
7. Lomen,Carl J., *Fifty Years in Alaska*,David McKay Co.,N.Y.,1954,pp.42.
8. Nome *Gold Digger*, Oct.9,1901.

Chapter 12
1. Diary, Sept.24,1901.
2. Ibid, Oct.27,1901.
3. Ibid, Apr.5,27,28,1902.
4. Ibid, Dec.27,1911.
5. Ibid, Jan.31,1916.
6. Ibid, Feb.27,1917.
7. Ibid, Mar.25,26,1929; Mar.27,1930.
8. Ibid, Oct.22,1901.
9. Ibid, Dec.26,1901.
10. Ibid, Mar.27,31,1902.
11. Ibid, Jan.1,Feb.28,1902.
12. Ibid, Sept.16,1901.
13. *Alaska Forum*, Dec.21,1901.
14. Diary, June 9,1902.

15. Nome *Nugget*, June 18,1902.
16. Nome *News*, Sept.12,1902.
17. Diary, Jan.10,11,1902.
18. Ibid, Jan.12,Feb.7,1902.
19. Nome *News*, Mar.4,1902.
20. Diary, Mar.16,22,25,28;Apr.17,1902.
21. Ibid, Apr.28,May 18,27,1902.
22. Seattle *Post Intelligencer*, Apr.1,1902.
23. Nome *Nugget*, June 4,1902.
24. *Alaska Forum*,Rampart,Oct.24,1903.
25. Old Yukon, pp.378.

Chapter 13
 1. Diary, Feb.20,1903.
 2. Ibid, Dec.29,1902;Jan.29,1903.
 3. Ibid, Sept.25,1901.
 4. Ibid, Jan.22,1900.
 5. Fairbanks *News-Miner*,Golden Days ed.,July 20,1955.
 6. Diary, Apr.12,1903.
 7. Ibid, Apr.22,1903.
 8. Ibid, May 12,1903.

Chapter 14.
 1. A facsimile of *The Fairbanks Miner* was included in an unpublished mss submitted by Wickersham to the Boone & Crockett Club, Chas. Sheldon Papers, mss.,Box 4, mss 45, University of Alaska archives.
 2. Ibid, pp.70-153.
 3. Diary, Mary 20,1903.
 4. Ibid, May 28,1903.
 5. *Old Yukon*, pp.260.
 6. Diary, June 3,1903.
 7. It is known today as "Wickersham Wall," having been named by Bradford Washburn about 1945, Dictionary of Alaska Place Names,U.S.Geol.Sur.professional paper 567.
 8. Diary, June 25,1903.

Chapter 15
 1. *Old Yukon*, pp.415.
 2. Diary, Sept.13,1903.
 3. *Old Yukon*, pp.426-27.
 4. Wickersham's *Alaska Reports*,vol.2,pp.134,Nov.28,1903.
 5. Diary, Feb.10,1904.
 6. Ibid, Feb.13,1904.
 7. San Francisco *Chronicle*,May 3,1904.
 8. Diary, Aug.1,1904.
 9. Ibid, Sept.13,16,1904.
10. Ibid, Aug.12,13,1904.

Chapter 16
 1. Ibid, Nov.22,1904.
 2. Ibid, Dec.23,1904;Jan.30,Feb.10,11,16,1905.
 3. Nome *Nugget*, Dec.21,1904.
 4. Diary, Feb.8,1905.

5. Seattle *Times*, Mar.25,1904.
6. *Old Yukon*, pp.445.
7. Ibid, pp.450.
8. Diary, Oct.27,1905.
9. Fairbanks *Evening News*, Aug.4,1905.

Chapter 17
1. Diary, Jan.15,19,20,1906.
2. Ibid, Jan.23,1906.
3. Ibid, Jan.30,1906.
4. The story came out during Grover Cleveland's campaign for the presidency, that he had fathered a child by a woman to whom he was not married, 11 years earlier.
5. Nome *News*, Feb.13,1906.
6. Diary, Feb.11, 1906.
7. Ibid, Feb.16,1906.
8. Ibid, Feb.20,1906.
9. Ibid, June 9,1906.
10. Ibid, May 0,1906.
11. Ibid, Máy 21,23;Dec.15,1906.
12. Ibid, June 5,1906.
13. Ibid, June 22,1906.
14. Fairbanks *Daily News*, June 27,1906.

Chapter 18
1. *The Miners' Union Bulletin*,Fairbanks,Jan.13,1907.
2. Fairbanks *Evening News*, Sept.14,1906.
3. Diary, Sept.20,1906.
4. *The Miners' Union Bulletin* ran a weekly series of articles on the judge's fight for confirmation, under the general title: "Story of a Crime: Being the True Story of the Wickersham Fight From Start to Finish," Dec.1906 through Jan.1907.
5. Seattle *Post-Intelligencer*, Jan.6,1907.
6. Diary, Feb.21-23,1907.
7. Ibid, Apr.8,15,1907.
8. Ibid, Apr.27,1907.
9. *Record-Miner*, June 4,1907.
10. *Alaska Dispatch*, Apr.28,1907.
11. Diary, May 9,1907.
12. Ibid, June 29,30,1907.
13. Seattle *Times*, July 14,1907.
14. *Dispatch*, Feb.4,1908.
15. Diary, Aug.10,11,1907.
16. Ibid, Aug.22,25,1907.
17. Fairbanks *Times*, Aug.5,1910.

Chapter 19
1. Fairbanks *Times*, May 26,1906.
2. Fairbanks *Evening News*, Sept.28,1906,quote from Juneau *Transcript*.
3. *Dispatch*,July 10,1906.
4. Skagway *Alaskan*, Oct.15,1906.
5. Nome *Pioneer Press*, Oct.26,1907.
6. Fairbanks *Times*, July 6,1908;*Alaska Record*, May 27,1908.
7. Skagway *Alaskan*, Apr.1,1908.
8. Tanana *Miner*, July 28,1907.

Chapter 20
 1. Diary, Sept.10,1907.
 2. Ibid, Nov.14,1907.
 3. Tanana *Miner*, Nov.17,1907,quote from Seward *Gateway*.
 4. *Dispatch*, Sept.28,Oct.1,1907.
 5. *Alaska-Yukon* magazine,Vol.IV,no.3,Nov.1907,pp.266-67.
 6. *Dispatch*, Oct.15,1907,quote from Tacoma *News*.
 7. Diary, Jan.7,1908.
 8. Fairbanks *News*, Nov.4,1907.
 9. *Alaska Daily Record*, Sept.28,1907.
10. Diary, Nov.7,1907.
11. Ibid, Feb.3,1908.
12. Fairbanks *Times*, Nov.19,1907.
13. *Old Yukon*, pp.433-34.

PART FOUR
Chapter 21
 1. Diary, Dec.10,1907.
 2. Ibid, Jan.20,1908.
 3. Ibid, Apr.8,1908.
 4. Ibid, Dec.1907.
 5. Ibid, Mar.15,1908.
 6. Ibid, Feb.15,1908.
 7. *Dispatch*, Sept.20,1907.
 8. Fairbanks *Daily Times*, Sept.17,18,1907.
 9. Tanana *Miner*, Jan.5,1908,quote from Seward *Gateway*.
10. *Dispatch*, May 14,1908.
11. Diary, May 14,1908.
12. *Dispatch*, May 14,1908.
13. *Alaska-Yukon* magazine, vol.IV,no.6,Feb.1908,pp.506-07.
14. Tanana *Miner*, June 23,1907.

Chapter 22
 1. Fairbanks *News*, June 25,1908.
 2. Skagway *Alaskan*, Aug.4,1908.
 3. Diary, July 4,6,7,1908.
 4. Ibid, July 17,1908.
 5. Tanana *Miner*, July 30,1908.
 6. Ibid, July 23,1908.
 7. *Miners' Union Bulletin*, July 20,1908.
 8. Diary, July 25,1908.
 9. Ibid, July 31,Aug.1,1908.
10. Ibid, Aug.4,1908.
11. *Dispatch*, Aug.10,1908.
12. Nome *Nugget*, Aug.11,1908.
13. Diary, Aug.20,1908.
14. Fairbanks *Times*, Aug.25,26,1908.
15. *Dispatch*, Oct.26,1910,certified returns by canvassing board.
16. Ibid, Aug.13,1908.
17. Diary, Aug.20,1908.
18. Tanana *Miner*, Aug.13,1908.
19. Fairbanks *Times*, Aug.12,1908.

Chapter 23
1. Seattle *Post-Intelligencer*, Jan.27,1909.
2. Skagway *Alaskan*, Nov.2,1909.
3. Juneau *Record*, Feb.17,1909.
4. Seattle *Post-Intelligencer*, Feb.22,1909.
5. Nome *Gold Digger*, Mar.13,1909; Fairbanks *Times*, Mar.14,1909; Diary, Mar.14, 1909.

Chapter 24
1. *Dispatch*, Apr.2,1909.
2. *News-Miner*, Nome *Gold Digger*, Skagway *Alaskan*, all editorials on Apr.3,1909.
3. Diary, Mar.20,1909.
4. Ibid, Apr.22,1909.
5. Ibid, June 2,Nov.16,1904; Dec.19,1905.
6. Ibid, May 21,1909.
7. Ibid, May 23,24,1909.
8. Fairbanks *Times*,May 22,1909.
9. *Dispatch*,May 25,1909
10. Fairbanks *Times*,Sept.4,1909.
11. *Dispatch*,July 28,1909,quote from Katalla *Herald*.
12. Nome *Gold Digger*, May 19,1909.
13. Fairbanks *News-Miner*, May 20,1909.
14. Fairbanks *Times*, June 8,1909; *Dispatch*, June 6,1909.
15. *Dispatch*, June 8,1909.
16. Ibid, Sept.21,1909.
17. Ibid, Sept.29,30,1909.
18. *News-Miner* and Fairbanks *Times*, Oct.2,1909.
19. Fairbanks *Times*, Oct.1,1909.
20. *Dispatch*, Oct.1,1909.
21. Fairbanks *Times*, Sept.29,1909.
22. Ibid, Oct.19,1909.
23. Ibid, Nov.20,1909.
24. Fairbanks *News-Miner*,Jan.28,1910.
25. Ibid, Mar.3,1910.
26. Diary, Dec.8,1909.

Chapter 25
1. Fairbanks *News-Miner*,Nov.19,26,1909;Mar.12,26,1910.
2. Robert B. Heinl,Wash.correspondent for *Leslie's Weekly*, accompanied Sec.of Int. Fisher to Alaska;articles appeared in Oct.,Nov.,Dec.,1911.
3. *News-Miner*, Aug.4,1933.
4. Ibid, Dec.26,1914.
5. *Alaska Life* magazine,Jan.1941,pp.18-19,27-30.

Chapter 26
1. Diary, Jan.16,1910.
2. Ibid, Jan.16,1910.
3. Nichols, pp.26-29.
4. *Dispatch*, Jan.24,1910;Fairbanks *Times*, Jan.25,1910.
5. *Dispatch* and *News-Miner*, Jan.27,1910.
6. Washington *Times*, Feb.16,1910.
7. *Dispatch*, Mar.21,1910.
8. Fairbanks *Times*, Feb.9,1910.

9. Fairbanks *News-Miner*, Mar.24,1910.
10. Nome *Gold Digger*, Apr.22,1910.
11. Diary, Apr.30,1910.
12. Cong. Rec. H.R.,June 16,1910.
13. Diary, June 22,23,1910.

Chapter 27
1. Skagway *Alaskan*, Jan.24,1910,quote from Cordova *North Star*.
2. Fairbanks *Times*, June 30,1910.
3. *Dispatch*, July 5,1910,quote from Ketchikan *Miner*.
4. Ibid, Feb.25,1910.
5. Diary, June 29,1910.
6. *The Optimist*, Iditarod, Aug.8,1910.
7. Fairbanks *News-Miner*, Aug.3,1910.
8. Fairbanks *Times*, Aug.6,1910.
9. Diary, July 21,1910.
10. *Dispatch*, July 19,1910.
11. Fairbanks *Times*, Sept.21,1907.
12. Ibid, Aug.3,1910.
13. Nichols, pp.361-62.
14. H.Res.213,217,218mH.Repts.56,145(Cong.Rec.pp.3908-09.)   Hearings H.Com.on Judiciary,July 13,24,31,1911.
15. *Dispatch*, Sept.9,1921.
16. Fairbanks *Times*,Aug.10,1910.
17. *Commoner*, Apr.4,1914.
18. Iditarod *Nugget*, Sept.7,1910.
19. Fairbanks *Times* and Fairbanks *News-Miner*, Aug.31,1910; *Dispatch*,Oct.6,1910.
20. *Dispatch*, Nov.10,1910.
21. Diary, Sept.1,8,1910.
22. Ibid, Sept.23,1910.
23. Skagway *Alaskan*, Oct.11,1910; Fairbanks *News-Miner*,Dec.12,1913.
24. Skagway *Alaskan*, Oct.11,1910.
25. Diary, Oct.18-31,1910.

Chapter 28
1. Diary, Dec.15,1910.
2. Washington *Post*, Feb.24,1911.
3. Diary, Feb.23,1911.
4. *Dispatch*, Feb.27,1911.
5. Nome *Nugget*, June 16,1911.
6. Cordova *Daily Alaskan*, May 4,1911.
7. *Dispatch*, June 26,1911.
8. Seattle *Times*,June 13,1911.
9. *Dispatch*, Aug.11,1911,quote from Portland (Ore.) *Telegram*.
10. Ibid, June 22,July 15,1911; *Alaska Citizen*,July 17,1911.
11. Fairbanks *Times*,June 24,25,1911; *Dispatch*,June 23,26,1911.
12. Nome *Nugget*, June 24,1911.
13. Fairbanks *Times*,Oct.27,1911.
14. Baltimore *North American*, Apr.19,1911; Diary,Apr.19,21,1911.
15. Diary, Dec.19,1910.
16. Baltimore *North America*, July 10,1911.
17. Hearing,House Com. on Terri.(H.R.38),May 17,20,24,1911.
18. Skagway *Alaskan*, May 31,1911.

Chapter 29
1. Fairbanks *Times*,Aug.2,1911.
2. Diary, Nov.25,1911.
3. Fairbanks *Times*,Aug.29,1911.
4. Diary, Sept.3,1911.
5. Fairbanks *Times*, Oct.19,1911.
6. *Dispatch*, Dec.23,1911.
7. Fairbanks *News-Miner*, Oct.7,1911.
8. Fairbanks *Times*, Oct.11,1911.
9. Cordova *Daily Alaskan*, Nov.14,1911.
10. *Alaska-Yukon* magazine,vol.XIII,no.1,Feb.1912,pp.68-72.
11. Diary, Dec.18,1911;Fairbanks *Times*, Dec.23,1911.
12. Seattle *Times*, Dec.29,1911.
13. Fairbanks *Times*, Feb.28,1912.
14. Cong.Rec.,62nd Cong.,2S.,Apr.24,1912.
15. *Dispatch*, May 10,1912.
16. Fairbanks *News-Miner*, Apr.25,1912.
17. Skagway *Alaskan*, Apr.27,1912.
18. *Dispatch*, Fairbanks *Times*, Fairbanks *News-Miner*,Feb.28,1912.
19. Diary, July 27,1912.
20. *Dispatch*, Apr.15,1912.
21. Valdez *Miner*, Apr.7,1912.
22. Fairbanks *Times*, Apr.5,1912.
23. Cordova *Alaskan*,Apr.13,1912.
24. Valdez *Miner*, Apr.21,1912; Diary, May 7,1912.
25. Valdez *Miner*, June 2,1912.
26. For various versions of the convention see: *Dispatch*,Mar.30,Apr.1,3,5,1912;Cordova *Alaskan*,Mar.29,Apr.2,1912; Fairbanks *Times*,Mar.30,Apr.2,June 11,26,1912;Fairbanks *News-Miner*, Apr.23,1912.
27. Valdez *Prospector*, Apr.25,1912.
28. Diary, June 16,22,1912.
29. Ibid, June 26,1912.
30. Ibid, July 5,1912.
31. Ibid, Aug.6,1912.

Chapter 30
1. *Alaska-Yukon* magazine,vol.XIII,no.1,Feb.1912,pp.202.
2. Skagway *Alaskan*, July 5,1912.
3. Valdez *Miner*, June 26,1912.
4. *Dispatch*, June 19,1912.
5. *Alaska Citizen*, Aug.12,1912.
6. Skagway *Alaskan*, July 15,1912.
7. Fairbanks *News-Miner*, Aug.14,1912.
8. Ibid, Nov.6,1912.
9. New York *Times*, Aug.15,1912.
10. Diary, Aug.20-28,1912.

Chapter 31
1. Diary, Sept.5,1912.
2. Fairbanks *News-Miner*, Dec.9,1912.
3. *Dispatch*, Mar.4,1913.
4. Fairbanks *Times*, Sept.24,1912.
5. Valdez *Prospector*,Mar.12,1913;Fairbanks *Weekly Times*,Mar.17,1913.

  6. *Dispatch*, Mar.11,1913.
  7. *The Commoner*, Mar.22,1913.
  8. Diary, Mar.10,1913.
  9. Ibid, Oct.12,1912.
 10. *Sat.Eve.Post*, Sept.22,1914.
 11. Diary, Apr.1,1913.
 12. *News-miner*, Apr.9,1913;Fairbanks *Times*, Apr.10,1913.
 13. Cong.Rec.,extension of remarks by Wickersham,Jan.28,1914.
 14. *Alaska Times*, Feb.17,1914;*Alaska Citizen*, Mar.2,1914.
 15. *News-Miner*, Mar.10,1914.
 16. Diary, Jan.15,1914.
 17. Washington *Times*, Mar.13,1914.
 18. Diary, Mar.22,1914,clipping from Seattle *Times*.
 19. Ibid, Mar.18,1914.

Chapter 32
  1. *Alaska Citizen*, Mar.9,1914.
  2. U. of A. Archives,Bunnell Papers,correspondence,1907-20,Box 1,letter from John Cobb to Wilson Anslev,sec.Demo.Club,Iditarod,Apr.21,1914.
  3. *Alaska Citizen*, Mar.9,1914.
  4. *Dispatch*, June 7,1914;Fairbanks *Times*, June 4,1914.
  5. Diary, Apr.16,May 16,1914.
  6. *News-Miner*, June 2,1914.
  7. Fairbanks *Times*,June 11,1914;*Dispatch*,July 17,1914.
  8. Cordova *Alaska*, Nov.3,1913.
  9. *Dispatch*, July 25,1914.
 10. Diary, July 31,1914.
 11. *The Commoner*,June 13,July 18,1914.
 12. *Dispatch*,Aug.7; Oct.27,1914.
 13. *The Commoner*,Aug.29,1914,quote from *Progressive*.
 14. *News-Miner*,Sept.14,1914;Fairbanks *Times*,Sept.13,1914.
 15. *Dispatch*, Sept.16,30,1914.
 16. Fairbanks *Times*, Oct.27,28,1914;*News Miner*,Oct.24,25,1914.
 17. *The Commoner*, Sept.19,1914.
 18. *News-Miner*, Sept.26,1914.
 19. *Alaska Sunday Morning Post*, Oct.25,1914.
 20. *Dispatch*, Oct.20,1914.
 21. Diary, Oct.31,1914.
 22. *News-Miner*, Nov.4,1914.

Chapter 33
  1. *Dispatch*,Jan.13,1915,quote from Tacoma *News*.
  2. Valdez *Prospector*, May 4,1915.
  3. Valdez *Miner*,May 30,1915,quote from *Socialist News*.
  4. Ibid, May 2,1915.
  5. Ballaine,John,"Seward:Its Beginning and Growth," *Alaska-Yukon* magazine, July 1911.
  6. *News-Miner*, Oct.18,1936.
  7. Los Angeles *Tribune*,Mar.18,1915.
  8. *The Commoner*, June 21,1913.
  9. Diary, July 12, Oct.11,14,16,20,1915.
 10. Anchorage *Daily Times*, Aug.24,1957.

11. Cashen,Wm.R.,*Farthest North College President*,U. of A. Press,Fairbanks,1972,pp. 114-20.
12. Diary, Nov.12-16,1915.

Chapter 34
1. Diary, Jan.18,1916.
2. *News-Miner*, Jan.8,1916;*Dispatch*,Jan.8,1916.
3. Diary, Mar.10,1916.
4. Ibid, Apr.8,1916.
5. *News-Miner*,Apr.19,29,1916;*Dispatch*,Apr.19,20,1916.
6. Diary, Apr.18,Aug.2,1916.
7. *News-Miner*, Jan.22,1916.
8. Katalla *Herald*, Feb.22,1908.
9. *News-Miner*, Dec.14,1916;*Dispatch*,Dec.21,1916.
10. Hearings before Hse.Com.on Merchant Marine and Fisheries,H.R.9527,64th Cong., 1s,June 7,8,1916.
11. *Alaska Evening Post*, Jan.15,Nov.6,1916.
12. Diary, Jan.22,1916.
13. *Dispatch*, Mar.30,1907.
14. Diary, Dec.27,1915;Jan.18,1916.

Chapter 35
1. Fairbanks *Sunday Times*, Aug.27,1916.
2. Anchorage *Times*, Oct.28,1916.
3. Nome *News*,Apr.7,1903;Nome *Nugget*,Apr.30,June 11, 1904.
4. U. of A. Archives,Strong Papers, correspondence files,1913-17,box 1,file 37,1913, letter from Gov.Strong to Hon.Melvin Grigsby.
5. Ibid,box 2,file 68,letter from Strong to Dr.B.L.Myers.
6. *Dispatch*, Dec.21,1916,quote from Cordova *Times*.
7. Diary, Nov.18,1916.

Chapter 36
1. *Dispatch*, June 16,1917,quote from Anchorage *Times*.
2. Diary, Feb.20,21,26,1917.
3. Ibid, Dec.8,1923.
4. A detailed account of the case can be found in a pamphlet published by the Wash. Govt.Printing Office,1917,Alaska Hist.Lib.,Juneau; also in files of *Alaska Daily Dispatch*,Mar.2,3,13,21,23,24,25;Apr.3,8,14,July28,29,1917;Apr.2,3,1918.
5. *Dispatch*, July 29,1917.
6. Diary, Jan.14,1919;Anchorage *Times*, Jan.13,1919.

Chapter 37
1. *Dispatch*, Mar.8,1918;Valdez *Miner*,Apr.13,1918.
2. Valdez *Miner*, May 4,1918.
3. Nome *Industrial Worker*, Aug.3,1918.
4. Anchorage *Times*, Aug.6,1918.
5. Diary, Oct.6,1918.
6. *News-Miner*, Mar.26,28,1919.
7. Cordova *Alaskan*, Mar.22,1919.
8. *Dispatch*, Feb.19,22,1919.
9. Seattle *Union*, Mar.17,1919.
10. Anchorage *Times*, June 5,1919.

11. Ibid, July 2,1919.
12. Diary, Aug.23,24,1919.

Chapter 38
 1. Sutherland Papers, U. of A. Archives,box 1, letter from Wickersham to Sutherland, Dec.12,1919.
 2. Diary, Oct.11,1920.
 3. Ibid, Feb.28,1921.
 4. Ibid, Mar.4,1921.
 5. Ibid, Apr.4,7,May 10,1921.
 6. Ibid, Mar.14,16,17,1921.
 7. *News-Miner*, June 1,1921.

Chapter 39
 1. Diary, Aug.27,1921.
 2. Ibid, Sept.16,Oct.11,24,Nov.6,1921.
 3. Ibid, Dec.7,1921.
 4. Ibid, Oct.21,1922.
 5. Ibid, June 21,July 7,1923.
 6. Ibid, July 11,1923.
 7. Seattle *Times*, July 27,1923.
 8. *News-Miner*, July 30,1924.
 9. Anchorage *Daily Alaskan*, Aug.23,1924.
10. Diary, June 2,17,1923.
11. Ibid, July 11,1923.
12. U. of A. Archives, Sutherland Papers,May 15,1926.
13. Diary, Jan.11,1929;Sutherland Papers, letter from Wickersham to Sutherland,Jan. 15,1929;Feb.11,1929.
14. Diary, Feb.17,1929.

Chapter 40
 1. *Alaska Journal*,Vol.5,no.4,autumn 1975,pp.214.
 2. Anchorage *Times*, Nov.5,1926.
 3. Diary, Nov.23,24-30,1926.
 4. Ibid, Dec.4,7,9,24,1926.
 5. Ibid, Aug.19,21,23,24,1925.
 6. Anchorage *Times*, Mar.21,1927.
 7. Ibid, Mar.31;Apr.7,14,1927.
 8. Ibid, Apr.16,18,30,1927.
 9. Sutherland Papers, May 28,1929.
10. Diary, Mar.20,1928.
11. Ibid, May 20,1928.
12. Ibid, June 20-26,1928.

Chapter 41
 1. Diary, July 7,10,1928.
 2. Sutherland Papers, Apr.9,1929.
 3. Ibid, Apr.24,1929.
 4. Ibid, Oct.10,1929.
 5. Diary, Nov.6,1929.
 6. *News-Miner*, Apr.10,1930.
 7. Ibid, Apr.25,1930.
 8. Anchorage *Times*, Apr.10,1930.

9. Ibid, Apr.19,1930.
10. *News-Miner*, Apr.12,1930.
11. *Stroller's Weekly*,Dec.21,1929;Diary,Mar.12,20,24;Nov.15,1929;Sutherland Papers, Dec.9,1929;Mar.9,1930.
13. Sutherland Papers, June 28,1930.
14. Ibid, Nov.22,1930.

Chapter 42
1. Lomen, Carl J.,*Fifty Years in Alaska*, David McKay Co., 1954.
2. Diary, Mar.13,1931;Jan.19,Mar.25,1932.
3. Valdez *Miner*, July 7,1932.
4. Diary, Jan.19,20,1932.
5. Ibid, Jan.26,Apr.2,1932.
6. Ibid, July 11,29,30,1932.
7. Ibid,Mar.29,Nov.24,1931;June 14,23,24,July 1,11,16,19,20,Sept.20,Oct.14,17,1932.
8. Ibid, Sept.2-9,1932.
9. *News-Miner*, Aug.30,Sept.2,1932.
10. Diary, Apr.1,1932.
11. *News-Miner*, Oct.27,1932.

Chapter 43
1. *Empire*, Apr.19,1933.
2. Diary, Apr.24,1938.
3. Ibid, May 14,1938.
4. Ibid, Dec.27,1932.
5. Ibid, Oct.6,1933.
6. Ibid, July 30,Nov.4,Dec.31,1936.
7. Ibid, Sept.14,1935.
8. Ibid, Apr.7,8,1936.
9. *Empire*, June 3,5,6,8,10,11,1936;Anchorage *Times*,June 5,6,10,1936;Diary,June 5,1936.
10. Diary, Aug.24,1937.11.
11. Seattle *Star*, July 7,1938.
12. *Empire*, Oct.27,1939.
13. *Alaska Weekly*,Seattle,Oct.30,1939.

Chapter 44
1. Bonney,vol.II,pp.94-100;pamphlet entitled "Is It Mt. Tacoma or Rainier?",Seattle Pub.Lib.,1917,97.
2. Hunt,vol.II,pp.94-96.
3. Diary, May 2,1917.
4. Tacoma *News-Tribune*, Oct.25,1939,pp.6.
5. Diary, Apr.25,1916;Jan.3,1920.
6. Seattle *Press-Times*, Mar.16,1893,pp.4.
7. Diary, Feb.12,1937.
8. *Washington Historical Magazine*,vol.1,no.1,Oct.1893,Tacoma Pub.Lib.,979,7W27, A12359.
9. Diary, June 1,9,15,24;July 18,1939.
10. Seattle *Times*, Aug.27,1939,E7.
11. Diary, Mar.17,21,25,1927.
12. Letter from Ruth Coffin Allman,May 5,1976.
13. Diary, Sept.1,1925.
14. Ibid, June 30,1936.

15. Ibid,Mar.9;June 2,9,18,19,30;July 1,2; Aug.3,10;Sept.6,1936.
16. Ibid,Jan.1;Oct.29;Nov.11,1937;Mar.5,1938.
17. *Alaska Weekly*, Nov.11,1928.
18. Diary, Feb.25;Mar.2,1939.

Epilogue
 1. Paper delivered before the Wash.State Hist.Soc.,by John P. Hartman of Seattle,Feb. 3,1940.
 2. *Empire*, Aug.25,1957.
 3. *News-Miner*, Aug.23,25,1958.
 4. *Empire*, Aug.24,1960.

INDEX

435